The Army and Politics in Argentina
1945–1962

Robert A. Potash

The Army & Politics in Argentina
1945–1962

PERÓN TO FRONDIZI

Stanford University Press, Stanford, California 1980

Source of photographs: Archivo
General de la Nación, Buenos Aires

320.982
P859
v. 2

Stanford University Press, Stanford, California
© 1980 by the Board of Trustees of the
Leland Stanford Junior University
Printed in the United States of America
ISBN 0-8047-1056-2
LC 79-64220

For Janet and Ellen

Preface

This volume continues the detailed examination of the Argentine Army and its political role that was initiated in *The Army & Politics in Argentina, 1928–1945: Yrigoyen to Perón*. The principal focus, as in that volume, is on the changing relationships between the nation's highest political authorities and the men who comprised the officer corps. Encompassing a time period of equal length, the present volume deals essentially with three administrations: the nearly ten-year presidency of General Juan D. Perón; the three-year military regime known as the Liberating Revolution; and the truncated civilian government of Dr. Arturo Frondizi. A brief overview of the military's political role since 1962 is provided in a concluding chapter.

As in the case of the earlier volume, this one will not attempt to provide a comprehensive history of the period; rather, it will emphasize those issues and events in which the military had a special interest or played a crucial role. Because the nature of Argentine politics was radically changed by Perón's rise to power, the specific issues that evoked military concern differed from those of the earlier years. Greater attention will consequently be paid to social and economic matters, although the primary focus will continue to be political.

Another difference from the previous volume lies in the increased attention that must be paid to the other military services, especially the Navy. The Navy's emergence as a separate political force in 1955 and the continuing efforts of Navy officers to exercise political roles that previously had been monopolized by their Army colleagues add a new dimension to the civil-military relationship. Thus, though neither Navy nor Air Force is mentioned in the title, this volume will explore their interactions with the Army and with the governing authorities during periods when the latter had to look to the sea and air as well as the land to calculate the dangers to their political survival.

The research for this volume was begun in 1969 with the aid of a grant from the Joint Committee on Latin American Studies of the American Council of Learned Societies and Social Science Research Council. I should like to acknowledge here my appreciation to that body, as well as to the University of Massachusetts Research Council for their financial assistance.

The individuals in Argentina and elsewhere who have helped me in the course of this study are too numerous to mention. Those who were kind enough to provide me with documents from their private archives are mentioned at appropriate places in the notes; those who consented to be interviewed are listed in the bibliography. I am grateful to all of them for showing confidence in this work. I should like, however, to express my particular gratitude to the following, whose constant kindness and cooperation greatly facilitated my research: Dr. Roberto Etchepareborda, General (Ret.) Emilio Forcher, General (Ret.) Juan E. Guglialmelli, Admiral (Ret.) Isaac F. Rojas, General (Ret.) Tomás A. Sánchez de Bustamante, and two Argentine historians who have recently passed away, Ricardo Caillet-Bois and José Luis Romero. I also want to thank General (Ret.) Roberto Arredondo, General (Ret.) José Embrioni, Félix Luna, Dr. Carlos M. Muñiz, Admiral (Ret.) Jorge Palma, Admiral (Ret.) Jorge Perren, General (Ret.) Benjamín Rattenbach, and Dr. Alberto Rodríguez Galán for their invaluable assistance. None of these individuals, however, bears any responsibility for the opinions or judgments expressed in the book.

This is an appropriate place to record my appreciation to the staffs of various institutions who have been helpful in the location of materials. In particular, I want to mention the librarians and archival personnel of the Argentine Army's Dirección de Estudios Históricos, Escuela Superior de Guerra, and Círculo Militar; the Division of Spanish and Portuguese Studies of the Library of Congress; the Diplomatic Branch, Civil Archives Division, of the National Archives; the John F. Kennedy Library; and the University of Massachusetts Library. Moreover, I specifically want to acknowledge the assistance of my former student, Dr. Celso Rodríguez, who aided in the transcribing of interview tapes. Finally, for her unwavering encouragement during these many years of research and for her helpfulness with the manuscript in all its stages, my deepest thanks go to my wife, Jeanne.

R.A.P.

Contents

Eight pages of photographs follow p. 210

The Army and Politics in Argentina
1945–1962

Chapter 1

The Setting: Post-October 1945

As the year 1945 drew to a close, the Argentine people found themselves summoned to participate in a major political decision: the choice of a constitutional successor to the military regime that had governed the country for the past two and a half years. During this period, no elected officials had served in executive or legislative posts at national or provincial levels. In the forthcoming elections the voters would be choosing the president of the nation and a national congress as well as provincial governors and legislatures. For many Argentines, especially young men from ages eighteen to 26, this would be their first chance to help select a president. Not since 1937 had there been a presidential election, and that one, by general account, had suffered the taint of widespread fraud. Given this precedent, and others that could be recalled, many voters probably wondered whether the coming election in which Colonel (Ret). Juan Domingo Perón was a presidential candidate would be free of the defects that had characterized earlier electoral struggles.

But Argentine concerns transcended the technical aspects of the electoral process. A widespread awareness existed that Argentina was now at a historical watershed; that changing conditions at home and abroad made this election especially important, one that could affect the country's orientation for the foreseeable future. On the international side, the war that had so deeply influenced the country economically while dividing it politically was now over. The United States, from whom Argentina continued to be estranged diplomatically, had emerged from the war as the dominant military and

economic power. Germany, to whom certain elements, military and
civilian, had looked hopefully as a counterweight to the influence of
both the United States and Great Britain, was no more. And even
Great Britain, whose economic influence over the country had been
the target of nationalistic attack, was now heavily in debt to Argentina as well as dependent on U.S. assistance to recover from the
economic strains of six years of conflict. Argentines, at least the more
perceptive ones, were also aware that their own country was undergoing profound social and economic changes, partly as a result of
the war, but in reality deriving from the Great Depression. These
changes may be summed up though not adequately described by the
terms urbanization and industrialization. The mid-1930's had witnessed the beginnings of a massive movement of rural and small-
town Argentines into cities. By 1943, a larger percentage of the entire
population was living in cities of 100,000 or above than was the
case in the United States or Canada.[1] The flight from the rural areas
was such that in the next census, to be taken in 1947, only a quarter
of the economically active population was found to be engaged in
agriculture, forestry, or related pursuits.[2] The principal mecca of
this internal migration was the national capital and its environs.
Each year tens of thousands of men and women, and after 1943 over
100,000 annually, came to Greater Buenos Aires looking for jobs
and excitement. The presence of these nearly one million newcomers
from other parts of the country was gradually altering the character
of the metropolitan area, giving it a mass of people whose ties and
traditions were linked to the interior rather than to Europe.[3]

The growth of industry was related to the urbanization trend, but

[1] Report of the National School Census Bureau (Dirección del Censo Escolar
de la Nación) in *La Prensa*, Nov. 22, 1945. According to this report, 34.2 percent of Argentina's population lived in cities of 100,000 or over. The total
population at the close of 1945 has been calculated at 15.520,000, of whom
2,968,000 resided in the Federal Capital. Greater Buenos Aires, which included
the Federal Capital and the seventeen surrounding counties located in the
province of Buenos Aires, had approximately 4,500,000 people (Ministerio de
Hacienda, Dirección Nacional de Estadística y Censos, *Informe demográfico
de la república argentina, 1944-1954* [23], Tables 1, 4, 12). (An abbreviated
form of source citations is used in the notes of this book. The bracketed number that accompanies the citation refers the reader to the full title in the Bibliography, pp. 383–402.
[2] Germani, [109], p. 129. Table 59.
[3] *Ibid.*, pp. 74–78.

not wholly responsible for it; actually, more people found employment in service activities than in manufacturing. Even so, it was the manufacturing sector that became the dynamic element in the economy. Whether or not industrial growth was an explicit goal of the economic policy makers after 1933 is still debated, but the fact is that manufacturing was responsible for much of the overall growth for the next six years. The impact of World War II slowed down the growth rate of the manufacturing sector as it did the economy as a whole. Nevertheless, by 1945, industry's contribution to the gross domestic product exceeded that of agriculture.[4]

The industrialization that Argentina was experiencing revealed special characteristics. Geographically, most of the activity was concentrated in the city and province of Buenos Aires. The industrial establishments tended to be small and to require a low level of technology. Most of the capital invested in industry went into the production of consumer goods; relatively little went into heavy industry or infrastructure. The one significant exception to this pattern was the development of the petroleum industry, where the state-owned Yacimientos Petrolíferos Fiscales (YPF) had been increasing its output down to 1943 at the very respectable annual rate of 8.2 percent.[5]

The war years created an illusion of prosperity, especially for industrial labor, whose real wages had fallen in the earlier years of expansion (1935–43) and only began to climb in 1943, partly in response to labor shortages and partly to Perón-inspired government policies. Also contributing to the sense of prosperity was the expanded production of textiles and similar consumer goods and the fact that Argentina was able to export such goods to other parts of Latin America. Less evident to the average Argentine, but nevertheless real, was the serious deterioration in the capital stock of machinery and equipment. Such basic industries as transport, metal processing, and oil refining had run down. Thus, although at the end of the war in 1945, the country had huge reserves of gold and foreign exchange, some of it in blocked sterling, it also had an industrial plant and transport network sadly in need of replacements

[4] Díaz-Alejandro [247], Chapters 2 and 4, and Statistical Appendix, Table 18 (p. 417).
[5] *Ibid.*, p. 119, note 53; pp. 241–46.

and a pent-up demand for gasoline, trucks, automobiles, and, as the military saw it, armaments, most of which could be obtained only from the United States, or with its consent.[6]

To understand the political environment of Argentina in the months preceding the February 1946 elections, it is necessary to take a close look at the two most powerful nontraditional political forces that could influence the results: the military and the labor movement. Although neither of these had played a significant role when Argentina last went to the polls in the 1942 congressional elections, perceptive individuals might have seen in the expanding labor movement a force as capable of providing political support for an elected government as the military was of overturning it.

The Argentine military confronted the impending elections and restoration of constitutional government from the mixed perspectives of budgetary affluence, organizational growth, and internal political division. The past three years had witnessed an increasing allocation of funds to defense purposes, so that by 1945 almost half of all government expenditures (43.3 percent) went to the armed forces. Stated in other terms, military outlays that year absorbed 6 percent of Argentina's gross domestic product, an extremely high level for a country that was not involved in actual war. Indeed, Argentina's military outlays for 1945 exceeded the combined total for Chile, Colombia, Peru, Venezuela, and Brazil.[7]

The Argentine Army was, as usual, the principal beneficiary of the defense budget, with 65 percent of the 1945 total allocated to its needs. Although the construction of military bases and the development of armaments plants accounted for substantial sums, the calling up of large numbers of conscripts and the overall expansion of force levels constituted the major drain on revenues. In 1945, the Army had incorporated some 104,000 conscripts and had an overall authorized strength of 138,000 men, the largest force in its history. The budget for 1946 anticipated a reduction of conscripts to 87,000, but the retention of noncommissioned (NCO), volunteer, and officer personnel at close to existing levels meant that the overall author-

---

[6] *Ibid.*, p. 103 and Statistical Appendix, Table 133; see also Zuvekis [282], p. 26. Real wages rose in 1944 but turned down in 1945.

[7] Heare [157], Tables 1 and 19. The Brazilian figures exclude war expenditures.

ized strength in peacetime would still exceed 125,000. This might be compared with the 51,000-man Army of 1939, before World War II exerted its influence on Argentine defense policies.[8]

The attitudes and actions of the professional officer corps, not the enlisted men or the NCOs, largely determined the Army's role as a political force, and, within the officer corps, the officers of the combat branches rather than the auxiliary services exercised the greatest influence. At the close of 1945, the authorized strength for combat officers was 3,454. These officers were distributed in a rank pyramid comprising at the bottom 2,380 junior officers (sublieutenants, lieutenants, first lieutenants, and captains); in the middle, 870 field grade officers (majors and lieutenant colonels), and at the apex 204 superior officers (colonels and generals).[9]

Data are not available on the social origins of the officer corps as a whole, but, as Table 1 reveals, at least 50 percent of the generals on active duty in January 1946 were immigrants' sons.[10] Metropolitan Buenos Aires was the birthplace of the largest number of generals (eighteen, or 40 percent), followed at some distance by the essentially rural provinces of Corrientes (six, or 14 percent) and Entre Ríos (five, or 11 percent). If one can extrapolate from these data, the officer corps as a whole, although drawn from many parts of the country, reflected in its membership the demographic preponderance of the national capital.

In their educational background these combat officers shared one common experience: from the most senior general to the lowliest sublieutenant, they had all started as cadets in the Military Academy (Colegio Militar) and had been commissioned upon completion of its requirements. No other route to commissioned status existed for career combat officers. In their preacademy background, however, these officers varied considerably; some had completed only the

---

[8] *Ibid.*, Table 7; Ministerio de Guerra, *Boletín Militar Reservado* [14], No. 2466 (Anexo), Feb. 6, 1946.

[9] Decree No. 21,381, Sept. 12, 1945, *Anales de legislación argentina* [1], V, 634. Hereafter all citations of decrees and laws will be to texts reproduced in volumes V–XXII of this collection. Although the authorized strength for generals was 52, the actual strength dropped early in 1946 to 44 and stood at 42 as of June 30, 1946. Ministerio de Guerra, Dirección General del Personal, *Escalafón del ejército argentino . . . hasta 1 de julio de 1946* [16].

[10] In the 1920's, 40 percent were immigrants' sons. See Potash, *The Army & Politics in Argentina, 1928–1945* [188], p. 22.

TABLE 1.—GENERAL OFFICERS ON ACTIVE DUTY, JANUARY 1946

Name and Rank	Date of Birth	Birthplace	Academy Class	Nationality of Father
Lieutenant General:				
Carlos von der Becke	1889	Santa Fe	1908	German
Major Generals:				
Juan Pistarini	1882	La Pampa	1903	Italian
Eduardo Lápez	1888	Buenos Aires	1908	Argentine
Diego Mason	1887	Buenos Aires	1908	Argentine
Edelmiro Farrell	1887	Avellaneda (B.A. prov.)	1908	Argentine
Juan Carlos Bassi	1889	Buenos Aires	1909	Italian
Juan Carlos Sanguinetti	1890	Buenos Aires	1909	Argentine
Pablo Dávila	1891	Buenos Aires	1909	Argentine
Víctor J. Majó	1890	San Luis	1909	Spanish
Estanislao López	1887	Santa Fe	1908	Argentine
Brigadier Generals:				
Jorge J. Manni	1890	Zarate (B.A. prov.)	1909	Italian
Baldomero de la Biedma	1891	Buenos Aires	1909	Italian
Ricardo Miró	1889	San Nicolas (B.A. prov.)	1909	Argentine
Ernesto Florit	1889	Buenos Aires	1909	Spanish
Santos V. Rossi	1889	Buenos Aires	1910	Italian
Luis Perlinger	1892	San Juan	1910	Argentine
Alberto Guglielmone	1888	Buenos Aires	1909	Italian
Manuel Savio	1892	Buenos Aires	1910	Italian
Elbio C. Anaya	1887	Buenos Aires	1910	Uruguayan
Carlos Kelso	1891	Corrientes	1910	Australian
Raúl González	1891	Mendoza	1910	Argentine
Angel Solari	1892	Entre Rios	1912	Argentine
José Humberto Sosa Molina	1893	Mendoza	1912	Argentine
Laureano Anaya	1890	Buenos Aires	1912	Argentine
Moisés Rodrigo	1894	Corrientes	1912	Spanish
Julio Checchi	1892	Buenos Aires	1912	Italian
Enrique D. Quiroga	1892	Buenos Aires	1912	Argentine
Pedro D. Abadíe Acuña	1891	Corrientes	1912	French
Alfredo L. Podestá	1891	Santa Fe	1912	Italian
Aristóbulo Vargas Belmonte	1891	Jujuy	1912	n.d.
Lorenzo Yódice	1891	Entre Rios	1912	Italian
Pedro R. Jandula	1891	Salta	1912	Argentine
Alfredo P. Escobar	1891	Entre Rios	1912	Argentine
Ramón Albariño	1891	Entre Rios	1912	Argentine
Ernesto O. Trotz	1891	Buenos Aires	1912	German
Felipe Urdapilleta	1890	Corrientes	1912	Argentine
Otto Helbling	1892	Santa Fe	1912	Swiss
Francisco Sáenz	1891	Entre Rios	1912	Spanish

TABLE 1 (Continued)

Name and Rank	Date of Birth	Birthplace	Academy Class	Nationality of Father
Ambrosio Vago	1895	Marcos Paz (B.A. prov.)	1913	Italian
Virginio Zucal	1892	Santiago del Estero	1913	Austrian
Armando Raggio	1893	Buenos Aires	1912	n.d.
Isidro I. Martini	1893	Corrientes	1913	Italian
Juan F. Velazco	1892	Corrientes	1913	Argentine
Leopoldo T. Peña	1895	Buenos Aires	1915	Argentine

Sources: Secretaría de Guerra, Dirreción General del Personal, "Nómina de los S.S. Generales que se encontraban en actividad en el año 1946," MS; *Boletín Militar Reservado*, various issues.

Note: This table does not include non-line generals of the auxiliary services.

sixth grade of elementary school; others had finished one or more years of secondary school. The recently established requirement of four years of secondary school meant that future officers would bring with them a greater uniformity in their intellectual baggage, but for the officer corps of 1945 or 1946, diversity rather than homogeneity of premilitary educational background was the rule.[11]

Once commissioned, however, these officers shared in the common experiences of peacetime soldiers, interspersing service in line units with attendance at various army schools. A select few as captains were chosen to take courses at the War Academy (Escuela Superior de Guerra) or the Superior Technical School (Escuela Superior Técnica), and, starting in 1943, newly promoted colonels were required to attend a special one-year course in national strategy.

Exposure to such professional experiences might be presumed to have encouraged a common outlook, but the fact is that Army officers did not share the same attitude toward the issues or the candidates involved in the 1946 electoral campaign. The divisiveness reflected in the unsuccessful effort to terminate Perón's political career in October 1945 had not disappeared, although the colonel's most active opponents who were not already on retired status were either put on inactive duty or assigned to innocuous posts in remote parts of the country.[12]

[11] Secretaría de Guerra, Dirección General del Personal, "Nómina de los S.S. Generales que se encontraban en actividad en el año 1946," MS. I am indebted to José Luis de Imaz for providing me a copy of this document which was prepared at his request.

[12] For reassignments of known opponents see *Boletín Militar Reservado* [14],

It would be a mistake, however, to conclude that the Army leadership was uniformly sympathetic to Perón's political aspirations. Rather, their viewpoints ranged from a minority of ardent supporters at one extreme to a minority of ardent opponents at the other. In the middle was the politically neutral majority, whose members carefully avoided identification with either camp, although privately they may have inclined in one direction or another.

Because Army regulations prohibited career personnel on active duty from engaging in partisan political activity (although not from accepting candidacy to a national elective post) and because elementary prudence encouraged officers to keep their political preferences private, it is not possible to establish with certainty the political orientation of all key officers. Nevertheless, by using a reputational approach, how officers were perceived by their colleagues, reasonably accurate conclusions may be drawn about political sympathies.

Table 2 identifies the orientation vis-à-vis Perón's candidacy of the 44 generals on the active list as of January 1946, as recalled by three retired Army officers in 1973. Five categories are used: Peronist, anti-Peronist, Neutral, Neutral-anti (neutral but believed to be opposed), and Neutral-pro (neutral but thought to be sympathetic). Subjective elements inevitably enter into the designations, but the fact that the sources are themselves identified with three distinct orientations, Peronist, Anti-Peronist, and Neutral, lends credence to those designations on which they all agree or on which their perceptions differ in only minor degree.[13]

The three sources are in complete agreement in designating six generals as Peronist (Juan Pistarini, Edelmiro Farrell, José Humberto Sosa Molina, Ramón Albariño, Isidro Martini, Juan Velazco) and are very close on two others (Laureano Anaya, Aristóbulo Vargas Belmonte). If, however, one accepts a designation as persuasive when at least two of the sources agree, then thirteen of the generals may be classified as Peronists (Pistarini, Farrell, Juan Carlos Sanguinetti, Sosa Molina, L. Anaya, Vargas Belmonte, Lorenzo Yódice, Albariño,

---

Nos. 2408, Oct. 19; 2415, Oct. 31; 2419, Nov. 10; 2431, Nov. 30, 1945. The pages of *La Prensa* from Oct. 20 to the end of the year also report numerous military changes.

[13] The three sources are all retired senior generals. To protect them from any recriminations their names will not be cited.

TABLE 2.—ORIENTATION OF ACTIVE DUTY GENERALS WITH RESPECT TO PERÓN'S CANDIDACY, JANUARY 1946

Name and Rank	Assignment	Source A	Orientation Source B	Source C
Lieutenant General:				
Carles von der Becke	Commander-in-Chief	Neutral	Neutral	n.d.
Major Generals:				
Juan Pistarini	Vice-President	Peronist	Peronist	Peronist
Eduardo Lápez	n.d.	Neutral-anti	Opponent	n.d.
Diego Mason	Commanding General of the Interior	Neutral	Neutral	n.d.
Edelmiro Farrell	President	Peronist	Peronist	Peronist
Juan Carlos Bassi	Chief, Army General Staff	Neutral-anti	Neutral-anti	n.d.
Juan Carlos Sanguinetti	Inspector-General of Instruction	Peronist	Neutral	Peronist
Pablo Dávila	Commanding General of Military Regions	Neutral-pro	Neutral-anti	n.d.
Víctor J. Majó	Quarter Master General of the Interior	Neutral-anti	Opponent	n.d.
Estanislao López	Commanding General, Second Army	Neutral	Neutral-pro	n.d.
Brigadier Generals:				
Jorge J. Manni	n.d.	Neutral-pro	Opponent	n.d.
Baldomero de la Biedma	National Defense Council	Neutral-anti	Opponent	n.d.
Santos V. Rossi	Commanding General, First Army	Neutral-anti	Opponent	n.d.
Luis Perlinger	Commander, Patagonian Groupment	Opponent	Opponent	n.d.
Ricardo Miró	Pres., Armaments Purchasing Commission	Neutral	n.d.	n.d.
Ernesto Florit	Commander, Anti-Aircraft Defense of Interior	Neutral-anti	Opponent	n.d.
Alberto Guglielmone	Commander, 4th Military Region	Neutral-anti	Neutral-pro	n.d.
Manuel Savio	Director-General of Military Industries	Neutral-anti	Opponent	n.d.
Elbio C. Anaya	Commander, 5th Military Region	Opponent	Neutral-anti	n.d.
Carlos Kelso	Commander of Cavalry	Opponent	Opponent	n.d.
Raúl González	Commander, 7th Infantry Div.	Neutral-anti	Opponent	n.d.
Angel Solari	Commander, 1st Infantry Div.	Peronist	n.d.	n.d.
José H. Sosa Molina	Minister of War	Peronist	Peronist	Peronist
Laureano Anaya	Inspector of Infantry	Peronist	Neutral-pro	Peronist
Moisés Rodrigo	Commander, 4th Cavalry Div.	Opponent	Neutral-anti	n.d.
Julio Checchi	Inspector-General of Antiaircraft Artillery	Neutral	Neutral-pro	n.d.
Enrique D. Quiroga	Unassigned	Opponent	Opponent	n.d.
Pedro B. Abadíe Acuña	Commander, 5th Infantry Div.	Neutral	Opponent	n.d.
Alfredo L. Podestá	Director, Center of Higher Studies	Neutral	Neutral-anti	n.d.
Aristóbulo Vargas Belmonte	Commander, Cuyo Groupment	Peronist	Neutral-pro	Peronist
Lorenzo L. Yódice	Commander, 6th Infantry Div.	Peronist	Peronist	n.d.
Pedro R. Jandula	Director-General of Remount Service	Peronist	Neutral-anti	n.d.
Alfredo P. Escobar	Director-General of Administration	Neutral-anti	Opponent	n.d.
Ramón Albariño	Chief, Camp de Mayo Garrison	Peronist	Peronist	Peronist
Ernesto O. Trotz	Commander, 1st Cavalry Div.	Neutral-anti	Opponent	n.d.
Felipe Urdapilleta	Minister of Interior	Peronist	Peronist	n.d.
Otto Helbling	Military Geographic Institute	Neutral-anti	Neutral-anti	n.d.
Francisco Sáenz	Commander, 3rd Infantry Div.	Peronist	Peronist	n.d.
Ambrosio Vago	Commander, 4th Infantry Div.	Neutral-pro	Peronist	Peronist
Virginio Zucal	Director-General of Personnel	Neutral-anti	Opponent	n.d.
Armando Raggio	Military Governor of Comodoro Rivadavia	Neutral	Opponent	Peronist
Isidro I. Martini	Commander, 2nd Infantry Div.	Peronist	Peronist	Peronist
Juan F. Velazco	Chief, Federal Police	Peronist	Peronist	Peronist
Leopoldo T. Peña	Commander, 2nd Cavalry Div.	Peronist	Neutral-pro	n.d.

Sources: Interviews and correspondence conducted in 1973 with three retired Army generals whose military careers can be identified with three distinct orientations: (A) Anti-Peronist; (B) Neutralist noninvolvement; (C) Peronist. Source C preferred to designate those clearly close to Perón without passing judgment on the others; hence the large number of "no data" entries. The military assignments were obtained from the *Boletín Militar Reservado*, various issues.

[a] Five categories are used to classify the political orientation of officers; Peronist = a known friend or supporter of Perón; Opponent = a known opponent to Perón's political aspirations; Neutral = did not reveal or have a political preference; Neutral-anti = neutral but believed to be inclined against Perón; Neutral-pro = neutral but believed to be inclined in favor of Perón.

Felipe Urdapilleta, Francisco A. Sáenz, Ambrosio Vago, Martini, Velazco).

The designation of generals as anti-Peronists is complicated by the fact that Source C did not comment on this issue and one is forced to rely on only two sources. These two agree, however, in viewing three generals as anti-Peronist (Luis C. Perlinger, Carlos Kelso, Enrique D. Quiroga) and differ only slightly on twelve others (Eduardo Lápez, Víctor Majó, Baldomiro de la Biedma, Santos Rossi, Ernesto Florit, Manuel Savio, Elbio Anaya, Raúl González, Moisés Rodrigo, Alfredo Escobar, Ernesto Trotz, Virginio Zucal).

Combining the designations where there is actual or near agreement yields a total of thirteen Peronists and fifteen anti-Peronists. Conceding that these numbers are not to be taken as absolutely certain, one may nevertheless conclude that the politically committed generals comprised two groups about equal in size and each a minority of the whole. The remaining sixteen officers constituted enough of a neutral core to enable the Army to maintain its balance and continue to function as an independent institution.

Although the two groups of generals, pro-Perón and anti-Perón, may not be representative of their counterparts at the lower grades of the officer corps, each group had certain characteristics in common. Of the thirteen pro-Perón generals, only five, or less than 40 percent, were immigrants' sons, whereas of the fifteen anti-Perón generals, nine, or 67 percent, fall into this category. Any assumption that Perón attracted the "new" Argentine as against the member of the more established family receives little support here. In terms of their place of origin, the Perón supporters among the generals also differ from their rivals. The former were overwhelmingly men of the interior (ten of thirteen) whereas the anti-Peronists were more evenly divided between natives of Greater Buenos Aires and those born elsewhere (seven and eight, respectively). It is apparent, then, that Perón's staunchest support among the generals tended to come not from first-generation *porteños*, but from first- and second-generation provincials, especially men from Entre Ríos and Corrientes.

Although the Peronist and anti-Peronist generals were apparently quite evenly divided in number, their assignments were not of equal political or military significance. Of the thirteen Peronist generals, five held key political posts: President, Vice-President, War Minister, and Chief of the Federal Police; eight held major troop commands, including four infantry divisions and the Campo de Mayo Garrison, and two held bureaucratic posts. Of the fifteen anti-Peronist generals, two were apparently without assignment, six held administrative posts, and seven held troop commands; but of these, only three were at the divisional level and all three were far removed from the capital. Perón's friends among the generals clearly were in stronger positions than his enemies.

It is equally significant, however, that the generals who held the two highest posts in the Army belonged to neither camp. The Commander-in-Chief, General Carlos von der Becke, and the Commanding General of the Interior, General Diego Mason, had reputations for being completely neutral. The presence of such men at the apex of the hierarchy acted to preserve the image of the Army in the eyes of most of its officers, including the politically oriented, as a professional institution dedicated to national interests and not to pretorianism.

In turning from the Army to consider what would later be regarded as the most important political force in Argentina, labor, one finds a situation vastly different though equally complex. The labor movement in its rank and file was much less disciplined than the military; the response of the average worker to labor leaders, unlike that of the enlisted man to his officer, was not always predictable. The labor leaders, in turn, differed among themselves in background, experience, and orientation and in their attitude toward the government. What they had in common, however, was an increasing conviction that the trade unions would and should play an active role in the forthcoming political campaign.

This conviction was the product of the contrasting experiences of the labor movement over the past four years. Prior to the military takeover in June 1943, trade union efforts to gain salary increases or other benefits for their members through direct negotiations with employers met with limited success; resort to strikes had increased sharply—in 1942, 113 were called as against 54 the previous year—but in the absence of a sympathetic government, the results had been disappointing for all but a few of those who went on strike. With Perón's creation of the Secretariat of Labor and Welfare in November 1943, the situation changed radically. Trade unions that collaborated with Perón found little difficulty in winning benefits for their members; grievances that derived from the failure of past governments to enforce existing social legislation were eased; and large sectors of the labor force that in the past had failed to benefit either from trade union efforts or from social legislation were now encompassed by one or the other or both.[14]

From an organizational viewpoint, the most notable change in the labor movement was the sharp increase in the number of recognized unions—from 356 in 1941 to 969 in 1945. Unions now operated in many of the interior provinces. In terms of paid-up membership, however, the increase was less dramatic. The 528,523 listed in 1945 constitute only a moderate increase over the 441,412 reported in 1941 and still represented less than 15 percent of the nonagricultural labor force. The proliferation of unions, however, meant that a new generation of leaders was emerging to join or compete with those who had been active on the labor scene over the past decades.[15]

For the younger leaders, the implications of cooperating with the Secretariat of Labor were less traumatic than for the older generation, many of whose members were identified with the antimilitary and antifascist traditions of the socialist, communist, anarchist, or syndicalist movements. The reluctance to seek benefits from a government agency so closely associated with the political ambitions of Colonel Perón created a dilemma for many old-line union leaders. Some, placing ideological consistency above all other considerations, refused to have anything to do with the Secretariat; others were quick to associate with it in view of the practical benefits they anticipated for their unions or themselves; still others agonized over the appropriate course to follow, and some who initially placed confidence in Perón later broke with him, while others who had held off at first finally chose to collaborate.[16]

The experiences of labor leaders who dealt with the Secretariat of

[14] Murmis *et al.* [266], p. 91; Baily [238], pp. 74–78. For an interpretation that downgrades the benefits labor received between 1943 and 1945, see Stickell [279], pp. 38–48.

[15] Durruty [250], Table 1, p. 114. According to a United Nations study, Argentina's economically active population, exclusive of those engaged in agriculture, averaged 3,679,000 in the 1940–44 period (*United Nations, Departamento de Asuntos Económicos Sociales* [35], I, 37). The 528,523 unionized workers come to 14.4 percent.

[16] Examples are the Railway Union leader, José Domenech, an early Perón supporter who later broke with him, and Angel Borlenghi, the Confederation of Commercial Employees head, who opposed him at first and later became a

Labor demonstrated the importance of having a strong and dependable voice in the government. While some saw in Colonel Perón the embodiment of that voice, others privately questioned whether he could be counted on at all times to defend labor's interests. Would it not be desirable for labor to organize politically, to form a separate political party that would represent worker interests in future governments and thus serve as insurance against arbitrary changes of policies or personalities?

The idea of creating a national labor party had been the subject of informal discussions among labor leaders since 1943. It was only in the month of October 1945, however, that concrete steps were taken to translate the idea into action. The first of these steps was the inclusion in the newly promulgated statute governing trade unions of their right to engage in political activities on a temporary or permanent basis. Who was responsible for the drafting of this provision is not clear, but it provided the legal basis for unions to act should they decide to do so.[17]

The first move to take advantage of the law came from among labor leaders generally regarded as friendly with Perón. Contrary to the general impression, their action took place before the October 9–17 crisis and was motivated more by suspicion of Perón's intentions than by a desire to provide him with support. The specific steps were taken at a meeting of trade union leaders held without Perón's knowledge at the Secretariat of Labor on Saturday morning, October 6. At this meeting, which was convoked and presided over by Aurelio Hernández, the decision was taken to proceed with the formation of a party along the lines of the British Labor Party. A document proclaiming the creation of the party was drawn up and signed by the 24 union leaders present. All but two of them, moreover, stated their determination to proceed with the formation of the party with or without Perón.[18]

---

staunch supporter. On the socialist background of many of those who joined Perón, see Sylvester [280], Chapter XVII.

[17] Belloni [239], p. 56; see also Articles 33–36 of Decree No. 23,852 of Oct. 2, 1945.

[18] Interview with Agustín Hernández, June 14, 1962. I am indebted to Sr. Hernández for showing me the relevant document. Not present at this meeting but later accepting the idea of forming a labor party was Cipriano Reyes; also not present but opposed to the idea, according to Hernández, were Luis

According to Hernández, the main motivation behind the summoning of the October 6 meeting was the fear that Perón might sell out the workers to advance his presidential ambitions. He had been meeting recently with leaders of the Sabattini wing of the Radical Party, and the possibility that he would make a deal to secure their support could not be discounted. The creation of a party to be made up exclusively of trade unionists was a move to defend labor interests, whichever course Perón adopted.

As it turned out, both the concerns that led to the October 6 meeting and its decisions were soon overtaken by events. The feared Perón-Sabattini political alliance did not materialize. Rather, dissident military leaders forced Perón's ouster from his offices on October 9, only to be followed after a week of confusion and indecision by the massive labor demonstration of October 17 that enabled Perón to regain control of the political situation and to proceed with his candidacy. For trade unionists who actively organized the October 17 movement, as well as for those who joined it belatedly, this successful intervention of labor onto the political stage strengthened the determination to create a permanent political vehicle. Accordingly, on October 24, some 50 trade union leaders met to draw up the bases for the Partido Laborista that was to play a major role in Perón's quest for the presidency.[19]

At the close of 1945, both the labor movement and the armed forces as well as the general Argentine public directed increasing attention to the election campaign. It was the military government headed by General Edelmiro Farrell, however, that was directly responsible for determining the conditions of the campaign; and it is to an examination of the nature of that government and its specific policies that one must turn to understand the process that led to the eventual results.

Gay and Angel Borlenghi. The two trade unionists who conditioned their support on Perón's acceptance came from the Light and Power Union, which traditionally tried to get along with the government.

[19] Interview with Hernández; Fayt, *La naturaleza del peronismo* [252], pp. 116–34, provides extensive data on the party based in part on information supplied by Luis Gay.

Chapter 2

The Guaranteed Election, 1945–1946

The main goal of General Farrell's government after the hectic events of October 9–17, 1945, was to hold elections that would put an end to military rule. In working toward that goal, the government pursued two objectives: first, to maintain or create conditions that would favor victory for their erstwhile colleague, Colonel (Ret.) Juan D. Perón; and second, to guarantee that the forthcoming elections would be free of the fraud and violence that had disfigured past contests, thereby redeeming the President's pledge of honor, given on behalf of the armed forces, that they would assure an honest vote. To understand how such seemingly contradictory aims could be simultaneously pursued, it is necessary to examine the nature of the reorganized government and of the roles played by its component parts.

The changes that took place in the highest levels of the national government after October 17 preserved or even intensified its military character. The number of cabinet posts that had been held by civilians prior to October 9 was reduced from four to three, and the politically significant Interior Ministry was now held by an Army officer. Civilian influence was accordingly restricted to the Ministries of Foreign Affairs, Justice and Public Instruction, and Agriculture; Army officers headed the aforementioned Interior post, Finance, Public Works, Labor and Welfare, Industry and Commerce, and, of course, the War Ministry; Navy and Air Force officers directed the Navy Ministry and Air Secretariat, respectively. In contrast to the instability that had characterized the government earlier in 1945, these appointments were to prove remarkably permanent. The Secretariats of Air, Labor and Welfare, and Industry and Commerce changed hands after October, but only one of the eight ministerial posts experienced a change between October 1945 and the assumption of the new administration in June 1946.[1]

The fact that military personalities controlled most of the key posts in the government did not mean that uniformity of viewpoint prevailed in regard to the specific policies to be followed. Indeed, within a matter of weeks, it became apparent that differences existed within the government as to which of the two objectives, honest elections or a Perón victory, should be pursued the more vigorously. The chief proponents of building up confidence in the electoral promises were found in the Interior and War Ministries. Much to the surprise of those who knew of his long-standing friendship with Perón, the newly appointed Interior Minister, Colonel (Ret.) Bartolomé Descalzo, set about vigorously to create conditions for an open political campaign. Combining public assurances with a series of concrete measures, he succeeded in a matter of days in giving some credibility to government assurances of impartiality. On November 2, however, it was suddenly announced that Descalzo had resigned for reasons of health and was to be replaced by an active duty officer, General Felipe Urdapilleta, until recently commander of the Campo de Mayo garrison.[2]

The shift from Descalzo to Urdapilleta was apparently a response to pressure brought by Perón and his closest adherents to have

[1] The civilian ministers were: Juan I. Cooke, a holdover in Foreign Affairs; José M. Astigueta in Justice and Public Instruction; and Pedro Marotta in Agriculture. The military ministers were: Colonel (Ret.) Bartolomé Descalzo in Interior; Colonel (Ret.) Amaro Avalos in Finance; General Juan Pistarini, a holdover in Public Works and also sworn in as Vice-President; General Humberto Sosa Molina in War; and Admiral Abelardo Pantín in Navy. The Air Force Secretary was Commodore Edmundo J. Sustaita; the Labor and Welfare Secretary was Colonel Domingo Mercante; and the Commerce and Industry Secretary was Lieut. Colonel Mariano Abarca (Decrees No. 25,723, Oct. 18; 25,855–58 and 25,861, all of Oct. 20, 1945). General Felipe Urdapilleta replaced Colonel Descalzo on Nov. 2 (Decree No. 27,497); Brigadier Bartolomé de la Colina replaced Air Force Secretary Sustaita on Nov. 7 (Decree No. 28,158); and Colonel Joaquín I. Sauri replaced Lieut. Colonel Abarca on Dec. 1 (Decrees No. 30,961–63).

[2] For a report on the War Minister's views, see U.S. Embassy, Buenos Aires, Dispatch 1242 to the Secretary of State, Nov. 3, 1945, National Archives, Record Group 59, File No. 835.00/11-345 (hereafter cited as Embassy BA, item, date, and file number); on Descalzo, Embassy BA Dispatch 1288, Nov. 10, 1945, 835.00/11-1045. The Embassy, it should be noted, was skeptical at first about the significance of the differences.

someone more in tune with their view of the appropriate tactics to follow. If so, General Urdapilleta must have been a disappointment, for he soon made it clear in word and deed that he was disposed to follow the path outlined by his predecessor. Moreover, as Interior Minister, he worked closely with the War Minister, General Humberto Sosa Molina, in trying to prevent too obvious a tilt in favor of Perón's candidacy. The continuing presence in the Interior Ministry of Lieut. Colonel Arnaldo Sosa Molina, who had been appointed its secretary-general by Colonel Descalzo and retained under General Urdapilleta, is indicative both of the continuity of policy and the link to the War Ministry.[3]

The War Minister himself, General Sosa Molina, took special pains to publicize the Army's commitment to free elections, and he did so in a manner designed to convey this pledge to the United States and other members of the international community. At a reception held on October 31 for foreign military attachés accredited to Argentina, he issued a lengthy statement designed to eliminate doubts. He told his listeners that the Argentine government with the support of the Army had the "unchangeable intention of assuring free elections." The government, he promised, "will maintain a position of strict neutrality" in these elections, and "has already given strict instructions to all those holding posts in the national administration." General Sosa Molina also asserted that the Army was returning to its professional tasks and that "the fact that some officers are occupying public posts is the result of the Executive's desire to guarantee the free exercise of the will of the people and in line with the firm intention of assuring honest elections."[4]

To his own subordinates the War Minister repeatedly emphasized that the Army must return to its professional duties and preserve the strictest neutrality vis-à-vis the political campaign. In his first general

---

[3] *The Times* (London), Nov. 5, 1945, discussed the significance of the Descalzo resignation; on the existence of a Sosa Molina–Urdapilleta alliance, Embassy BA Telegram 2800, Nov. 7, 1945, 835.00/11-745; also Dispatch 1370, Nov. 21, 1945, 835.00/11-2145; on Arnaldo Sosa Molina's presence in the Interior Ministry, Ministerio del Interior, Subsecretaría de Informaciones, *Las fuerzas armadas* [12], II, 638.

[4] Enclosure 1 to Embassy Dispatch No. 1242, cited above in note 2. Here and elsewhere in quotations throughout the book, ellipsis dots have been omitted at the beginning and end of passages in accordance with the editorial policy of Stanford University Press.

order, issued on October 30, he stated that the only promise he had made in accepting the post was "to carry out the most impeccable electoral process in the entire political history of the country."[5] A month later, reminding the Army of its obligations, he directed all officers to refrain from expressing their political feelings either in public or private and called for any officer knowing of violations to report them to his superior.[6] In his commencement address at the Military Academy in December, the War Minister again sounded the theme that the Army should restrict its activities to the military sphere and suggested that any Army man whose ambitions were too great to be satisfied with the usual rewards of Army service should resign rather than bring discredit on the institution.[7]

The firmness with which the War and Interior Ministries were committing the government to the path of free elections was apparently a cause of deep concern to Perón and his closest supporters. Although the restructured cabinet was presumably made up of his sympathizers, its actions were not sufficiently responsive to what he and his political advisors regarded as their electoral needs. Accordingly, they attempted to force changes that would bring into the cabinet such unconditional supporters as Federal Police Chief General Juan F. Velazco and Air Force Commodore Bartolomé de la Colina. These efforts proved only partly successful; Colina replaced the incumbent Air Secretary on November 7, and the Secretary for Industry and Commerce was replaced by Colonel Joaquín Sauri on December 1, but no other changes took place. The cabinet thus remained divided, with one group consisting primarily of Labor and Welfare Secretary Domingo Mercante, Air Force Secretary Colina, and Industry and Commerce Secretary Sauri, aided of course by the Federal Police Chief Velazco, devoting their energies to securing Perón's election by any means, while another group led by War Minister General Sosa Molina, and including the Ministers of Interior, Navy, Finance, Agriculture, and Justice and Public Instruction,

[5] General Order No. 29, *Boletín Militar Reservado* [14], No. 2414, Oct. 30, 1945.

[6] General Order No. 30, *ibid.*, No. 2428, Nov. 27, 1945.

[7] Excerpts of the speech are contained in Embassy BA Dispatch No. 1618, Dec. 19, 1945, 835.00/12-1945, and also in *La Vanguardia*, Dec. 18, 1945, p. 2. In its December 4 issue, however, this Socialist Party daily claimed that the Army's monthly propaganda bulletins were highly partisan and hostile to the anti-Perón Democratic Union.

worked to create the appearance, and as much of the substance as possible, of official neutrality.[8]

It should not be thought that General Sosa Molina was opposed to Perón's candidacy or was trying to prevent his election. Quite the contrary, his stance seems to have been premised on the belief that Perón could win in a free election. Soundings taken by Army officers indicated that he enjoyed widespread support in the interior of the country as well as in the industrial belt around Buenos Aires.[9] An election, therefore, that was free of the fraud that had stigmatized the choice of presidents since 1930 would have several advantages. The Army as guarantor of such an election could return to its professional duties with its honor intact, its reputation enhanced, and a persuasive claim for benevolent treatment from the future government. That government, moreover, would enjoy a legitimacy of origin possessed by no administration since Hipólito Yrigoyen's ouster; and, hopefully, it would have a stability that would permit the Army to concentrate on the urgent tasks of acquiring modern equipment and incorporating the military lessons of World War II.

But if the War Minister and his like-minded colleagues were prepared to risk a Perón defeat, the same was not true of the coterie of officials most closely associated with the candidate. Counting on the influence of Perón with President Farrell, they were prepared to convert their offices into parts of Perón's electoral machine. Sosa Molina's injunctions against military men engaging in political proselytization apparently did not extend to Lieut. Colonel Domingo Mercante, who now headed the Secretariat of Labor and Welfare; and it seems to have had only an intermittent effect on certain other Army officers who were holding nonmilitary posts.

[8] On Perón's effort to get Velasco into the cabinet, Embassy BA Telegram 2800, Nov. 7, 1945, 835.00/11-745; on the rival blocs within the government, Embassy BA Dispatch 1370, cited above in note 3; Telegram 2917, Nov. 21, 1945, 835.00/11-2145; Telegram 2933, Nov. 22, 1945, 835.00/11-2245.

[9] For example, General Carlos Kelso, Commander of Cavalry, told the Assistant U.S. Military Attaché on December 15 that he had just returned from an inspection trip that had taken him by automobile to all parts of Argentina and that as a result of the survey he had made of public opinion he "was convinced that Colonel Perón will be elected President in free elections." Kelso was personally opposed to Perón's candidacy. See Enclosure to Embassy BA Dispatch 1678, Dec. 29, 1945, 835.00/12-2945. Colonel Franklin Lucero, Undersecretary of the War Ministry, was also reported as saying that in a free election "Perón will win with votes to spare" (Enclosure to Embassy BA Dispatch 1388, Nov. 24, 1945, 835.00/11-2445).

The Labor and Welfare Secretariat, which had been a major instrument of Perón's ambitions from its creation in November 1943 to October 1945 when he became an avowed presidential candidate, was to continue serving his interests under the leadership of Lieut. Colonel Mercante. With a bureaucratic apparatus that extended throughout the country, the Secretariat was in a position to provide the basic organization and a good deal of the funding needed to give viability to the recently founded Partido Laborista. Complaints by independent trade unionists and opposition newspapers that the Secretariat was openly engaging in electoralist activities were ignored.[10] Indeed, once the new party reached the stage of selecting its nominees for the national and provincial posts to be filled in the forthcoming election, a number of the Secretariat's personnel graduated into candidates. Most notable among these was Secretary Mercante himself. Having been promoted to full colonel in December 1945, presumably in recognition for services other than military, he accepted the Laborista Party nomination for Vice-President, asked for retirement from the Army, and resigned from his cabinet post.[11]

Paralleling the partisan political activities of the Secretariat of Labor and Welfare were those of other Perón supporters in the provincial administrations. No major shakeup of provincial interventors had taken place after October 1945, and, consequently, the direction of provincial affairs remained for the most part in the hands of men who were appointed to their offices during the years of Perón's predominance in the national government. Only four of the provinces were under military interventors; the other ten were under civilians. In several of the latter, despite explicit instructions from Interior Minister Urdapilleta, the interventors personally attended political rallies for Perón, and lesser officials used their positions and public funds to promote his cause. More serious was the arbitrary use of

[10] On the political activities of the Labor Secretariat and the complaints made by anti-Perón groups, see Embassy BA Dispatch 1313, Nov. 14, 1945, 835.00/11-1445; Embassy BA Telegram 3408, Dec. 6, 1945, 835.00/12-645; *La Vanguardia*, Nov. 6, 1945; *La Prensa*, Nov. 13, 1945.

[11] *La Prensa*, Jan. 15, 16, 1946. Mercante later exchanged the vice-presidential nomination for that of governor for Buenos Aires province. His military promotion was in keeping with Army legislation that allowed time spent in nonmilitary posts under assignment by the Executive Power to count as military service. See Decree No. 29,375 of 1944, Article 86. On the acceptance of Laborista Party nominations by other Labor Secretariat personnel, see *Review of the River Plate*, Feb. 22, 1946, p. 4.

administrative authority to discourage or disrupt the political activities of the Radical, Socialist, and Progressive Democratic parties, which had joined, together with the Communist Party, in forming the Unión Democrática to put up a single presidential slate against Perón. Post Office officials in various provinces interfered with the distribution of newspapers that supported the Unión Democrática, while allowing pro-Perón papers to circulate freely. Provincial police under the direction of partisan interventors were also employed to harass supporters of the Unión Democrática.[12]

In the city of Buenos Aires it was the activities of the Federal Police under the direction of Perón's Military Academy classmate, Colonel Velazco, that aroused frequent and bitter complaints by representatives of anti-Perón political parties, civic groups, and independent trade unions. Colonel Velazco was not only a fervent supporter of Perón, but maintained close ties with the nationalist groups that, despite earlier misgivings about Perón's opportunism, now came out in support of his candidacy. Bands of armed nationalist youths, confident that the police would not deal harshly with them, were thus able to roam the streets, assaulting opponents or engaging in anti-Semitic depredations. Official repudiations by the Interior Minister of such acts seem to have had little effect, and despite rumors at one time that General Urdapilleta was seeking to oust the Police Chief, nothing of this sort occurred. Colonel Velazco's control of the Federal Police was too important an asset to Perón, and only a major political crisis of the sort the government wanted to avoid might have produced such a change.[13]

Despite the freewheeling partisan activities of Perón's supporters within the national and provincial administrations, and perhaps to some extent because of them, Interior Minister General Urdapilleta worked to establish equitable ground rules for the electoral campaign. To be sure, some of his pronouncements reflected a heavy-handed defensiveness about the government's prerogatives and an

[12] See complaints against Interventors of La Rioja, Jujuy, Salta, and Córdoba in *La Prensa*, Nov. 19, 27, Dec. 3, 30, 1945.

[13] For Urdapilleta's rumored effort to have Velasco transferred, see Embassy BA Telegram 3048, Dec. 6, 1945, 835.00/12-645; for Democratic Union complaints of police favoritism to Perón supporters, *La Prensa*, Nov. 23, Dec. 10, 1945; for a proud acknowledgment that those who tried to disrupt Democratic Union meetings and engaged in shootings were nationalist youths, see Ibarguren (h.) [61].

insufficient sensitivity to the needs of political groups that had frequently suffered over the past two years from repressive measures; but his decisions on a number of important issues gradually and grudgingly won for him a degree of credibility.

The first test of his sincerity arose over the disposition of property that had been confiscated from the political parties after their dissolution in 1943. Under the decree issued by his predecessor on October 30, 1945, these parties were again legalized and their representatives were authorized to apply for the return of their former buildings, equipment, and papers. When members of the pro-Perón Radical Party splinter group, the Junta Reorganizadora led by Hortensio Quijano, presented themselves as the legitimate owners of the Radical Party documents, their claim was rejected and the materials were turned over to the anti-Perón leadership of the regular party.[14]

The Interior Minister was quick to respond to charges of Post Office interference with the circulation of newspapers associated with anti-Perón groups. When the Socialist Party complained that its daily *La Vanguardia* was not being delivered through the mails, he ordered this practice halted, although he could not refrain from observing that under existing laws, national and international, the Post Office was authorized to halt the distribution of publications that insulted the legally constituted government. Two weeks later, when the representatives of the Unión Democrática accused the Post Office of interfering with the distribution of both newspapers and closed mail, the Interior Minister issued explicit instructions to the Director-General of the Correos y Telecommunicaciones to take steps to assure the normal circulation of all periodical publications and to prevent delays in the handling of political party mail. That official, an Army lieutenant colonel, did in fact warn the personnel of the postal service that anyone using his official function to help or harm any political party would be subject to punishment. Apparently, however, such warnings did not have universal effect, for complaints of postal interference with the circulation of newspapers continued to be registered in several provinces.[15]

The inability of the Interior Minister to eliminate partisan political activity among public employees was evidenced in the series of in-

---

14 Embassy BA Dispatch 1313, Nov. 11, 1945, 835.00/11-1145.
15 *Las fuerzas armadas* [12], II, 116, 125–27.

structions he felt compelled to issue. Here again it was Colonel Descalzo in his brief tenure as Interior Minister who had given the
provincial interventors a detailed set of instructions, calling on them
among other things to "issue instructions to their subordinates to the
effect that state personnel are absolutely forbidden to engage in
political activities of any sort and that they must act with complete
impartiality in the electoral process that is beginning."[16] General
Urdapilleta, on assuming the Interior Ministry post, endorsed these
instructions as his own, but when complaints continued about partisan behavior by the personnel of the Labor Secretariat and certain
provincial administrations, General Urdapilleta prepared a decree,
which the entire cabinet endorsed, to spell out the rules of behavior
for federal civil servants. With the exception of university professors,
high school teachers, and medical personnel, government employees
were not to serve on political committees or in leadership posts
within political parties, sign manifestos of a political character, or
involve themselves in the electoral struggle. On December 17 the
Interior Minister directed provincial interventors to issue similar
regulations, but ten days later he felt obliged to remind the interventors of Tucumán, Jujuy, Santiago del Estero, La Rioja, Santa
Fe, and Salta of their obligation to fulfill these instructions strictly.
Early in January, Urdapilleta called on the Subsecretary of Information to supply him daily with any newspaper reports of public
employees engaged in political activities; and a few days later, he
was again reminding provincial interventors of their duties, specifically that the laws forbade officials from coercing their subordinates into affiliating with any party or voting for any candidate.[17]

Two conclusions seem to follow from this review of the Interior
Minister's efforts to prevent government employees from engaging
in partisan actions: first, that General Urdapilleta was sincere in his
attempt to assure government neutrality; second, that the tradition of
the *calor oficial* whereby the "ins" do whatever possible to assist their
political friends was not easily eradicated, even when an Army general served as Minister of Interior.

Although the Interior Minister failed to eliminate partisan use of

[16] *Ibid.*, p. 113.
[17] *Ibid.*, pp. 115–16, 118–19, 167, 179, 196, 204–5; Decree No. 32,577 of
Dec. 14, 1945.

public office in support of Perón's candidacy, his efforts to establish equitable arrangements in another area of vital concern to the contending groups, radio broadcasting, proved more successful. Since 1943 the military government in general and Colonel Perón in particular had made effective use of the radio to justify their activities. It was obvious that radio would play a larger role in the forthcoming political campaign than in any previous national election. This gave special significance to whatever rules were established for the allocation of radio time for campaign purposes.

Argentine radio facilities consisted of some 45 privately owned stations distributed in a score of cities plus the government-owned station, LRA, located in the capital. Privately owned networks were still rudimentary, but government-controlled facilities located at LRA made it possible to hook up the private stations into a national network and to replace local programs with broadcasts emanating from the state radio. The creation of an equitable system of allocating broadcast time, therefore, required regulating both the private radio sector and the use of the government station. As an initial step, the Interior Minister issued instructions to LRA that it could transmit public events only with express prior permission of the Ministry, and he made it plain that such permission would be given only for events organized by government bodies. In the private sector, in apparent response to suggestions of the Minister, the owners' association met and worked out an arrangement for guaranteeing impartial use of their facilities. Each station would sell to each political party participating in the election the same amount of time of comparable quality on a daily basis. Apart from these time spaces, the stations pledged not to carry any political advertising.[18]

The text of this agreement, when published in the press, produced varying reactions. A spokesman of one traditional party complained about the commercial aspect, contending that the stations should provide the time as a public service, but the Unión Democrática leadership was primarily concerned that there should be no prior censorship of the campaign material going out on the airwaves. On the Peronist side, there was little public comment, but privately, according to the account of one station owner, Perón tried to disrupt the agreement. Apparently counting on his and Evita's long-standing

[18] *Las fuerzas armadas* [12], II, 138–42; *La Prensa*, Nov. 15, 1945.

ties with Jaime Yankelevich, the owner of Radio Belgrano, Perón proposed that the entire air time of that station be turned over for his propaganda. Yankelevich was urged to resign from the broadcasters' association and was promised a subsidy to make up for the loss of advertising revenue, a subsidy that supposedly would be paid by the Buenos Aires Electric Company. His refusal to go along with the Peróns' demand produced an angry scene and was followed by harassment in the form of repeated inspections of Radio Belgrano's premises.[19]

The Interior Ministry, accepting the owners' agreement for the allocation of time, issued special regulations to govern the content of political broadcasts. Under these regulations, the government refrained from exercising a direct censorship role, but made the station operators responsible for guaranteeing that such broadcasts did not violate standards of decency and order. The texts of all political broadcasts had to be submitted in advance to the station operators, who were obliged to excise materials that showed disrespect for national institutions, compromised social harmony, exploited racial or religious differences, insulted or defamed persons or parties, or might prejudice the country's international relations.[20]

In practice, the system of guaranteeing equal access to radio time was not without flaws. Private station owners, sensitive to their accountability to the government for the content of all broadcasts, tended to be chary about allowing Unión Democrática speakers to criticize actions of the government or its officials or to comment adversely on the country's international situation. Meanwhile, Perón's supporters in the Secretariat of Labor were able to use the facilities of LRA for what were ostensibly "official" functions. Moreover, on at least one occasion, the time space of the Unión Democrática presidential candidate was interrupted by the compulsory hookup in order to broadcast an LRA news program. Despite such annoyances and the obvious inequities in the use of LRA, the various parties were able to utilize the radio to set forth their messages. Furthermore, as the campaign progressed, the government relaxed the re-

---

[19] On the reactions of the Democratic Union, *La Prensa*, Dec. 4, 1945; on the Perón effort to take over Radio Belgrano's air time, Military Attaché Report from Argentina R-779-45, Nov. 29, 1945, National Archives Record Group 59, Department of State, Argentine Blue Book Files (hereafter Blue Book Files).

[20] *Las fuerzas armadas* [12], II, 140.

quirement for prior submission of texts of speeches of presidential and vice-presidential candidates.[21]

More serious to the anti-Perón forces than radio-related issues was the government's insistence on maintaining the state of siege throughout the political campaign. Despite persistent demands from numerous groups, including the Chamber of Commerce, the major newspapers, independent trade unions, and, of course, the political parties that made up the Unión Democrática, the government was unwilling to give up its emergency powers. This meant that those who took an active part in the political campaign did so in the realization that the constitutional guarantees of the rights of expression and assembly and against arbitrary arrest depended on the will if not the whim of the government.[22]

Whether its retention of the state of siege was motivated, as some critics insisted, by the desire to aid Perón's candidacy, or by fear that it could not otherwise guarantee the electoral process, the government's decision placed on it a heavy responsibility for evenhanded use of its powers. This was especially true in regard to authorizing political gatherings, for under the state of siege, the Interior Ministry decided when and how people could exercise the right of assembly.

Within a few days of assuming his post, General Urdapilleta announced that political parties were thenceforth free to hold meetings in indoor locales. This right was subsequently extended to such other groups as professional associations, civic groups, and independent trade unions, and the police were ordered not to interfere. The real test, however, was the handling of requests for outdoor assemblies. Under existing police edicts based on the state of siege, such meetings were not permitted, although the police had the authority to make exceptions. A request for an exception had to be submitted at least ten days before a proposed public meeting.[23]

During the month of November, Peronist adherents engaged in street demonstrations on several occasions, usually in front of the Labor Secretariat, without police interference. Whether prior permission had been sought is not known, but when the directors of the Unión Democrática requested permission to hold a mass meeting

[21] *Ibid.*, pp. 154, 172, 218; *La Prensa*, Dec. 16, 25, 1945.
[22] *Las fuerzas armadas* [12], II, 125, 128, 153–55.
[23] *Ibid.*, pp. 116, 123.

near the Congress for Saturday afternoon, December 1, Police Chief Velazco turned them down. Only after repeated protests to the Interior Minister did the latter overrule the Police Chief and authorize the meeting that was now rescheduled for December 8.[24]

This first open-air mass meeting called by Perón's political opponents attracted some 200,000 participants. It was intended by its organizers, the executive board of the Unión Democrática, to exhibit the unity, strength, and orderliness of their supporters, as well as to give exposure to the man who would shortly thereafter be their standard-bearer in the presidential election, Dr. José Tamborini. A heavy-set man with slicked-down hair, Tamborini was a veteran Radical Party politician who had served several terms as a national deputy beginning in 1918, had been a cabinet member under President Alvear (1925–28), and most recently (1940–43) a national senator from the Federal Capital.

The meeting called by the Unión Democrática amply fulfilled the expectations of its organizers; its finale, however, illustrated the fragile character of the political scene. Nationalist youths, having unsuccessfully tried to disrupt the meeting by scuffling with the men posted as guardians, resorted to gunfire. Shots were exchanged for over half an hour before the police, whose headquarters were only two blocks away, made their appearance. When the casualties were counted, four were dead (two Radicals, one Socialist, one Communist) and 30 were wounded.[25]

This tragic incident further embittered the relations of the anti-Perón forces with the government. The Unión Democrática leaders, denouncing the behavior of the police, demanded the ouster of Colonel Velazco, but the Interior Minister, although deploring the shootings, refused to blame the police. Colonel Velazco even tried to make the participants in the meeting responsible for the violence, an effort that could not efface the fact that armed nationalist youths had initiated the fracas. Even Colonel Perón found it prudent to issue a statement denouncing "irresponsible persons [who] to cries of viva Rosas, death to the Jews, viva Perón, hide their indignity in order to

[24] Peronist street demonstrations were reported by *La Prensa* on Nov. 10 and 28, 1945; on the efforts of the Democratic Union to get permission for its rally, *ibid.*, Nov. 22, 23, Dec. 7, 1945.

[25] For a good account of the rally and the accompanying shootings, see *The Times* (London), Dec. 10, 1945; see also Ibarguren (h.) [61].

sow alarm and confusion" and to deny that any of the groups supporting his candidacy were responsible.[26]

Despite the violence that accompanied this first open-air mass meeting, the political campaign had reached the point where it could no longer be confined to indoor meetings. Six days after the Unión Democrática rally, the Laborista Party held its first open-air assembly, a massive affair, at the Plaza de la República. And by the close of the month the Interior Minister was authorizing provincial interventors to use their own discretion in permitting outdoor meetings even as he distributed new instructions on how to prevent clashes before, during, or after such gatherings. Nevertheless, the pattern of political violence that had characterized the beginning of the political campaign was to continue until practically the eve of the February election.[27]

Even as the political campaign unfolded to reveal an Argentine nation passionately divided into hostile communities, each convinced of the sanctity of its cause, the armed forces were readying themselves to carry out a new assignment. Over the past decade, occasional voices had urged without success that the safeguarding of the election process be entrusted to the military rather than to the often partisan-controlled police forces. Now, however, the Farrell government, in conjunction with its December 1 decree detailing the offices to be filled and the rules that would apply in the February 24 general election, proclaimed that the armed forces would assure "access to the polls, the free exercise of the vote, and custody of the ballot boxes."[28]

Anticipating the role the Army would be called on to play, War Minister Sosa Molina sought to instill a heightened sense of discipline and unity. Hierarchical authority, which had suffered in the past from the existence of personal networks that competed with the chain of command, was now emphasized.[29] The War Minister also

---

[26] For the Democratic Union's reaction to the violence, see *La Prensa*, Dec. 10, 1945; for Perón's reaction, see *ibid.*, Dec. 12, 1945; for the Interior Minister's response, see *Las fuerzas armadas* [12], II, 158–59.

[27] *Las fuerzas armadas* [12], II, 191; *La Prensa*, Dec. 14, 15, 1945, for its back-page treatment of the Laborista Party meeting.

[28] *Las fuerzas armadas* [12], II, 142–44. The quoted words are in Article I, Paragraph i, page 143.

[29] General Kelso, the anti-Peronist Commander of Cavalry, told the Assistant U.S. Military Attaché in early November that for the first time he was really

sought to ease some of the bitterness that derived from the political clashes of the past several months. A dozen officers who had been expelled from the military for participating in the abortive Córdoba uprising in September were reincorporated, although in retired rather than active status. Even a group of eighteen teachers, many of them Socialist Party members, who had been ousted in August from the Liceo Militar San Martín were restored to their positions.[30]

Steps such as these could not, of course, erase the differences of viewpoint that existed within the officer corps. The Minister of War, however, shrewdly played on their sense of professionalism while carrying out a balancing act in making assignments and recommending promotions. The year-end promotion list, as approved by President Farrell, reflected at the top levels the contradictory pressures at work. Of the five brigadier generals promoted to major general, only one was regarded as a Perón supporter; but of the four colonels raised to the rank of brigadier general, certainly three, and possibly all four, were in that category. Moreover, two of these colonels, the Police Chief, Velazco and a cavalry officer, Leopoldo Peña, were promoted even though they were not general staff officers and lacked the equivalent training usually required for advancement to the highest ranks. From a professional viewpoint, their promotion could only be viewed as a political reward for services to Perón's cause.[31]

A similar interpretation could be made of the decision to assign General Ramón Albariño to head the important Campo de Mayo garrison. The center of a scandal because of charges that as Interventor of Buenos Aires province he had used his personal bank account to funnel political contributions to pro-Perón newspapers, Albariño resigned the post in January 1946 under heavy pressure

---

in control of his command (Embassy BA Telegram 2800, Nov. 7, 1945, 835.00/11-745).

[30] See *La Prensa*, Nov. 23, 1945, for the names of the teachers; *ibid.*, Jan. 1, 1946, for the names of the officers. Among the former were Luis Arocena, José Luis Romero, and Julio César González; among the latter, Generals Arturo Rawson and Osvaldo Martín.

[31] The promotions were authorized by Decree No. 34,517, Dec. 31, 1945, which is reproduced in *Senadores* [3], 1946, VII, 1170–71. The new major generals were: Juan C. Bassi, Juan Carlos Sanguinetti, Pablo Dávila, Víctor J. Majó, and Estanislao López; the new brigadier generals were: Armando S. Raggio, Isidro I. Martini, Juan F. Velazco, and Leopoldo T. Peña. For their political orientations see Table 2 above.

from the Navy, only to be rewarded with the prestigious Campo de Mayo assignment. The War Minister's defense of this assignment, in the face of newspaper criticism, as nonpolitical and based on the needs of the service was hardly persuasive. The appropriate action would have been to place Albariño in unassigned status (*disponibilidad*) until the judicial investigation into his conduct had been completed.[32]

Navy involvement in the Albariño affair was an unanticipated by-product of the decision to share responsibility for guaranteeing the elections among the three armed forces. An agreement worked out at cabinet level had provided for the creation of an Electoral Command Coordinating Committee consisting of the Army Commander-in-Chief, the Chief of the Naval General Staff, and the Commander of the Argentine Air Force, to be chaired by its senior member, Lieut. General Carlos von der Becke. This Coordinating Committee in turn had appointed commandants for each of the provinces and the Federal Capital, which comprised the country's fifteen electoral districts. Army officers were appointed as commandants in thirteen districts, an Air Force officer for the province of San Luis, and a Navy admiral for Buenos Aires province, in recognition of the fact that most Argentine naval forces were located on the coast of that province. When the Albariño affair broke, the insistence of that admiral, supported by his fellow officers, that the electoral guarantees in his province should be free of any doubt resulted in Albariño's resignation from the interventorship.[33]

A similar sense of responsibility seems to have characterized most if not all of the military men appointed as electoral commandants. Table 3 lists these officers and their districts and, where known, their political orientation. In the ten cases where such data are available—all Army generals—two are listed as Peronist, three as anti-Peronist, and five as neutral. These political labels indicate their personal inclinations and, in the absence of other evidence, do not mean that the officers used their positions to assist the candidates of their choice.

[32] *La Prensa*, Jan. 30, 1946, prints the War Minister's defense of the Albariño assignment. On the detailed charges made against him, *ibid.*, Jan. 16, 17, 1946.

[33] *Las fuerzas armadas* [12], II, 144–51, and 168–71, for the creation of the Electoral Command and the designation of officers; on the Navy's role in forcing General Albariño out of the interventorship, *La Prensa*, Jan. 17–21, 1946.

TABLE 3.—ELECTORAL DISTRICT COMMANDANTS

District	Name and Rank	Service	Political Orientation
Federal Capital	Maj. Gen. Diego Mason	Army	Neutral
Buenos Aires	Rear Adm. José Zuloaga	Navy	Unknown
Córdoba	Brig. Gen. Ambrosio Vago	Army	Peronist
Santa Fe	Brig. Gen. Pablo Dávila	Army	Neutral
Tucumán	Brig. Gen. Estanislao López	Army	Neutral-pro
Mendoza	Brig. Gen. Víctor J. Majó	Army	Neutral-anti
San Juan	Brig. Gen. Carlos Kelso	Army	Anti-Perón
Santiago del Estero	Brig. Gen. Ernesto Florit	Army	Anti-Perón
Salta	Brig. Gen. Pedro Abadíe Acuña	Army	Neutral-anti
San Luis	Vice Commodore Roberto Bonel	Air Force	Unknown
Corrientes	Brig. Gen. Raúl A. González	Army	Anti-Perón
Entre Ríos	Brig. Gen. Francisco A. Sáenz	Army	Peronist
Catamarca	Col. Julio B. Montoya	Army	Unknown
La Rioja	Col. Emilio Taft Olsen	Army	Unknown
Jujuy	Col. Guillermo C. Genta	Army	Unknown

Sources: *Fuerzas Armadas*, II, 168–69; and Table 2 above.

Indeed, in the case of General Ambrosio Vago, listed as Peronist, the available information indicates that he took great pains as electoral commandant for Córdoba to prevent interference with the electoral process. He issued sharp warnings to provincial policemen who disregarded the standing orders to maintain neutrality, suspended violators, and did not hesitate to transfer police from their usual districts to prevent incidents. Perhaps the best evidence that General Vago took his responsibilities seriously is that on election day, the Unión Democrática won a narrow victory.[34]

But if, despite his presumed personal inclinations, General Vago put duty above politics, the record in Entre Ríos, where another Perón sympathizer, General Francisco A. Sáenz, was in charge, is less clear-cut. Here, allegations of partisanship have been directed not against General Sáenz himself, but at the newly promoted General Leopoldo Peña, who, as Second Cavalry Division commander at Concordia, was also the local electoral commandant serving under the orders of General Sáenz. General Peña's aide, the then First Lieutenant Alejandro Lanusse, no Peronist sympathizer himself, later recalled the various ways his chief showed favor to the Laborista Party at the expense of the Unión Democrática. When representatives of

[34] Interview with General (Ret.) Ambrosio Vago, Aug. 1, 1962.

the latter group tried to see the electoral commandant, they were forced to cool their heels, while Laborista Party men were ushered in immediately. In issuing permits to hold public meetings, General Peña limited the Unión Democrática to remote areas at inconvenient hours, while allowing the Laboristas to hold meetings in the central plaza right after stores closed. Lanusse believed that though the electoral act was totally clean, "all that preceded it was saturated with favoritism."[35]

The creation of the Electoral Command Coordinating Committee and the appointment of the fifteen electoral commands were but the first steps in a carefully worked-out plan for guaranteeing the February 24 election. Operation orders comparable to those issued in time of war or national emergency flowed from the Coordinating Command headquarters, assigning units to be employed and specifying the steps to be taken to assure free access to the polls and the custody of the ballot boxes.[36]

A key issue to be resolved, one that in some ways was a test of the government's sincerity in pledging a free election, was the degree of control that the military electoral commanders would exercise over the police. Would the police be placed under military control, or would they function as an independent force, free to harass Unión Democrática supporters on orders from provincial interventors or their own leaders? The government at first appears to have preferred the latter arrangement, for the original directives issued by the Coordinating Committee stated only that the armed forces would "collaborate, whenever necessary, with the local police in the maintenance of general order."[37]

Within a week, however, a cabinet-level decision redefined the relationship between armed forces and police. Whether this derived from military pressure or from a desire to increase public confidence in its pledges is not clear, but the cabinet agreed that the military electoral commanders should have control over local police forces from the day before the election through the day after. Accordingly, the Coordinating Committee instructed the district commanders to

[35] Interview with General (Ret.) Alejandro A. Lanusse, Aug. 23, 1973.

[36] Ministerio de Guerra, *Memoria . . . 4 de junto de 1945–4 de junio de 1946* [20], pp. 32–72.

[37] Directive No. 1 for Electoral District Commanders, Article 1b, Dec. 24, 1945, *Las fuerzas armadas* [12], II, 173.

get full information on the existing distribution of police so as to be able to order whatever changes they felt necessary during the three-day period beginning February 23.[38] As the date of the election approached, the cabinet, apparently under pressure from high Army and Navy officers, decided to extend the period of military control. On February 8, it was announced that all police forces would be subordinate to the electoral commanders as of February 19. This meant that for the last four days of the electoral campaign, as well as on election day, the military were in an unchallenged position to enforce the pledge of official neutrality.[39] To whatever degree official favoritism or police interference had violated that pledge before, the finale of the campaign was designed, provided military men followed the orders of their superiors, to be an honorable experience above reproach.

The ten weeks before the election, however, witnessed a series of explosive political maneuvers, plots, charges, and countercharges, some of them of external origin, that served to raise the political temperature to new heights. The first of these bombshells was a government measure, ostensibly unrelated to the election, yet one that had greater repercussions in the short and long term than any event since October. On December 20, the Secretary of Labor and Welfare, Colonel Mercante, at a ceremony attended by President Farrell, announced the promulgation of a new wages and salary policy. Under the terms of Decree 33,302, employers would be required to pay a minimum wage geared to the cost of living, salary scales that reflected among other things the economic capacity of their enterprises, and annual bonuses equal to one month's pay. In addition, the decree increased severance pay benefits and set up a government-controlled institute to administer the entire policy. Full implementation of these benefits was expected to take time, but the decree mandated that employers must pay the first annual bonus and an emergency wage increase at the close of the current month.[40]

The decree, to be sure, did not include a profit-sharing provision

[38] Directive No. 2 for Electoral District Commanders, Article 1, Jan. 7, 1946, *ibid.*, p. 198. The cabinet decision was made on Dec. 31, 1945 (*ibid.*, p. 197).
[39] *Ibid.*, pp. 238–39.
[40] *Anales de legislación argentina* [1], 757–66; on Colonel Mercante's nation-wide radio speech giving credit for the decree to Perón, see *La Prensa*, Dec. 21, 1945.

that Perón from outside the government and Mercante from within had championed, but even so its provisions were too much a break from traditional employer prerogatives for business to swallow them quietly. On the other hand, the provisions were so clearly designed to widen support for the Laborista candidate as to create a major dilemma for his political opponents. If the latter accepted without criticism the wage decree, they were endorsing its appropriateness and by extension the wisdom of the man regarded as its originator, Colonel Perón; but if they attacked its provisions, they lent substance to his charge that the Unión Democrática was simply a front for reactionary elements with no concern for the working classes.

In this situation the Unión Democrática maintained an official silence, but not so the business community. With an energy rarely before displayed, employer associations representing trade, industry, and producers organized to resist the decree. A series of meetings culminating on December 27 in an assembly at the Buenos Aires Stock Exchange of almost 2,000 persons denounced the decree as unconstitutional, called on businessmen not to pay the bonus, and appointed an executive committee with authority to call for a nation-wide shutdown of economic activities if the government insisted on enforcing it.[41]

The legal period for payment of the bonus ended on January 7, and when that date passed with the employers still firm in their re-sistance, workers in one city after another went out on strike. In the heart of Buenos Aires, employees occupied many businesses includ-ing some of the larger stores; elsewhere, workers seized factories. An atmosphere of crisis spread, and to some it seemed that another October 17 was in the making. For their part, unable to persuade the government to rescind the decree, employer groups resorted to their ultimate weapon: the lockout. For three days in mid-January fac-tories and stores throughout the country shut down; the economy ground to a halt, and the cities of Argentina took on a deserted ap-pearance. But businessmen could not afford indefinite suspensions and when the government gave no sign of wavering, one by one different enterprises came to terms with their workers over the bonus payment. By the end of the month the employer rebellion was a thing of the past, but because major spokesmen for business interests

[41] *La Prensa*, Dec. 28, 1945.

were also open supporters of the Unión Democrática, the entire episode served both to reinforce Perón's appeal to the wage earner and to strengthen those union leaders supporting his election at the expense of Socialist and Communist rivals affiliated with the opposition.[42]

Even as the furor over the bonus payment was subsiding, rumors of impending revolutionary action contributed a new source of tension. The origin of these rumors lay, on the one hand, in the activities of an anti-Perón resistance movement, and, on the other hand, in what appeared to be Perón's determination to gain the presidency by any means, fair or foul. The anti-Perón resistance movement, which was headed by civilians but included a number of retired officers, had been trying to organize an uprising against the Farrell government ever since their failure to oust it in October 1945. Through the efforts of Colonel (Ret.) José F. Súarez and other retired officers including Bartolomé Gallo and Miguel Mascaró, supporters had been recruited among younger officers in the Army. How many active duty officers became involved cannot be established, but Lieut. Colonel Carlos Toranzo Montero, Commander of the Eleventh Cavalry Regiment in Entre Ríos, is known to have been one.[43]

The acquisition of weapons to arm the members of the resistance movement was a continuing preoccupation of its organizers. Efforts were made to purchase weapons in neighboring countries and even in the United States. Numerous inquiries were made of the U.S. Embassy in Buenos Aires about establishing contacts with arms dealers; and, through a U.S. businessman acting as an intermediary, Assistant Secretary Spruille Braden was approached in late November to ask whether the State Department could furnish arms, especially submachine guns and bazookas. The request was categorically rejected.[44]

[42] *Ibid.*, Jan. 10–30, 1946; for a good discussion of this episode and its political impact see Luna, *El 45* [262], pp. 444–51.

[43] Embassy BA Telegram 2800, Nov. 7, 1945, 835.00/11-745; Dispatch 1747, Jan. 9, 1946, 835.00/1-946; interviews with Generals (Ret.) Bartolomé Gallo, Feb. 23, 1970, Carlos Toranzo Montero, March 22, 1970, and A. A. Lanusse.

[44] U.S. Military Attaché, Uruguay, Report No. R-484-45, dated Dec. 18, 1945, Blue Book Files; Department of State Memorandum of Conversation between Mr. R. B. Smith, General Manager, Will L. Smith, S.A., Buenos Aires, and Mr. Braden, Nov. 26, 1945, 835.00/11-2645; Embassy BA Dispatch 1747, Jan. 9, 1946, cited in note 43.

The effort to acquire arms continued through early January 1946. Without additional weapons it seemed unlikely that civilians could constitute a military force of any significance. Nevertheless, in the week of January 21–28, rumors of an imminent uprising intensified. The attacks by Perón supporters on the presidential campaign train of Unión Democrática candidate Tamborini, the appointment of a known Perón supporter as Interventor of Buenos Aires province replacing General Albariño, the assignment of police to watch the Navy officers who had demanded his ouster, and the appointment of Albariño as Campo de Mayo commandant all served to convince the anti-Perón activists that the government would not permit an honest election. With only a month remaining to election day, an attempt to force a change in the government had to be made soon.[45]

Over the next several days Buenos Aires was swept by fantastic rumors, many of them emanating from Uruguayan radios. None of the dire predictions materialized in deeds; but within the government, behind the scenes a significant struggle was taking place that would decide which of its dual objectives would take priority: assuring Perón's succession or guaranteeing the honesty of the forthcoming election. The issue that apparently provoked the cabinet conflict was a Perón proposal to postpone the elections at the provincial level. The competing ambitions of his Laborista and Unión Cívica Radical Junta Renovadora (UCRJR) supporters had delayed the nomination of gubernatorial candidates in several provinces, and time was needed to resolve the differences. But the proposal for delaying the provincial elections, if adopted, implied a retreat from the government's well-publicized promise to hold general elections on February 24. Because the prestige of the armed forces was involved in this commitment, their own integrity would be exposed to question.

The presence in the capital of all the electoral district commanders on January 31 when the cabinet took up the Perón proposal seems to have been more than a coincidence. At any rate, despite the urgings of Perón's adherents, the determined stance of the Navy Minister, combined with the attitude of certain Army officers, carried

[45] Embassy BA Telegrams 220, Jan. 21, 1946, 835.00/1-2146; 230, Jan. 22, 1946, 835.00/1-2246; 261, Jan. 25, 1946, 835.00/1-2546.

the day against postponement.[46] To preserve appearances, the Interior Minister issued an official statement on February 1, denying that the government had ever considered postponing the election in whole or in part.[47] But there is little doubt that the decision on this issue was a turning point; and taken together with a new War Ministry general order warning against political partisanship in the Army and a series of public meetings in which the President of the Electoral Coordinating Commission, General von der Becke, explained the plans for guaranteeing the election, the atmosphere of skepticism that had pervaded the Unión Democrática leadership, the independent press, and the diplomatic corps about the honesty of the forthcoming election began to dissipate.[48] The February 8 decision to advance the date when the military took control of the police, previously discussed, also served to increase optimism in opposition circles. Perhaps the best indication of Unión Democrática confidence in the honesty of the February 24 elections was a secret meeting a week before that date when vice-presidential candidate Dr. Enrique Mosca apprised members of the anti-Perón resistance movement that he was aware of their activities and urged them to desist.[49]

Buoyed by their expectations of victory in a free election, the leadership of the Unión Democrática now intensified their verbal assaults on Perón. Their entire campaign had sought to draw a distinction between themselves as the champions of freedom and democracy and Perón as the incarnation of fascism and Nazism. Now with the fraudulent road to electoral victory closed, they charged Perón with planning to take power by the only route available: insurrection.

On February 10, the national interparty executive committee of the Unión Democrática presented a written denunciation to War Minister Sosa Molina and to General von der Becke of a Perón plan to prevent the holding of the elections. The outlines of the alleged plan had already been set forth a few days before by Progressive Democratic Party leader Julio Noble. Perón would make a spectacu-

[46] Embassy BA Telegram 349, Feb. 1, 1946, 835.00/2-146; see also *La Prensa*, Feb. 1, 1946, editorial; *Las fuerzas armadas* [12], II, 221.
[47] *La Prensa*, Feb. 2, 1946.
[48] *Las fuerzas armadas* [12], II, 223–24, 225–27.
[49] Interview with General (Ret.) Lanusse.

lar resignation of his candidacy; his followers would gather in a mass demonstration as on October 17 and proclaim him president by "plebiscite." Military support to be provided by four infantry regiments, the capital police, Air Force units, and 2,000 armed civilians would neutralize the expected reaction from the Navy and the public. The political rally called for February 12 by the Laborista, UCRJR, Alianza Libertadora Nacionalista, and other pro-Perón groups, ostensibly to proclaim the candidacy of Perón and Quijano, was expected to provide the occasion for the coup.[50]

Whether there was any substance to these charges cannot be established with certainty. The War Minister immediately appointed the Chief of the Army General Staff, Major General Juan C. Bassi, an officer regarded as politically neutral but with little liking for Perón, to conduct an investigation of the possible involvement of Army personnel. Even as General Bassi was in the process of gathering data, including taking testimony from the accusers of Perón and from some 60 officers of the Army units alleged to be involved, the February 12 Peronist political rally took place without incident. The preceding day, however, General von der Becke, in an off-the-record interview, had stated flatly that the Army "would suppress whatever attempt might be made to prevent fulfillment of the promise of honest elections." Moreover, he stated explicitly that force would be used if necessary to maintain order against Perón partisans.[51]

The Bassi investigation turned up no concrete evidence to support the allegations of the Unión Democrática leaders. They had refused his request to identify the persons who had supplied them with their information; in turn, the officers of the units supposedly involved in the plot flatly denied the imputations made against them. It is quite possible, therefore, that the alleged plot was more imaginary than real and that its public denunciation was in part a political ploy intended to put Perón on the defensive, in part a test of the armed forces' determination to guarantee the election. On the other hand, if Perón adherents had been contemplating an extraconstitu-

[50] *Las fuerzas armadas* [12], II, 237–38, 247–49; *La Prensa*, Feb. 11, 15, 1946.

[51] *La Prensa*, Feb. 12, 1946; *Las fuerzas armadas* [12], II, 249–53; see Embassy BA Telegram 451, Feb. 11, 1946, 835.00/2-1146, for von der Becke's remarks.

tional move, the firm position adopted by the Army and Navy leadership may have discouraged any steps to implement it.[52]

Even before General Bassi's investigation had run its course, public attention was diverted from domestic charges of plots and counterplots to a new and explosive denunciation emanating from Washington, D.C. On February 11, the Department of State distributed copies of its "Argentine Blue Book." Compiled from a variety of sources including captured German records and interrogations of former German officials, the Blue Book charged numerous members of the military regime and especially Colonel Perón with having been Nazi accomplices during World War II and with creating a Nazi-fascist state in Argentina. The major thrust of the Blue Book was to document the protection given to Nazi espionage and economic interests, the totalitarian character of the Farrell regime, and the threat it presented to neighboring countries.[53]

The publication of the Blue Book was only the latest of a series of measures begun by the United States during World War II to bring Argentina into line with the rest of the hemisphere. With the close of the war, these efforts intensified, for there was little disposition on the part of substantial sectors of American opinion or of the man charged with directing the State Department's Latin American policy, Spruille Braden, to allow a man like Juan Perón to control the destinies of Argentina now that the Axis had been defeated. With a moralistic fervor reminiscent of Woodrow Wilson's campaign against the Mexican dictator Victoriano Huerta, Braden worked to bring down the Farrell military government and in the process to terminate the political career of Colonel Perón.

The complete history of the Blue Book episode from its conception through its preparation to its release deserves a separate monograph. Here the principal concerns are with its purpose, the timing of its release, and its impact within Argentina. Contrary to appearances, the idea of trying to influence the February 24 election had little to do with the original decision to prepare this special study on

[52] On the report of the Bassi investigation, *Las fuerzas armadas* [12], II, 249–50; *La Prensa*, Feb. 19, 1946; Luna, *El 45* [262], p. 464, flatly denies that the plot ever existed.
[53] *Consultation Among the American Republics with Respect to the Argentine Situation* [37].

the Argentine situation. When Secretary of State James Byrnes on October 25 authorized the creation of a task force to produce what ultimately became the Blue Book, the principal aim was to prepare a documented study supported, among other sources, by evidence obtained from official German records, so as to be able to persuade the other American republics to maintain a common front against the Argentine regime. Indeed, when the task force first assembled on October 30 to contemplate its work, Washington had little confidence that the Farrell regime would even hold elections. The magnitude of the work and the urgency of completing it were the major concerns of the men assigned to direct the project.[54]

Five weeks later, as the materials from Germany began to accumulate and the Argentine government's promise of elections took on credibility, the idea of utilizing the one to influence the other was suggested to Spruille Braden by a visiting Argentine newspaper editor, Hugo Stunz. Whether Braden had already given thought to his idea is not clear. Stunz's proposal was "to release a statement of the evidence found in Germany about twenty days before the elections scheduled for February 24."[55]

A different approach was recommended by the U.S. Chargé d'Affaires in Buenos Aires, John Cabot. Anxious that the German material should be placed before the Argentine public, but sensitive to the possible charge of intervention, he urged the earliest possible publication of the material, even if only a part of it. "Any publication after January 1," he cabled on December 4, "is certain to be pounced on by Perón clique as [a] clumsy effort to influence election and consequently as further alleged intervention in Argentine internal affairs."[56]

Cabot's advice influenced the State Department decision to allow him to release a preliminary body of material on January 17 in the form of photocopies of thirteen telegrams from the German Embassy in Buenos Aires. These telegrams documented the extent of German

[54] Department of State, Memorandum of Meeting, Oct. 30, 1945. Subject: Preparation of Material concerning the Argentine Situation and Enclosure, Departmental Order No. 1353, dated Oct. 25, 1945, issued by James F. Byrnes, 835.00/10-3045.

[55] Department of State, Memorandum of Conversation between Mr. Hugo Stunz, editor of *El Dia* in La Plata and Mr. Braden, Dec. 3, 1945, 835.00/12-345.

[56] Embassy BA Telegram 3033, Dec. 4, 1945, 835.00/12-445.

subsidies to Argentine newspapers during the war. The fact that two of the newspapers currently supporting Perón's candidacy, *La Epoca* and *Tribuna,* had traceable links to the publications financed by the Germans was apparently not without influence on the decision.[57]

As January turned into February and the prospects for the Unión Democrática improved, Cabot became leery of any further official release of material before February 24. When he learned on Friday, February 8, that the State Department planned to release the completed text of the Blue Book the following Monday, he urged delay: "Perón has suffered a series of disasters recently and majority of observers now think he cannot win elections. To throw 'atomic bomb' directly at Argentine Government in present supercharged atmosphere is to court incalculable results. Opinion will be universal that we are trying to influence election results."[58]

Cabot's concern, however, was not shared by his superiors in the State Department. Spruille Braden was not one to be deterred at this late date by charges of intervention; if the Unión Democrática forces were gaining on Perón, then the publication of the damning materials would provide the coup de grace to his candidacy. And in any case, if Cabot was apprehensive about the impact on the election of releasing the document, Argentine politicians, including the Unión Democrática vice-presidential candidate, Dr. Enrique Mosca, favored immediate release.[59]

Apart from political calculations, the Blue Book project had acquired a bureaucratic momentum of its own. For over three months scores of people had been working on it under pressure in both the United States and Germany. Data had been sifted from tons of records dispersed in that country; task force members had prepared lengthy memorandums that were reduced to a single rough draft only by the morning of February 4. Over the next several days this draft was polished into the final text and made ready for the printer in the early hours of Saturday, February 9. To have to shelve the product of all these efforts, even if only temporarily, was too much

[57] Department of State, *Foreign Relations of the United States, 1946,* [39], XI, 183–84, 187–90.

[58] Cabot to the Secretary of State, Buenos Aires, Feb. 8, 1946, Telegram 430, *ibid.*, pp. 201–2. A follow-up telegram (No. 432, Feb. 9, 1946) gives Cabot's second thoughts on the matter (*ibid.*, pp. 203–4).

[59] Secretary of State to Cabot, *ibid.*, p. 204; on Dr. Mosca's approving attitude see Embassy BA Telegram 435, Feb. 9, 1946, 835.00/2-946.

to expect. The view from Washington, after all, was not the same as that from the Embassy in Buenos Aires.[60]

The release of the Blue Book reverberated through Argentina with the force of a wild pampero. The anti-Perón press, which included most of the dailies in Buenos Aires and the provinces, devoted more space to the Blue Book than to any event since the close of the war. Day after day, their columns were filled with reproductions of the Blue Book text, editorials, and ancillary stories. The pro-Perón newspapers, for their part, carefully refrained from printing any of the text. Instead, in headlines and articles, they denounced the issuance of the Blue Book as the grossest form of intervention in Argentine internal affairs, denied the accuracy of its charges, and published countercharges of United States espionage in Argentina. Given the barrage of words printed in the Argentine press between February 13 and 23, it is difficult to conceive of a voting-age person who had not heard of the Libro Azul in one context or another.[61]

The immediate response of the Farrell government to the issuance of the Blue Book, a copy of which did not officially reach its hands for several days, was on the whole restrained. Although some cabinet members urged a break in relations, the government limited itself to the issuance of statements critical of the Blue Book as an act of interference in domestic affairs. It promised a detailed response to the charges in due time and meanwhile reaffirmed Argentina's observance of its hemispheric obligations. The detailed response, in the form of a Foreign Ministry publication directed to the other American republics, was issued a month after the elections.[62]

Within the armed forces, reactions to the Blue Book varied, but the predominant feeling among most Army and Air Force officers was one of deep indignation. Many of the officers who were named in the Blue Book as Nazi sympathizers or worse published denials in the form of paid advertisements that appeared in the press. In the Navy, where opposition to Perón had been most widespread, the

[60] On the work required to produce the Blue Book, see Roland D. Hussey's typed statement dated Feb. 13, 1946, that is pasted to the inside cover of the master copy located in the National Archives, Argentine Blue Book Files, Box No. 1.

[61] Embassy BA Dispatch 2087, Feb. 20, 1946, 835.00/2-2046.

[62] Embassy BA Telegrams 506, Feb. 16, 1946, 835.00/2-1646; 518, Feb. 17, 1946, 835.00/2-1746; 520, Feb. 18, 1946, 835.00/2-1846; Ministerio de Relaciones Exteriores y Culto [28].

sense of satisfaction generated by the Blue Book was tempered by concern that its appearance only days before the election would prejudice the anti-Peronist cause. Some Unión Democrática leaders feared that Army officers, stung by the Blue Book, would do everything in their power to ensure that the government remained in friendly hands.[63]

For Colonel Perón, the Blue Book provided both a challenge and an opportunity, and indeed he lost no time in employing the publication for his own advantage. With the political instinct that had served him so well over the past two years, he made no effort to defend himself against its charges, but rather used the occasion of its appearance to attack Spruille Braden and make foreign domination a main issue of the campaign. In the closing words of his February 12 proclamation address delivered before a mass meeting of his followers in Buenos Aires and broadcast nationwide, he defined the choice for his countrymen: "Let those who vote on the twenty-fourth for the Oligarchic-Communist alliance know that they are simply voting for Mr. Braden. The question of the hour is this: Braden or Perón. Paraphrasing the immortal phrase of Roque Sáenz Peña—let the people know how to vote."[64]

The final week of the electoral campaign unfolded under the influence of the Blue Book affair. Perón supporters distributed handbills by the thousands and plastered city walls with posters all bearing the simple but incisive three-word message: "Braden or Perón." On the final day of the campaign, Perón issued a pamphlet reply to the Blue Book designed to demonstrate Braden's control over vital Argentine institutions that were supporting the Unión Democrática and also to document instances of U.S. Embassy espionage. Perhaps the most significant aspect of this hastily prepared and poorly printed pamphlet, which appeared on the stalls the night of February 22, was its effective title: Libro Azul y Blanco. Once again, this time through reference to the national colors, the point was made that a vote for Perón was a vote for the defense of national sovereignty.[65]

[63] Embassy BA Telegrams 515, Feb. 16, 1946, 835.00/2-1646; and 569, Feb. 23, 1946, 835.00/2-2346.

[64] Cabot to the Secretary of State, Feb. 13, 1946, in *Foreign Relations of the United States, 1946* [39], XI, 210–11.

[65] Embassy BA Telegrams 556, Feb. 21, 1946, 835.00/2-2146; and 569, Feb. 23, 1946, 835.00/2-2346; Luna, *El 45* [262], pp. 534–39.

The final week also witnessed a recrudescence of the violence that had punctuated the campaign since the beginning. The most serious episode occurred in Buenos Aires on February 19, after the Tamborini-Mosca campaign train returned to the city from a tour of the interior. Although the candidates themselves were not hurt, three persons were killed and six wounded when shots were fired into the waiting crowd at Plaza Once. The next day, at the funeral for one of the victims, even though military forces were assigned to provide protection, shots were again fired at the participants. These episodes caused deep concern among Unión Democrática supporters, who took them as indication that the February 24 election, despite all the promised guarantees, would turn out to be a violent affair.[66]

Such pessimism proved to be unwarranted. Perhaps because under the law the political campaign had to close at midnight on February 22, thus allowing a day of quiet for passions to subside, perhaps because of the presence of a horde of foreign newsmen to report on the event, but more likely because of the clear determination of the armed forces not to allow the process to be sullied, the February 24 election was one of the cleanest, if not the cleanest, in Argentine history. Voters turned out in record numbers to cast their ballots in orderly fashion. The deployment of troops in each electoral district assured peaceful access to the polls throughout the day and safeguarded the ballot boxes from subsequent violation. The military had indeed guaranteed the honesty of the vote, and their performance won praise from all political sectors, the press, and foreign observers. Among those who were quick to salute the military was Dr. José Tamborini, the Unión Democrática presidential candidate. Convinced of his own victory, he greeted "the rebirth of brotherhood between the people and the armed forces."[67]

For a week after the elections, as the vote count proceeded with exasperating slowness, Unión Democrática supporters continued to believe in Tamborini's victory. Only after the returns from the Federal Capital, Santa Fe, Mendoza, and Entre Ríos began to mount up were their illusions destroyed. Contrary to their original belief,

[66] Embassy BA Telegram 564, Feb. 22, 1946, 835.00/2-2246; *La Prensa*, Feb. 16, 20, 21, 1946; Luna, *El 45* [262], pp. 471–72.

[67] *Las fuerzas armadas* [12], II, 329–30; for military reports on their election day activities, *ibid.*, pp. 331–49; on foreign reaction, *The Times* (London), Feb. 25, 1946.

Perón had won the presidency in an honest vote. In addition, his followers gained overwhelming control of both Houses of the national Congress and all the governorships but one.[68]

The achievement of the Peronists in the congressional and gubernatorial races, where the parties that made up the Unión Democrática ran competing tickets, has tended to obscure the narrowness of Perón's victory in the presidential contest. It has often been stated that his margin of victory over Tamborini was in excess of 54 percent.[69] Yet a recent survey of the election statistics, based on the official vote counts from each district kept on file in the Ministry of Interior, reveals that Perón received only 52.4 percent of the 2,839,507 votes cast and had a margin over his opponent of only 280,806.[70]

These figures suggest that the Unión Democrática anticipation of victory was not without foundation. A shift of only 140,500 votes away from Perón would have given Tamborini the popular majority. More to the point, a shift of only 37,350 votes in five electoral districts would have given him a majority in the electoral college.[71]

The narrowness of Perón's electoral victory makes it more than likely that the Blue Book served to swing the balance in his favor. This does not discount the fact that working-class men voted overwhelmingly for him. But as recent studies have shown, Perón received substantial support from other social sectors.[72] One category of voter that would seem to have been particularly sensitive to U.S. intervention was the young man casting his vote in a presidential election for the first time. Over 700,000 more registered voters were eligible to cast ballots in 1946 than in 1937, a figure that approxi-

---

[68] Luna, *El 45* [262], pp. 576–81.

[69] Smith, *Argentina and the Failure of Democracy* [272], p. 103, refers to a "solid 54 percent majority"; Luna *El 45* [262], p. 583, states that "55 percent of the electorate had voted for Perón."

[70] The complete vote, with percentage of the overall total in parentheses, was as follows: Peronist, 1,487,886 (52.40); Democratic Union, 1,207,080 (42.51); National Democrat, 43,499 (1.53); Lencinista UCR, 3,918 (0.14); Bloquista UCR, 13,469 (0.47); Santiago del Estero UCR, 12,362 (0.44); Blank, 23,735 (0.84); Unidentified remainder, 47,558 (1.67) (Cantón, *Materiales para el estudio de sociología política en la argentina*, [105], I, 129).

[71] The breakdown is as follows: 21,700 votes in the Federal Capital; 7,559 in Entre Ríos; 5,489 in Mendoza; 1,976 in Catamarca; and 619 in La Rioja (based on election data given in *ibid.*).

[72] Smith, "The Social Base of Peronism" [274], pp. 67–68; Llorente [261], pp. 61–68.

mates the number of young men who had come of voting age since the fraudulent Ortiz election.[73] Although social class, family tradition, and even religious considerations exercised their influence on most voters, it is probable that many young men, hitherto uncommitted, or even leaning to the Unión Democrática candidate, voted for Perón out of patriotic resentment.[74]

What would have happened in Argentina had the figures been reversed and Dr. Tamborini emerged victorious is beyond the historian's obligation to discuss. Interviews with Peronist Army officers a quarter century later, however, produced unanimous agreement that the Army would have upheld the electorate's decision. This, of course, was the declared position of the armed forces at the time, but fortunately or unfortunately, depending on one's viewpoint, it never had to be put to the test. The "rebirth of brotherhood between the armed forces and the people" that Tamborini spoke of with reference to his own supporters applied with even greater force to the masses that voted for Perón. Unlike its role between 1932 and 1943 as the defender of essentially unpopular and minority governments, the Army could look ahead to a more comfortable role as the protective arm of a duly elected constitutional government.

[73] Cantón, *Materiales* [105], I, 119, 129, gives the number of registered voters in 1937 as 2,672,750 and in 1946 as 3,405,173, or an increase of 732,423. Military conscription data indicate that approximately 112,000 young men turned eighteen in 1937 and the next two years. Projecting this number for the period 1938–45 would give approximately 896,000 men in the 18–25 age group who had never before voted for a president ("Cantidad de ciudadanos sorteados . . . para cada uno de los años 1920 a 1939," Ministerio de Guerra, *Memoria . . . 1940–1941* [19]).

[74] The view that the Blue Book provided the margin of victory for Perón is stated by General (Ret.) Carlos von der Becke in *Destrucción de una infamia* [130], p. 274. Von der Becke was the President of the Electoral Coordinating Committee in 1946. Perón himself expressed the belief that he owed his victory to Spruille Braden's intervention in a conversation with U.S. Ambassador George Messersmith which the latter quoted in a letter of February 26, 1947, to William Pawley. I am indebted to Ray Sadler for bringing this to my attention.

Chapter 3

The Perón Presidency: Consolidation, 1946–1948

The inauguration of Juan D. Perón as constitutional president of the Argentine nation on June 4, 1946, marked a new phase in the political career of this talented figure, even as it raised hopes for a kind of normalcy after three years of military government. For Perón the week that saw him donning the presidential sash marked the culmination of two ambitions: on May 29 the outgoing government had decreed his restoration to active duty status and promotion to the rank of brigadier general. Not quite 51 years of age, Perón had thus fulfilled the aspiration of every career Army officer even as he joined the select company of those elected to the Argentine presidency.[1]

What did this dual status as general and president mean for the nature of the forthcoming administration? To what extent would military concerns and a military mentality shape its style, goals, and methods? How would Perón reconcile his inaugural pledge to uphold the constitution and to be President of all the Argentines with a military man's tendency to prefer uniformity to diversity, to equate loyalty with obedience, and to regard public criticism as bordering on the subversive? Moreover, given his political debt to the laboring classes, to whose social betterment he committed himself anew in his inaugural address, how would he reconcile the demands of his various constituencies, military and civilian?

Perón, of course, was not the first general to serve as an elected president. General Agustín Justo, the last individual to hold both

[1] Perón was born on October 8, 1895. For his reincorporation and promotion see Decree No. 15,656 in Ministerio de Guerra, *Boletín Militar Público* [13], No. 767.

distinctions, had, perhaps because of the dubious nature of his election, downplayed his military ties by retiring from active duty just prior to his inauguration and by eschewing the uniform for civilian dress.[2] General Perón, in contrast, wore the uniform and thus drew attention to his military personality, at the same time expressing his pride at "having reached the highest office through the consensus of wills that repudiated alien pressure, through the assent of all those who wished justice to prevail over interest"—in short, through a popular awakening.[3] Aware of his widespread popularity and confident that the legitimacy of his election could not be impugned, General Perón stressed his military status, perhaps both as a warning to those at home and abroad who might still be disposed to obstruct his government and as a signal to his supporters that in the administration that was about to unfold, their role was to follow, his was to lead.

Indeed, he did more than signal, for in his inaugural address to the assembly of recently elected senators and deputies, he made very plain his determination to be an active chief executive, exercising to the full the powers of the presidency to carry out his mandate from the people.[4] Moreover, he announced, "I will always give more importance to immediate practical achievements than to involved discussions about organizational structure. . . . More than good planners we need ready performers."[5]

In the light of this preference for action-oriented administrators rather than planners, it is useful to examine the President's choice of collaborators. The cabinet he appointed was overwhelmingly civilian; of the twelve ministerial and secretariat positions, only the three armed service posts and the Public Works Ministry went to military men. In this last case, the choice went to a holdover from the previous government, the 63-year-old General (Ret.) Juan Pistarini, who had served continuously as Minister of Public Works since December 1943 and who was to establish a service record by remaining in that post until 1952. Perón's choices for the other cab-

---

[2] For Justo, see Potash, The Army & Politics in Argentina, 1928–1945 [188], Chapter 4.
[3] The text of the inaugural message is reproduced in Diputados [2], 1946, I, 39–47. The quoted words are on page 40.
[4] Ibid., p. 42.
[5] Ibid., p. 43.

inet posts differed in several respects from earlier cabinets. First, the members were young, with the youngest, the Finance Minister, Dr. Ramón Cereijo, only 33, and the oldest civilian, the Secretary of Labor and Welfare, José María Freire, all of 44. A second distinctive feature was the appointment of three men drawn from the ranks of organized labor. In addition to the Labor Secretariat, the important and prestigious Ministries of Interior and Foreign Affairs went to Angel Borlenghi and Dr. Juan Bramuglia, respectively, the former the veteran head of the commercial workers with long experience in trade union politics, the latter a labor lawyer who had drafted much of the labor legislation decreed by the military government.[6]

In terms of education and prior experience, Perón's first cabinet did not break sharply from past tradition. Six of the eight civilian appointees were university trained and had had prior government experience.[7] Including the military appointees, three of the members were holdovers in the same posts from the previous administration (War Minister Sosa Molina, Secretary of Industry and Commerce Rolando Lagomarsino, and Public Works Minister Pistarini), and a fourth, the Agriculture Minister Picazo Elordy, had moved up from the undersecretariat of Industry and Commerce. This was not, then, a cabinet devoid of experience or ability, as some contemporary critics held. What it lacked, however, with perhaps one or two exceptions, were individuals of personal distinction, men of acknowledged prestige and professional stature, who could command the respect of opponents as well as supporters of the new government.[8]

[6] The Ministers were: War, General J. Humberto Sosa Molina; Navy, Captain Fidel Anadón; Justice and Public Instruction, Dr. Belisario Gache Pirán; Finance, Dr. Ramón Cereijo; Interior, Angel Borlenghi; Foreign Relations, Dr. Juan Bramuglia; Agriculture, Juan C. Picazo Elordy; Public Works, General (Ret.) Juan Pistarini. The State Secretaries were: Air Force, Brigadier Bartolomé de la Colina; Public Health, Dr. Ramón Carrillo; Industry and Commerce, Rolando Lagomarsino; Labor and Welfare, José María Freire.

[7] The exceptions were Interior Minister Borlenghi and Labor Secretary Freire. Lagomarsino and Elordy had both attended the National University of Buenos Aires (UNBA), but apparently did not complete a degree program. Carrillo, Gache Pirán, and Cereijo were all graduates of UNBA; Bramuglia had received his degree at the National University of La Plata.

[8] The most distinguished member was probably Dr. Carrillo, a neurosurgeon and full professor at UNBA Medical School, from which he had graduated in 1929 with the *medallo de oro* or gold medal as the outstanding student in his class.

But then again, this was not a traditional Conservative or Radical administration, but one that was identified with a charismatic leader and with a program of accelerating the economic and social changes he had initiated during the military regime.

Although the President turned primarily to civilians to staff the cabinet, military men received appointments to head several key agencies. The Federal Police was again entrusted to Perón's nationalistic academy classmate, General Juan F. Velazco; General Ramón Albariño, whose role in the electoral campaign, as noted earlier, had aroused much controversy, was named to head YPF, the state petroleum agency; and another political ally, General A. Vargas Belmonte, became the head of the National Transportation Bureau that had jurisdiction over highways and railroads. With these and other appointments, Perón sought the dual objective of rewarding loyal supporters while giving the Army a sense of participation in such areas of strategic interest as energy, transportation, and internal security.[9]

Within the Casa Rosada or Government House, the President also provided for an added military presence. Beyond the usual staff of military aides, the Casa Militar, Perón began his administration by creating a centralized presidential intelligence office and an office called the Military Secretariat. The intelligence office, known usually by its initials CIDE, was headed by a senior Army officer and served to coordinate the foreign and domestic intelligence activities of the armed forces and other departments of government. The CIDE was to be a permanent part of the Perón administration.[10] The Military Secretariat, however, proved to be more ephemeral.

Created apparently to parallel the Political and Technical Secretariats, which were respectively headed by Perón's close advisors, Ramón Subiza and José Figuerola, the Military Secretariat provided a place in the Casa Rosada for Colonel (later General) Oscar Silva. Silva, a longtime Perón adherent, was identified with extreme nationalists in and out of the armed forces, and his appointment, together with that of the like-minded Police Chief, General Velazco, was designed to give those elements a degree of representation in

---

[9] For the various appointments see *La Prensa*, June 6–15, 1946. Colonel (Ret.) Bartolomé Descalzo was continued as head of the National Energy Bureau.

[10] The CIDE was created by Decree No. 337 of June 13, 1946. I am indebted to General (Ret.) Oscar Uriondo for providing data about this agency, which he headed from 1949 to 1953 (interview Aug. 5, 1973).

the administration. In little over a year, however, policy and personality differences led to the resignations of both Velazco and Silva and to the total dissolution of the Military Secretariat.[11] Shortly thereafter, in response to concerns voiced in military circles about official corruption, the President created another office under a military man to report directly to himself. Known as Control de Estado, its functions were to watch over administrative morality and see that presidential directives were enforced.[12] Through the mechanisms of CIDE and Control de Estado, the President was in a position to be well informed about the operations of his own administration at all levels and, whenever he so chose, to root out the corrupt as well as the disloyal. As will be shown, his reluctance to act against corruption was conditioned by the fact that key figures within the administration and even members of the presidential household were believed to be using their public position for private profit.

No effort to understand the inner dynamics of the Perón administration would be complete without attention to two individuals who were responsible in their separate ways for much of its controversial image in its first three years. These were, of course, the President's wife, María Eva Duarte de Perón, and his principal economic advisor and policy maker, Miguel Miranda.

At a time when a woman in politics was a rarity and in a country where presidents' wives had usually remained behind the scenes except for an occasional social or charitable event, Mrs. Perón's activities produced shock waves among her countrymen. Unwilling to accept the restricted role of her predecessors, she transformed the initial influence inherent in her position as wife of the President into genuine political power. She became a political partner with her husband, and not necessarily the junior partner. Indeed, one official who served for five years in the cabinet later recalled, "I never knew who was governing whom."[13]

Except in certain matters, Eva Perón seemed less concerned with policy issues than with personalities. She had a penchant for intrigue

[11] For data on the background leading to these resignations and the dissolution of Silva's office see Embassy BA Telegram 673, June 4, 1947, 835.00/6-447, and Airgram 468, July 25, 1947, 835.00/7-2547; also *Qué*, July 29, 1947, p. 6.

[12] Interview with General Uriondo.

[13] Interview with Carlos Emery, July 22, 1971. Emery was Perón's second Minister of Agriculture from August 1947 to June 1952.

and enjoyed the sensation of manipulating people. Within the cabinet and presidential entourage, she had her own clique of favorites, and she did not hesitate to use her position to advance their interests as against their rivals. She could be overbearing, and more than one cabinet official found himself the target of her vindictiveness. To men resentful of a woman's presence to begin with, and this included not a few military officers, her behavior was a source of deep concern. One officer who had served as a presidential military aide from 1946 to 1948 recalled with distaste how Mrs. Perón ordered cabinet officers around, employing the familiar "tu" to summon them to her side. This same officer proudly noted that, fortunately, she never tried this with him, but added that he was relieved to get a foreign assignment in 1949.[14]

Evita's principal interests lay in the constituencies she staked out for herself in the trade union movement, in charitable work, and in women's rights. From an office in the Labor and Welfare Secretariat, she supervised the relations of the administration with the trade unions, converting the Secretary, José Freire, into a mere puppet.[15] Not only did Evita in effect take over this agency, but she began to play an active role in trade union politics. Her intervention led to the unseating of Aurelio Hernández, the Secretary-General of the CGT (General Confederation of Labor), in December 1947 and the election in his place of a man with practically no trade union experience, José Espejo.[16]

Evita was passionately committed to improving the lot of the working classes, especially that of lower-class women and children, with whom, because of her own background, she could readily identify. With funds obtained from a variety of private sources, and not always voluntarily, Evita directed a charitable foundation organized in her name. The operations of this foundation, which were never subject to public scrutiny, had the commendable aim of alleviating the condition of the distressed. The results, however, were often something else. Evita lacked the training or skills needed to direct a

---

[14] Interview with General (Ret.) Juan José Uranga, July 27, 1971.

[15] *Ibid.*; also interview with Aurelio Hernández, June 14, 1962. Hernández, CGT Secretary-General from January to December 1947, provided details on the selection of Freire and on the humiliating treatment to which he was subjected.

[16] Hernández interview. See also Alexander [283], pp. 110–11.

charitable foundation of this magnitude efficiently and was frequently victimized by swindlers who took advantage of her sentimental impulse to assist those who claimed to be life's tragic victims. Nevertheless, her activities benefited many with genuine needs and helped create for herself in the hearts of the poor an indelible image of generosity and compassion.[17]

Next to the President and Mrs. Perón, no member of the administration was to attract so much attention at home and abroad as the Central Bank president, Miguel Miranda. Originally an industrialist in the food-processing sector, Miranda had developed a close relationship with Perón beginning in 1944, when he served on the board of the state industrial bank (Banco de Crédito Industrial) and later on the National Postwar Council, a body Perón had set up to define priorities for future economic development. Miranda shared Perón's ideas for promoting economic independence while raising living standards and, almost alone among Argentine businessmen, stood by Perón in the October 1945 political crisis and subsequent electoral campaign.[18]

Following the February 1946 election, Miranda, in collaboration with others, drafted the series of economic reform measures that were issued in decree form by the outgoing Farrell regime a few weeks before Perón's inauguration. These measures gave the new administration legal instruments that could be employed at once, and without congressional debate, to gain control over vital economic processes. Through the nationalization of the Central Bank and the redefinition of its relationships with other banks, the government gained control of the allocation of credit; and through the creation, under the Central Bank, of the innocuously named Argentine Institute for the Promotion of Trade (IAPI, Instituto Argentino de Promoción del Intercambio), an agency was established with broad power to control the marketing of Argentine exports and imports.[19]

As president of the Central Bank, and therefore also of IAPI,

[17] Interview with Carlos Emery.

[18] Miranda furnished this information in a speech to the Bolsa de Comercio reported in *La Prensa*, Dec. 17, 1946.

[19] *Ibid.* Miranda's collaborators were Orlando Maroglio and Rolando Lagomarsino. See Decrees No. 14,957, 14,959, 14,961, and 14,962 all dated May 24, 1946, and No. 15,350 of May 28, 1946.

Miguel Miranda emerged in 1946 as the most powerful economic figure of the administration, overshadowing both the Finance Minister and the Secretary of Industry and Commerce. Given the broad authority he exercised in matters that affected every Argentine business activity, little wonder that the man and his policies should arouse heated controversy. But despite periodic attacks against those policies and despite allegations that Miranda was using his position to benefit his own enterprises, he retained Perón's confidence and a place of power for several years.

Perón's reluctance to dispense with Miranda's services in the face of successive waves of criticism from military as well as civilian circles suggests not only his own basic agreement with the industrialist's policies, but the lack of a suitable replacement. Perón apparently felt that he needed an experienced businessman to run the economy; but given his own alienation from the business community, a man who combined Miranda's talents with proven political loyalty was not easy to find. Perón preferred, therefore, to make face-saving adjustments to pressures, changing Miranda's titles, but retaining his services as his key economic advisor until 1949.[20]

Much of the military criticism directed against Miranda, Evita, and other members of Perón's cabinet in the first year of the administration involved charges of corruption and came from a small group of ultranationalist officers, headed by Generals Velazco and Silva. Perón was able to contain this group, easing the two officers out of their posts in the national administration and preventing disaffection from spreading, through the firm control exercised by his War Minister, General Humberto Sosa Molina, over the Army as a whole. Indeed, Sosa Molina performed for Perón a role similar to that which President Justo's War Minister, Manuel Rodríguez, had played in the 1930's. In both cases the task was to revive the sense of professionalism after a period of political involvement.[21]

[20] For comment on Perón's difficulties in getting businessmen to work with him, see Embassy BA Dispatch 3060, Oct. 6, 1947, 835.00/10-647. In July 1947, Miranda resigned his post as head of the Central Bank and of IAPI but was named at once to a newly created cabinet-level post as President of the Economic Council. Orlando Maroglio, regarded at this time as a Miranda supporter, moved into the vacated posts (*Qué*, July 22, 1947, p. 3).

[21] *Qué*, July 29, 1947, p. 6; Embassy BA Telegram 1037, Aug. 21, 1947, 835.00/8-2147.

Originally an infantry commander with mountain troop experience, General Sosa Molina had a reputation in the Army as an energetic officer and a harsh disciplinarian, who demanded a great deal from himself and from his subordinates. He was not the kind one would rebel against lightly. His reputation for authority was such that when he assumed his cabinet post, even Perón, it was felt, would have to treat him with deference. The War Minister, in short, was looked upon as one who would try to isolate the Army from politics, concentrating his efforts on restoring discipline and developing its professional capabilities.[22]

Sosa Molina's handling of his post demonstrated his sensitivity to the need to maintain the morale of the officer corps while supervising their return to professional duties. Even before Perón's inauguration, while serving as War Minister to the outgoing Farrell regime, he approved an amendment to the basic military law that reduced the time needed for promotion to captain and substantially increased the number of slots at that level and also at the grades of major and colonel. On May 23, he authorized an increase in the basic pay scale for all commissioned officers that primarily benefited the senior ranks.[23]

In his handling of personnel assignments, the War Minister was careful to balance professional requirements with President Perón's understandable desire to have politically friendly officers in the key commands in and around the capital. Thus, although the posts of Campo de Mayo garrison commander and that of the Palermo division went to Perón loyalists,[24] the two top Army posts of Commander-in-Chief and Commanding General of the Interior went to the senior officers on the rank list, Generals Mason and Bassi, both of whom were viewed in the Army as politically neutral. A similar balancing of the professional and political was reflected in the year-

[22] This image of General Sosa Molina emerges from interviews with several retired generals including Lieut. General Emilio Forcher (July 4, 1971), Brig. General J. J. Uranga (July 27, 1971), and a man I shall call Brig. General "X" who asked not to be identified (Aug. 8, 1973). General "X" was a onetime aide to Sosa Molina and served closely with him for several years.

[23] Decree No. 14,584, May 21, 1946; No. 14,753, May 23, 1946. The pay increase was subsequently embodied in the next budget bill.

[24] Brigadier Generals Angel Solari and Lorenzo L. Yódice respectively (Decree No. 1377, June 25, 1946).

end promotion lists in 1946 and again in 1947. At the senior level, the officers promoted to the prestigious rank of major general were predominantly professionals without ties to Perón. The newly minted brigadier generals were a mixture of Perón loyalists and political neutrals, but all seem to have been qualified for advancement.[25]

The data on promotions and assignments during General Sosa Molina's first two years in the War Ministry are incomplete, but available information suggests that professional competence rather than political fealty held the key to career advancement. A competent officer who devoted himself exclusively to the profession could look forward to a normal career; at least before 1949, it was not essential to make an overt show of political faith. To be sure, officers who were both effective professionals and personal friends of the President enjoyed advantages in assignments in the Buenos Aires area. Sosa Molina, however, would not put up with indiscipline even among such officers, and in one instance he placed a general under arrest for not going through channels before seeking an audience with the President.[26]

But such evidence of evenhanded enforcement of military regulations, however, cannot obscure the fact that Sosa Molina was ever sensitive to the presence in the officer corps of anti-Peronists. The latter, in turn, especially those who did not hide their view, often felt themselves to be the victims of harassment. Lieut. Colonel Carlos S. Toranzo Montero, for example, did not receive a fair evaluation of his performance during the 1946 Entre Ríos maneuvers, but found himself the object of unjust criticism in the War Minister's field critique. Toranzo Montero, accompanied by his fellow officers of the Eleventh Cavalry, all of them weary and dirty from their activities, stepped forward and with hand on sword challenged the

[25] The data presented in Table 2 above indicate that none of the three officers promoted in December 1946 to major general (Santos Rossi, Luis C. Perlinger, and Manuel Savio) was a close Perón supporter. In 1947 nine new major generals fell into three groups: four may be designated as Perón supporters (Humberto Sosa Molina, Angel Solari, Laureano Anaya, and A. Vargas Belmonte); one was clearly opposed (Carlos Kelso); and four were neutral but inclined to be unsympathetic to Perón (Raúl González, Moisés Rodrigo, Pedro Abadíe Acuña, and Alfredo L. Podestá).

[26] Interview with Carlos Emery (Emery was an eyewitness to this episode); interview with Brig. General (Ret.) Dalmiro Videla Balaguer, Feb. 26, 1970.

accuracy of the War Minister's remarks. A potentially ugly confrontation in the presence of 4,000 officers was averted when the War Minister accepted the suggestion of General Carlos Kelso, the Commander of Cavalry, to recheck his information; but there is little doubt that the impetuous lieutenant colonel was ever after a marked man.[27]

At the junior ranks, a reputation for hostility to Perón unaccompanied by overt actions was not fatal to a military career, as is illustrated by the experience of a cavalry first lieutenant, Alejandro Lanusse. Stationed at Tandil in 1947, he was accused by a soldier of conspiratorial activity. A thorough investigation by the divisional commander found the charges baseless, and the soldier himself was later discharged. Even so, Lanusse fully expected that he would be passed over for promotion at year's end. Much to his surprise, he was given his captaincy, assigned to Campo de Mayo in 1948 for the course required of officers at that level, and permitted to enter the general staff course in the War Academy the following year.[28]

General Sosa Molina was far less tolerant of officers who engaged in overt acts of opposition against Perón. In this category were a number of field and senior grade officers who were still on active duty despite their involvement in the abortive October 1945 movement. Having survived the personnel review decisions at the end of that year, they apparently hoped that the episode would be regarded as closed. Late in 1946, however, the War Minister ordered the newly convoked officer qualification boards to reexamine the individual cases, ostensibly on the grounds that new evidence was available that raised questions about the character deficiencies of the officers. The evidence was a document drawn up long before October 1945 in which the officers had signed a pledge of loyalty to the then Colonel Perón. In view of the War Minister's directive to give great weight to a broken pledge as evidence of moral incapacity, the qualification boards ruled that scores of officers were unfit to continue. Although a few successfully petitioned to have their cases reconsidered, the rulings resulted in the retirement during

[27] Interview with Lieut. General (Ret.) Carlos S. Toranzo Montero, March 22, 1970, and Major General (Ret.) Héctor Solanas Pacheco, May 28, 1970.
[28] Interview with Lieut. General (Ret.) Alejandro Lanusse, Aug. 23, 1973.

1947 of four generals, thirteen colonels, and 50 other field grade officers.[29]

Whether the initiative for getting rid of these officers originated with the War Minister or President Perón himself is not clear. Presumably, both saw it as a means of purging the officer corps of unreliables and warning others who might be tempted to act against the government. For the officers in question, however, the termination of their careers was an act of political reprisal that encouraged them to join with other disaffected citizens, watching the policies of the Perón administration and waiting for it to give them the opportunity to seek revenge.

Down to 1948, however, the Perón administration gave little hope to such critics. On the contrary, with his supporters in control of the Congress and confident of the loyalty of the armed forces, the President was in a position to embark on the policies designed to promote the "new Argentina" he had promised the voters. A key factor that conditioned the optimism of the administration was the existence of unprecedented holdings of gold and foreign exchange, the accumulated balances of the war years, and the continued prospect of high-level exchange earnings from a war-torn Europe avid for Argentina's agricultural exports.[30]

Encouraged by the favorable international economic situation, Perón committed his administration to a vast program of expenditures designed simultaneously to transform the economy, extend health and social welfare benefits, and strengthen national defense. Sketched out in his address at the opening of the congressional sessions on June 26, the program was spelled out with considerable fanfare in the Five-Year Plan that the President announced to the public in October 1946. Although the Plan included measures for reorganizing administrative, judicial, and educational institutions and

[29] The enforced retirement of these officers was the subject of a polemic between Radical Party Deputy Raúl Uranga and the War Minister. For Uranga's criticism see *Diputados* [2], 1947, III, 278ff., 465; IV, 387; V, 32–34; for Sosa Molina's reply see his letter to the Chairman of the Committee on National Defense, Sept. 15, 1947, *ibid.*, V, 594–605. The *Boletín Militar Reservado*, various issues but especially Nos. 2617, 2631, 2640, and 2669, contain data on the retirements; the totals mentioned in the text are those provided by Deputy Uranga in *Diputados* [2], 1950, IV, 3536.

[30] The gold and foreign exchange reserves stood at $1.6 billion in June 1946. For a view that the economic situation was not favorable to long-term reliance

encouraging immigration, its principal concern was with promoting the industrialization of the country.[31]

Perón's decision to foster industrialization has sometimes been ascribed to his military background or to the influence of the military on his administration. A foreign diplomat in 1948 thus wrote: "The Argentine government is interested in industrialization of the country and sometimes carries it almost to the point of absurdity. One of the reasons for the intense interest in industrialization lies in the military aspects of the question and the desire for military industrialization."[32]

Although military concerns played a part in the considerations that led to the promulgation of the Five-Year Plan and military men participated in the drafting of the preparatory studies, the justifications for the industrialization program transcended the military aspects and appealed to widely diffused aspirations. Industrialization, it was argued in the text of the Plan, would produce an array of economic, social, and financial benefits. Foremost among the anticipated economic benefits was an increase in the national income, the absorption of unexportable agricultural surpluses, and a greater stability in domestic prices. The anticipated social benefits lay in the increased employment opportunities and higher salaries that an expanding industrial sector would offer. From a financial viewpoint, the expansion of industry would offer new opportunities for productive investment and new sources for government revenues that would be more stable than those tied to the fluctuations of foreign trade.[33]

Over and above these tangible benefits, the promotion of industry was expected to have political consequences of which the first and most significant would be "to increase and strengthen national economic and political independence."[34] It was this exhilarating pros-

---

on agricultural exports, see Jorge Fodor, "Public Policies for Agricultural Exports, 1946–1948: Dogmatism or Common Sense," in Rock [114], pp. 135–61.

[31] For the June 26 address, see *Diputados* [2], 1946, I, 58–72; for the text of the Five-Year Plan, see *Senadores* [3], III, 82–308.

[32] Embassy BA Dispatch 338, June 3, 1948, 835.00/6-348. The quoted passage is on page 11.

[33] See Section XI of the Five-Year Plan, especially the passage "Razones que justifican la industrialización," in *Senadores* [3], 1946, III, 186.

[34] *Ibid.*

pect of making Argentines masters of their own house, of reducing what a later generation would describe as "dependency," that Perón played upon effectively before his election and that he now proclaimed as the central goal of his administration's economic policies. Industrialization would not only bring specific advantages, it would open the gate to the achievement of the moral and material greatness that many Argentines, and not just military men, believed to be the destiny of their nation.

The Five-Year Plan outlined in graphic detail the public works projects to be undertaken and presented the prepared drafts of 27 pieces of legislation to be sought from the Congress. The Plan, however, was imprecise if not deceptive on two vital questions: What would be the total cost? How was this to be financed?

The Plan offered a set of figures described as an estimate of organization and investment costs for the 1947–51 period amounting to 6.66 billion pesos (U.S. $1.27 billion).[35] But this total almost certainly excluded the acquisition of military equipment and military factories proposed for the armed services; it also omitted any sums for the public health and housing construction programs; and it made no reference to the foreign-owned public service industries whose acquisition, in one way or another, was an implicit part of the program to achieve economic independence. In fact, the purchase contract for the U.S.-owned United River Plate Telephone Company, entered into only a few weeks before the announcement of the Five-Year Plan, involved a price of 419 million pesos; the acquisition of three French-owned railway lines, approved in December 1946, came to 183 million pesos; and the biggest operation of all, the purchase of the British-owned railway system, agreed to in February 1947, came to over 2 billion pesos. Clearly, then, a price tag of 10 billion pesos would have been a more realistic figure for the Five-Year Plan.[36]

The provisions for financing as well as the total cost of the Five-Year Plan were uncertain. There was no detailed projection showing how and in what sequence the external costs of the various projects

[35] *Ibid.*, p. 225.

[36] For the purchase of the telephone company assets see *Qué*, Sept. 14, 1946, and *Senadores* [3], 1946, II, 241ff.; for the two French-owned lines, *La Prensa*, Dec. 18, 1946; on the British railway purchase see below at note 46.

were to be met. All that was certain was that there was to be no reliance on foreign borrowing. The Perón government was in the process of paying up the last of Argentina's foreign debt as another step
toward achieving economic independence. Some other instrument
would have to be called upon to generate the foreign exchange.

The instrument to which the Perón administration turned in 1946
was the Argentine Institute for the Promotion of Trade, commonly
known as IAPI. This agency, under the control of the Central Bank,
was the exclusive buying and selling agent for grains and certain
other crops. By fixing the domestic prices paid to farmers considerably below the prices it was able to obtain in the international mar-
kets, IAPI could generate huge profits; and as the exclusive importer
of certain commodities, for which the Central Bank refused to make
foreign exchange available to private importers, it could earn large
profits from resale to private purchasers. So successful, indeed, were
IAPI's initial operations that its head and Central Bank president,
Miguel Miranda, anticipated in December 1946 that its profits by
the end of 1947 would reach 2 billion pesos—a forecast that IAPI's
subsequent failure to publish accounts makes difficult to substan-
tiate.[37]

For its importance in the history of the Perón administration, IAPI
merits a dispassionate and scholarly study of its own. No such study
has been made, and much of its operations remain shrouded in controversy. What does seem clear, however, is that the plans to have
it finance the Five-Year Plan broke down and that the responsibility
for this failure rested in part on the misjudgments and mistakes of
those who directed its activities, in part on factors beyond the power
of any Argentine official.

One problem, evident in hindsight, was the failure of the government to establish an effective system of priorities among the projects
for which overseas equipment was being purchased. The simultaneous purchase of elements for numerous projects, none of which
could be put into productive operation until additional heavy expenditures were made, meant that any future shortage of funds
would have a devastating effect. In the meantime, the port of Buenos

[37] Miranda's estimate was made in his Bolsa de Comercio speech, cited above
in note 18. IAPI's first published report, issued in 1950, covered only the previous year's operation. See *La Prensa*, Dec. 30, 1950.

Aires became congested with crates of equipment that seemed to have no particular destination. In the same category were numerous used trucks, surplus military models, that IAPI had purchased for resale to civilian users. The latter, however, preferred new vehicles, built to civilian specifications and with full sets of spare parts.[38]

Another factor that undermined IAPI's financial effectiveness and served to discredit it in many eyes was the pervasiveness of corruption. As the exclusive purchasing agents abroad for most government entities, IAPI officials had enormous opportunities to arrange for kickbacks. U.S. State Department and Embassy officials had the impression that IAPI purchasing contracts in the United States were deliberately placed with little-known suppliers, rather than established sources, to facilitate payoffs.[39] How much the Argentine government lost in this manner has never been established, but the diversion of substantial public funds into private pockets is suggested by one episode that was brought to the attention of the U.S. Embassy in Buenos Aires by Argentine Army Officers.

The Army's General Directorate of Military Factories was making plans to erect a sheet steel plant and had asked for bids from large firms in the United States and Great Britain, expecting to award the contract to the lowest bidder. This turned out to be an American firm, ARMCO. Miguel Miranda, however, without saying anything to Army officials or to President Perón, arranged to have the contract go to an obscure firm at a cost of $7 million above the lowest bid. The Army, on learning of this, protested to the President, who in turn ordered the Central Bank to cancel the arrangement; but when its directors met to do so, they discovered that the funds earmarked in the Bank for the steel mill were unaccountably short by some $2 million. Fearing that the situation might reach crisis proportions and that the stability of the regime might be affected if the President backed Miranda against the Army, high Army officers invited Ambassador Bruce to meet with them. He properly refused in the ab-

---

[38] Embassy BA Unnumbered Dispatch, Aug. 14, 1947, 835.00/8-1447, pp. 4–5; Airgram 626, Oct. 15, 1947, 800.5018/10-1547; on the unsold trucks see *Qué*, June 24, 1947, p. 13. To decongest the port of Buenos Aires, the Army under presidential orders issued in late August 1947 moved 7,783 vehicles, 7,524 crates containing motors and machinery, and 3,376 other crates (Ministerio de Guerra, *Memoria . . . 4 de junio 1947—4 de junio 1948* [22], p. xi).

[39] Embassy BA Airgram 731, Dec. 2, 1947, 835.656/12-247.

sence of an invitation from either the President or the Foreign Minister. The upshot of the affair was that, to prevent a national scandal, the Army agreed with the President to build the mill themselves, hiding the $2 million shortage in the cost of subsequent construction. But future Army purchases were removed from the jurisdiction of Miranda and IAPI.[40]

Mismanagement and corruption were self-inflicted blows against the success of the Perón government's industrial development plan. Its greatest problems, however, came from the collapse of its overly optimistic assumptions about the postwar economic order. The President and his economic advisors had counted on using European currencies, especially British sterling, earned by Argentina's high level of agricultural exports, to offset trade deficits to the United States; they had also hoped that a recovered Europe would soon be in a position to supply fuels, raw materials, and machinery needed for the development program. Neither of these expectations held up in the early postwar years. The most painful blow came in August 1947 when Great Britain, which had agreed the previous September to the free use of Argentina's current sterling earnings, was forced to abandon convertibility. Argentina, meanwhile, had been quadrupling its imports from the United States; but, unable to increase its sales in that market, found itself with a serious and persistent dollar problem.[41] By the close of 1948, Argentina's reserves of gold and foreign exchange were down to $258 million from the $1.1 billion of two years before; its commercial indebtedness to U.S. banks meanwhile had risen to over $200 million. The Five-Year Plan, launched amid great publicity two years before, had run aground.[42]

Moreover, it was becoming increasingly clear that despite the rhetoric of economic independence only a substantial infusion of U.S.-owned dollars would be able to refloat the Five-Year Plan. In 1948 Perón and his advisors hoped for such an infusion in external conditions over which they had no control: the possibility that de-

[40] *Ibid.* (this airgram was drafted personally by Ambassador Bruce); also Letter, Guy Ray to Cecil Lyon, Buenos Aires, Nov. 17, 1947, 835.50/11-1747.

[41] Jorge Fodor, "Public Policies," in Rock [114], p. 146, Table 6.1.

[42] Nonconvertible foreign exchange had risen in 1947 to the equivalent of $730 million but then dropped to $320 million by the end of 1948 (Díaz-Alejandro [247], p. 486, Table 73). For estimates of Argentine commercial arrears to U.S. suppliers, see Embassy BA Dispatch 128, Feb. 15, 1949, 835.00/2-154, p. 4.

teriorating United States–Soviet Union relations might lead to war; or the prospect, at times encouraged by the statements of U.S. officials, that Marshall Plan funds would underwrite the purchase of sizable stocks of Argentine agricultural products for consumption in Europe.[43] Neither of these prospects was to materialize. An alternative solution theoretically available to Argentina was to seek the participation of foreign capital in the development of the economy, but President Perón was too heavily committed to restricting the role of foreign investment to alter course at this time.

At the beginning of his presidency, Perón had not foreclosed all possibility of associating foreign capital in his development plans. A decree-law issued on the eve of his inauguration had provided a legal instrument for this in the "sociedad de economía mixta" or mixed corporation in which the state could join with private, including foreign, investors to operate enterprises of public interest. The president of such a corporation and at least one-third of its board of directors were to be appointed by the state and had to be native Argentines, but there were no nationality requirements for the other board members.[44]

Perón's awareness of the possibilities inherent in the mixed corporation may have derived from his military experience. Ever since 1941, the Army's General Directorate of Military Manufactures (DGFM) had been authorized to join with private capital in setting up companies to produce items needed in arms manufacture. During Perón's tenure as War Minister, two such enterprises had been set up in the chemical and metallurgical fields. More recently, in January 1946, in connection with the most ambitious undertaking ever sponsored by the DGFM, the establishment of an integrated steel mill, its president, General Manuel Savio, had entered into preliminary agreements with a number of private metallurgical firms including the Argentine affiliate of the American Rolling Mill Company, whereby they would become shareholders in joint enterprises. Clearly, then, the Army was not opposed on principle to enlisting

[43] For Argentine economic expectations in 1948, see remarks of Dr. Alfredo Gómez Morales incorporated as an appendix to Cafiero [241], pp. 405–6. Gómez Morales took over from Miranda as a key policy maker in 1949.

[44] Decree No. 15,349, May 28, 1946.

the cooperation of private, including foreign, capital in projects of great interest to it.[45]

Perón's inclination to accept a role for foreign capital, using the mixed enterprise system in significant sectors of the economy, was probably at its strongest in the first eighteen months of his presidency. During this period he publicly supported the reorganization of the railways embodied in the Miranda-Eady agreement with Great Britain, and he privately explored proposals for attracting United States investors into petroleum development.

The Miranda-Eady agreement, signed on September 17, 1946, dealt with a range of bilateral issues confronting Argentina and Great Britain, including future meat sales, payments matters, and the uses to which Argentine sterling balances, past and future, could be put. The railway settlement was but one part of the overall agreement. It called for the creation in Argentina of a mixed company that would take over the operating assets and liabilities from the existing companies, giving them shares in the new corporation. These shares were to reflect the capital investment of those companies, as determined by a joint valuation committee, and would be guaranteed an annual income of 4 percent based on the par value in pesos at time of issuance. The Argentine government was pledged to invest 500 million pesos over the next five years to rehabilitate the lines, for which it would receive shares that did not have the guarantee provisions. The corporation would enjoy a tax-free status on its operations and a duty exemption on the equipment and materials it imported save where they competed with Argentine manufactures.[46]

The opponents of the railway reorganization plan came from all parts of the political spectrum, including men who normally supported the administration as well as those from Radical, Socialist, and conservative circles. Among the critics were partisans of outright nationalization who condemned the agreement for preserving British

[45] Castiñeiras [138], pp. 11–32, gives the details of these agreements. ARMCO later withdrew as a shareholder because of a possible conflict of interest with its role as supplier of technical services.

[46] Drosdoff [249], pp. 197–206, reproduces the text of the Miranda-Eady agreement; for a recent treatment of the negotiations see Wright [281], Chapter 12.

control over the railways and denounced the mixed company as a British-inspired device for protecting their capital investment. These men paid little attention to the fact that under existing law governing mixed enterprises (Article 8), the president of the corporation would be a native Argentine appointed by the government and that he would have the authority to override the wishes of a majority of the board of directors or of the stockholders in matters of vital concern to the state. Nor did such critics give much thought to the provision of the Miranda-Eady agreement that authorized the Argentine government to acquire "at any time at par a part or all of the shares of the new company in the hands of any holder." In an era when inflation was already making itself felt, this would give the government the right to buy out the private shareholders at some time in the future when pesos had a fraction of their present value.[47]

Few of the critics, however, were prepared to concede this possibility, nor does it appear that President Perón fully appreciated its significance. In a matter of weeks, for reasons that are still not entirely clear, he apparently began to have second thoughts and postponed appointing the Argentine member of the joint valuation committee. There is no clear evidence that he was pressured from military quarters or from the powerful union of railway workers, although the protests from other sectors were vehement. Whatever his motivations, Perón seized the opportunity to abandon the mixed enterprise plan when the British, themselves under pressure from the United States because of the blocked sterling provisions, asked in December to reopen the terms of the Miranda-Eady agreement.[48]

A new round of negotiations began, this time on the basis of a British proposal for outright sale of the railways as a means of liquidating the blocked sterling account. The principal issue to be resolved was setting a valuation for the properties. Finally, in February 1947, after a month of bargaining, the Argentine government agreed to pay £150 million or 2.48 billion pesos at the current rate of exchange for the railways, their subsidiary companies, and the

[47] Wright [281], pp. 252–54; for contemporary criticisms, see the summaries in Irazusta, *Perón y la crisis argentina* [291], pp. 63–69.

[48] Wright [281], pp. 255–58, cites U.S. Secretary of the Treasury Snyder's complaints to Great Britain that the Miranda-Eady agreement violated the spirit of their 1945 loan agreement; Wright also alleges without citing his source that Argentines were fearful that Britain might transfer the railways to U.S. control.

real estate that belonged to them. This decision at once appeased nationalist sentiment within the ranks of administration supporters, but its political opponents, as might be expected, found new cause for criticism in the price, which they denounced as exorbitant.[49]

Although the hostile reaction to his initial handling of the railway question might have served as a warning on what to expect from any policy that seemingly favored foreign investors in a politically charged industry, in the latter part of 1946, President Perón began to give serious consideration to proposals for expanding the role of foreign capital in the highly sensitive petroleum industry. This was all the more surprising inasmuch as the recently issued Five-Year Plan gave little attention to expanding domestic oil production. The experts, both military and civilian, whose recommendations underlay the Plan's energy section, had felt that the country lacked sufficient quantities of oil to meet the long-term needs for energy and therefore gave highest priority to the development of renewable energy sources in the form of hydroelectric works. Perón had accepted this approach in issuing the Five-Year Plan. Yet within a matter of weeks, he was discussing an alternate solution to fuel needs in the secret conversations he was holding with the United States Ambassador George Messersmith and with Herman A. Metzger, the head of Standard Oil of New Jersey's local affiliate.[50]

How can Perón's actions be explained? No doubt, he was influenced by Argentina's growing dependence on imported petroleum products. The demand for industrial fuels and gasoline, which already exceeded domestic output, was bound to grow with the spread of automobile transport and the expansion of industry. But there were considerations of an international nature as well. Perón's con-

[49] The text of the February 13, 1947, agreement in English may be consulted in the *Review of the River Plate*, Feb. 24, 1947, pp. 15ff., and in Spanish in *La Prensa* of the same date. Wright [281], p. 259, errs in asserting that by this agreement "the British cancelled their wartime debt to Argentina." No mention is made in the text about the use of blocked sterling, and in fact the payment for the railways was financed largely from the value of Argentine exports to Great Britain in 1948 as provided in the February 12, 1948, agreement between the two countries. The text of this agreement, which is ignored by Wright, is reproduced in Drosdoff [249], pp. 207–12. For contemporary criticism of the price aspects of the purchase agreement see *Qué*, Feb. 18, 1947, pp. 2–3. The wisdom of the purchase has been a matter of controversy to the present day.

[50] Cafiero [241], pp. 284–85; Embassy BA Top Secret Dispatch 1196, Nov. 12, 1946, 835.00/11-1246; Letter, Ambassador Messersmith to W. L. Clayton, Nov. 12, 1946, 835.6363/11-1246.

versations with Messersmith and Metzger took place, it must be remembered, at a time when Argentine relations with the United States were still affected by wartime strains. The State Department was still adhering to the policy of Spruille Braden that insisted that Argentina had yet to demonstrate full compliance with its Chapultepec commitments to act against Axis interests and agents. To enforce this policy, the United States was maintaining an embargo on arms sales to Argentina from potential European as well as U.S. suppliers. Ambassador Messersmith, on the other hand, having convinced himself that the Perón administration was carrying out those commitments in good faith, was urging his superiors to act promptly to restore normal relations. Perón's willingness to discuss with him and Metzger the possibility of private investment in Argentine petroleum development may be viewed, therefore, as an effort to strengthen Messersmith's hand in his opposition to Braden's policy by enlisting the support of powerful U.S. business interests in behalf of early normalization of relations. An open attitude on oil might thus help Argentina regain its place as a full member of the hemispheric community and enable the arms-hungry military forces to replace their pre–World War II equipment.[51]

Whatever the international relations rationale, there still remained the problem of domestic opposition. Would not a move to abandon existing policy, which gave to the state petroleum agency, YPF, the dominant status in crude production, arouse heated protests? If, indeed, Perón sincerely intended to set up a mixed company with U.S. capital, he must have believed that he could contain the reaction, perhaps by identifying it with the opposition Radical Party, traditionally the most vociferous defender of YPF, and by appealing in partisan terms to his own supporters.

In any event, the President had no hesitation in revealing his views in private conversation with the U.S. Ambassador. In a top secret

[51] The Messersmith-Braden policy controversy is reflected in many State Department documents located in the National Archives. Of special interest is the sixteen-page memorandum prepared by Ambassador Messersmith in Buenos Aires on December 16, 1946, in anticipation of conversations with Secretary of State Byrnes and submitted later with a seven-page addendum to Secretary of State Marshall on January 24, 1947. The document, ironically bearing the notation "TOP SECRET NOT FOR THE FILES" is filed under 711.35/1-2447.

dispatch, Messersmith reported at length the substance of that conversation:

> He [President Perón] realized that the state did not have enough money under the best of circumstances to aid the YPF adequately in a broad program. He had come to the conclusion that every encouragement should be given to the foreign oil companies here to expand their programs. . . .
> He then asked me whether I thought American companies would be interested in entering into a mixed company—That is, into partnership between the companies and the Argentine government.[52]

A few weeks after this conversation, President Perón received Herman A. Metzger, who had sought the interview to discuss a memorandum prepared by his company two years before and resubmitted to Perón's technical secretary, José Figuerola, the previous July. In this memorandum, Standard Oil of Argentina set forth its interest in forming a mixed company and presented its view of the conditions for a possible agreement. These conditions envisaged a company that would receive a ten-year privilege to explore for oil in the area south of the 49° south latitude parallel. Standard Oil would supply all the working capital in the form of an interest-free loan. The government would receive a 12 percent royalty on all oil discovered and 51 percent of the eventual profits after the original investment or loan was paid back. The general management of the mixed company would be appointed by the five private directors on its board. The government would name the president and two directors, and the former would have a veto over board decisions in the cases where vital state interests were involved, as provided by Article 8 of the mixed enterprise statute.[53]

The Perón-Metzger conversation, which was attended by the YPF President, General Albariño, and the National Energy Director, Colonel (Ret.) Descalzo, went so well that Metzger decided to return to the United States to discuss the conversation with his principals in New York.[54] It was here that the first major stumbling block was encountered. Metzger, it turned out, had submitted his memorandum

[52] Embassy Dispatch 1196, Nov. 12, 1946, cited in note 50. The conversation in question took place some three weeks before this dispatch.

[53] *Ibid.*; Letter, L. F. McCollum, Standard Oil Company to Assistant Secretary Braden, New York, Sept. 25, 1946, and enclosures, 835.6363/9-2546.

[54] Embassy Dispatch 1196, p. 4.

to the Argentine government before clearing it with his home office. The New York officials of Standard Oil found the veto provision of Article 8 disquieting; and in view of the size of the projected investment, $25–30 million, they decided to make the revision of Article 8 a prerequisite for going ahead with the mixed company.[55]

Such a request was difficult for the Argentine government to accept because it would reduce the mixed company from a joint venture to a barely disguised direct concession to Standard Oil. But even if President Perón were personally prepared to go this route, he would have to ask Congress to weaken a statute already regarded by nationalistic critics as ineffective. This was a step he was not yet prepared to take. Indeed, although the negotiations with Standard Oil were supposed to be confidential, antiadministration voices were already being raised in Congress. At the end of January 1947, Radical Party deputy Arturo Frondizi declared categorically in the face of denials by administration supporters that plans were afoot to turn YPF over to a mixed company. A few weeks later Frondizi was joined by other members of the Unión Cívica Radical (UCR) bloc in submitting a series of resolutions to the lower house calling on the executive not to entertain any proposal for the formation of mixed companies between the state and private petroleum companies, asking for an investigation into all problems relating to petroleum resources and the activities of the international companies, and asking the executive to call a special session of Congress to consider the expropriation of the private companies and the nationalization of the entire industry.[56]

Although there was little likelihood that the Peronist-dominated Chamber would approve these resolutions, their purpose seems to have been to alert the supporters of YPF and embarrass the administration in its negotiations with Standard Oil. The weekly news magazine *Qué*, a moderate critic of the government, joined in arousing public opinion by publishing an article entitled "What is Going

[55] Department of State, Memorandum of Conversation, Subject: Proposed Exploration Contract between Standard Oil Company, S.A. Argentina and the Argentine Government, Sept. 25, 1946, 835.6363/9-2546; Department of State, Memorandum of Conversation, Subject: Possibility of Standard Oil Company forming Company for Oil Prospecting with Argentine Government, Dec. 19, 1946, ARA Memoranda on Argentina, Vol. 8.

[56] *Diputados* [2], 1946, X, 25 and 671–72; Embassy BA Dispatch 788, Feb. 14, 1947, 835.00/2-447; *La Prensa*, March 6, 1947.

on with Petroleum" that reported growing resistance to any change in YPF status among its high-level officials, as well as among oil field workers.[57] The dilemma for nationalistic Peronist deputies, should the President ask for legislative endorsement of an arrangement with Standard Oil, was a real one.

Although President Perón subsequently restated to Ambassador Messersmith, on the eve of the latter's permanent departure from Argentina, that he had no hope of YPF satisfying the fuel needs of the country, that its operations had been unsatisfactory for years, and that the best solution lay in arrangements between the government and foreign, preferably American, companies, the negotiating prospects with Standard Oil, or indeed any foreign company, were poor.[58] Foreign companies, aware of the difficulties that already affected their marketing operations, wanted guarantees that any new investments would be protected; but the Perón administration, despite the stated views of the President, found itself unable to move ahead. As of September, when the new U.S. Ambassador, James Bruce, presented his credentials, the President felt compelled to state that, after talking to his congressional leaders, he was now convinced of the impossibility of getting a law through Congress that would permit foreign companies to carry out explorations and develop Argentina's petroleum resources.[59]

Perón faced not only congressional resistance, but a sharp split within his own administration. The President's view of the advantages to be gained from foreign investment in the exploration and exploitation of oil was shared by Miguel Miranda, President of the Economic Council, and by Foreign Minister Bramuglia, but YPF had staunch supporters within the cabinet in the persons of the newly appointed Secretary of Industry and Commerce, José C. Barro, Finance Minister Cereijo, and Air Secretary De la Colina. Together

[57] *Qué*, March 18, 1947, pp. 30–31.

[58] Embassy B.A. Dispatch 2691, June 17, 1947, 835.6363/6-1747, p. 4. Perón apparently made no reference in this June 14 conversation to any external factor affecting YPF's performance. For a view that ascribes the state oil agency's difficulty in expanding oil production to a U.S. government policy of restricting the sale to it of drilling equipment, refinery apparatus, and replacement parts, see Solberg [278], pp. 164–65. For evidence that IAPI purchasing policies prevented YPF from acquiring such equipment, see Embassy B.A. Airgram 626, Oct. 15, 1947, 800.5018/10-1547.

[59] Embassy BA Dispatch 2924, Aug. 27, 1947, and enclosed memorandum of conversation between President Perón and Ambassador Bruce, 711.35/8-2747.

with Julio Canessa, a government engineer-bureaucrat who temporarily took charge of YPF while General Albariño was on sick leave, they initiated a campaign designed to end once and for all the threat to YPF's position.[60]

The first step was a YPF notification to the private companies, issued by Julio Canessa on September 30, to the effect that the existing agreement allocating their shares of the domestic market would lapse at the end of the required six months' notice.[61] Secretary Barro followed this up with a flat statement to private company representatives of his personal view that petroleum production in the future should be monopolized by the government and that, if need be, the private properties should be expropriated.[62] This, indeed, was the goal of the YPF supporters; their problem was to win the President over to their viewpoint.

YPF takeover of the private oil-producing properties was discussed in two lively cabinet meetings early in December. In the first, on December 4, Secretary Barro, Minister Cereijo, and Air Secretary De la Colina presented a vigorous case for expropriation. Only the President, Bramuglia, Miranda, and Orlando Maroglio, the new Central Bank president, argued against it. The rest of the cabinet, including the War and Navy Ministers, although apparently inclined to favor the takeover, held back from active participation in the discussion. No decision was taken at this meeting, but the advocates of a YPF production monopoly, possibly with the President's knowledge, although this was later denied, embarked on a risky ploy to get the foreign companies to sell out voluntarily.[63]

The local heads of the Standard, Ultramar, and Shell companies were summoned to a meeting in Miranda's office on Friday, December 5, where Industry and Commerce Secretary Barro and YPF Director Canessa explained that the government wanted to announce on December 13, the annual celebration of Petroleum Day, that Argentina had recovered all its oil properties. The private companies

[60] Embassy BA Dispatch 3265, Dec. 1, 1947, 835.6363/12-147; Letter, Guy Ray to Cecil Lyon, Buenos Aires, Dec. 12, 1947, 835.6363/12-1247.

[61] Department of State, Memorandum of Conversation, Subject: Argentine Petroleum Situation, Nov. 25, 1947, 835.6363/11-2547.

[62] Embassy Dispatch 3265, cited in note 60.

[63] Letter, Guy Ray to Cecil Lyon, cited in note 60. *La Prensa*, Dec. 5, 1947, reports a three-hour cabinet meeting the previous morning at which the petroleum production issue was discussed, but gives no details on the controversy.

were requested to reply by December 9 whether they would be willing to sell their producing properties in return for a long-term marketing and refining arrangement with "generous profits" guaranteed. When pressed by the private company representatives as to whether a refusal to sell would mean expropriation, the Argentine officials said they were not prepared at present to answer.[64]

Although their proposition was couched as a "request," the four-day limit for reply, which included a weekend, gave it the tone of an ultimatum. What followed was presumably not what its originators had in mind. Guy Ray, in charge of the U.S. Embassy in the temporary absence of Ambassador Bruce, at once sought out Foreign Minister Bramuglia to find out whether the President himself approved of the plan and to protest the unfairness of expecting so important a decision in so short a time. The British Ambassador, concerned with the Shell interests, took a similar course. Bramuglia assured Ray on behalf of the President that he was unaware of the demands made on the companies, that no action would be taken, and that the President had "no intention whatsoever [of] expropriating oil or any other American properties."[65] The day after the expiration of the deadline, both Standard and Shell turned down the "request."[66]

The critical phase of the intragovernmental struggle over petroleum policy was reached in a cabinet meeting held a few days before the President was to deliver his Petroleum Day speech. The more nationalist members of the cabinet exerted intense pressure on Perón to buy or expropriate the foreign-owned wells and to proclaim in his address a policy of nationalizing all of Argentina's petroleum resources. This time, however, the War Minister actively intervened and, in contrast to his earlier stance, warned that any threat of expropriation or forced sale would be damaging to the interests of the country. The President, pointing to the refusal of the companies to sell and the strong protests already received from the U.S. and British embassies, made the final decision.[67]

Whatever political advantages he might have seen in the proposed course, the President was very much aware that Argentina was de-

[64] Embassy BA Telegram 1416, Dec. 5, 1947, 835.6363/12-547.
[65] Embassy BA Telegram 1417, Dec. 15 [sic], 1947, 835.6363/12-1547. The date is obviously in error since No. 1417 was filed one hour after No. 1416.
[66] Embassy BA Telegram 1435, Dec. 10, 1947, 835.6363/12-1047.
[67] Letter, Guy Ray to Cecil Lyon, cited in note 60.

pendent on imported fuels for at least one-third of its needs. Any move that alienated both the Standard and Shell corporations could very well interrupt the flow of imported oil and produce unwanted international complications. But in refusing, as he did, to authorize the takeover of the wells, Perón found himself less able to resist the nationalists' pressure for what might indeed have been their secondary objective: a public policy declaration that no further concessions would be given to foreign companies and that no mixed enterprises with foreign capital be approved. Perón, perhaps reluctantly, incorporated their wishes in the final paragraph of his December 13 address. In language that was anything but direct he announced:

Argentine petroleum policy must be based on the same principles that underlie its entire economic policy: absolute conservation of Argentine sovereignty over our subsoil wealth and rational scientific exploitation by the state. It should be made clear that when the state retrieves immediate and direct control over the nation's resources, it cannot relinquish the privilege of administering them; it must not share functions with other interests that do not belong to all Argentines.[68]

Thus, after more than a year of secret discussion, private negotiations, and domestic controversy, Argentina's petroleum policy remained where it had begun. The status quo as regards state versus private exploitation was preserved; the government had taken no action that would significantly accelerate domestic production or reduce Argentina's growing dependence on imports. This internal controversy, however, is of special interest for the light it throws on Perón's exercise of power and on the role of the military at this time. It is clear that in petroleum matters Perón was far more pragmatic than his public rhetoric about economic independence implied; it is also clear that despite his image as a dictatorial figure, he did not feel free to impose his own solutions. His cabinet ministers were certainly not puppets, but were able to advocate a course of action that they knew differed sharply from his own preferred position. In the end, after what he would call one of the worst struggles he had with his administration, he headed off the most extreme demand,

[68] "Discurso pronunciado por el presidente de la Nación, general Juan Perón, con motivo de celebrarse en la fecha el Día del Petroleo," enclosure to Embassy BA Dispatch 3328, Dec. 17, 1947, 835.6363/12-1747.

but in the process had to sacrifice, at least for the next several years, his hope of developing the domestic oil industry. To this extent, then, by 1948 he had become a prisoner of his own nationalistic rhetoric.

The most striking aspect of the Army's role in the oil policy controversy was its relative passivity. In a matter of such strategic importance as petroleum development, it seems surprising that the Army did not have a clearly defined position. Yet the hesitant and inconsistent actions taken by key officers suggest that they lacked such a position. In contrast to the Air Force Secretary, who clearly wanted to give YPF a monopoly of all oil production, Army spokesmen were ambivalent. Even the fact that an Army officer, General Albariño, was the president of YPF did not convert him into a champion of its ambitions. Albariño, it will be recalled, was present and supportive when Perón discussed the mixed company plan with H. A. Metzger, and it was only when the general was on sick leave that other YPF officials launched their plan to take over the private oil properties. The Minister of War, on the other hand, appeared to sympathize with this plan when it was first brought up in the cabinet, but he was far less vocal than his colleague from the Air Force. General Sosa Molina spoke out vigorously only in a later cabinet meeting, this time in opposition to expropriation.[69]

The War Minister's decision to come down hard against this action reflected less a concern over petroleum policy per se than alarm over the possible effects of expropriation on other vital Army interests, especially its arms procurement plans. The War Minister's sensitivity to this possibility had been raised by conversations with Guy Ray, Counselor of the U.S. Embassy, and with a high-ranking U.S. Army officer, Lieut. General Willis Crittenberger, who by coincidence was in Argentina on an official visit to discuss its military modernization needs when the YPF proponents launched their squeeze against the oil companies. General Sosa Molina's subsequent warning to the cabinet that this could damage the interests of Argentina was an understandable position for one whose consuming interest ever since he took office had been to replace the Army's outmoded equipment

[69] Other Army officers, meanwhile, were said to be pressuring Perón to act against the foreign oil companies (Embassy BA Airgram 748, Dec. 11, 1947, 810.6363/12-1147).

and transform its components into a post–World War II fighting force.[70]

The desire to redress the regional military balance that had swung against Argentina during the armament-starved years of World War II was a major goal of the military establishment in the years that followed Perón's inauguration. The pursuit of this goal influenced the government's handling of foreign relations, even as it shaped the specific plans for military modernization.

The immediate preoccupation of Argentina's armed forces was with acquiring the latest in military equipment to replace obsolete pre–World War II materiel: planes for the Air Force; ships and planes for the Navy; antiaircraft guns, tanks, artillery, and whatever was needed to equip mechanized and motorized units for the Army. But of comparable concern was the longer-term goal of developing a domestic arms industry. The recent war had demonstrated once again Argentina's dependence on external arms sources and its vulnerability to decisions taken by other powers. The military planners wanted to reduce this vulnerability by establishing factories to produce heavy weapons and by developing a steel industry.

In seeking to acquire military equipment, the Perón administration found itself confronted with the continuation of the arms embargo that the United States had instituted during the war. This embargo aimed to secure from Argentina satisfactory compliance with the commitments it had undertaken in connection with the Chapultepec agreements.[71] The embargo applied not only to sales or transfers of weapons from the United States, but also, through a gentlemen's agreement with the respective governments, to weapons produced in Canada and Great Britain. Even neutral Sweden was pressured by the United States not to make deliveries on arms that had been contracted years before.[72]

[70] Letter, Guy Ray to Cecil Lyon, cited in note 60. Ray's information on intracabinet discussions was provided by Foreign Minister Bramuglia.

[71] President Truman, on July 22, 1946, reaffirmed the policy, including the arms embargo, that Secretary of State Byrnes had set forth on April 8 after Perón's election. For a detailed rationale of this policy by its principal proponent, see Letter, Spruille Braden to Will Clayton, Aug. 15, 1946, and enclosed memorandum on the Argentine situation, 835.00/8-1546.

[72] Department of State, Memorandum of Conversation, Subject: Bofors Arms and Argentina, July 30, 1946, ARA Memoranda on Argentina, Vol. 6; Spruille Braden to Will Clayton, memorandum dated Sept. 19, 1946, *ibid.*, Vol. 7.

The first significant breach in this embargo was achieved by Argentina early in 1947, when Great Britain notified the United States that it proposed "henceforth to treat Argentina in all respects on the same footing as other Latin American countries."[73] The timing of this announcement, January 27, coinciding with the ongoing British-Argentine negotiations that led to the February 13 agreement to sell the railways, suggests a linkage between the two. Perhaps to get Argentina to pay the agreed-upon price, Great Britain intimated a willingness to enter into arms purchase negotiation. Supporting this hypothesis is the fact that the railway agreement made no reference to the use of the blocked sterling as had been proposed by the British in December. Apparently under pressure from the military, the Perón government decided to utilize some of the accumulated sterling to acquire new "iron" in the form of weapons rather than the old iron of the rail lines.

In any event, Argentina soon opened negotiations with British firms looking forward to the purchase of military aircraft and naval combat vessels. In May, despite the objections of the United States, the British government approved contracts whereby its aircraft manufacturers undertook to supply 100 Meteor jet fighters and a number of Lincoln bombers. The total value of the aircraft and naval vessels ordered from Great Britain was reportedly about £20,000,000.[74]

While Argentina turned thus to Great Britain to satisfy a principal goal of its Air Force, its weapons acquisition policy for the Army continued to rest on the premise that sooner or later relations with the United States would be fully composed. The Perón administration was committed to reequipping the Army within the framework of the hemispheric defense pact anticipated by the Chapultepec agreement and to the standardization program for weapons, training, and organization recommended by the Inter-American Defense Board.[75] Nationalistic Army elements, on the other hand, unhappy

[73] Department of State, Memorandum of Conversation, Subject: Relations with Argentina, Jan. 27, 1947, 711.35/1-2747. A copy of the Aide-Memoire presented by the British Ambassador to Washington is enclosed.

[74] Spruille Braden to Mr. Acheson, Memorandum on Argentine-British Armament Negotiations, March 25, 1947; R. S. Atwood to Mr. Tewksbury, Memorandum on Argentine Purchase Contracts with British, Nov. 5, 1947, both in ARA Memoranda on Argentina, Vols. 7 and 8; also *Foreign Relations of the United States 1947* [40], VIII, 219–25, 233.

[75] See the conversation between Foreign Minister Bramuglia and Ambassador

with the measures insisted upon by the United States to compose relations, were presumably urging the purchase of weapons elsewhere. In the face of the continued embargo, even War Minister Sosa Molina apparently sought a reconsideration of the policy that precluded major purchases from European suppliers such as Skoda.[76] Nevertheless, Perón, persisting in his course, achieved a major aim when on June 3, 1947, almost a year to the day after his own inauguration, President Truman announced in Washington that the United States was now satisfied with Argentina's compliance with the provisions of the Chapultepec agreements and was ready to resume discussions with other hemispheric countires about concluding the mutual defense pact. The long-deferred Rio conference could now be scheduled.[77]

In regaining for Argentina, vis-à-vis the United States, a status of equality with the rest of Latin America, President Perón had made no major sacrifices of principle or interest. To be sure, he had proceeded with the acquisition en bloc of Axis-owned companies and had turned over for deportation an additional number of Axis agents, although nothing like the complete list submitted by the United States.[78] Nevertheless, even these measures alienated ultranationalist elements from the Perón administration. In the weeks that followed President Truman's announcement, a number of such individuals, civilian and military, were separated from their government posts. The resignations of General Velazco as Federal Police Chief and General Silva as head of the Military Secretariat of the Presidency, though linked to domestic differences with the President, may thus be regarded as by-products of his determination to seek United States support for the Army's modernization and the related industrialization program.[79]

Messersmith of March 18, 1947, reported in Embassy BA Dispatch 2119, March 31, 1947, 711.35/3-3147.

[76] Miguel Miranda in a conversation with Ambassador Messersmith claimed to have blocked a War Ministry move to take up a Skoda arms offer (Embassy BA Dispatch 2023, March 12, 1947, 835.516/3-1247).

[77] *New York Times*, June 4, 1947.

[78] Memorandum from Mr. Mann to Mr. Braden, May 13, 1947, 711.35/5-1347.

[79] See Embassy Telegram 1037 cited in note 21; for the resignation of Santiago Peralta, the notoriously anti-Semitic National Director of Immigration, see Embassy BA Telegram 791, June 27, 1947, 835.00/6-2747.

The assiduity with which the Perón administration sought to gain United States friendship and support was reflected in the unprecedented degree of cooperation shown by its delegates at the Inter-American Conference at Rio de Janeiro. Even before the opening of the Conference, Foreign Minister Bramuglia privately assured the U.S. Chargé in Buenos Aires that internationally Argentina would support the United States completely and that any indications to the contrary were strictly for domestic consumption. Bramuglia, in fact, proposed that the two countries enter into a secret anticommunist agreement and, though critical of some United States measures vis-à-vis Russia, stated explicitly: "In any case, Argentina will enter any war with Russia from beginning on side of U.S."[80]

In agreeing to the terms of the mutual assistance treaty that Bramuglia signed at Rio on September 2, Perón and his Foreign Minister yielded up some of the independence of action that Argentine governments had insisted on in past inter-American agreements. No longer would Argentina be able to use the requirement of unanimous consent as it had in 1942 to oppose collective measures that a two-thirds majority of the American republics could henceforth invoke against a state that attacked one of its members.[81] But if acceptance of the binding power of a two-thirds vote, which, to be sure, did not extend to the use of military forces without the consent of each member, seemed to imply a sacrifice of independence, Perón's conception of his country's place in the inter-American system was certainly not that of a satellite of the hemisphere's strongest power, but rather a powerful partner with a predominant role in its southern reaches.

This was demonstrated most clearly in Argentine attitudes toward the U.S.-sponsored proposal for the standardization of military equipment in the hemisphere. The Minister of War enunciated the views of the Army as well as of the administration in a July speech at Villa María when he stated that Argentina was in a position to produce its own equipment and that the "nation cannot abandon for any principle of arms unification all that it had already accomplished for its own defense." The Minister continued: "We agree to the uniformity of armaments on condition that our own industry, which has the

[80] Embassy BA, Top Secret Telegram 985, Aug. 8, 1947, 710 Consultation 4/8-847.
[81] Conil Paz and Ferrari [230], pp. 144–47.

capability, produces them. We cannot give up this reality which belongs to the entire Argentine people."[82]

This view that Argentina should produce its own weapons, howbeit on the basis of U.S. models and with equipment obtained from that country, was widely shared among friends and foes of the Perón administration. Argentina would thereby be free to arm as it saw fit, independent of any quota that the United States might set for it. Argentina could become the arsenal of southern South America and, in case of war, could take care of its own needs as well as those of its neighbors. The country's traditional aspiration for preeminence in its part of the hemisphere would thus have an additional foundation on which to rest.[83]

The tasks of promoting the development of the Argentine arms industry fell primarily to the Army's General Directorate of Military Manufactures (DGFM). General Savio as director of the DGFM pushed for both the establishment of an integrated steel mill and the erection of weapons factories. Savio's steel industry plan, introduced into Congress with administration backing, won approval in legislation enacted in June 1947. This law provided for the creation of a mixed company under military control with a capitalization of 100 million pesos, 80 percent of which would be supplied by the state. The initial target was a steel mill that would be in operation by 1951 with a capacity to produce annually 300,000 tons of cast iron and finished products of various types, including steel sheets.[84] General Savio sought to install three specific weapons factories: a plant to manufacture artillery pieces, including 90mm. antiaircraft guns; another to produce machine guns of various calibres; and a third to produce all types of ammunition. The cost of acquiring the necessary equipment for these three factories was estimated at about $14 million.[85] The combined cost of the steel mill and the arms factories that

[82] *El Mundo*, July 5, 1947. *La Prensa's* July 5, 1947, version of the speech has the Minister state: "La Nación no puede abandonar, frente a ningún principio de solidaridad americana, todo cuanto lleva realizado," which has a more nationalistic tone than the *El Mundo* text.

[83] Letter, Guy Ray to James Wright, Buenos Aires, July 28, 1947, and enclosed memorandum, 710 Consultation 4/7-2847; Embassy BA Dispatch, Aug. 14, 1947, p. 8–9, 835.00/8-1447.

[84] Law No. 12,987. The extensive Chamber of Deputies debate over this measure can be followed in *Diputados* [2], 1947, I, 257ff.

[85] Department of State, Memorandum of Conversation, Subject: Proposed

General Savio was promoting thus amounted to approximately $40 million.

Simultaneously with these efforts to develop Argentina's steel and arms manufacturing capacities, the War Ministry was seeking to acquire a variety of materials and weapons for immediate needs. The initial aim was to equip the Army's branch schools so as to be able to test the equipment for suitability to Argentine needs. For those items found most suitable, the War Ministry would seek the necessary machinery and technical advice to enable manufacture within the country. Items Argentina could not produce would be sought abroad.[86]

Here again it was from the United States that the Army hoped to obtain the equipment, although, in the face of what seemed like dilatory responses from the U.S. authorities, President Perón was not above threatening to accept weapons offers from other sources. In one such instance involving the possible purchase from the Czechoslovakian Skoda Works of 200 88mm. antiaircraft guns, Perón in October 1947 was able to maneuver Ambassador Bruce into interceding with his Washington superiors. The result was that in less than two months, the U.S. War Department found that it could make available to Argentina its 90mm. antiaircraft equipment and the State Department approved the sale of an initial 50 guns.[87]

From this point on, contacts between the Argentine and United States military establishments intensified. Lieut. General Willis Crittenberger visited Argentina in late November and early December, inspecting units and installations and receiving from the War Minister's hands a detailed listing of Argentine Army needs as well as a request for U.S. Army personnel to be assigned to Argentina as advisors in the use of the materiel to be acquired. Following several

---

Establishment of Arms and Ammunitions Plants in Argentina, Nov. 5, 1947, in ARA Memoranda on Argentina, Vol. 8.

[86] Memorandum to the Chief of Staff, United States Army, from Willis D. Crittenberger, Commander-in-Chief, Caribbean Command, Subject: Informal Staff Conversations with Argentina, Dec. 15, 1947, and enclosure entitled "Bases for the Direct Understanding" submitted by Minister of War General Sosa Molina, 835.20 Missions/1-1648 (hereafter referred to as the Crittenberger Memorandum).

[87] *Foreign Relations 1947* [40], VIII, 230–31; *Foreign Relations 1948* [39], IX, 325; Memorandum from John Dreier, Division of Special Inter-American Affairs, to Colonel Kingman, Dec. 5, 1947, ARA Memoranda on Argentina, Vol. 8.

months of written exchanges, General Sosa Molina, accompanied by a delegation of officers, paid an official visit to the United States touring installations and discussing the availability of military equipment. The climax of the visit was the understanding reached in Washington in June 1948 whereby the War Minister scaled down his original shopping list for complete organic units and accepted an offer by the United States Secretary of the Army to sell from its stocks the organizational equipment, exclusive of vehicles, for six mechanized troop units. The details of assigning U.S. Army advisors were subsequently worked out and made part of a formal military mission agreement that was signed by representatives of the two governments in October 1948.[88]

This purchase of organizational equipment involved only part of the materiel that the Argentine War Ministry hoped to acquire. Accordingly, it obtained permission to set up a purchasing mission in the United States that could negotiate directly with private industry for additional materiel as well as manufacturing equipment. Meanwhile, through sources in Belgium, the Ministry continued its program of acquiring surplus but serviceable American tanks and other vehicles. How much was expended for these military purchases in the United States and Europe cannot be stated with precision, but certainly it must have ranged in the millions of dollars.[89]

The domestic counterpart to the overseas acquisitions was an ambitious military construction program, the broad aims of which were set forth in the Five-Year Plan. Not only were new Army bases to be built to permit the deconcentration of units currently located at Campo de Mayo, but the program envisaged the construction of military hospitals; housing at interior bases for the families of officers, noncommissioned officers, and civilian employees; and even summer vacation lodgings, at appropriate places, for such families.[90]

[88] Crittenberger Memorandum; Memorandum to the Department of State from Colonel P. L. Freeman, Latin American Branch, War Department General Staff, with enclosures, June 5, 1948, 835.20/6-548; *Foreign Relations 1948* [41], IX, 321; Department of State, *Bulletin* [36], XIX, No. 485 (Oct. 17, 1948), p. 494.

[89] As of April 30, 1949, Argentina had acquired at cost from the U.S. Government $1.4 million worth of military equipment under U.S. Public Resolution 83 and an additional $6.8 million worth of equipment at the surplus property price of $748,000 (Department of State, *Bulletin* [36], XXI, No. 534 [Sept. 26, 1949], pp. 479–81). For data on Argentina's purchases in Europe, see *Foreign Relations 1948* [41], IX, 310–16; also *Diputados* [2], 1949, VI, 5132–35.

[90] *Diputados* [2], 1946, III, 148.

Under the Perón administration, the military enjoyed far greater autonomy in selecting and implementing construction projects than had been the case under pre-1943 constitutional governments. Whereas the 1941 Congress, in approving the long-term outlay of up to 127 million pesos for Army construction, had itemized the projects to be built, a 1947 decree regulating the 1941 law authorized the Army's Bureau of Engineers to draw up an annual construction plan, for approval by the Ministers of War and Finance, that would be kept secret from public scrutiny. Moreover, when the Congress, at the request of the administration, voted in 1948 to authorize an additional 458 million pesos for military construction, none of the projects to be built with the funds was spelled out in the law. The Peronist majority apparently accepted the administration contention that "the prosecution of military constructions is unavoidable in order to satisfy the normal increase of the Army and its plan of modernization which the War Department has outlined."[91]

Congressional acquiescence to military-related fund requests during the first three years of the Perón administration assured the armed forces of a substantial if somewhat declining share of the budget. From a 1945 peak of 43.3 percent of the central government outlays, the armed forces share dropped about 5 percent each year, reaching 24.9 percent in 1949. Actual outlays, measured in current pesos, increased, but because of continuing inflation, their value, measured in constant pesos, declined.[92]

With its share of the armed forces budget, a share that declined sharply from 1945 to 1946 as the separate Air Force was organized but then remained fairly stable at just under half of the total, the War Ministry proceeded to reshape its forces. Contrary to some impressions, the Argentine Army declined in strength, dropping by some 14 percent between 1946 and 1949. This reduction was achieved primarily by cutting back sharply on the number of one-year conscripts while retaining the number of permanent enlisted men at about the same level. What stands out, however, in the reshaping process was the Army's reduced reliance on reserve officers and the

[91] Law No. 12,737, Sept. 30, 1941; Decree No. 1434, Jan. 24, 1947; the quoted passage is from the Executive Power's message to Congress, Aug. 8, 1947, *Diputados* [2], 1947, III, 203. The request was enacted as Law 13,227, Aug. 19, 1948.
[92] Heare [157], Table 1, p. 11.

substantial growth in the authorized strength for regular officers. By 1949, in contrast to three years before, the Army budget provided for more than 900 additional regular officers to command a force that was smaller by 17,000 men; and as Table 4 reveals, this trend toward a larger regular officer component in an overall smaller force was continuing.

Coinciding as it did with the substantial troop reduction, the decision to permit the steady growth of the officer corps requires explanation. Was this decision based on an anticipation of military need should the worsening of the international situation require mobilization? Or was it related to the social and political policies of the administration? Did Perón and His War Minister, in keeping with the former's populist orientation, see an opportunity here to open up careers for the sons of working-class families and other social sectors not represented in the officer corps? Was the Army serving, thus, as an instrument of social integration, amalgamating in its leadership ranks elements from all social strata? Given the importance of labor support to Perón, such a policy would have had much to commend it on political grounds alone. Moreover, in view of the trade union origins of many Peronist congressmen, government initiatives to open up military careers to all would presumably have received enthusiastic support.

An examination of the congressional record, however, shows that

TABLE 4.—ARGENTINE ARMY, AUTHORIZED FORCE LEVELS, 1946–50

Grade	1946	1947	1948	1949	1950
Enlisted personnel					
Conscripts	87,273	81,500	77,500	71,900	68,500
Others[a]	32,185	26,786	31,598	30,543	29,848
Total	119,458	108,286	109,098	102,443	98,348
Officer personnel					
Regular	4,754	5,025	5,389	5,661	5,766
Reserve	1,547	1,705	1,648	402	300
Total	6,301	6,730	7,037	6,063	6,066
Combined Totals	125,759	115,016	116,135	108,506	104,414

Sources: *Boletín Militar Reservado*, Nos. 2466, 2626, 2765, 2947, 3092.

a Includes positions for permanent (noncommissioned and volunteer) ranks, reserve noncommissioned ranks, cadets, and candidates in enlisted men schools. The number of permanent posts was as follows: in 1946, 20,865; in 1947, 21,102; in 1950, 21,280.

the War Ministry during the first three years of the Perón administration made little effort to alter its system of recruiting future officers
and that the opposition Radical Party initiated whatever moves were
made to democratize officer selection. A main thrust of these proposals was to loosen the monopoly the Military Academy had been
exercising since the beginning of the century in preparing line officers,
a monopoly the Radicals denounced as discriminating against the
poor and the non-Catholic. The War Minister defended the Academy
against such charges, pointing to recent increases in scholarships and
denying that there was a religious qualification for admission. He
did admit that such a restriction existed until May 1945, but claimed
that Perón as War Minister directed the Academy at that time to
cease requiring evidence of baptism and profession of Catholicism
as part of the admission application.[93]

The Radical Party proposals to open up Army officer status to
lower social sectors took two forms: one was to try to eliminate all
fees at the Academy, placing every cadet on full scholarship; the
other was to provide a route to commissioned status outside the
Academy for noncommissioned personnel, most of whom came from
the lower classes. Specifically, Radical deputies submitted bills on
at least three occasions between 1946 and 1948 calling for the establishment of an officer candidates school (Escuela de aspirantes a
Oficial) to which sergeants and corporals with two years of service
might apply via an examination and, on successful completion of the
course, be commissioned as sublieutenants.[94]

None of these bills, however, emerged from the Peronist-controlled
Chamber Committee on National Defense. The War Ministry was
little inclined to encourage the commissioning of noncommissioned
personnel, and even when a later Congress, in the new organic-mili-
tary statute of 1950, authorized all three services to develop their
own procedures to facilitate such promotions, the War Ministry dog-
gedly refused to take action.[95] Only in 1953 did it seem to fall into

[93] *Diputados* [2], 1946, II, 136.

[94] *Diputados* [2], 1946, I, 123; *ibid.*, V, 120; *Diputados* [2], 1948, I, 161.

[95] Cf. Law 13,996 (1950) article 39 with the *reglamentación* of this article in
Decree No. 20,493 (Oct. 12, 1951), articles 112 and 114, and the amended regulations embodied in Decree No. 11,321 (Nov. 21, 1952). Neither decree provided
a means for elevating noncommissioned personnel to officer status.

step when it established a procedure whereby selected sergeants and corporals might be admitted as third-year cadets in the four-year Military Academy program. As far as is known, however, not a single sergeant or corporal ever obtained a line officer's commission in this manner while Perón was in power.[96]

During the 1946–49 period, the only apparent concession the Army was prepared to make in the way of democratizing officer recruitment related to its *liceos militares*. These were secondary schools run by the Army. Their graduates received commissions as reserve officers, although some of them went on to the Military Academy and upon graduation obtained regular commissions as line officers. Transfer to the Academy was not automatic, however, and for most of the students who attended the Liceo General San Martín or the Liceo General José Paz, the principal benefit was exposure to a rigorous education.

The opportunity for boys of low-income families to obtain such an education was substantially enhanced in September 1947, when the Congress approved a bill providing for scholarships at the liceos for the sons of workers, noncommissioned officers, employees, pensioners, and others whose monthly income did not exceed 400 pesos. The law specified, moreover, that 50 percent of the entering classes in the two existing liceos, and any others established in the future, should be made up of these scholarship winners.[97]

Although a French scholar has interpreted this law as a subtle move by Perón to ingratiate himself with the popular sectors as well as an effort to "democratize the recruitment of the Military Academy,"[98] the legislative history of the law reveals something quite different. The law did not originate with the administration, but rather with the Radical Party, six of whose deputies drafted the original bill.[99] Referred to the Chamber's Committee on National Defense, it won the support of the Peronist majority, who found themselves unwilling to oppose a move of such populist nature. Even

[96] Decree No. 9278, May 28, 953; interview with General Uranga.

[97] Law 13,024, Sept. 30, 1947.

[98] Rouquié [205], p. 86. The law, of course, did not deal with the Military Academy, but with the liceos.

[99] *Diputados* [2], 1946, II, 271. The authors were Gregorio Pomar, a retired officer, H. Pueyrredon, Arturo Frondizi, Emilio Ravignani, Luis Dellepiane (son of an officer), and Raúl Uranga.

so, the initial reaction on the part of the War Ministry was anything but enthusiastic. In arguments that anticipated those used in the United States in the 1970's to oppose affirmative action programs to benefit minority students, General Sosa Molina contended that the bill set up social class qualifications for admission to the liceos and might result in students who received poor grades in the entrance examination receiving preference over more able candidates simply because they were sons of workers. The War Minister also objected to having the scholarships come out of his budget.[100]

The Committee took cognizance of this objection by assigning the cost of the scholarship program to the Justice and Education Ministry; but it insisted on giving absolute preference to young men in the specified categories.[101] The War Minister is not known to have voiced further objections, and the bill in this form was subsequently enacted into law by vote of both houses. Nine months later, however, Radical Deputy Atilio Cattaneo, a former officer himself, rose in the lower chamber to complain with reference to one of the liceos, "Up to this moment there isn't one instance of an NCO's son who has been able to enter this school."[102]

One is left to wonder whether any of the other intended beneficiaries were in fact admitted, and indeed to what extent the Army implemented the law in future years. No firm conclusion can be ventured until studies are made of the social origins of students admitted to the liceos militares before and after 1947; but it may well be that here as in the case of opening up commissions for sergeants and corporals, the War Ministry found ways to avoid being pushed into directions it was reluctant to follow.

If War Minister Sosa Molina was able to preserve the Army's autonomy from unwanted civilian intrusion, he was also highly successful down to 1949 in keeping the Army from becoming involved in civilian politics. In part, this resulted from the sense of professional well-being that President Perón fostered through pay increases, improved housing, and other social benefits, and through the energetic support he gave to weapons acquisition and the construction

100 *Diputados* [2], 1947, IV, 440–41.
101 *Ibid.*, pp. 440–48.
102 *Diputados* [2], 1948, IV, 2629.

of new military facilities. Also contributing to the political neutrality of the Army was its absorption in the tasks of adapting to U.S. organizational concepts and equipment. At the War Academy, for example, the study of English took on new importance since, as its Director pointed out at the opening of the 1948 courses, "All, or almost all, that can interest us professionally we are going to find in the armed forces of the United States . . . [and] moreover, many of the future general staff officers will be summoned to participate in inter-American military organizations where they will have to exchange opinions and come to terms with the American representatives among others."[103]

Reinforcing the effects of these factors was the emphasis that the War Minister and senior officers placed on the traditional values of obedience and discipline. General Sosa Molina tried to discourage Army personnel from expressing aloud their political opinions, and although he could not have been completely successful, down to 1949 the atmosphere in the Army was one in which professional rather than political concerns were uppermost.[104] A few officers undoubtedly reacted privately, but there was no collective or uniform response to the political measures taken by the administration. It may be assumed that officers responded differently, and not necessarily for partisan reasons, to such positive breaks with tradition as the extension of the vote to women and to noncommissioned officers, enacted in 1947 and 1948, respectively. On the other hand, to the extent that they had any regard for constitutional procedures and guaranties, some officers might have viewed with alarm such drastic measures as the impeachment of the Supreme Court, the silencing of opposition newspapers, and the harsh treatment accorded outspoken critics, whether Radical Party deputies or one-time Perón supporters, who refused to submerge their identities in the single party Perón insisted on.

None of these measures, however arbitrary, produced any shock waves within the Army. As a professionally oriented officer later recalled, it was not a question of the Army supporting Perón, but one of obedience. "The Army still followed for many years the traditional

[103] *Revista de Informaciones*, XXVI, No. 276 (March–April 1948), p. 152.

[104] The War Minister periodically issued general orders warning against political discussion. See General Order No. 34 of June 6, 1946, and that of Sept. 20, 1948, issued just after the vote was given to noncommissioned personnel.

process of obedience, of loyalty, of discipline until a limit is reached
. . . when the thing is so great that even the most simple-minded
realizes that this cannot continue, but it takes time."[105] For most
officers, as of the close of 1948, that limit had yet to be reached.

[105] Interview with Lieut. General (Ret.) Benjamín Rattenbach, April 8, 1970.

Chapter 4

The First Warnings, 1949–1951

As the year 1949 opened, President Juan Perón could take satisfaction in the strength of his position and the popularity of his administration. Despite the bitter criticism voiced by political opponents at home and echoed in the world press, the Argentine voters had twice shown their steadfast and, indeed, increasing support for their leader. In the congressional elections of March 7, 1948, the Peronist candidates won 60 percent of the votes as against 54 percent two years before and easily assured the administration of a two-thirds majority in the lower house. In the December 5 elections for delegates to the constituent assembly that was to meet in January 1949, the Peronists received 66 percent of the vote and obtained two-thirds of the seats.[1]

The Peronist movement was still not free of the internal wranglings that had characterized it since its rise to power, but Perón's lieutenants were learning how to control the heterogeneous elements that went to make it up. The opposition of erstwhile supporters like the Laborista Cipriano Reyes was countered by direct measures. Reyes himself was arrested in September 1948 and accused, together with John Griffith, a onetime United States Embassy official in Buenos Aires, now a private citizen in Uruguay, of plotting the overthrow of the government and the assassination of both the President and his wife. The anti-American atmosphere that was

---

[1] The election results may be found in the contemporary press. See also Embassy BA Dispatch 304, April 12, 1948, 835.00/4-1248; ARA Office Memorandum from Mr. Dearborn to Mr. Tewksbury, Jan. 10, 1948 (this is obviously misdated for 1949 and is misfiled under 835.00/1-1048).

whipped up in connection with this sensational but unproved charge was eventually allowed to die down, but Reyes was to remain in jail for the next seven years, and his fellow Laboristas were forced into inactivity or exile.[2] Meanwhile, under the leadership of Señora Perón, newly enfranchised women were encouraged to become active politically. Although delays in the preparation of voter registration lists prevented their participation in a national election until 1951, everything indicated that when women exercised the right to vote, they would show themselves to be even stronger supporters of the Peróns than their male counterparts.

The core of Perón's support now as in the past was in the working class. Despite the efforts of Socialist and other anti-Peronist labor leaders to exploit resentment against rising prices, labor support for Perón was, if anything, growing, buttressed by a series of accomplishments to which the Peróns could point with pride: the rise of real wages over the past three years; the extension of retirement systems to include additional groups; fringe benefits from paid vacations to medical assistance that amounted perhaps to half again the value of money wages; and an attack on the housing shortage through the direct construction of low-cost units and the provision of inexpensive home loans through the state-controlled banks.

The identification of many Argentines of modest circumstances with the Perón administration rested on emotional as well as pragmatic considerations. Evita Perón's charitable activities and her many public appearances helped create a sense of personal contact with the President and his administration. The trade unions, through Evita's influence and the frequent presence of the secretary-general of the CGT at high-level meetings, could give their members a sense of vicarious participation in the making of policy. The linkage between the masses of workers and the Perón government was further strengthened by its frequent denunciations of other political parties as the agents of exploitive property owners and of foreign imperialism. Sensational revelations such as the Griffith "plot" served to exploit nationalist sensitivities to alleged external intervention against

[2] The accusations against Griffith generated a flood of reports from the U.S. embassies at Buenos Aires and Montevideo, most of which are filed under 835.00, starting with BA Telegram 955, Sept. 24, 1948. For Laborista explanation of the "plot" see the Beveraggi Memorandum transmitted in Embassy BA Dispatch 642, Oct. 14, 1948, 835.00/10-1548.

Perón and to induce a fanatical quality in the outlook of his followers.[3]

Nevertheless, despite his assurance of popular support, President Perón's position was not invulnerable. For, beginning early in 1949, his administration had to face a series of economic crises that contributed to a sense of political and social unease. The economic crisis of 1949 manifested itself in several ways: in a severe payments problem with the United States that practically halted imports including fuel and machinery needed by various industries; in a sharply increased inflation rate that eroded the value of wage increases; in a reduced level of agricultural exports, caused in part by an unrealistic price structure that was to be aggravated at year's end by a severe drought; and in a general lowering of economic activity.[4]

What seemed at first a temporary setback to the pattern of strong economic growth that had characterized the past three years proved to be more enduring. The decline in real national income, observable in 1949, was repeated in 1950. Favorable international factors led to an upturn in 1951, but the second severe drought within three years plunged the country in 1952 into the most difficult straits it had experienced since Perón first took office. With inflation rates at historic peaks and real incomes continuing to decline, Argentines were asked by their government to curb their consumption of beef and wheat in order to generate supplies for export abroad.[5]

The response of the Perón administration to the economic crisis of 1949 was to maintain a public stance that defended existing policies while denying the gravity of the overall situation. In speech after speech, the President proudly listed the measures that had achieved Argentina's "economic independence," but either passed over in silence or minimized the seriousness of the current problems.[6] Behind

[3] The manner in which the Peronists exploited the plot charges is covered in Embassy BA Dispatch 609, Oct. 1, 1948, 835.00/10-148.

[4] Díaz-Alejandro [247], *passim*, and Statistical Appendix, Tables 34, 37, 64, 123, 124, and 133. For contemporary comments on the economic situation, see Embassy BA Dispatches 7, Jan. 4, 1949, 611.3531/1-449, and 128, Feb. 15, 1949, 835.00/2-1549. As of January 1949 the Embassy placed the Argentine debt to U.S. suppliers at over $300 million.

[5] Díaz-Alejandro [247], Statistical Appendix, Tables 11, 123, and 124. For the institution of meatless days, see *La Nación*, Jan. 31, 1952.

[6] See for example his February 18 address to labor attachés in which he

the scenes, however, these problems sparked a series of efforts to force the President to abandon his closest advisors and shift his policies. In the early months of 1949, this movement precipitated an internal political crisis that seemed to threaten the stability of the government.

The nature and ramifications of this movement and the identity of its participants have never been clearly established. Apparently involved were certain cabinet members, including War Minister Sosa Molina and various military friends of Perón acting as individuals. An interested observer, if not an active participant, was Foreign Minister Bramuglia. Their first target was the economic boss, Miguel Miranda, who had survived so many previous efforts to unseat him. This time, however, for reasons of her own, Evita Perón lent her support to those demanding Miranda's ouster, and the result was his formal resignation in the latter part of January.[7]

The departure of Miranda created a void that Perón sought to fill by naming to the cabinet Dr. Roberto Ares, a Foreign Ministry economic officer and close associate of Dr. Bramuglia; and Dr. Alfredo Gómez Morales, a trained economist with long government experience, most recently in the Secretariat of Commerce and Industry. The appointment of these men to the newly created posts of Secretary of Economy and Secretary of Finance, respectively, did not, however, produce agreement within the government on the appropriate measures for meeting the economic crisis. The basic issue was how much of the Miranda economic structure and policies to change.

---

claimed that "today we owe nothing," summarized in Embassy BA Dispatch 143, Feb. 23, 1949, 835.00/2-2349; also his Campo de Mayo address of March 10, in *La Prensa*, March 11, 1949; his "State of the Nation" address to Congress on May 1, in *Diputados* [2], 1949, I, 11–35; and his "camaraderie" dinner address to the armed forces in July 1949 reproduced in Perón, *Perón habla a las fuerzas armadas, 1946–1954* [99], pp. 51–65.

[7] According to U.S. Ambassador Bruce, Evita's decision to press for Miranda's ouster came when she learned that he was collecting a 3 percent kickback for issuing wool export licenses and claiming that he was doing it on her behalf (Embassy BA Airgram 39, Jan. 21, 1949, 711.35/1-2149). For other information on Miranda's resignation, which was informally offered on January 18 and confirmed on January 26, see *La Prensa*, Jan. 19, 1949, and *New York Times*, March 6, 1949.

The new appointees, especially Dr. Ares together with Foreign Minister Bramuglia, were apparently urging sweeping changes: the abolition of IAPI, the dismantling of export controls, and greater cooperation with the United States. They seemed to view with favor Argentina's eventual membership in international economic and financial organizations and looked to the possibility of securing a dollar credit to ease the current payments crisis. The more nationalist officials, however, supported strongly by Evita Perón, were adamantly opposed to any restoration of private interests to positions of dominance in foreign trade; they opposed concessions to foreign business interests and regarded membership in the international organizations as incompatible with economic independence. The idea of seeking anything resembling a foreign loan was anathema to them.[8]

So intense were the policy divisions within the government that early in February reports were circulating to the effect that Bramuglia, Ares, and Gómez Morales were all threatening to resign. Another account had the President himself stalking out of a meeting of officials, also threatening to resign. Although none of these threats materialized, it is evident that Perón was laboring under a great deal of stress, that he was not at all certain how to resolve the economic problems, and that his health was showing signs of strain.[9]

To complicate the President's situation, the War Minister, supported by certain senior officers, chose this critical period to launch an attack against Evita's role and influence within the government. Such prestigious retired officers as Lieut. General von der Becke, a former Commander-in-Chief, and Lieut. General Pistarini, the Public Works Minister, joined with General Sosa Molina in privately urging the President to send Evita out of the country, preferably to Europe, or at least make a public declaration that she would have no further connection with the government.[10]

[8] Embassy BA Dispatch 128, Feb. 15, 1949, 3, 835.00/2-1549; Memorandum of Conversation between Dr. Juan Scarpati, Economic Counselor, Argentine Embassy, and Mr. Tewksbury *et al.*, Department of State, Feb. 9, 1949, 835.50/2-949; Memorandum of Conversation, Mr. Sohar R. del Campo, Ambassador James Bruce, and Mr. Tewksbury, Department of State, March 11, 1949, 835.50/3-1149.

[9] Embassy BA Telegram 145, Feb. 9, 1949, 835.00/2-949, and Dispatch 128, Feb. 15, 1949, 835.00/2-1549. Perón was reported to be having problems with his teeth and his blood pressure.

[10] Embassy Dispatch 128.

In thus pressing for the First Lady's retirement to private life, the War Minister seems to have been responding to concerns felt by certain officers of his own or older generations rather than to demands for action emanating from younger members of the officer corps. General Sosa Molina was not one to allow any assembly of officers to discuss such a matter, and there is no evidence that he took it up even with those holding general's rank. Moreover, the War Minister in presenting the request for Evita's removal to the President chose not to have key troop commanders present. Thus, the Commanding General of the Third Army, who had jurisdiction over all combat units in the Buenos Aires area, took no part in the meeting with Perón.[11]

General Sosa Molina and those who did participate with him in this delicate undertaking seem to have operated upon two assumptions: first, that maximum privacy could soften the potentially humiliating aspects of their mission and thus facilitate its success; and second, that brotherly advice from older comrades in arms would be sufficient to achieve the goal. To minimize public attention, the officers held off making their move until after the President and Mrs. Perón began a brief vacation on February 8 at their *quinta* in San Vicente, some 25 miles from the capital. By fortuitous circumstance, the day the Peróns went out to San Vicente coincided with a newspaper blackout in Buenos Aires. A printers' strike that day shut down all the dailies in the capital and kept them from publishing for several weeks. Thus, no major paper, whether pro- or antiadministration, was able to inform its readers of the fact or significance of the visits to San Vicente by the War Minister and several other high-ranking officers. Through word of mouth, however, the news soon circulated within diplomatic circles, among foreign correspondents, and among a good many Argentines that the Army was pressuring Perón to relegate Evita to privacy. In the continuing absence of local newspapers, rumors transformed the episode into a major political crisis.[12]

[11] Interviews with Major General (Ret.) Oscar Uriondo, Aug. 5, 1957; Lieut. General (Ret.) Angel Solari, Aug. 10, 1973; and Lieut. General (Ret.) Emilio Forcher, Aug. 1, 1973. Solari served as Third Army Commander, Forcher as Second Infantry Division Commander, and Uriondo as Chief of the Army Intelligence Service (SIE) in early 1949. None of these officers recalled hearing of or attending a meeting at which the First Lady's activities were discussed.

[12] See *New York Times* stories "Peron Not at Parley; Tension is Reported,"

The War Minister and his colleagues were not prepared to do much more than urge their views upon the President. In assuming that they could persuade him to deprive himself of Evita's political appeal, and possibly also of her affections, they vastly underestimated both Perón's loyalty to his wife and his sense of political realities. He refused their request while making vague promises about limiting her activities to the social welfare field; in essence, he was challenging them to do without him. But this was not a re-enactment of October 8, 1945, when emissaries of aroused Campo de Mayo troop commanders, ready to march on the capital, secured Perón's dismissal. The War Minister and his colleagues wanted Perón to remain in office; they had little confidence that any other leader could gain the necessary support for running the government, and they were fearful of provoking a revolution.[13]

Reluctant, therefore, to follow their original initiative to its logical conclusion, the War Minister and his group had little alternative but to accept Perón's promises about Evita and work together to try to patch up the images of the administration and the Army. To this end, a well-publicized presidential visit to military bases was arranged, followed by a luncheon at Campo de Mayo attended by the President and Mrs. Perón, the three military ministers, and the ministers' wives. In his radio broadcast speech that followed, the President combined words of high praise for the War Minister with an optimistic review of the economic situation. Wishing his comrades "to hear from my own lips the truth, but absolutely the truth," he assured them that ever since his own youth "the Argentine Republic has never enjoyed the well-being or economic possibilities that it does at present."[14]

The War Minister, in his address, identified the Army with the

datelined Buenos Aires, Feb. 11, and "News Strike Spurs Argentine Rumors," datelined Feb. 12, 1949; also Embassy BA Telegram 152, Feb. 14, 1949, 835.00/2-1449; and Dispatch 128, Feb. 14, 1949, 835.00/2-1549.

[13] Embassy BA Telegrams 162, Feb. 16, 1949, 835.00/2-1649, and 190, Feb. 23, 1949, 835.00/2-2349; Dispatch 207, March 22, 1949, 835.00/3-2249. In an interesting coincidence von der Becke, who was supporting Sosa Molina's efforts, was one of the emissaries who had obtained Perón's resignation in October 1945.

[14] *La Prensa*, March 11, 1949; Embassy BA Telegram 242, March 11, 1949, 835.00/3-1149. The prepared text of the speeches given at the luncheon may be found in Embassy BA Dispatch 177, March 11, 1949, 835.00/3-1149.

administration's Five-Year Plan and with its principles of popular sovereignty, social justice, and economic independence. Taking note of the recent spate of rumors, he flatly denied that the Army involved itself in political affairs or was opposed to either the social program or the economic policies of the government. Then, in words directed to Mrs. Perón, General Sosa Molina tried to rewrite the recent past. Noting that her work for the poor and the needy entitled her to everyone's respect, he asserted:

Her presence among us today as a special guest of honor is intended as a flat denial of the rumors that the Army opposes her and opposes the people who support her, rumors designed to arouse their distrust of the Army. Let the country know that the armed forces as a living part of their people appreciate with equal fervor the great work of social justice that she stands for as the stoic flagbearer of their struggles. Far from interfering with her useful work which demands such great sacrifice and vigilance, the armed forces are ready to provide her humanitarian and fraternal mission with the frank cooperation that it requires from all.[15]

Although the War Minister's speech at Camp de Mayo was carefully worded to praise only her social welfare work, it represented a capitulation to Mrs. Perón and her determination to exercise influence within the administration. In a matter of days, it was evident that her activities transcended the social welfare field and that her views were again a significant factor in the councils of the administration.[16] A diplomatic observer who was not particularly sympathetic to those views wrote a few weeks later: "There is no indication that she is restricting her activities and in fact there is every indication that no step of major importance can be taken without having her interfere. She probably has more intestinal fortitude and energy than all the so-called good members of the Cabinet, and she knows how to throw her weight about."[17] The appointment of her protégé, Raúl Apold, to the sensitive post of Undersecretary of Press and Information underscored her power. Apold was to be in a position to shape the news presented by the government-controlled radio and pro-administration press as well as to exercise leverage over

[15] "Discurso pronunciado por S. E. el señor Ministro de Guerra en las Guarniciones de El Palomar y Campo de Mayo," Embassy Dispatch 177.

[16] Embassy BA Dispatch 207, March 22, 1949, p. 5, 835.00/3-2249.

[17] Embassy BA Dispatch 322, April 28, 1949, p. 5, 835.00/4-2849.

other papers through his administration of the recently established official monopoly of newsprint allocation.[18] The silent treatment accorded by the government-controlled media to the activities of Foreign Minister Bramuglia, for whom Mrs. Perón had little love, was a clear example of her influence.[19]

The resurgence of Evita's influence was matched by the deterioration of General Sosa Molina's personal prestige. In the eyes of at least some of his subordinates he was no longer the tough, energetic defender of the Army and its institutional interests, but rather the increasingly bland instrument of the Peróns.[20] His issuance of a general order, a week after the Campo de Mayo affair, requiring the formal reading before all officers and noncommissioned personnel of the President's speech and repeating his own disclaimers of hostility to Mrs. Perón's social work could have done little to alter this impression.[21]

Even the President came to feel the need for a change at the head of the Army, but here one can only speculate on his motives. It is quite possible that despite the conclusion of the recent episode, Perón still viewed Sosa Molina as too independent a figure, and therefore too dangerous, to leave in his present position. A younger officer, one with less professional stature and greater personal ties to Perón, would serve his needs better. It is also possible that Mrs. Perón, anxious to exact retribution for the recent experience, urged her husband to move against the Minister.[22] A convenient opportunity for an initial step presented itself in the cabinet reorganization called for by the recently completed constitutional reform. Perón named Sosa Molina to the newly created post of Minister of Defense, allowing him to retain his former position on an acting basis only. After seven months of speculation as to who would permanently head the Ministry of the Army, as it was now called, Perón entrusted the post to

[18] *La Prensa*, March 8, 9, 1949.

[19] Embassy BA Dispatch 368, May 17, 1949, 835.00/5-1749.

[20] Interview with General (Ret.) "X," Aug. 8, 1973. This officer asked to remain anonymous, but the posts he held, some of them in close proximity to the War Minister, lend special weight to his observations.

[21] General Order No. 38, March 18, 1949, in Annex to *Boletín Militar Reservado*, No. 2955, March 18, 1949.

[22] During the recent crisis Mrs. Perón was reported to have requested Sosa Molina to resign and to have received a blunt challenge in reply (Embassy BA Dispatch 157, March 1, 1949, 835.00/3-149).

his former subordinate and close friend, General Franklin Lucero. Sosa Molina, as Minister of Defense, continued to serve in the councils of government, but his was essentially an administrative post; he no longer had direct authority over troop commanders, the colonels and generals whose support was necessary to influence events.[23]

Almost coincident with these politico-military tensions was the completion of the work of the constituent assembly that began its task of revising the nineteenth-century charter late in January. Disregarding the minority of Radical Party delegates who challenged the legitimacy of the convention and finally walked out of it on March 9, the majority proceeded to approve a document that bore an unmistakable Peronist stamp. The tone of the charter was set forth in the new preamble that, while retaining much of the original language, spoke of "ratifying the irrevocable decision of constituting a nation socially just, economically free, and politically sovereign." In keeping with this thrust, the revised constitution embodied two new chapters, one devoted to the rights of the worker, the family, and the elderly and to education, the other to property rights and economic activity. This latter chapter, reflecting the statist and nationalistic fervor of its authors, assigned to the state direct control over foreign trade; permanent ownership of all minerals and natural sources of energy including petroleum deposits; and ownership, original and inalienable, of public service enterprises. Such enterprises that were currently in private hands were to be acquired by the state through purchase or expropriation, and in the latter case, at a price that would reflect the deduction from original investment cost of both amortization and any profits regarded as excessive. A constitutional basis was thus provided for the takeover at minimal or no cost of the remaining foreign-owned utilities.[24]

The revised charter differed markedly in its collectivist tone from its liberal predecessor, but preserved the existing formal structure of government with its separation of powers and federalist character. A number of articles were altered and still others suppressed. The net effect was to add to the powers of the President at the ex-

[23] For the U.S. Military Attaché's comment on Sosa Molina's appointment to be Minister of National Defense, see Embassy BA Dispatch 230, March 29, 1949, 835.20/3-2949.

[24] The text of the revised constitution, as well as the report of the committee favoring the change, may be consulted in *Anales* [1], IX-A, 1–184.

pense of other authorities. The most significant change, however, and the one that critics insisted was the ultimate purpose of the entire reform, was the lifting of the barrier to presidential self-succession. With the elimination of the earlier requirement of an intervening term, it was a near certainty that Perón would seek to remain in power another six years after the expiration in 1952 of his current term. Little wonder that in his state of the nation address on May 1, he described the constitutional reform as "the most serious and transcendent matter of all that the Executive Power has had to confront in the past twelve months."[25]

The President's satisfaction with the reform was not without reservations, however. In particular, he was discomfited by the formula for determining the compensation for expropriated public service enterprises that was embodied in the last paragraph of Article 40. This formula, by threatening to eliminate the distinction between expropriation and confiscation of what were in most cases foreign-owned enterprises, brought protests from the international community. The paragraph had been inserted by nationalist delegates at the last minute and, despite objections by President Perón, was retained in the final text of the revised constitution.[26]

Unable, or unwilling for political reasons, to push too hard in behalf of unpopular foreign-owned utilities like the notorious Compañía Argentina de Electricidad (CADE), President Perón tried to reassure the Belgian, Swedish, Dutch, and United States governments that as long as he was in office he would never invoke the controversial provision. Such assurances did not dispel concern, however, and the existence of Article 40 became a complicating factor in Argentine efforts to obtain United States cooperation in the solution of the dollar shortage and other problems affecting the relations between the two countries.[27]

[25] *Diputados* [2], 1949, I, 12. In his address to Congress just one year before, Perón had categorically opposed amending Article 77 to permit presidential re-election (*ibid.*, 1948, I, 17–18); it was only in the final hours of the convention that this article was amended. For an account of Eva Perón's role in securing this amendment, see Luna, *Argentina de Perón a Lanusse, 1943–1973* [112], pp. 57–58.

[26] Embassy BA Telegram 230, March 9, 1949, Airgram 134, March 14, 1949, *Foreign Relations of the United States 1949* [42], II, 485–87.

[27] *Foreign Relations 1949* [42], II, 490–97; Embassy BA Dispatch 207, March 22, 1949, 835.00/3-2249.

In a further move to eliminate concern over Article 40, President Perón encouraged the visiting executive of one of the affected companies, International Telephone and Telegraph, to propose interpretive legislation that the Argentine executive might submit to Congress. This attempt to draw up a law that could negate the effect of a constitutional provision ended logically in failure. But as an alternative, the ITT executive, Sosthenes Behn, proposed a statement that he felt Perón might make with salutary effect. Perón's eagerness to overcome the detrimental effects of Article 40 was evidenced in his verbatim inclusion of that statement in his May 1 state of the nation address to Congress.[28] In passages that few of his listeners knew were drafted by the head of a United States–based multinational corporation, the President explained his policy toward public service enterprises. His purpose, he stated, as in the past, was to recover these enterprises for the nation, but this was not intended to discourage private initiative in the fields of industry, commerce, and finance; the public service designation was limited to those services that by their nature should be offered by some branch of the state. In recovering public service enterprises he would rely on direct negotiations as he had in the case of the railways and telephones. The purchase through mutual agreement between proprietors and the government "will be adopted by my government as a uniform policy," he announced, and expropriation would be resorted to only when the owners refused reasonable solutions "which we are disposed to offer at every moment." The statement continued with the assertion that his policy was amply supported by Article 40, the relevant text of which (paragraph three) he proceeded to quote, carefully omitting the controversial final paragraph. "On the basis of the transcribed constitutional precept," he continued, "my government will proceed to recover for the nation at the proper time the public services that are still in the possession of private enterprises, according the same reciprocal and equitable purchase conditions and resorting to the alternative of expropriation, with prior indemnification when it may be necessary."[29]

[28] Memorandum of Conversation, Colonel Sosthenes Behn and Mr. Thomas Blake of International Telephone and Telegraph, Mr. Daniels and Mr. Martin, Department of State, May 20, 1949, 835.50/5-2049.

[29] *Diputados* [2], 1949, I, 27. For the statement "Servicios Públicos" prepared

The promulgation of the revised constitution in March 1949 produced no immediately overt impact on Perón's relationship with the armed forces. Within the Army officer corps, whose members, like all government employees, had to take an oath to uphold the new charter, the predominant reaction was one of automatic acceptance. Most officers, absorbed in their professional duties, gave little thought either to its contents or to the oath requirement. A certain number, however, especially those with family ties to members of Radical or other traditional parties, saw the new charter as a document designed primarily to enable Perón to prolong his presidency. To be asked, therefore, to take an oath to uphold this constitution—and oath taking was a serious matter among military men—was tantamount to being asked to swear support for Perón. They presumably recalled the effective use Perón had made of oaths taken by fellow officers in his rise to power before 1945 and the punishment later meted out to certain officers on the grounds of having violated such oaths. To be sure, an officer could avoid the oath by asking for retirement, but this was a heavy price to pay. Most officers, therefore, took the oath, but the necessity of doing so with mental reservations was deeply resented by some of these men and served as a festering source of discontent. With the passage of time, their critical view of the 1949 constitution, enhanced by the violence done to their consciences, was to permeate the thinking of a growing number of officers. Indeed, by 1950 a sense of *malestar*, of uneasiness, was taking on significant dimensions within the Army.[30]

Contributing to this uneasiness was a gradual but perceptible change in the outlook of the Perón administration and its use of its powers. With the enactment of the constitutional reform, Perón and his supporters took the view that Peronist doctrine, symbolized in the watchwords of social justice, economic independence, and political sovereignty, had ceased to be a partisan matter. It was now

by Colonel Behn, see enclosure to Memorandum of Conversation, cited in note 28.

[30] Interviews with Generals (Ret.) Emilio Forcher, July 4, 1971; Benjamín Rattenbach, April 8, 1970; Julio Alsogaray, Aug. 6, 1973; Juan Uranga, July 24, 1971; José Embrioni, May 19, 1970; Admiral (Ret.) Samuel Toranzo Calderón, April 6, 1970; and General (Ret.) "X" Aug. 8, 1973; also interview with Colonel (Ret.) A. Pérez Amuchástegui, Feb. 18, 1970.

national doctrine, and so was the movement that supported it. Those who disagreed with Peronism (or justicialism as it now came to be called) were, therefore, either consciously serving antinational interests or were the victims of ignorance and in need of reeducation. Although the President insisted that his goal was national union, not a single party, he made plain his view that the existing parties did not merit the term and were simply political gangs. In their place, he stated in a revealing speech in December 1949, he would like to see an opposition party formed by decent men who desired the public good, a party to which the government could be entrusted if the people should so decide in free elections. The greatest legacy he could leave to the republic would be two parties, his own and a decent organic opposition party; in other words, a two-party system, both of them Peronist.[31]

Operating from such premises, the Perón administration proceeded to narrow the already restricted opportunities for political opposition and independent criticism. In the latter part of 1949, new legislation was adopted forbidding the formation of electoral coalitions and obstructing the creation of any new political parties. The enactment of amendments to the penal code establishing heavy penalties for offending the dignity of public officials (*desacato*) gave the government a new weapon for intimidating opposition, whether on the public platform or through the printed word.[32] The Peronists used their overwhelming majority within the Congress to restrain their opponents, voting the expulsion of two outspoken Radical Party deputies, who immediately sought exile to avoid arrest, and depriving another of his parliamentary immunity so that he could be tried under the desacato law for remarks made in a campaign speech.

[31] *La Nación*, Dec. 10, 1949. The remarks were made to a delegation from the Ateneo Bancario. See also Embassy BA Dispatch 931, Dec. 13, 1949, 835.00/12-1349.

[32] For the *desacato* penalties, see Law 13,569, article 4; on the new rules for political parties, see Law 13,645; both were promulgated on October 10, 1949. Further restraints on political criticism were imposed by the Law for the Repression of Acts of Espionage, Sabotage and Treason (Law 13,985), enacted the following year, which broadened the definition of espionage to include (article 6) the publication or dissemination of "economic, political, military, financial or industrial data which without being secret or confidential are not intended for publication or issuance" and imposed a prison sentence of from one month to four years for violators.

Arrested in March 1950, Ricardo Balbín, the parliamentary leader of the Radical minority, remained imprisoned for the next ten months, a symbol both of the increasingly repressive character of the government and of the resistance it was generating.[33]

The administration revealed its desire for conformity in its increasingly arbitrary treatment of the press. Although Perón had not hesitated in the past to close down individual newspapers, his government, late in 1949, initiated a campaign of wholesale harassment against independent papers. An ad hoc congressional committee, created to investigate allegations of police tortures as well as anti-Argentine activities, served as the principal instrument for intimidating those newspapers not already in pro-government hands. This committee began by seizing the business records of various newspapers and news agencies. In 1950, using as a pretext the failure to obey a congressional directive requiring the printing on their mastheads of an allusion to the centennial of the national hero San Martín, it shut down provincial newspapers by the score. By the close of 1950, the process of transforming the once-variegated press into a uniform chorus of approving voices was well under way.[34]

The major obstacles to complete uniformity were two family-owned organs of independent conservatism, *La Nación* and *La Prensa*, both of which had been in existence for over 80 years and enjoyed international reputations for the quality of their coverage. The government chose the more outspoken of the two, the Paz family's *La Prensa*, as the target for its pressure in January 1951. What started out seemingly as a news vendors' strike forced it to suspend publication and ended up, despite a wave of international protests, in the seizure of the newspaper from its owners. A transformed *La*

[33] For the debate on Balbín's loss of immunity, see *Diputados* [2], 1949, VI, 4257–96; on his subsequent sentencing, Embassy BA Dispatch 782, Nov. 30, 1950, 735.00/11-3050; on his release, *La Prensa*, Jan. 3, 1951. The expelled deputies were Agustín Rodríguez Araya on June 9, 1949, and Atilio Cattáneo for charging Perón with enrichment in office, on Dec. 12, 1949. For the debate preceding Cattáneo's expulsion, *Diputados* [2], 1949, VI, 5259–66. The Chamber President suppressed his accusations from the record, but they are reported in Embassy BA Dispatch 1010, Dec. 27, 1949, 835.00/12-2749.

[34] On the activities of the Visca-Decker committee, as it was known, see Embassy BA Dispatches 836, Nov. 28, 1949, 835.00/11-2849; 865, Dec. 5, 1949, 835.00/12-549; 56, Jan. 12, 1950, 735.00/1-1250; 64, Jan. 12, 1950, 735.00/1-1250; 129, Jan. 20, 1950, 735.00/1-2050, 154, Jan. 25, 1950, 735.00/1-2550. See also Rabinovitz [296], pp. 116–21.

Prensa subsequently reappeared as the house organ of the CGT, leaving a subdued and cautious *La Nación* as the only national newspaper to maintain independence from the government.[35]

Why President Perón, with his overwhelming majorities in the Congress and his broad popular support, should have felt impelled to move in the direction of greater control of Argentine society in the years after 1949 is a complex matter that no simple observation can explain. To argue that this trend was the inevitable consequence of Perón's totalitarian mentality or to ascribe it to his military background ignores the timing and has little overall explanatory value. History has known civilian leaders of seemingly unimpeachable democratic inclinations, Indira Gandhi for example, to clamp down on the press and persecute their opponents. In Perón's case, a more plausible explanation may be that his actions were a defensive response to the seriousness of the economic situation.[36]

For all of his public insistence that the Argentine economy was sounder than ever, the President was aware that the policies of the past few years would have to be modified in ways that could cause discontent in the ranks of labor, the bureaucracy, and among his more nationalistic followers. Restraints on salaries and wages, demands for greater productivity, reductions in public works expenditures, a lowering of domestic consumption to increase agricultural exports, diversion of income to the agricultural sector, incentives for foreign investment, all had to be considered if inflation were to be stopped and the economy revived.[37] The political damage such measures might do to Perón's support could be minimized, however, if the administration had thorough control of the communications media and if the opposition were fragmented and discredited.

To view the shift toward greater control as a political expedient induced by the economic crisis may seem to deny any ideological thrust to the Peronist movement. Given the fervor it was able to

[35] The details of *La Prensa's* difficulties with the news vendors and the Peronist administration may be followed in the columns of *La Nación* beginning January 28, 1951, and in many foreign newspapers including the *New York Times*.

[36] For an interpretation that rests almost exclusively on the economic crisis of 1949, see Ferns [107], p. 194.

[37] For a memorandum purportedly presented by President Perón to his cabinet setting forth the need to consider precisely these steps, see enclosure to Embassy BA Dispatch 517, July 25, 1949, 835.00/7-2549.

generate among its supporters, not only in its palmy days, but even in the bitter years that followed the ouster in 1955, one must concede the presence of a mystique, of a sense of commitment to a new society, even if the details were vague and the accompanying rationale lacked intellectual vigor. But what of the leader? Did Perón share the faith of his most dedicated followers, or was he a complete opportunist saying whatever had to be said and doing whatever had to be done to stay at the top? Judgments will inevitably vary, but there seems to have been more than simple expediency in his exercise of power. He was after all identified with changes in the distribution of power and income within Argentina, changes in the balance between industry and agriculture, changes of style and of substance in Argentina's economic and political relationships with the outside world. This was his "revolution," and it would appear that the thrust toward even greater domination of Argentine life after 1949 was designed to create a permanent structure that would make impossible a return to the past.

This thrust coincided with increasing rhetoric emphasizing the need for organization. In speech after speech in 1950, Perón sounded the importance of organization at the level of the government, the state, and the nation, in order to give Peronist achievements a permanence that would transcend his stay in office. Greater organization at the national level meant spreading Peronist consciousness among the people. As he explained to a meeting of provincial and territorial governors: "At present, it should be a matter of pride for an Argentine citizen to be a Peronist. We should be impressing this view, and our ideas, on children, youth, women, men, and all sectors of society. We do so not for politics but for national reasons because we are persuaded that our ideas are saving the country."[38] But in calling for action to strengthen the Peronist majority, he threatened with destruction those who would not share his outlook: "No longer would it be conceivable in the Peronist Argentina placed under our custody and our government, that anyone, absolutely anyone, can rise up against the majority will of the nation. Whoever does this will suffer the consequences of his action."[39]

[38] *Hechos e Ideas*, XIX, No. 74/75 (May–June 1950), p. 205. The full text of Perón's address to the governors is reproduced here under the title "La organización del Gobierno, del Estado y de la Nación."

[39] *Ibid.* For other speeches that sounded the themes of organizational achieve-

Whatever his underlying motives, as Peronism increasingly pre-empted the political stage and arrogated to itself the monopoly status of a national movement, the President's relations with the Army were bound to change. He could no longer be satisfied with the relative autonomy that the armed services had enjoyed between 1946 and 1949. It was now essential that the military institutions themselves be increasingly integrated with the political movement. This was of course a delicate process, one whose ultimate goal could neither be openly proclaimed nor hastily pursued. If ever achieved, it would mean nothing less than the elimination from the Army of the traditional professional norm of political neutrality and the imposition of the overt politicization characteristic of the armies of one-party states.

The man chosen to direct the process of integrating the Army with the Peronist movement was Perón's former War Ministry aide and devoted supporter, General Franklin Lucero, who took over as Minister of the Army on October 15, 1949.[40] As suggested above, the process would be gradual. It involved efforts to promote a sense of personal identification and ideological affinity with the President and his movement; it also involved measures that would strengthen the military men's sense of appreciation, personal and professional, for favorable treatment accorded them and their institutions.

On the institutional level, the administration's capacity to provide such treatment was hampered by the general economic situation. It was no longer able to afford major equipment purchases for the Army, or anything involving heavy outlays of foreign exchange. The plight of the Army-sponsored mixed steel company, SOMISA, is a case in point. The original authorized capital of 150 million pesos had proved far too low, partly because of a decision to increase the capacity of the basic plant from 315,000 to 500,000 tons annually,

---

ment in the government and the need to organize the economic forces, see his May 1, 1950, state of the nation address to Congress, *Diputados* [2], 1950, I, 7–13, and his remarks at the annual armed forces camaraderie banquet in July 1950, *Perón habla a las fuerzas armadas* [99], pp. 76–77.

[40] *La Prensa*, Oct. 16, 1949. Lucero had been serving as Subsecretary of the Army Ministry since March 18, 1949. Prior to that he had been Military Attaché in the United States. His friendship with Perón dated from an early phase in their respective careers and was consolidated between 1944 and 1945 when Perón was War Minister and he was the Undersecretary. For Lucero's own comments on their ties, see his *El precio de la lealtad* [65], pp. 22–23.

but even more because of rising costs. To meet this situation, the directors of SOMISA had petitioned the government in 1948 to increase its authorized capital to 500 million pesos. Only in 1950, presumably in response to a presidential directive, did the Congress enact legislation authorizing the Executive Power to "increase the capital of . . . [SOMISA] to whatever sum is essential to fulfill the aims of the Argentine steel plan, Law No. 12,987."[41] Any rejoicing in SOMISA circles would have been premature, however, for the administration made no contribution to the augmented capital either in 1950 or 1951, nor would it authorize the company to seek foreign credits to finance the purchase of the needed equipment.[42] Other economic needs, especially the liquidation of commercial debts, had a higher priority, and continued postponement of tangible steps to assure completion of the steel mill remained the order of the day. Although the Economic Council in 1949 discussed the possibility of an Export-Import Bank loan for the steel mill, the government did nothing to obtain such a loan. The $125 million credit eventually arranged with that bank in May 1950 was to pay off commercial arrears owed to private U.S. banks; nothing was sought for the steel plant.[43]

In the sphere of personnel benefits, however, where scarcity of foreign exchange was not a constraint, the Perón administration acted energetically. To combat the erosion of inflation on salaries, it provided periodic wage adjustments. Although civilian employees also received increases, the amounts assigned to the military tended to be more generous. In March 1952, when the maximum cost-of-living increment authorized for anyone on the civil list, including the judiciary and legislature, and even for senior members of the Federal Police, was 500 pesos, Army generals in a separate decree of the same date received from 1,100 to 1,300 pesos; colonels, 1,000;

[41] Article 4, Law 13,997, enacted Sept. 29, 1950. For the earlier requests to Congress to increase SOMISA's capital see *Diputados* [2], 1948, II, 809, and 1949, I, 678–79.

[42] Castiñeiras [138], pp. 41, 42, 52–54, 66.

[43] Embassy BA Dispatches 322 and 323, both April 28, 1949, 835.00/4-2849; *Foreign Relations 1949* [42], II, 504; *Foreign Relations 1950* [43], II, 711–24. As further evidence of current Argentine priorities, the government canceled a $5.6 million order for military equipment that had been placed in the United States in 1948 (*ibid.*, II, 729, n. 3).

and the lowliest sublieutenant, 450 pesos. Not surprisingly, the text of the latter decree was not published.[44]

The administration also enabled Army officers to share the benefits of a special system it had instituted to provide government officials, trade union leaders, and others with new automobiles at far below their going price. The system, introduced in 1949, required commercial automobile dealers, as a condition for getting import permits, to agree to turn over half the imported units to the Ministry of Industry and Commerce. The Ministry designated the recipients of the vehicles and fixed their prices, using an artificially low exchange rate to translate the dollar costs into pesos. The resulting "list price" of these automobiles was half or less of what the ordinary purchaser had to pay to obtain the comparable unit from the undersupplied commercial channels. This two-tiered price structure allowed an individual fortunate enough to obtain a purchase authorization from the Ministry either to use it himself or to resell it for a handsome profit.[45]

The inclusion of Army officers as participants in this system was initiated some time around April 1951 when, as Army Minister Lucero later observed, "through express order of His Excellency the President of the nation, the benefits of the *obra social* which the Army conducts were broadened with the assignment of 441 automobiles at list price for interested officers."[46] The opportunity to acquire these vehicles was suspended a year later, but in that period 435 officers from first lieutenant to lieutenant general and six civilian employees of the Ministry took advantage of it. Not all of the officers on the list of recipients were enthusiastic Perón supporters, suggesting that General Lucero either hesitated to apply a political test or, more likely, hoped to use the automobile transactions as a means of

[44] Decree No. 6000 of March 25, 1952, authorized salary increases for all government employees save the military; an unpublished decree of the same date, No. 6019, authorizing military salary increases is reproduced in *Boletín Militar Reservado*, No. 3350, April 7, 1951. Earlier the military had shared in both the general cost-of-living increase granted by Decree No. 7025 of April 13, 1951, and the adjustments of military base pay and emoluments authorized by Decree No. 21,087 of Oct. 24, 1951.

[45] See the testimony of Minister of Industry and Commerce, José C. Barro, to an investigating committee in 1955 after Perón's fall, Comisión Nacional de Investigaciones [10], I, 168–69.

[46] *Boletín Militar Reservado*, No. 3351, April 8, 1952, p. 502.

converting them. What is beyond dispute, however, is that a number of officers who later broke with Perón were not averse at this time to using the favoritism implicit in the "list price" system for their own benefit. It would seem that neither the administration that provided the opportunity nor any of the officers who utilized it saw anything wrong in it at this time.[47]

Over and above providing automobiles and cost-of-living benefits, the Perón administration displayed a sensitivity to other standard concerns of military men: the desire for more rapid promotions, on the one hand, and for a less rigid system of obligatory retirement, on the other. The bill it submitted to Congress in September 1950 to revise and unify the basic statutes affecting the three military services afforded an opportunity for some accommodation to both aspirations. On the promotion side, this bill, which Congress was quick to approve, cut down the minimum time that had to be spent in each grade from first lieutenant to brigadier general. Thus, an academy graduate fortunate enough to win promotion in each grade at the earliest permissible moment could now become a major general in just 22 years, as against the 29 previously required. Most of the time reductions, moreover, took place at the grades of captain and above, thus making for an accelerated movement in the prestigious categories of *jefes* (majors and lieutenant colonels) and of *oficiales superiores* (colonels and generals).[48]

The other side of the coin was the compulsory retirement system. The Argentine military, like most career services, operated on an up-or-out basis; to create promotion vacancies, it was sometimes neces-

---

[47] The names of the 441 recipients are listed in *ibid.*, pp. 502–512. Presumably these vehicles, which were distributed before April 8, 1952, were included in the figure of 481 that the 1955 testimony of J. C. Barro (see note 45 above) specified as having been distributed to persons recommended by Army Minister Lucero. Barro also stated that another 168 vehicles were assigned to individuals recommended by the Defense Minister, General Humberto Sosa Molina. These presumably went to Army, Navy, and Air Force officers assigned to his Ministry.

[48] The changes in minimum times were as follows:

Rank	1946	1950	Rank	1946	1950
Brig. Gen.	4	3	Captain	6	4
Colonel	4	3	1st Lieutenant	3	2
Lieut. Col.	4	3	Lieutenant	2	2
Major	4	3	Sublieutenant	2	2

The figures for 1946 are from Decree No. 14,584, and those for 1950 from Law 13,996.

TABLE 5.—CHANGES IN AUTHORIZED STRENGTHS FOR SUPERIOR OFFICERS,
1950–55

	1950	1951	1952	1953	1954	1955
Generals	61	66	72	71	76	90
Colonels	214	224	236	244	251	299
All officers	6,066	5,721	5,820	5,753	5,753	5,753
All enlisted	98,348	101,617	103,427	103,101	103,101	103,101
Total strength	104,414	107,338	109,247	108,854	108,854	108,854

Sources: Annexes to *Boletín Militar Reservado*, Nos. 3092, 3208, 3368, 3415, 3486, 3555, 1950–55.

sary to compel the retirement of officers who stood at the bottom of their respective merit lists. Under prior legislation, one-fourth of the budgeted positions at the grade of major and above had to be renewed each year, and if sufficient openings were not available as a result of upward promotions, disability retirements, and other factors, officers fully qualified for continued service could be forced out. For the less than outstanding officers in each grade, the threat of being "sent home" was demoralizing as well as a waste of trained manpower. The 1950 legislation did nothing to alter the basic system, but it did give the military ministries greater flexibility in operating it, allowing them the option of extending by decree the period in which the turnover in a given grade had to be completed. The Army thus had the authority, although it was careful in its use, to retain a number of field grade and superior officers who otherwise would have been forced to retire.[49]

With the greater flexibility provided by the new legislation, Perón and his Army Minister, General Lucero, embarked on a promotions policy that had the effect of compressing the rank pyramid at the junior levels and expanding it elsewhere, especially at the senior grades. As Table 5 demonstrates, the authorized strength of the entire Army grew by about 4 percent between 1950 and 1953 and then remained level for the next two years. The officer corps actually declined between 1950 and 1953, to remain thereafter at a fixed size, but the number of positions for senior officers grew steadily. Between

[49] Article 189, Decree No. 29,375, of Oct. 26, 1944, as amended by Decree No. 14,584 of May 12, 1946; article 89, Law 13,996/1950. The 1950 law enabled majors and above to remain in grade for a period up to twice the minimum time fixed for the grade or up to six years. In 1952 (Law 14,163) this was extended to three times the minimum or up to nine years.

1950 and 1955, the openings for colonels increased by 85, or 40 percent; the openings for generals in that same period jumped 48 percent, increasing from 61 in 1950 to 90 in 1955. Lest it be thought that these budget projections were unrelated to reality, the rosters of active duty officers show 76 general officers on the last day of 1952 and 96 at the end of 1954.[50] The authorized figures in Table 5 seem to understate the actual situation at this level.

Although the trend toward top-heaviness is unmistakably clear, the reasons remain a matter of speculation. Professional needs other than overall growth, such as the accommodation of unpromoted officers, would seem to have justified some upward adjustment in the rank profile. But it is difficult to resist the conclusion that political considerations were even more responsible. At a time when the administration could not satisfy institutional aspirations for new armaments or other equipment, promotions to and within the coveted status of general must have seemed a practical way of advancing the process of integrating the Army into the "national" movement.

Here again the gradualness and unevenness of the process must be emphasized. At the close of 1950, professional officers without Peronist inclinations could still gain promotions at these high levels. The year-end promotion list in December included several from this category among the fifteen officers raised from brigadier to major general.[51] To be sure, the top positions in the command structure were now overwhelmingly in the hands of Perón supporters, in contrast to the situation only two years before.[52] Those generals whose sympathies were in any way uncertain found themselves in bureaucratic posts. The one exception to this pattern among the newly promoted major generals was Eduardo Lonardi, who, for reasons not at all

---

[50] Ministerio de Ejército, *Escalafón del ejército argentino . . . hasta 31 de diciembre de 1952* [17]; *Escalafón del ejército argentino . . . hasta 31 de diciembre de 1954* [18]. Nine of the 96 generals listed in 1954 were scheduled to retire in the early part of 1955, but this still left 87 on active duty.

[51] Generals Fosbery, Rattenbach, Lonardi, and Corti are the more obvious ones.

[52] Prior to 1948 the post of Army Commander-in-Chief had been held by Generals von der Becke (1944–46) and Mason (1946–48), and the post of Commanding General of the Interior by Generals Mason (1945–46) and Juan Bassi (1946–48), all of whom had reputations for political neutrality. As of the close of 1950, Generals Angel Solari and Laureano Araya held the two posts, both of them officers who were viewed by their peers as strong Peronists. See Chapter 1, Table 2.

clear, was moved from his position as director general of administration in the War Ministry to a major command, head of the First Army located in Rosario, Santa Fe. If, as some believe, Perón's desire to compensate for an old injury he had done to Lonardi led him to approve this assignment, he would later have reason to regret his generosity.[53]

Efforts to identify the Army with the goals, ideology, and rhetoric of the Peronist movement constituted a significant aspect of the integration process. Perón, by virtue of his triple position as Chief Executive, Commander-in-Chief of the armed forces, and head of the Peronist movement, was the natural prime mover of these efforts. Every visit to a military installation, every speech to a military audience, carried political overtones. This was evident whether he was addressing the colonels' course at the War Academy or speaking to the officers assembled at the annual July camaraderie dinner. At the 1950 dinner, for example, after presenting his view of Argentina's future as that of an "organized community marching toward the conquest of clear objectives," he defined the role of the armed forces in these words: "Within the organized community the armed forces of the nation are something like the spinal column that is the backbone of every organism; they form a part of the national unity, but not an inert part, rather a living organism that is part of every other, and is integrated by all the rest."[54]

If there was any doubt about his meaning, his observation in the same speech that there was only one creative political force currently in existence should have dispelled that doubt. In still other speeches, the President promoted the idea that the Argentine people and their

[53] In 1937 Lonardi replaced Perón as Argentina's Military Attaché in Santiago, Chile. Perón who had arranged for a transfer of materials in violation of Chilean espionage laws, left it to Lonardi to pick up the data without briefing him as to the nature or illegality of the operation. The trap that Chilean authorities had prepared for Perón was sprung on the innocent Lonardi, who was arrested and held in a Santiago police station until the Argentine Embassy could secure his release. This episode came close to ending Lonardi's active military career, but he was allowed to continue partly through the intercession of a friend and classmate, Benjamín Rattenbach, who was related to the War Minister. General Rattenbach believes that Perón had a sense of guilt about this affair and that this affected his subsequent relations with Lonardi (interview with Lieut. General (Ret.) Rattenbach, April 8, 1970).

[54] *Perón habla a las fuerzas armadas* [99], p. 77; for his address inaugurating the colonels' course in March 1949, see *Revista de Informaciones*, XXVII, No. 282 (March–April 1949), pp. 121–28.

armed forces were closely linked to one another because of their mutual belief in the principles of his movement. "The armed forces," he observed in his 1951 state of the nation address to Congress, "have understood perfectly well these principles of justicialist doctrine; and the greatest praise that I can give them before your honors is to affirm that at this moment the people of the nation trust and love their Army, Navy, and Air Forces because they see in them not only the instruments of their security but the effective causes of their happiness and greatness. They have learned to acquire the only thing that has value for us: the affection of the people."[55]

Sharing with the President the effort to strengthen the armed forces and the Peronist movement were his military ministers and other high-ranking officers. In some instances, their contribution was mainly symbolic, such as the attendance of the Defense Minister at the July 1949 congress of the Peronist Party. More often, the contribution took the form of linking traditional military concerns to the rhetoric of Peronism. General Laureano Anaya, Quarter-Master General of the Army, for example, gave a detailed lecture at the Círculo Militar designed to show that the Army was a contributor to progress rather than a financial burden to the nation. The one conclusion he chose to stress, however, was that "the Army constitutes an optimum reserve force to achieve the ideals set forth in the preamble of the new Magna Carta: A Fatherland socially just, economically free, and politically sovereign."[56] In somewhat similar fashion, General Eduardo Garimaldi, a military engineer, published an essay that discussed the obstacles in the way of industrial mobilization. His analysis of the existing situation inclined him, he admitted, to a pessimistic view, but it was necessary to consider what the President had proclaimed about economic independence and the need to organize the nation's economic forces. General Garimaldi's conclusion was, therefore, appropriately optimistic; he looked forward to "the effective reality of our balanced economic potential, thanks to the extraordinary effort of the GOVERNMENT OF THE NATION, so that we are a country politically sovereign, socially just, and economically free."[57]

---

[55] *Diputados* [2], 1951, I, 42.
[56] Anaya, "El Ejército" [125], p. 232.
[57] Garimaldi, "La defensa nacional y el progreso industrial" [148], pp. 351–52.

In this atmosphere of deliberately cultivated harmony between the armed forces and the Peronist movement, it was only natural that the traditional legal barriers to military men engaging in politics should be reexamined. Ever since the beginning of the century, when the professionalization of the Army got under way, active duty officers had been banned by statute from taking part directly or indirectly in partisan political activity. To be sure, the same laws permitted an officer to accept election to a national post, but if he did so he was placed in a status (*disponibilidad*) that froze his promotion prospects. He could not count the time spent in elective office toward promotion; moreover, only if he held a national office, not a provincial or local one, would the time be credited toward his retirement. These disincentives were undoubtedly a factor in shaping the decision of career-minded officers when urged by friends to take a flyer into politics.[58]

A group of Peronist deputies took the initiative in seeking to narrow the demarcation line between military and political careers. In 1948, they proposed a bill that would allow active duty officers, with prior permission of the executive, to serve in any elective post, federal, provincial, or municipal, without loss of either promotion or retirement credit. The bill passed the lower chamber, but got no further.[59] The Congress did, however, enact special exceptions to the rules, in one case allowing an Air Force brigadier to serve as Peronist governor of Córdoba without any loss of privileges; in another, approving promotion for Perón to major general despite the fact, noted by the opposition, that he had been in disponibilidad since his last promotion in 1946 and could not have earned any promotion time.[60]

The idea of easing the path for officers who wanted to enter politics was finally examined in the Executive Branch in 1950 when the President and his military ministers reviewed the draft of a proposed

[58] Article 59, clause 1e and Article 86, clause 5 of Decree No. 29,375, Oct. 26, 1944, were currently in effect. For earlier legislation governing political activity, see Article 31, clause 4, of Law 9765 of 1915, Article 6 and Article 24 of Law 4707 of 1905, and Article 6 of Law 4031 of 1901.

[59] *Diputados* [2], 1948, V, 3567, 3983ff.

[60] Law No. 13,339 of Sept. 1948 authorized Brigadier Juan I. San Martín to become governor of Córdoba; Law No. 13,896 of May 1, 1950, promoted Perón. For the Chamber debate see *Diputados* [2], 1950, I, 34ff; the Senate had already acted on this earlier (*Senadores* [3], 1949, III, 2851–57).

military statute that would apply uniformly to the Army, Navy, and Air Force. It is not known whether they seriously considered legalizing open affiliation with the Peronist Party, but this must at least have come under discussion. After all, the President was known to be affiliate number one of the party, and the desire to emulate him must have been strong. Indeed, the commander of the Patagonian Army Group, Brigadier General Julio Lagos, perhaps anticipating a change in policy, had openly joined the branch of the party where he was headquartered. Probably to his surprise, he found himself punished by being relieved from his command, though this did not prevent his continuation in service and later promotion. Apparently the President and his ministers decided that the time was not ripe for so open a breach with the traditions of the profession.[61]

Accordingly, when the administration submitted its bill to reform and unify existing military statutes in September 1950, the text retained some of the existing restraints.[62] Active duty personnel were enjoined "not to participate in the activities of political parties."[63] This obligation, however, was specifically waived for those "summoned to discharge federal elective functions, for the period of their mandate."[64] The text specified that such officers would be able to have their time in office credited for both promotion and retirement purposes, but repeated the traditional ban against their wearing of the uniform or insignia of rank at political meetings.[65] The Congress, for its part, enacted the bill promptly with a few amendments, one of which provided for the President's promotion to General of the Army; another for the extension of promotion and retirement credits to officers serving in any elective post, not just federal ones. When this latter provision was first proposed in the Senate, the Defense Minister spoke against it. The Chamber of Deputies, however, insisted on its inclusion in the final bill.

[61] For General Lagos's removal, see *Boletín Militar Reservado*, No. 3135, June 12, 1950. He was subsequently named Commander of Communications under the Army Commander-in-Chief (*ibid.*, No. 3264, June 14, 1951) and a few months later Second Army Commander (*ibid.*, No. 3306, Nov. 13, 1951) with promotion in December 1951 to major general.

[62] The complete text of the bill is reproduced in *Senadores* [3], 1950, II, 1084–1101.

[63] Article 5, clause 6, *ibid.*, p. 1085.

[64] Article 54, clause 5, *ibid.*, p. 1090.

[65] Article 54, clause 5, and Article 56, *ibid.*, p. 1090.

Thus, by the close of 1950, under the new unified statute, Army, Air Force, and Navy officers on active service could accept political party nominations for any elective post, municipal, provincial, or federal, without fear of slowing their careers. The one common requisite was that they obtain permission from their respective service ministry before accepting. Given the President's view of the illegitimacy of the opposition parties, it seems clear that only officers interested in Peronist Party candidacies were likely to take advantage of the new legislation.

In seeking to identify the armed forces with himself and his movement, Perón paid special attention to the permanent enlisted personnel, the *suboficiales,* or noncommissioned officers (NCOs). Indeed, the cultivation of their support was a goal that he had been pursuing for some time. Having served at the Escuela de Suboficiales at earlier stages in his own career, Perón had a wide acquaintance among army sergeants and a keen insight into their professional and personal concerns. He was aware that efforts to reduce distinctions between them and the commissioned ranks would have a profound impact, and he was prepared to make changes in areas that did not affect basic hierarchical principles. The 1948 enactment that extended the franchise to permanent enlisted men was an example of such changes. Others included the substantial improvements in housing and social benefits provided for their families and changes in the official uniform that enabled senior NCOs to appear more like officers.[66]

Perón's appeal to the noncommissioned ranks, however, transcended the professional sphere. After all, his movement was directed to the social classes from which most enlisted men came; the same social programs and policies that generated support among working men and women could be expected to have a comparable impact on

[66] Another "benefit" was the 1950 legislation authorizing the creation of a procedure whereby an NCO could become an officer. In Chapter 3, at note 96, I pointed out that this enactment (Article 39 of Law 13,996) was not implemented by specific decree until May 1953, when it was established that a qualified NCO by completing the last two years at the Colegio Militar could win a commission. The Army Ministry in 1951 did, however, allow three NCOs who passed the qualifying exams to enter the Military Academy as first-year students (*La Nación,* May 5, 1951). Whether any of these students finished the course is not known, but it is clear that they received only limited credit for their prior military experience.

their relatives in uniform. The effect of this combination of class appeal and professional benefits was demonstrated in various ways: in the warm welcomes accorded the President and his lady when they visited military bases; in the banners strung up in barracks, contrary to military practice, in praise of Evita; and in such occurrences as the *acto de homenaje* organized by NCOs of the three services at the Olivos residence in January 1951. The singing of an "himno a Perón" composed by a suboficial mayor and the presentation of gifts to the President and Mrs. Perón marked the tone of the affair. Perhaps no less indicative of the relationship between the Peróns and a good many permanent enlisted personnel were the words with which Mrs. Perón concluded her speech of thanks to those present: "I hope that you transmit to your wives and relatives this affection from comrade Evita who knows that the suboficiales, like the entire Argentine people, have raised in their hearts an altar to the most renowned of all Argentines, General Perón." [67]

Not all Argentines, by any means, civilian or military, were prepared to raise such altars. Quite the contrary. In the face of the government's increasing curbs on overt political opposition, certain members of the Radical, Socialist, Progressive Democratic, and Conservative parties began to contemplate the possibility of insurrection. Their problem was to put aside old differences and find sufficient military support.

For several years a limited number of retired officers had been discussing among themselves the possibility of overthrowing Perón. Many of these officers had been identified with the liberal, or pro-Allied, sector of the Army rather than the nationalist, or pro-Axis, wing at the time of Ramón Castillo's ouster in 1943; most of them became involved in one way or another in the abortive efforts to prevent Perón's rise to power in 1944 and 1945 and had seen their own careers terminated in consequence. Since then they had sought to influence the outlook of their active duty colleagues, often through the circulation of anonymous handbills and propaganda pamphlets designed to expose the excesses of the Perón administration. Such

[67] *La Nación*, Jan. 26, 1951, covers the event and reproduces the speeches; on the presence of banners in the barracks, interview with Lieut. General (Ret.) Emilio Forcher, July 4, 1971.

activities kept alive the spirit of resistance of their authors, but had seemingly little effect on the troop commanders whose support would be essential for any serious undertaking. Even among retired officers, where old differences still influenced current attitudes, there was no unity of outlook, no agreement on what, if anything, should be done, or who should do it.[68]

This situation began to change in the increasingly charged atmosphere that engulfed Argentina in 1950 and 1951. Contributing to the change was the firm evidence that Perón was preparing for his reelection and the less firm but still electrifying news that Evita would be his running mate.[69] This prospect, however gratifying to her supporters, was one to set the teeth on edge of many Argentine males, especially those in uniform, for whom the idea of this woman, or indeed any woman, as constitutional successor and consequently Commander-in-Chief of the armed forces was still inconceivable.

Also contributing to the changed situation were developments in the social, economic, and foreign policy spheres suggesting that Perón was more vulnerable now to concerted opposition than at any time since 1946. Under the impact of inflation, divisions in labor's ranks became more evident. A series of strikes in defiance of government orders during 1950, culminating in the January 1951 railway strike that Perón broke by ordering the military mobilization of the workers, suggested that his hold on the labor movement was not as extensive as might have been imagined.[70]

---

[68] Interview with Gen. (Ret.) Bartolomé Ernesto Gallo, Feb. 23, 1970; "Alocución pronunciada por el General de Brigada (RE) Bartolomé Ernesto Gallo, en homenaje a la Revolución Libertadora . . . 16 de septiembre de 1969," MS in my possession. From 1945 to 1951 Gallo and José Francisco Suárez, both retired colonels, took leading roles in promoting resistance to Perón.

[69] "Perón's Wife Seen as Running Mate," *New York Times*, Sept. 4, 1950.

[70] Worker unrest was reflected in the port workers' strike that lasted three months despite a government order declaring it illegal, in strikes in the meatpacking and banking sectors, and in the temporarily successful protest against the CGT-sponsored move to hold back the wages that would have been paid out for October 12 and donate them to the Eva Perón Foundation (*La Prensa*, Oct. 14, Dec. 22, 1950; Jan. 16, 1951). The railway strike that broke out in December, seemingly settled and then renewed in January, was as much a protest against the officially recognized leadership of the Unión Ferroviaria as it was for wage increases. Both Eva Perón and Transport Minister Castro tried without success to resolve the differences. In the end Perón fired the Transport Minister, placed the workers under military control, and ordered the arrest of numerous Socialist Party leaders whom he held responsible for the strike. *La Prensa* gave

Shortages of fuel and other economic difficulties also continued to plague the country, although increased exports to the United States, generated by the outbreak of the Korean War, were easing the dollar payments problem. But even here, the administration opened itself to criticism by abandoning its pledge never to borrow money abroad. To be sure, the $125 million loan, accepted from the Export-Import Bank in May 1950, was disguised as a credit and was extended to a group of private banks, not to the Argentine government itself. But the Central Bank guaranteed ultimate repayment of the sum, and government officials had gone to the United States to work out the preliminary arrangements.[71] Among nationalist elements, whose support of Perón was predicated on his commitment to economic independence, his credibility was bound to suffer, even though government spokesmen continued to insist on the differences between a loan and a credit.

More serious were the allegations, baseless in fact but nevertheless widely believed, that one condition for securing the Ex-Im credit was Argentina's ratification of the Rio Treaty, signed in 1947. Perón had held up submitting the treaty to the lower chamber after its approval by the Senate in 1948 because of nationalist criticism. Two days after the outbreak of the Korean War, however, the treaty was placed without warning before the Chamber of Deputies and rammed through in a single session.[72] The ratification of this treaty raised questions about Perón's alleged commitment to a third position (neither pro-United States nor pro-Soviet) in international affairs. So did his Foreign Minister's open-ended response to a United Nations request for support of the war in Korea.[73] Rumors spread wildly that the government was planning to send troops to Korea,

detailed coverage to the activities and statements of the dissident unionists, a fact that may have influenced the decision, apparently reached in a meeting between Mrs. Perón and the leaders of the news vendors union on January 19 (*La Nación*, Jan. 20, 1951) to have the latter force the shutdown of the paper a week later.

[71] Central Bank officials José Brignoli and Julio Juncosa were in Washington from September 1949 participating in a U.S.-Argentine study of trade problems.

[72] *Diputados* [2], 1950, I, 681, 746–47; for the State Department's denial that Perón had promised ratification of the Rio Treaty as a *quid pro quo* for U.S. financial assistance, see the Department's secret circular to U.S. embassies in Latin America dated June 7, 1950, in *Foreign Relations 1950* [43], II, 727–28.

[73] For the text of his statement see *La Prensa*, July 1, 1950.

and a number of protest meetings were held, possibly inspired, as the Federal Police Chief claimed, by enemies of the regime.[74] Given the clear evidence of popular opposition to any break with Argentina's 80-year tradition of peace, the President announced that he would do only "what the people wanted." His Foreign Minister clarified his communication to the United Nations, insisting that the sending of troops was never intended.[75] The entire episode, however, gave those not firmly committed to Perón an impression of vacillation, not of the firmness expected from a strong President.

Under the impact of these developments as well as of the general thrust of Perón's policies, Argentines in 1950 found it increasingly difficult to maintain an independent stance that was neither pronor antigovernment. Put in other terms, a process of polarization was forcing hitherto uncommitted Argentines to take sides, a process that the Peronists themselves were actively promoting by their view that "for us . . . there are only Peronists and anti-Peronists."[76] Although Peronist leaders obviously hoped to strengthen their movement as a result, and many a teacher and civil servant joined the official party simply to hold onto their posts, the effects of polarization were not necessarily all on one side. Within the ranks of the military, both active and retired, conformity was promoting attitudes of resistance on the part of a growing number of officers.

Indications of such feeling among retired officers who had long been regarded as politically neutral may be seen in various minor episodes that would normally not attract attention. For example, in July 1950, Perón abruptly replaced Colonel (Ret.) Bartolomé Descalzo as director of the Sanmartinian Institute and Museum, charging that its staff was not permitting humble groups to visit the premises and claiming that its building was being used for antigovernment activities. It is noteworthy that serving on the Institute's Council and

[74] Radio talk by Federal Police Chief, General Bertollo, *La Prensa*, July 19, 1950.

[75] Perón's statement was made to a CGT-sponsored meeting at the Teatro Colón. See *La Prensa*, July 18, 1950. For the Foreign Minister's clarification, see *ibid.*, July 19, 1950.

[76] Quoted from the remarks of Alberto Teisaire, President of the Superior Council of the Peronist Party to the Conference of Governors, *La Prensa*, June 15, 1950. President Perón enunciated a similar view in his "Twenty Truths of Justicialism," which he proclaimed to the crowd assembled to celebrate "Loyalty Day" on October 17, 1950. Truth number six stated: "For a Peronist there can be nothing better than another Peronist."

working with Descalzo were a number of retired senior officers, including Lieut. Generals Mason, Bassi, and von der Becke, none of whom had had a reputation for political partisanship and all of whom now submitted their own resignations from the Institute Council.[77]

Whatever the validity of Perón's charges, the increasing difficulty officers found in maintaining a neutralist stance is suggested by von der Becke's presence a few days later at a lecture given by General (Ret.) Adolfo Espíndola under the aegis of *La Prensa's* Instituto Popular de Conferencias. In this, the centennial year of San Martín's death, Espíndola was lecturing on the topic "San Martín—First Soldier of Liberty." The subject matter alone might have attracted von der Becke, but the location of the lecture, the reputation of the speaker, and the identity of other members of the audience suggest otherwise. The *La Prensa* Institute lecture series had become a center of cultural opposition to Perón and Peronism; pro-administration speakers never graced its platform, but when an anti-Peronist like Colonel (Ret.) Roque Lanús spoke there a month before, or when the equally hostile General Espíndola lectured now, the crowded audience was a veritable *Who's Who* of figures who had dominated Argentine politics and society before Perón's rise to power. Present also were numerous retired officers, some of them like the speaker, former activists who had suffered imprisonment, others like von der Becke or the recently retired Moisés Rodrigo, who had kept their noses out of trouble. All, however, could appreciate the broader connotations of Espíndola's concluding remarks when he stated: "May God wish that Argentina in the endless course of time continue to produce free men and that they, animated by the spirit of the first soldier of liberty, never permit the sun to be eclipsed from our beloved and glorious flag."[78] Although it cannot be argued that von der Becke, Rodrigo, or any other officer in attendance was thereby a

[77] *La Prensa*, July 27–30, 1950. Descalzo also resigned as head of the National Energy Bureau, an agency within the Industry and Commerce Ministry. For an indication that criticism of Evita was a factor in his removal from the Sanmartinian Institute, see Embassy BA Dispatch 169, Aug. 7, 1950, 735.00/8-750.

[78] The text of Espíndola's lecture and a story identifying prominent members of the audience, civilian and military, are given in *La Prensa*, Aug. 5, 1950; for the Roque Lanús lecture and a description of his audience, see *ibid.*, July 1, 1950.

member of a conspiratorial group, their presence symbolized the growing concern among retired officers with the tendencies of the Perón administration, a concern that would deepen with the action of the police in September in putting an end to the Institute lecture series and with the forced shutdown in January 1951 of *La Prensa* itself.[79]

It was not only among civilian groups or retired military officers that what seemed to be the increasingly totalitarian character of the Perón government was arousing deep concern. Within the ranks of active duty officers a similar reaction was taking place. Among Army officers assigned to military installations in various parts of the country, among Air Force officers, and within the Navy, hostility to Perón was growing, fed by the clear evidence that he was preparing for his reelection and by the incipient campaign to elevate Evita to the vice-presidency. The greatest concentration of hostile officers, however, was found in the staffs of military and naval colleges in the Buenos Aires area and in the institution that was the intellectual centerpiece of the Army's professional training system, the War Academy. Of its more than 400 officers, including course directors, professors, and officer-students, perhaps 80 percent were alienated from Perón in 1951. It is not surprising then that War Academy officers should have been deeply involved in efforts to organize a revolutionary movement that could oust Perón before his reelection could take place.[80]

The officers committed to this goal, however, had to contend not only with the vigilance of the government and of loyal officers, but also with internal divisions in their own movement. Indeed, several separate strands made up the movement, not all of which meshed readily with one another. Lack of coordination and a rivalry over

[79] The Federal Police notified that Institute on September 26 that henceforth it would need prior police permission to hold further lectures. The Institute's directors thereupon voted to suspend the series. Four months later, on January 26, 1951, the newspaper itself was forced to shut down (*La Prensa*, Sept. 27, 1950).

[80] Interviews with Generals (Ret.) Bernardino Labayru, May 14, 1970; Juan E. Guglialmelli, July 13, 1970; Julio Alsogaray, Aug. 6, 1973; Admiral (Ret.) Adolfo Estévez, March 24, 1970; and another officer interviewed on Aug. 14, 1973, who asked not to be identified and who shall be referred to henceforth as General (Ret.) "Z." The 80 percent figure for alienated War Academy officers comes from General (Ret.) "Z."

leadership plagued the movement practically from the start. The basic rivalry was between two groups of officers, one led by Major General Lonardi, whose current post was First Army Commander in Rosario, the other led by Brigadier General (Ret.) Benjamín Menéndez, a cavalry officer whose active service had ended in 1942.

Lonardi, a 55-year-old artillery officer with a first-class professional reputation, had never been known to mix into politics before, even though he had personal reasons dating back to the 1930's for disliking Perón.[81] Indeed, because of his quiet temperament, his open manner, and his dedication to duty, he was the last person that fellow officers who knew him since cadet days could conceive of as a possible caudillo of a revolution.[82] His decision to get involved now suggests the extent to which the polarization process promoted by Perón could affect the outlook of an officer who otherwise was enjoying a successful professional career. Family pressure—Lonardi had married into a traditional but highly nationalistic family in Córdoba—may have played a part in his decision. But it appears likely that certain officers at the War Academy also had something to do with it. For late in 1949, a group of the Academy's officer professors and senior staff, including the subdirector, the then Colonel Pedro Aramburu, began discussing the idea of ousting the government. In searching for an officer who might be persuaded to lead an eventual movement, they fixed on General Lonardi, then serving as the War Ministry's Director General of Administration. Presumably they thought of Lonardi partly because he was a general of great personal prestige, partly because they were aware of his personal distaste for the Perón administration. In any event, they established contact with Lonardi through one of their number, Lieut. Colonel Bernardino Labayru, and thus began a period of discussion and exploration that extended for more than a year. When General Lonardi, now assigned to Rosario, finally decided to organize a revolutionary movement in March 1951, he looked to the War Academy in Buenos Aires rather than to his First Army headquarters for his principal collaborators. Colonel Juan C. Lorio, the chief of the Academy's general staff course, together with several lieutenant colonel professors, took

[81] See above, note 53.
[82] Interview with General (Ret.) Benjamín Rattenbach, April 8, 1970.

on additional duties as General Lonardi's revolutionary general staff; in Rosario apparently only his personal aide was aware that the First Army Commander was involved in a conspiratorial movement.[83]

General Menéndez, Lonardi's chief rival in organizing the subversive movement of 1951, was almost his antithesis in temperament and career experience. Impetuous rather than reflective, Menéndez had led a stormy life, punctuated by duels, challenges to politicians, and involvement in a series of conspiracies, none of them successful. Popular among fellow cavalrymen, he had been disappointed not to be invited to play a major role in the successful coup of 1943 and had viewed Perón's subsequent rise to power with distaste. On the sidelines for the next several years, he had maintained contacts within the Army partly through his two sons, both cavalry officers. He had also mellowed from his earlier nationalistic antipolitician stance and had developed ties with civilian political figures, especially members of the conservative National Democratic Party. By 1950 he believed that Perón's military support was waning and, in 1951, moved by his own sense of outrage at the treatment of the opposition as well as encouragement from his civilian friends, he began actively to conspire. Tall, erect, and with a bearing that belied his 66 years, this was the man who wanted desperately to tap the anti-Peronist feeling within the armed forces and to lead a successful coup for the first time in his career.[84]

The existence of two competing conspiratorial groups was a natural source of confusion to the would-be participants, especially when representatives of both groups solicited pledges of support from the same officers or the same units. Nevertheless, in the months of March and April 1951, the movement seemed to be taking shape. General Lonardi received a pledge of support from the retired officer

[83] Interviews with Generals (Ret.) Bernardino Labayru, May 14, 1970; Bartolomé Gallo, Feb. 23, 1970; Alejandro A. Lanusse, Aug. 23, 1973; Colonel (Ret.) Luis M. Terradas (telephone conversation), Aug. 21, 1973. I am also indebted to Gen. (Ret.) Tomás Sánchez de Bustamante for obtaining replies to my questions from Lieut. Colonel (Ret.) Abel Almeida. Almeida had served in Rosario in 1951 as aide to General Lonardi; Terradas was a member of the general staff of the Third Military Region in Rosario.

[84] Interviews with General (Ret.) Benjamín Menéndez, March 23 and 27, 1970; see also Potash, *Army & Politics in Argentina, 1928–1945* [188], pp. 111, 149–51, 156.

group led by Colonel (Ret.) José Francisco Suárez, which had been carrying on the anti-Peronist pamphlet campaign of the last several years. Lonardi also received promises of support from various civilians, including the Radical leader Miguel Angel Zavala Ortiz and the Socialist leader Américo Ghioldi, many of whose party colleagues had been jailed after the January railway strike, and who was himself in hiding from the police. Through intermediaries, Lonardi was sounding out officers in all three services in Greater Buenos Aires, in Córdoba, and in such places as Tandil, where the Air Force jets and Army cavalry division were located. The replies obtained were encouraging but not sufficiently firm to permit adherence to the original plan for launching the uprising in June or July. General Lonardi preferred caution to precipitous action and postponed fixing a firm date in spite of the understandable impatience of certain civilian supporters.[85]

The passage of time permitted additional efforts to secure support, but also increased the risk of discovery by authorities. In June, the Army Ministry announced the arrest of five junior officers on charges of participating in a plot to break up the unity of the officer corps. Shortly thereafter, it was announced that Suárez had been arrested, accused of plotting the overthrow of the government. Fortunately for General Lonardi, the authorities had no firm evidence implicating him, even though Army Intelligence observed his movements as it did those of other officers. Perhaps Lonardi was protected by the fact that the Army Commander-in-Chief, General Angel Solari, was a close professional and personal friend. Fully aware, from private conversations over the past several years, that Lonardi did not share his own enthusiasm for Perón, Solari nevertheless was reluctant to

[85] Interviews with Generals (Ret.) "Z," Aug. 14, 1973, Bartolomé Gallo, Feb. 23, 1970, Señores Miguel Angel Zavala Ortiz, July 22, 1971, Américo Ghioldi, March 20, 1970; Admiral (Ret.) Adolfo Estévez, March 24, 1970, Francisco Pérez Leirós, May 16, 1962. The difficulty of coordinating the military and civilian elements in the conspiracy is illustrated by the events of August 1, 1951. In the understanding that the military uprising would take place that day, Socialist leaders arranged to have the main railway lines coming into Buenos Aires blown up. Late in July, General Lonardi sent Estévez to advise Ghioldi that the military move would have to be postponed. It was too late to call off the saboteurs, however, and the explosions went off in the early morning of August 1 to the general mystification of the public. The Peronist government proceeded to tighten up its vigilance, warning the opposition parties of severe consequences and ordering further arrests of suspected individuals.

believe that his fellow professional would actually take part in a rebellion.[86]

The government nevertheless stepped up its vigilance of suspected high-ranking officers, in a few cases by assigning loyal officers to their staffs to counteract possible moves.[87] For the most part, however, the authorities directed their efforts to strengthening the sense of discipline and unity within the ranks. Army Minister Lucero, in a series of general orders, lectures, and visits to garrisons, preached the need for maintaining professional ethics and developing pride in one's unit. In his presentation to officers he stressed the necessity of exclusive dedication to specific functions and "sincere spiritual harmony" vis-à-vis the government, one's superiors, and the rest of the Army to assure its well-being and also to promote the prestige of the individual unit. In this connection, General Order No. 6 pointed out that "any component of the officer corps who on or off a military base criticizes or comments unfavorably on the established govern- ment . . . injures the prestige of his unit."[88]

Lucero did not act alone in his efforts to preserve the loyalty of the officer corps; he sent other senior officers out to lecture at various garrisons. It was the fate of the Inspector of Instruction, Emilio Forcher, to be sent to Rosario, where at an assembly presided over by General Lonardi, he delivered a forceful lecture, emphasizing the unequivocal obligation of the soldier, regardless of conditions, to support the civilian authorities. Lonardi, patently distressed, invited General Forcher to his lodgings afterward to present his own view that the current state of affairs could not be allowed to continue. Forcher, however, held to his position and, unaware that his host

[86] Interview with General (Ret.) Angel Solari, Aug. 10, 1973. For the an- nouncement of the arrests, see *La Nación*, June 23 and July 1, 1951.

[87] Interview with General (Ret.) Miguel Iñíguez, Aug. 21, 1973; recollections of Air Force Brigadier Mayor Samuel Guaycochea, published in *La Prensa*, Sept. 29, 1961, in a series of articles entitled "A diez años de un intento para derrocar la dictatura."

[88] See *La Nación*, March 13 and 14, 1951, for the meeting of officers of the Federal Capital and Buenos Aires region and the text of Lucero's General Order No. 6; for the Army Minister's visit to various garrisons in Córdoba, where he commented on this same general order, see *La Nación*, May 31 and June 2, 1951. In late August, General Lucero circulated throughout the Army a printed pam- phlet that reproduced several of his previous homilies on norms of proper con- duct including General Orders No. 6 and No. 7 of August 16 on strict fulfillment of military duty. *La Nación*, Aug. 25, 1951, published a summary of this pamphlet.

was already involved in a revolutionary movement, left Rosario to present his lecture at other garrisons.[89]

Such efforts to shore up military loyalty may have slowed, but certainly did not halt, the conspiracy in gestation. A more serious obstacle to its success was the unresolved issue of who was to lead the movement. Late in July, in view of Lonardi's failure to act and spurred on by the government's sudden decision to advance the election date by three months to November, General Menéndez made his bid to take over sole leadership. At a secret meeting attended by leading figures of the chief opposition parties, Arturo Frondizi of the UCR, the Socialist Américo Ghioldi, Reynaldo Pastor of the National Democrats, and Progressive Democrat Horacio Thedy, General Menéndez presented himself as the "jefe natural" of the impending revolution. After outlining his plans to set up a patriotic and decent government based on the 1853 constitution, with the aid of the parties represented at the meeting, and after announcing his determination to oust Perón before the November elections, he asked for the collaboration of those present. All four political leaders agreed, although Ghioldi, noting his own links to Lonardi, urged that the two conspiratorial groups be united.[90]

The next few weeks saw several attempts to bring about such unity through the urging of military men as well as civilians. Certain Air Force and Navy conspirators were especially eager to see their Army counterparts join forces, although they themselves were prepared to join whichever revolutionary group moved first. In the effort to bring about unity, a face-to-face discussion was arranged between

[89] Interview with General (Ret.) Emilio Forcher, July 4, 1971. General Forcher recalled these events as having taken place sometime after the September 28 military uprising led by General Menéndez (see text below), but it is clear from documentary evidence that his talk with Lonardi had to have taken place prior to late August 1951. General Lonardi at his own request was relieved of his command and placed in disponibilidad status on August 28; named to replace him as First Army Commander was General Felipe Urdapilleta, who was formally installed in the post on August 30 (*Boletín Militar Reservado*, No. 3284, Aug. 29, 1951; *La Nación*, Aug. 31, 1951). If further evidence were needed, Lieut. Colonel (Ret.) Abel Almeida, who served as General Lonardi's aide, recalls the Forcher lecture and his subsequent meeting with Lonardi and. insists that they took place prior to Lonardi's relief from his post.

[90] Interviews with General (Ret.) Menéndez, March 23, 1970; General (Ret.) Julio Alsogaray, Aug. 6, 1973; and Américo Ghioldi, March 20, 1970; also "A diez años de un intento para derrocar la dictadura," *La Prensa*, Sept. 28, 1961, published interview with General Menéndez.

Generals Menéndez and Lonardi. To avoid detection, the two met in the cramped quarters of the small diesel-consuming Mercedes Benz owned by the War Academy captain who was serving as Menéndez's aide. Neither this meeting nor a second one held in similar fashion produced the hoped-for joining of forces.[91]

What the meetings did accomplish was to reveal something of the differences between the two leaders, differences that extended to the tactical aspects of the revolutionary phase as well as to the policies that would follow a successful ouster of the incumbent regime. Menéndez proposed to establish an interim dictatorship, to revoke the 1949 constitutional changes, and to make a fresh start by canceling most of the Peronist legislation. General Lonardi, on the other hand, saw the necessity of preserving many of the Peronist social measures. As regards tactics, General Lonardi insisted on continued efforts to obtain additional pledges of support, with the idea of action later in the year, perhaps in November. Menéndez, on the other hand, was committed to moving as soon as possible; he thought a surprise blow with a small force that included Campo de Mayo units and the Military Academy would rally the entire nation.[92] It would appear that in both his tactics and his conception of future policies, he was looking back to the 1930 coup of another retired general and ignoring the vast social and political changes that had taken place since.

But the biggest obstacle to agreement between the two generals was apparently not revolutionary tactics or future policies, but something even more powerful: personal dignity, pride, and ambition. Neither one was prepared to subordinate himself to the other.

The prospects for the proposed revolution, however, were to depend not only on the attitudes of the two generals, but on political decisions reached by Perón. On August 22, his carefully orchestrated renomination campaign came to a climax in a monster rally organized by the CGT. There, in the presence of hundreds of thousands of enthusiastic supporters, the Juan Perón–Eva Perón candidacies

[91] *La Prensa*, Sept. 29, 1961, published interviews with Air Force Brigadier Major (Ret.) Guaycochea and Admiral (Ret.) Vicente Pio Baroja; also interviews with Generals (Ret.) Menéndez, March 23, 1970, and Alsogaray, Aug. 6, 1970. Alsogaray was the owner and driver of the Mercedes; Lieut. Colonel Labayru accompanied General Lonardi in the first automobile meeting, Colonel Juan C. Lorio in the second one.

[92] Interview with General (Ret.) Menéndez, March 27, 1970.

for president and vice-president were formally proclaimed. But, although the President indicated his acceptance, his wife asked for a few hours before giving her reply. The few hours in fact turned into nine days before Evita, in an emotional radio address on the night of August 31, announced that she preferred her present status and would not accept the nomination.[93]

What had happened? Was it Evita's awareness of her physical deterioration, the cancerous growth that would hospitalize her for surgery in just two months, that led her to decline the nomination? Or did the Army, as some writers have contended, force the President to censor his wife's political ambitions?[94] This writer has been unable to uncover any evidence that Army officers, either alone or in groups, ever approached the President with such a demand. A more likely explanation is that Perón used the nine days to make his own assessment of military reactions. Through his military ministers he had available a network of intelligence agents who could report officer attitudes to the proposed nomination. It is even possible that in the officers' clubs, opponents of the nomination gave vigorous expression to their views, knowing full well that Army Intelligence Service (SIE) members would pass them on to their superiors. Perón could easily have come to the conclusion that Evita's nomination was too dangerous to insist on.[95]

Curiously, General Lonardi himself may have contributed to Perón's decision. On August 27, the First Army Commander in a blunt note to the Army Minister asked for immediate relief from his assignment. "Well-known recent political events," he wrote, "have created for the undersigned a state of mind incompatible with support for the acts of the government which Your Excellency's Directives and General Orders establish as a necessary condition to merit the con-

[93] For a detailed account of this huge rally, which its sponsors called the "Cabildo Abierto de Justicialismo," and of the speeches and exchanges between Evita and the crowd, see *La Nación*, Aug. 23, 1951. For the text of Sra. Perón's renunciation of the nomination see *La Nación*, Sept. 1, 1951. In August 1973 this "renunciation speech" was rebroadcast on Argentine television as part of a special program devoted to Evita, and I was able to make a tape recording of it.

[94] For interpretations that posit overt Army pressure see Magnet [113], p. 100; Whitaker, *The United States and Argentina* [117], p. 161; and Ferns, *Argentina* [107], pp. 196–97.

[95] Interviews with General (Ret.) Angel Solari, Aug. 10, 1973; General (Ret.) Oscar Uriondo, Aug. 5, 1973; and General (Ret.) "X," Aug. 8, 1973.

fidence of superior authority."[96] Perón may have reasoned that if General Lonardi, whom he still presumed to be a loyal officer, could no longer reconcile his private views with his sense of duty and asked for retirement, what might be expected from officers who lacked his professional qualities? At any rate, on August 31 it was announced that the incumbent Vice-President Quijano would accompany Perón on the reelection ticket.[97]

The elimination of Evita's candidacy, and with it one of the immediate sources of discontent among military men, undoubtedly influenced the prospects of the revolution in preparation. General Menéndez, however, was undeterred and continued with his plans for an early blow. General Lonardi, on the other hand, began to vacillate. At the time of his replacement as First Army Commander on August 28, his intentions apparently were to return to Buenos Aires and use his presence there to garner additional support and coordinate the still dispersed revolutionary effort. Some time over the next two weeks, however, he decided to desist from further activity. Probably his awareness that General Menéndez was about to move, but perhaps also the feeling that such a move was doomed to failure, led him to step aside. In any event, his decision was communicated to his supporters, enabling those who were impatient with further delays to cast their lot with General Menéndez.[98]

The actual uprising on September 28 suffered from inadequate planning and poor execution. Because Menéndez placed great emphasis on secrecy and surprise, he allowed supporters to leave for the interior unaware that the uprising was imminent. He and his staff depended too much on chance and thus failed to anticipate that the tanks of the Campo de Mayo regiment they counted on seizing would require fueling, or that NCOs would oppose their efforts.

[96] For the complete text of this note and the subsequent exchanges between Lucero and Lonardi, see Lonardi [161], pp. 340–43.

[97] The possibility exists that Perón had decided well before Lonardi's August 27 note that Evita would not be a candidate. In a book written eight years later Lucero claims that he had given Lonardi private assurances as a friend that Mrs. Perón would reject the nomination and was therefore surprised to receive his request for relief and retirement (Lucero [65], pp. 41–42).

[98] Interviews with General (Ret.) Federico Toranzo Montero, Feb. 24, 1970, and General (Ret.) Alejandro Lanusse, Aug. 23, 1973; statements of Lieut. Colonel (Ret.) Abel Almeida (see note 83, above), interview with Admiral (Ret.) Vicente Pio Baroja, as published in *La Prensa*, Sept. 29, 1951.

The delays involved in provisioning the vehicles enabled a loyal officer and several NCOs to obstruct their plans and upset their timetable. But the basic error of General Menéndez was one of perception. He assumed that the overwhelming majority of military men felt as he did and that a brave handful of men by simply defying the government would attract sufficient support to bring it down. Even on this assumption, the minimum requirement was a resounding initial success that could persuade the undecided to take part, but the scraggly column of three tanks and 200 men that left Campo de Mayo for the Military Academy offered little incentive to officers who were sympathetic but not yet openly involved to gamble away their careers.[99]

The Menéndez revolt was limited in geography, character, and duration. Its principal foci were Army and Air Force installations in the northwestern outskirts of the capital and the naval air base at Punta Indio. Only at Campo de Mayo were there any casualties, and their limited nature, one killed and four wounded on both sides, underlines the fact that this was not a do-or-die revolt, but an attempt to exploit the presumed alienation of the officer corps. Army Minister Lucero, however, was able to mass overwhelming force under loyal commanders and to effect the surrender of Menéndez in a matter of hours. Meanwhile, Peronist workers, summoned by the CGT, rallied to defend the government from an attack that never came. With the surrender of Menéndez, rebel Air Force and Navy aviators, who had earlier showered the city with leaflets proclaiming the rebellion, abandoned their bases to advancing loyal forces and flew off to seek refuge in Uruguay.[100]

Although Lucero subsequently tried to minimize the significance of the September 28 episode and even tried to assure the public that the day of revolutions in Argentina had passed, the uprising was to

[99] Interviews with Admiral (Ret.) Adolfo Estévez, March 13, 1970; General (Ret.) Benjamín Menéndez, March 23 and 27, 1970; and General (Ret.) Julio Alsogaray, Aug. 6, 1973.

[100] *La Nación*, Sept. 29, 30, 1951, provided contemporary coverage of the events; the detailed accounts from the viewpoint of the Navy and Army Ministries were released to the press and published in *La Nación* on Oct. 7, 9, respectively; General Menéndez, while awaiting trial, prepared his own handwritten account, "Relato de los Acontecimientos Revolucionarios del 28 de Septiembre de 1951 (Para mis hijos Rómulo y Benjamín)," dated Oct. 3, 1951, a typed copy of which is in my possession.

have far-reaching consequences for the government, the country, and the armed forces.[101] The government's immediate response to the first news of the movement was to proclaim a state of internal warfare. Similar to a state of siege but without specific constitutional authority, this action permitted the Executive Power to suspend constitutional guarantees and to detain individuals without trial.[102] Under its terms, many individuals were arrested, not only over the next few days, but in succeeding months and years. For the state of internal warfare was declared without limit of time, and, with congressional approval of the original decree, Perón maintained it, except for election days, to the end of his tenure four years later. Thus, even though he enjoyed overwhelming support as measured by elections and the massive rallies periodically organized by the CGT, Perón felt compelled to utilize emergency legislation rather than the normal provisions of the constitution to maintain himself in power.

As a result the political atmosphere in Argentina became even more polarized than ever before. Peronist supporters increasingly viewed those opposed to the administration as traitors in league with imperialist forces. The opposition, in turn, found it increasingly difficult to make itself heard. For example, in the political campaign leading up to the November 11 elections, anti-Peronist parties operated under the handicap that they were denied all access to radio broadcasting. They could hold outdoor rallies only with police permission, and even when these were held, they were often subject to physical attack. The Socialist Party operated under the further disadvantage that both its presidential and vice-presidential nominees, as well as most of its congressional candidates in the Federal Capital, were either in detention or hiding from the police.[103]

[101] In his press conference of October 8, after presenting his account of Army operations on September 28, General Lucero observed: "This flash in the pan [*chirinada*] is proof that revolutions have disappeared from Argentina. The country possesses a moral, spiritual, and material stature in the eyes of the entire world and of its own people; it is a great nation and therefore revolutions are done for."

[102] Decree No. 19,376 of Sept. 28, 1951, and Law 14,062 of the same date. The 1949 revised constitution provided, in Article 34, for the declaration of a state of siege (under which constitutional guarantees could be suspended) and a more limited state of prevention and alarm, but said nothing about a state of internal warfare.

[103] For disruptions of Radical Party and Communist Party rallies, se *La Nación*, Oct. 28, Nov. 1, 1951; on the detained or fugitive status of the Socialist

The impact of the abortive Menéndez rebellion on the armed forces themselves was immediate and extensive. Perón replaced his Air Force and Navy Ministers and ordered an investigation into the conduct of every officer and noncommissioned officer during the emergency.[104] The effects were felt not only by the active participants in the uprising, but by others who had been aware of the conspiratorial atmosphere or who had not acted promptly to repress it. Within the Army, a vigorous shakeup began that affected particularly its most prestigious schools, the War Academy, the Technical Academy, and the Military Academy at El Palomar. A number of officers attending courses at the War and Technical Academies were dropped, some to be discharged from the service and sentenced to imprisonment, others to be forced into premature retirement. The generals who directed all three institutions were replaced, and one of them, the Military Academy director, who had refused to join Menéndez on September 28, was discharged from the Army and sentenced to three months' confinement. By a curious irony, the retired general who presided over the military court that issued this sentence was himself a former director of the Military Academy and in that capacity in 1930 had joined the ultimately successful Uriburu revolution.[105]

Party candidates, see *ibid.*, Nov. 6, 1951, and *Nuevas Bases*, Oct. 13, 1951. Embassy BA Dispatch 76, Nov. 9, 1951, 735.00/11-951, provides commentary on the general atmosphere of the preelection period.

[104] The newly designated ministers were Air Force Brigadier Juan San Martín and Navy Captain (later Admiral) Aníbal Olivieri. San Martín, who resigned the governorship of Córdoba to take the Air Ministry post, assured the President that "yesterday, today, and always my unqualified identification with the Peronist movement could not be more absolute and decisive" (*La Nación*, Oct. 4, 1951). For the President's order for a general investigation of the role of the military personnel during the crisis, see *Boletín Militar Reservado*, No. 3297, Oct. 16, 1951. The Congress speedily enacted Law 14,063 on Sept. 28, 1951, to authorize special military boards to review the conduct of every military man who in any way participated in the events of that day and to recommend promotions, retirements, or discharges as warranted by that conduct. *Boletín Militar Reservado*, No. 3295, Oct. 5, 1951, contains the order creating the special board for the Army.

[105] *Boletín Militar Reservado*, Nos. 3294–3307, Oct. 3–Nov. 13, 1951; *La Nación*, Nov. 15, 1951. General (Ret.) Francisco Reynolds, a key participant in the 1930 revolution, presided over the court that sentenced General Héctor Ladvocat to dismissal. General Eneas Colombo, Director of the War Academy, was allowed to resign, but General Guillermo Streich of the Technical Academy was apparently cleared of any involvement and was given a new assignment.

It was this military court that conducted the trial for rebellion of General Menéndez and other leading participants in his movement. Although Peronist newspapers demanded the death penalty, the court sentenced Menéndez to fifteen years in a Patagonian prison and discharge (*destitucion*) from the service. Even here, the court refrained from ordering the more severe penalty of degradation, as authorized by the military code of justice. Menéndez's chief aides were also sentenced to from four to six years' imprisonment, and those with less responsibility to shorter sentences. All in all, 111 Army, Navy, and Air Force officers were given jail sentences and discharged from their respective services; another 66 officers who failed to appear before the court, having fled the country or gone into hiding, were dropped as rebels. Including those not court-martialed, but compelled to retire by administration action, the total number of active duty officers who lost their careers as a direct result of the Menéndez uprising approached 200.[106]

Although most of these men were in the junior grades, the number of high-ranking officers who were indirectly affected by the aftermath of the abortive coup was also extensive. For Perón and his Army Minister undertook in November a sweeping shakeup of practically all major troop commands. Even the Army Commander-in-Chief, Lieut. General Solari, who had taken personal charge of repressing the uprising and was subsequently decorated both by the President and the CGT in a special ceremony on October 17, fell victim to this purge. The fact that he was replaced after serving only one year in this post when all his predecessors had served two suggests that the President no longer had confidence in him.[107]

---

[106] For the court-martial sentences, see *La Nación*, Oct. 5, 6, 15, 1951; for the discharges for rebellion of 34 Air Force officers see *ibid.*, Oct. 2, 1951; for the discharge by the Army of 22 officers see *ibid.*, Oct. 15, 1951. The ten naval officers who fled to Uruguay were presumably also dropped. Not included in the above were a number of retired officers who were condemned as perennial conspirators, dropped from the list of retirees, and deprived of their pension rights. See *La Nación*, Nov. 13, 1951, for the application of this penalty to General (Ret.) Arturo Rawson, General (Ret.) Bautista Molina, General (Ret.) Fortunato Giovannoni, Colonel (Ret.) José F. Suárez, Colonel (Ret.) Bartolomé Gallo, Lieut. Colonel (Ret.) Bernardo Guillenteguy, and Lieut. Colonel (Ret.) Carlos S. Toranzo Montero.

[107] For the decoration of General Solari and other officers with medals see *El Laborista*, Oct. 18, 1951, and *La Nación* of the same date; on the replacement of key commanders, see *Boletín Militar Reservado*, No. 3306, Nov. 13, 1951, and

Solari was followed into retirement by eight major generals and six brigadier generals. Of these fourteen senior officers, ten came from either the artillery or the cavalry, the branches with which Lonardi and Menéndez, respectively, were associated. Moreover, nine of the fourteen had been promoted only the year before and normally would have anticipated longer service before retirement. Clearly, then, by such wholesale changes, the President hoped to assure himself that only men of steadfast loyalty would henceforth serve in the top commands.[108]

As a further safeguard against a possible repetition of the recent events, the President authorized a series of institutional moves designed to strengthen the powers of the Interior Ministry at the expense of the military services. A decree issued on November 13 created under Interior Minister Borlenghi's chairmanship a new internal security body, the Consejo Federal de Seguridad, to coordinate the work of all police forces at the national and provincial levels. Borlenghi, who already controlled the 25,000-man Federal Police, was now given direct charge of the National Gendarmery, a militarized border force hitherto under Army control, and of the National Maritime Prefecture, a river and port police force previously under Navy jurisdiction. Perón clearly had great confidence in the loyalty of his Interior Minister and was seeking a way of increasing his government's invulnerability to potential military discontent.[109]

A similar aim underlay the decision to remove certain units from the Campo de Mayo–Greater Buenos Aires area and assign them to more remote garrisons. The actual transfers had to wait on the com-

---

La Nación, Nov. 15, 1951. On the far-reaching nature of the shakeup, interview with General (Ret.) "X," Aug. 8, 1973.

[108] For the retirement orders see *Boletín Militar Reservado*, Nos. 3320, 3321, 3327, 3328, 3340, Dec. 19, 1951–Feb. 27, 1952. Retiring after only one year in their present grade were Major Generals Fosbery and Cassagne (Cavalry), Rattenbach and Corti (Artillery), Genta and Daneri (Infantry), Brigadier Generals Elies (Cavalry), J. Sanguinetti (Artillery), and S. V. Alvarez (Engineers). Others placed in retirement were Major Generals Urdapilleta and Sáenz (Artillery), Brigadier Generals Roulier and Colombo (Cavalry), and Luis González (Infantry). Although some of these officers would have retired as part of the normal rotation process, the number far exceeded what was needed to create openings for promotions, especially if one bears in mind the vacancies created by the September retirements of Major Generals Lonardi and Vago and the dismissal of Brigadier General Ladvocat.

[109] *La Nación*, Nov. 14, 1951.

pletion of facilities, but it was not mere coincidence that the Cavalry School and the Armored Cavalry Reconnaissance Unit, both of which had been involved in the Menéndez uprising, were transferred from their bases in the vicinity of the capital to Corrientes province. Eventually, through the shift of other armored and infantry units, interior garrisons, especially that of the Córdoba region, acquired a military significance that undercut the traditional overwhelming importance of Campo de Mayo.[110]

As of the close of 1951, however, no amount of reshuffling of men or units could erase the hostility felt by hundreds of ousted officers, or guarantee that Perón's policies would not again alienate substantial opinion within the ranks of active duty personnel. For the present, Perón was firmly in control of the military establishment. The duration of that control, however, would depend not only on the vigilance of his police and intelligence services, but on how he would exercise the powers of office once elected to a second term.[111]

[110] For references to the relocation of military units see *La Nación*, Jan. 8, Nov. 19–20, 1953, and Jan. 31, 1954.

[111] The Navy as well as the Army underwent a severe shakeup following the September uprising. At year's end eight admirals and numerous lesser officers were retired (interview with Admiral [Ret.] Carlos Sánchez Sañudo, March 20, 1970).

Chapter 5

New Directions, 1951–1954

The national elections that the Menéndez coup had hoped to forestall took place without incident on November 11, 1951. Once again as in 1946 the military guaranteed the integrity of the balloting on election day; but the preceding campaign had been anything but fair. Their passions raised by recent events, Peronist supporters regarded the opposition parties not as rivals entitled to fair treatment, but as organizations of potential if not actual subversives. The candidates of these parties (those who were not already in detention or in hiding) found themselves severely restricted in what they could say and where they could say it. In contrast to 1946, they were denied access to radio facilities, and the daily press was now overwhelmingly sympathetic to the Peronist candidates. Only through public meetings could they present their program, and even here they were dependent on Peronist police authorities to approve the time and place of such meetings. Under such circumstances, it was perhaps remarkable that the chief rival to Perón in the presidential election, the Radical Party's Ricardo Balbín, received 2.4 million votes, or 32 percent of the 7.6 million cast. Whether he would have gained a majority in a fairly conducted campaign is much to be doubted, but Perón and his advisors were not prepared to run any risks, even at the cost of giving the opposition grounds for questioning the legality of the results.[1]

[1] For general coverage of the campaign see *La Nación*, Oct. 1–Nov. 11, 1951; for Socialist complaints about the treatment received by their candidates, *Nuevas Bases*, Oct. 31, 1951; for a sampling of Peronist views of their opponents, see the articles originally published in *Democracia*, Oct. 13–16, and reproduced in the pamphlet *La revolución de los tres tanques* [103]. On the results of the

For President Perón, the overwhelming vote in his favor—a 10 percent jump over his 1946 margin of victory—was a renewed mandate to govern as he pleased. Once again his supporters gained complete control of the Senate, chosen now for the first time, as was the President, by direct popular vote; they also obtained all but fourteen of the 149 Chamber of Deputies seats and elected the governors of every province.[2]

The election, moreover, proved the political astuteness of the Peronist leadership in dealing with the women's vote. Although the franchise had been extended by law in 1947, and several national and provincial-level elections had subsequently taken place, the November 1951 election was the first time that women were able to cast ballots. The authorities had justified the postponement on grounds of the need for time to prepare electoral registration lists. In fact, the time was used by Eva Perón to organize the Women's Peronist Party and to gain support for her husband. Her investment of time, energy, and the resources of her social welfare foundation produced political dividends in the election results. Women voters exceeded their male counterparts at the polls by over 137,000, and of these women, a higher proportion cast their ballots for Perón than did men (63.98 percent as against 60.98 percent). For the first time, moreover, six women senators and 21 women deputies, all of them Peronists, would occupy seats in the new national Congress when that body assembled in May 1952.[3]

The significance of the November electoral victory lay not only in its endorsement of Perón's continued control, but in its enhancement in the eyes of the military leadership of the legitimacy of his program. This was, after all, the first popular vote since the 1949 constitutional convention gave juridical status to Peronist ideology. In voting now by a two-to-one margin to continue Perón in office, the

---

election the best source is Cantón, *Materiales para el estudio de la sociología política en la Argentina* [105], I, 137–48.

[2] Deputies were now elected for six years and by congressional district as against the Saenz-Peña system that had allocated one-third of each province's seats to the runner-up party. The congressional districts for the 1951 election were drawn up in such a fashion that the Peronist candidates with just twice as many votes as the Radicals obtained ten times the number of seats.

[3] Cantón, *Materiales* [105], I, 137–40; *Diputados* [2], 1952, I, xiii–xvii.

electorate could be said to have ratified the transformation of Perón's philosophy, of what was called *doctrina peronista*, into a national ideology, *doctrina nacional*. Henceforth, the effort to identify the military with this doctrine could proceed apace; and, indeed, General Lucero ordered the incorporation of the study of doctrina nacional into the Army instructional program at all levels starting in 1952. Thenceforth, in accordance with ever more elaborate plans, Army personnel were required to attend lectures and classes where Perón's accomplishments, especially in the public works area, received unstinting praise, and where a revisionist view of Argentine history was presented that attacked the patriotism and effectiveness of the liberal and conservative figures of the past.[4]

Among certain opponents of Perón, however, the election results did nothing whatever to legitimize his exercise of power. Quite to the contrary, despairing of the electoral route to his ouster, and despite the widespread crackdown that followed the Menéndez fiasco, they mounted a new conspiratorial movement. Strictly speaking, it was not a new movement, but a reorganization of elements that had been involved in one or another of the previous plots. What was new was not the identity of the participants, but the desperate action they proposed to take: the assassination of the President and of Eva Perón. The leader of this movement was the inveterate conspirator ex-Colonel José Francisco Suárez. Associated with him were several hundred civilians, a number of retired Army officers, a retired police official, and a few Army and Navy officers who had managed to remain on active duty despite the post-Menéndez crackdown.[5]

The conspiratorial plan called for the simultaneous seizure of the Casa Rosada, the main post office, and the central police department, but its principal target was the presidential residence on Avenida Libertador. Heavy trucks were to be used to break down the surrounding iron fence, enabling a well-armed shock force to penetrate the building and liquidate the residents. The conspirators could not guarantee, however, whether the President would be sleeping at the

---

[4] Interview with General (Ret.) José T. Goyret, March 24, 1977, and other officers who asked not to be identified. The man who prepared the new instructional materials was the then Colonel Miguel A. Iñíguez.

[5] Interview with General (Ret.) Federico Toranzo Montero, Feb. 24, 1970; *La Nación*, May 22, 1952.

residence. On occasion he apparently slept elsewhere, including, ironically, the director's residence at the National Penitentiary, where many of his bitterest political foes were encarcerated.[6]

The Suárez conspiracy was planned for February 3 to coincide with the hundredth anniversary of the battle of Caseros that marked the defeat of the dictator Juan Manuel de Rosas. This was a historical event, close to the heart of Argentine liberals, which the Peronist government was studiously trying to ignore. Unfortunately for the conspirators, in their eagerness to give their supporters a double reason for celebrating February 3, they fell victim to their own carelessness; they had recruited into their midst an Air Force Intelligence agent who betrayed them to the authorities. Before they could act, the police moved in, seizing Suárez and his principal collaborators, and following up by arresting hundreds of members of the Radical Party and other opposition groups. Censorship kept the news from the pages of the daily press, but reports of the arrests and of the torture of Colonel Suárez and other prisoners soon circulated at home and abroad. Only in May when the investigating judge presented his indictments in open court did the general public learn the details of the plot, the names of the key participants, and their plan for the country's future.[7]

Perón's response to the violence planned against his person was not only to have the military and civil courts act against those directly involved and to have legislation enacted to penalize the families of military conspirators by taking away their pensions,[8] but also to authorize the secret planning of violent countermeasures should another attempt be made against him. Through a directive known as General Order No. 1, issued to high officials in the national and provincial governments on April 18 by the headquarters of Control de Estado, an office directly under the President, and through a re-

[6] Interview with General Federico Toranzo Montero; also interview with Admiral (Ret.) Adolfo Estévez, March 13, 1970.

[7] Embassy BA Dispatches 1245, Feb. 11, 1952, 735.00/2-1152 and 1458, March 28, 1952, 735.00/3-2852; *New York Times*, Feb. 4–5, 8–9, 1952; *La Nación*, May 22, 1952; *Nuevas Bases*, April 1952.

[8] *Senadores* [3], 1952, I, 366–67; Law 14,123, *Anales* [1], XII-A, 2; *Boletín Militar Reservado* No. 3343, March 7, 1952, and No. 3375, Aug. 7, 1952; *La Nación*, May 22, 1952; also interview with General (Ret.) Federico Toranzo Montero, Feb. 24, 1970.

lated directive known as the "Plan Político Año 1952" that was circulated among high-level Peronist Party officials, Perón established the policy that "one must answer an assault on the President of the nation with thousands of assaults." The Plan Político directed provincial party leaders to cooperate in the preparation of lists of enemy targets and in the organization of strongarm groups, to be made up of specially selected individuals from the party and the CGT, whose mission it would be to carry out personal attacks, bombings, and arson. Control de Estado distributed its own preliminary lists of enemies subject to expansion "as new investigations permitted their updating." The initial lists contained the names of 322 individuals, 50 foreign businesses, embassies, and individuals, 29 Argentine business firms with links to opposition elements, and locales of opposition political parties. The individuals were rated on a five-point scale in terms of their political importance as opponents. Those with the higher ratings presumably would be the first "to be suppressed at once in case of an assault against His Excellency the President of the nation."[9]

This remarkable policy of contingency planning against Argentine citizens and foreign residents raises questions about Perón's motives and sense of responsibility. It might be argued that his was a defensive measure, a response to a provocation, but to entrust to private squads the implementation of a policy of revenge against targets arbitrarily chosen by a combination of domestic intelligence agents and political partisans was an abdication of the legal procedures one associates with responsible government. Why, then, did the President authorize the reprisal plan with its dangerous implications for the future integrity of Argentine society? Was it his intention to intimidate the opposition against any repetition of the Suárez plot? If so, the secrecy associated with the directives militated against this. Was it a temporary aberration induced, on the one hand, by his sense of omnipotence and, on the other, by anger at the temerity of opponents in continuing to plot against him? Perhaps so, but it was one

[9] A copy of General Order No. 1 was found by General Benjamín Rattenbach in the safe of General Humberto Sosa Molina, Minister of National Defense, after Perón's downfall and turned over to the Tribunal Superior de Honor (interview with General (Ret.) Rattenbach, March 9, 1977). The text of the documents are reproduced in Comisión Nacional de Investigaciones [10], I, 82–83; and *Libro negro de la segunda tiranía* [11], pp. 110–13.

that could have dangerous consequences even if the directives were kept locked in the safes of high officials. Perón's willingness to contemplate a policy of violent reprisals must have been well known among key party and CGT officials. In February 1952 he approved the purchase of substantial quantities of pistols by the Eva Perón Foundation for distribution to the CGT and other recipients. Such purchases, forbidden under the law unless the Minister of Defense gave prior approval, were authorized a posteriori at the express request of the President.[10]

Rather than an emotional exercise in the arrogance of power, an indulgence in political machismo complete with pistols, Perón's reprisal directives seem to have been a response to very practical objectives: to identify and to eliminate from the provincial and national governments any employee not an avowed member of the Peronist Party; and, by focusing attention on political enemies, to stimulate the morale of the party and CGT leaders at a time when the deepening economic crisis was forcing Perón to retreat from the consumer-oriented policies of the past.[11]

On February 18, confronted with the effects of a disastrous harvest, stagnating industrial production, deteriorating terms of trade, and a sharply rising inflation rate, the President took the airwaves to announce an economic austerity program. It was a sober message in which Perón pointed out that the government over the past five years had not "asked the people for the slightest sacrifice to achieve their happiness and consolidate the greatness of the Fatherland," but that the time had now come to adopt a policy of consuming less and producing more. The specifics of Perón's message indicated that the government would now give priority to stimulating the agricultural and meat-raising sectors by providing incentive prices and by an easing up of restrictive labor practices on farms and in the meatpacking houses. The consumer, in turn, would be required to do

[10] On the purchase of the pistols, see the ruling of the Tribunal Superior de Honor in the case against General Humberto Sosa Molina, published in *La Nación*, Jan. 4, 1956.

[11] The "Plan Político" was very explicit in regard to the indoctrination of public employees. It stated the need to "destroy the false concept that the civil servant or employee is neutral in his action or function" and went on to assert that "when they don't have the confidence of the government they can be separated from their posts without further requisite than the discretionary act of the Executive Power" (*Libro negro* [11], p. 113).

without beef one day a week and to reduce his purchases of other exportable items.[12]

The Economic Plan for 1952, as the new policy was called, also sought to promote private savings and investment and to reduce the state's role in the housing industry in favor of private initiative. In the sensitive wage-price area, the government still proposed to maintain price controls as in the past, but wage agreements, once adjusted under a government formula to reflect recent price rises, were not to be reopened, save in special cases, for a minimum of two years.[13]

The Economic Plan of 1952 served as a transition to the longer-term statement of policy goals that President Perón announced to the Congress and the country in his Second Five-Year Plan issued in December 1952. Intended to guide Argentine development over the period 1953–57 and to promote as its fundamental objective "consolidation of Economic Independence so as to assure Social Justice and maintain Political Sovereignty," this Plan contrasted with the first Five-Year Plan in its definition of priorities. Top priority was now to be given to the development of the agrarian sector, energy resources, and mining and heavy industries, followed by improving the infrastructure (transportation, highways, sewer and water works). Of a projected 33.5 billion pesos to be spent over the five-year period, 42 percent was to go into public works and services and 33 percent into economic promotion activity with only 4 percent into social action. The remainder was to be distributed between the military (4 billion, or 12 percent of the total) and contributions to provincial plans (3 billion, or 9 percent). The largest single areas of projected investment were transportation (5 billion), fuels (4.6 billion), highways (3.5 billion), and electric energy (2.5 billion).[14]

While the Second Five-Year Plan optimistically assumed that the state could generate the necessary funds through public loans and

[12] *La Nación*, Feb. 19, 1952. Details of the new economic policy were spelled out in a March 5 speech that was published under the title "El Plan Económico 1952 Ejecución y Control" in *Hechos e Ideas* XXIII, No. 96 (March 1952), pp. 13–14.

[13] "El Plan Económico 1952."

[14] Perón submitted the text of the Plan in a message to Congress on December 1, 1952: the Plan was promptly enacted into Law 14,184. For the statement of fundamental objectives, see its Article 2; for the priorities in public outlays, see Chapter 30 of the Plan. The complete text in 31 chapters may be consulted in Subsecretaría de Información [32].

taxation, the text embodied the concept that private capital, both foreign and domestic, could be attracted to cooperate in the implementation of its objectives. In stipulating that the state would create "the necessary conditions and favorable circumstances" to attract such capital, the Plan opened the door to a shift away from the economic nationalism of recent years. The full significance of this shift in the direction of a more traditional economic stance became evident later in 1953 when Perón asked Congress to enact a new foreign investment law and began to speak out openly in favor of seeking foreign capital for such a sacred field as petroleum production.[15]

Contributing to this changing orientation was not only the pressure of economic realities, but the elimination from the scene of the administration's most ardent opponent of private business, Evita Perón. Operated on for cancer a few days before Perón's reelection, she seemingly had recovered enough to make a partial return to public life. On May 1, 1952, as in the past, she addressed the huge rally organized by the CGT, but this turned out to be her last public speech. Even though she managed by dint of enormous personal determination to attend the June 4, 1952, inaugural ceremonies, this once vibrant and beautiful woman was a tragic shadow of her former self, with only 56 days left to live.

The realization of Evita's moribund condition had a numbing effect on the Argentine scene, particularly in the Congress where the overwhelming Peronist majorities, the men and women elected the previous November, took their seats for the first regular session on May 1. For the next several weeks, these Peronist legislators indulged in an orgy of speechmaking, trying to outdo each other in expressions of affection and appreciation for the dying caudilla. Senate members, for example, having already taken the constitutionally prescribed oath, swore an additional oath of loyalty to the President *and* his wife on June 18.[16] Neither this gesture nor the resolution proclaiming Evita Spiritual Chief of the Nation, nor the vote to erect a monument to her in the Federal Capital, with replicas in every province

[15] *Ibid.*, Chapter 13 (Objective 6) and Chapter 30 (Objective 10), pp. 171, 347. See below for further discussion of the 1953 investment law.

[16] General (Ret.) Ramón Albariño, a newly seated senator, proposed this gesture (*La Nación*, June 19, 1952).

and territory, could halt the course of her dread disease, and on July 26, 1952, the once most powerful woman in Argentina passed away.[17]

Evita's death produced an outpouring of popular grief with few precedents in Argentine history, the closest perhaps being that which accompanied Yrigoyen's death in 1933. But Evita's death was also the occasion for elaborate funeral ceremonies, carefully planned and staged for maximum political impact, and incidentally preserved on film by cameramen hired for the purpose. For two weeks the body was on view at the Ministry of Labor, where ordinary Argentines by the thousands stood in line, often in the rain, to get a final glimpse. The remains were then moved with full military honors to the Congress, where they lay in state another day while Argentine workers throughout the country participated in a CGT-ordered general work stoppage from 6:00 A.M. to midnight. The funeral itself took place on August 10, when Evita's body, resting on a catafalque pulled by the arms of CGT leaders, solemnly moved through Buenos Aires's streets lined by military men holding back the grief-stricken crowds. At the hour of burial, throughout the country military units maintained a period of silence. The burial site was not a cemetery, however, but the headquarters building of the CGT. There Evita's remains, specially preserved in an airtight casket with a glass lid, were to have a temporary resting place, awaiting the construction of the already voted monument. Intended to be taller than the Statue of Liberty and to be financed by "voluntary" contributions, the monument was never destined to be completed.[18]

Evita's passing from the Argentine scene was inevitably to have its effects on personal and power relationships within the Peronist movement and the national administration. Perón, for example, decided not to allow any of the aspiring women Peronists to replace Evita as head of the Women's Peronist Party; he made the same decision in connection with the Eva Perón Foundation, and in both cases announced his intention to take personal charge. In the labor field, he moved to replace men who had owed their position in large part to his wife's influence. The Secretary-General of the CGT, José Espejo, finding himself the object of a barrage of jeers at the October

17 *Diputados* [2], 1952, I, 66–75, 180–297, 582–85; *La Nación*, July 27, 1952.
18 Pedro Santos Martínez [115], I, 170–74; *La Nación*, July 27–Aug. 11, 1952. Daniel Mallo's documentary film "Ni Vencedores Ni Vencidos" incorporates a good deal of contemporary newsreel footage on the funeral.

17 Loyalty Day rally, took the cue and submitted his resignation. A more graceful exit was afforded the Minister of Labor, whose poor health led him voluntarily to resign in April 1953. Perón selected a minor trade union official, Eduardo Vuletich, to head the CGT, and a Santa Fe politician, Senator Alejandro B. Giavarino, to become the new Minister of Labor.[19]

The April 1953 resignation of Evita's brother Juan Duarte from his Casa Rosada post as the President's private secretary was a further step in the housecleaning process. The circumstances both before and after that event were of a different and more sensational nature. It was not Perón who initiated the moves that led to the resignation, but his military aides, anxious to remove Duarte, his brother-in-law Orlando Bertolini, and other Casa Rosada staff persons whom they knew to be involved in illicit schemes. Aware of Perón's special feelings for Duarte, the military aides made Bertolini the focus of their accusations to the President, knowing full well that the trail of corruption would lead inevitably to Evita's brother.[20]

The timing of the charges against Bertolini coincided with growing public concern over skyrocketing food prices and with increasing criticism in Peronist as well as anti-Peronist circles about corruption in high places. Even CGT officials were suggesting that the operations of certain high officials might be behind the current meat shortage in Buenos Aires. In these circumstances, and given the risk that failure to act might lead his military aides to take their case to fellow officers, Perón agreed to their proposal that he appoint a prestigious Army officer with a reputation for independence, General León Bengoa, to carry out an investigation of Bertolini's activities.[21]

Entrusted by the President with broad investigatory powers and with direct access to his person at any time, General Bengoa began his investigation on April 6 with a small staff of officers and with the personnel of Control de Estado, over which he was given temporary charge. Each day Bengoa drew up a summary of his findings in a single handwritten copy and made a personal report to the President.

[19] *La Nación*, Sept. 13, Oct. 21–28, 1952; April 7–9, 1953.

[20] Álvaro Carvajal, "El caso Duarte" in *Esto Es*, No. 107 (Jan. 3–9, 1956), pp. 5–7; Santos Martínez [115], I, 174–77. Supplementing these printed accounts were data provided by a retired officer who was very close to the investigation but who prefers not to be identified.

[21] *Ibid.*

No obstacles were placed in his path, and he was able to unearth evidence in the files of Bertolini and Duarte and in testimony taken from various middlemen that implicated not only these two relatives of Evita but several other prominent officials in illicit transactions. Duarte was suspended the first day of the investigation and denied access to his office. Two days later, on April 8, the President, in a radio address, took cognizance of the public concern over price rises and the widespread rumors of official corruption, but insisted that both the shortages and the rumors were part of an antigovernment conspiracy. At the same time, however, he announced that he had ordered an investigation of the Office of the President "to establish the responsibility of each official beginning with myself. And wherever there is a crime it will go to justice, as has been my unshakable norm since I have been in the government.[22]

This "norm" was shaken the very next day when the body of Juan Duarte was discovered, the victim either of a self-inflicted bullet wound, as the police ruled, or of a murderous assault by parties unknown, as many Argentines then and since have thought. In any event, the President ordered General Bengoa to halt all further investigation and to make a final report. In a matter of hours, Bengoa turned over all of the evidence that had been collected, and there the matter died. A few individuals, apparently, were later transferred from the Casa Rosada to other positions, but apart from Juan Duarte, none of the major figures implicated in illicit activities suffered punishment. The image of the Casa Rosada as a sanctuary for the corrupt did not diminish.[23]

For all of the sensationalism surrounding the Duarte case, it was only one aspect of the crisis that confronted Perón in April 1953. Far less easily handled were the complaints about sharp increases in food prices and the undersupply of meat to the Buenos Aires area. Resentment over this situation, as noted earlier, lent strength to the charges circulating in various quarters about corruption and mis-

[22] *Ibid.*; for Perón's address, *La Nación*, April 9, 1953.

[23] See sources cited above in note 20. The cause of Juan Duarte's death has been the subject of continuing controversy. The leading exponent of the murder theory and of the belief that the police covered up for the crime has been Navy Captain (Ret.) Aldo Molinari, who as subchief of the Federal Police in 1956 directed an investigation into the matter. His views are set forth in the pamphlet, *Ratificación del Informe producido por la Comisión Investigadora No. 58 de la Policía Federal sobre la muerte de JUAN DUARTE* [33].

management in high places; and in the ranks of labor, spontaneous demonstrations were putting pressure on the CGT leadership either to obtain price rollbacks or to seek changes in the two-year wage contracts the government had insisted on the year before. The challenge to the President was somehow to appease consumer groups without abandoning his basic policy of preserving the wage-price stability.

Perón's initial response to the issue of food prices seemed to suggest that he had lost none of his political verve and that, even without Evita, he would be able to rally the masses behind him. With great publicity he convoked a joint meeting of the cabinet economic team, the national wage-price committee, and representatives of the CGT and General Economic Confederation (CGE), the employers' group, and ordered them into continuous session until they could agree on solutions. In his own remarks initiating the meeting he tried to strengthen the image of the CGT leaders by praising their aggressiveness in defense of the interests of consumers: "This is the first time that the Confederation has put a knife to my belly but [it has acted] with truth and justice." In equally blunt language, he promised personally to handle the suppliers responsible for the meat shortages even though this meant that "I am going to slaughter meat on Avenida General Paz and distribute it free, if need be. Those who have failed in their duty as suppliers will pay for it." This image of their President, a Lieutenant General of the Army, butchering meat on the outskirts of the capital must have had a curious impact on status-conscious Argentines; but the positive effect of his remarks on ordinary workers should not be discounted.[24]

Perón soon found that it was easier to give the appearance of seeking solutions to economic problems than to find them. In his nationwide radio address scheduled a week later to announce the new economic measures, Perón could offer little more than an extension of price controls to all food products and a pledge of vigorous enforcement. This speech of April 8, however, revealed a different President, a man who rambled almost out of control. Aware now of the need to cover up the Bengoa findings, of the continuing wave of public complaints, and of the lack of any real solution to the eco-

[24] For press coverage on the meeting of the economic team and the full text of Perón's remarks, see *La Nación*, April 2, 1953.

nomic dilemmas, Perón gave vent to a mixture of denunciations, warnings, and expressions of self-pity.

Taking cognizance of the charges that thievery and bribery were widespread, Perón with a bizarre logic placed the blame on the victims: "When a person is a thief, it is because some stupid person allows himself to be robbed. . . . And where there is a bribe-seeker, [it is because] there is a thief who pays the bribe." The failure of the ordinary citizen to refuse to pay more than the posted prices in the stores or to make formal charges against corrupt individuals also came in for scathing comment. Perón warned shopkeepers especially that he would make them abide by the posted prices, and if "they don't fulfill this, we will give it to them with inspectors; if this still doesn't work, I'm going to install troops and enforce compliance with bayonet thrusts."

It was ostensibly to the rumormongers, but in reality to the core of his supporters, that Perón directed another incoherent series of remarks that seemed to reveal a troubled state of mind:

And to the gentlemen who take charge of spreading rumors, whether they are enemies of the government or partisans of the government—they exist also—let them watch out. For if the people don't have the courage to squelch the spreaders, I'll take this task on, too. It's not going to surprise me. For ten years I have been exposing my chest to internal and external enemies and I will continue to do so as long as I have a breath of life, even though no one accompanies me, because I know that I do my duty. But, gentlemen, I am already wearying. There have been too many years of struggle and these fatigue and tire any person. I will continue as long as I feel supported. But what happened to Yrigoyen is not going to happen to me; they are not going to overthrow me with lies because I will leave a year before they overthrow me, whenever I don't feel supported by men, which is what is needed for this type of struggle.[25]

Whether Perón ever really contemplated resignation is much to be doubted. Rather, his remarks, however irrational and contradictory they appear in cold print, had as their aim to generate expressions of support. The CGT indeed translated his wishes into a call for a work stoppage and mass rally to be held in the Plaza de Mayo one week later on April 15. Once again, with thousands of faces looking up at him, Perón felt himself in complete control. Conceding that "perhaps

[25] *La Nación,* April 9, 1953.

in the heat of the struggle . . . [he had] let slip some expression of discouragement," he reaffirmed his intention to lead the country.

I am not one of those men who get discouraged in spite of the legion of the well-intentioned and bad-intentioned who beat permanently on my spirit and nervous system. I am not one of those men who get discouraged as they do marching between a legion of flatterers and a legion of pimps. If that could discourage me, if someday that might succeed in causing me to lose the unshakable faith I have in my people, I would have ceased to be Juan Perón.[26]

Not everything that occurred at the April 15 rally, however, went off according to Perón's plan. He had been speaking only a few minutes when two bombs exploded, causing temporary panic and a casualty list that was later reported as six dead and 93 wounded. Interrupted in his planned remarks, Perón lashed out at the perpetrators, promising that they would be identified and brought to justice. But when shouts arose demanding vengeance, Perón, apparently without premeditation, replied: "This vengeance you are advising me to take, why don't you begin [to take] it yourselves?"[27]

Whether this was the only signal given, or whether special instructions were issued separately, that night, roving bands of Peronist youths put into practice violent reprisals akin to those called for in General Order No. 1. They broke into the Socialist headquarters, the Casa de Pueblo, destroying its contents and setting fire to the building that housed its archives and library; this was followed by assaults on the Radical and Democratic Party buildings and by the total destruction of the Jockey Club. Symbol of the wealthy upper class, the club's downtown structure went up in flames with the loss of its library and some of its valuable paintings—to the indifference of the police and of the firemen who busied themselves primarily in protecting neighboring buildings.[28]

The events of April 15, 1953, raised domestic tensions to levels higher than at any time since the state of internal war was proclaimed in September 1951. Over the next several weeks the police detained scores of individuals as they sought the authors of the bombings and all over the country conducted searches for illegal

[26] *La Nación*, April 16, 1953.
[27] *Ibid.*
[28] *Ibid.*; also *New York Times*, April 17–19, 1953.

arms. Believing that the terrorists were linked to the exile community in Uruguay, the government tried to control all movement between the countries, keeping a close watch on launch traffic and banning all private plane movement over the zones bordering Uruguay and Brazil. Despite the initial efforts of the police, however, small explosive devices continued to go off at various places in the capital, including the vicinity of the Military Club. In the hours before the President was to give his annual state of the nation address to Congress, a half-dozen such explosions took place.[29]

Although Perón in his May Day labor rally speech placed the blame for these violent acts squarely on members of the Radical Party, it was in fact a group of young conservatives, some of them members of distinguished families, who had organized the bombing campaign.[30] But even after the police discovered the identity of its true authors and put a halt to their activities, the government continued to employ heavy-handed measures against other opposition parties. As of mid-May, such Radical leaders as Arturo Frondizi and Ricardo Balbín, Socialists Nicolás Repetto and Alfredo Palacios, and Democrats Adolfo Vicchi and Reynaldo Pastor joined the ranks of many of their fellow partisans under detention in the nation's jails.[31] Perón from the first took the position that foreigners were also involved, and, unhappy with what he regarded as deliberate distortions in the U.S. press, penalized U.S. news agencies by stopping their services to domestic newspapers.[32] It seemed as if a long, hard Argentine winter of political conflict, domestic and international, lay ahead.

The events, it turned out, were to prove otherwise. Perón himself was anxious to avoid prolonged political turmoil, for this could easily jeopardize his economic program, which was based increasingly on creating conditions that could encourage expanded agricultural activity at home and attract investment from abroad, especially from

[29] Details of additional bombings, arrests, and other security measures were reported almost every day by *La Nación*, between April 30 and May 30, 1953.

[30] *La Nación*, May 2, 5, 1953.

[31] *La Nación*, May 20, 1953; *New York Times*, May 16, 1953.

[32] For Perón's view that elements in the United States, including the news agencies, were deliberately fomenting difficulties for him in collusion with domestic foes, see his "State of the Nation" address to Congress on May 1, in *Diputados* [2], 1953, I, 11–12, 23. On the penalties imposed on the U.S. news agencies, see *New York Times*, May 10, 12, 1953.

the United States. Without such investment, the development of the fuel and energy resources, heavy industries, and transportation facilities to which the Second Five-Year Plan gave its highest priorities would simply languish. A climate of continuing tension could also adversely affect the prospects for implementing the policy of economic union with neighboring states that Perón had initiated in a state visit to Chile in February 1953, and in connection with which a return visit by Chilean President Carlos Ibañez was already planned.[33] From an economic development as well as an international relations viewpoint, then, the case for reducing the heightened tensions of the recent past and seeking some kind of long-term political truce had to be compelling.

A further consideration influencing Perón may have been a sense of heightened power, of invulnerability to political opposition.[34] The recent events had, if anything, increased his hold on his followers; the labor movement, despite the April tremors, was firmly under his control, and so, to all appearances, were the military. No officers on active service had been involved in the recent unrest, in contrast to the situation in 1951 and early 1952. The weeding out undertaken at that time had seemingly done its work. Moreover, under the direction of Defense Minister Sosa Molina and Army Minister Lucero, the process whereby the Army as an institution and Army officers as individuals were identifying themselves with the policies and person of the President was well advanced. Not only was his *doctrina nacional* a required subject in all military educational institutes, including the most advanced,[35] but Perón was now receiving expressions

[33] For the text of the Act of Santiago pledging Argentina and Chile to form an economic union see *La Nación*, Feb. 22, 1953; for Perón's references to the idea of a union of South American states see his speech to Congress, *Diputados* [2], 1953, I, 10.

[34] As early as February 1953, Perón was indicating a desire for conciliation with opposition political parties. See his series of radio addresses on the Second Five-Year Plan reproduced in *Hechos e Ideas*, XXIV, No. 106/109 (Jan.–April, 1953), p. 414.

[35] The newly established National War College (Escuela Nacional de Guerra, or ENG) gave major attention to the study of the *doctrina nacional*. For a revealing insight into Perón's views about the necessity for every functionary, civilian or military, to assimilate this doctrine, see his remarks at the inauguration of the first ENG class, *La Nación*, May 15, 1952. Five Army colonels, four Navy captains, and three Air Force commodores were among the 29 participants in the seven-month course (*Boletín Militar Reservado*, No. 3364, June 5, 1952; *La Nación*, Dec. 11, 1952). For its part, the Army Ministry disseminated its own indoctrination materials in its *Manual de doctrina y organización nacional* [15].

of institutional homage that would have been unthinkable a few years before. The most striking example was given on May 29, Army Day, when in lieu of the traditional parade ground formations honoring the founding of the first infantry regiments in 1810, the Army and Defense Ministers, Generals Lucero and Sosa Molina, organized a formal military testimonial to the President, complete with speeches and the presentation of a plaque.

The florid remarks which the Defense Minister addressed to Perón revealed the spirit of unlimited personal attachment that he and his fellow military ministers had been working to inculcate into their subordinates:

Sir, we are here to affirm solemnly to you before ourselves and others, and with the most sincere and resounding expression of our sentiments, that we are absolutely identified with the gigantic work you are carrying on in the government to better the Argentine people; and with the orientation of your international policy. . . .

We well know, sir, that in strict military practice this gesture of the armed forces is unusual, and that perhaps you do not feel it necessary as leader of the Argentine nation. But on this occasion we fully justify it and assign it great importance.

We are convinced that your policy interprets precisely the feelings of the Argentine people. The armed forces, who are an integral part of that people, feel impelled to state publicly and solemnly for all to know, ourselves and others, that in addition to the unchanging principle of subordination that guides them, they are united by a strong feeling of unbreakable adherence to His Excellency, the President, and the noble cause he represents.[36]

It was in an atmosphere conditioned by such assurances that the Perón administration began to move away from rigorous repression toward a policy of limited conciliation. Introduced haltingly over a six-month period beginning in June, this conciliatory phase was to survive, not without fluctuations, for about a year until its sudden abandonment in the final months of 1954.

The specific origins of the conciliatory policy are not entirely clear. The public beginnings can be traced to initiatives taken not by the government, but by members of the most conservative of the opposition groups, the Democratic Party. On June 30, a delegation of its members met with Interior Minister Borlenghi and presented him

[36] For the full text of these remarks see *La Nación*, May 30, 1953.

with a statement that urged the release of all political prisoners and the lifting of the state of internal war as essential steps for achieving spiritual unity. In a separate but apparently related move, the distinguished conservative Federico Pinedo, in a letter written from his jail cell, proposed a political truce in which the opposition would refrain from criticism in the interest of reducing passions, while the government, recognizing its triumph, would revoke the state of internal war and not resort to exceptional measures.[37]

What remains unclear, however, is whether preliminary contacts between administration spokesmen and the conservative leaders preceded the public moves. It is known that a few weeks earlier, in an address directed to the agricultural sector, the President came out clearly against agrarian reform in favor of preserving the existing land tenure system with its great holdings.[38] The Democratic Party was, of course, the political vehicle of the great landowners, and its leaders may have acted in response to what they regarded as an encouraging sign without the need for other, more specific contacts. In any event, the administration's immediate response to the petition of the Democratic Party delegation was to release from prison several of its leading members, including the president of its national committee.[39]

With this as a precedent, a pattern began of delegations from other sectors, the Enrique Dickmann dissident wing of the Socialist Party and the Progressive Democratic Party, visiting the Interior Minister, followed by the immediate release of some of their party colleagues. Neither the Radical Party national committee nor the regular Socialist leadership, however, was prepared to make this pilgrimage to Canossa or to endorse the Pinedo concept of a political truce. Interior Minister Borlenghi, in turn, cited the attitude of the Radicals, the largest opposition group, as justification for maintaining the state of internal war and kept up the pressure on the regular Socialists by recognizing the Dickmann group. Nevertheless, from the administration's viewpoint, the policy of limited conciliation was making progress. The selective release of prisoners had encouraged further political conversations, especially with the Democratic Party, at

[37] *La Nación*, July 1, 2, 1953; Orona, *La dictadura de Perón* [177], pp. 180–83.
[38] *La Nación*, June 9, 1953. For an approving editorial, *ibid.*, June 13, 1953.
[39] *La Nación*, July 2, 1953.

whose request even a few Radical and Socialist leaders were released in September. The government, moreover, was now preparing for a further step in the form of a seemingly broad, but in fact carefully qualified, amnesty for political offenders.[40]

As enacted by the Peronist-dominated Congress in December, the amnesty law made a sharp distinction between political crimes committed by civilians and those by military men and a further distinction within the ranks of trade union offenders. Civilians were to receive "a full general amnesty for political crimes committed prior to the present law"; political offenders under military jurisdiction were to receive the benefits of the law "only in those cases and only to the extent that the Executive Power should decide." In no case would the amnesty cover crimes of political terrorism. In the trade union field, the distinction was made between offenses committed prior to October 17, 1945, for which full amnesty was granted, and those committed since, which would be taken up on a case-by-case basis. In short, neither military men nor trade union leaders who committed anti-Peronist political acts in violation of law received automatic benefit from the amnesty legislation.[41] Obviously, Perón wanted to make sure that no one released under its provisions would again act to undermine his control in the two areas of greatest concern to him, the labor movement and the armed forces.

The promulgation of the amnesty law shortly before Christmas 1953 resulted in the liberation from prison of scores of individuals and the shelving of arrest orders against other political figures in exile or hiding. But none of the Laboristas, such as Cypriano Reyes, held in prison since 1947, or military men, such as Colonel (Ret.) José Suárez, implicated in the plots of 1951 and 1952, emerged from their places of incarceration. Even those civilian political figures who benefited from the law found that being out of jail or home from exile did not mean that they were free to speak out openly against the government. The state of internal warfare was still in effect; po-

[40] *La Nación*, July 3, 1953, for the Dickmann group visit; July 4 for the Progressive Democratic Party visit; July 4 for the UCR repudiation of the Pinedo proposal; July 12 for the Socialist Party position; July 17 for Interior Minister Borlenghi's policy statement. Amnesty bills were submitted to Congress on Nov. 11. See *La Nación*, Nov. 12, 1953.

[41] See the text of Law 14,296, enacted on December 18, 1953.

lice permission was still essential to hold public meetings; and the law of desacato still served as a deterrent to forthright criticism.[42]

But for Perón, the policy of limited conciliation continued to pay dividends, internationally because of Argentina's improved image to potential investors, a matter to be discussed below, and domestically because of the unsettling effects on the opposition. Within most of the traditional parties, internal wrangling over how to cope with the arbitrary power of the government grew more intense. This became evident in the reactions to the government's announcement that elections for Congress and for vice-president would take place on April 25, 1954.

The election announcement itself was an example of the arbitrary power that the Perón administration, under the existing constitution, was able to exercise. The post of vice-president, to which the elderly Hortensio Quijano was reelected in November 1951, fell vacant through his not unexpected demise on April 3, 1952, two months before his second term was to begin. For the next two years, the government made no move to have a successor chosen. Perón and his Interior Minister were waiting apparently for a moment when political passions were under control and only a moderate effort would be needed to secure the desired result. The decision to combine congressional elections with the choice of the vice-president was on the surface a practical one, eliminating the expense and disruption of two national elections, but here again the electoral periodicity called for by the constitution was stretched to the point of distortion. The congressional seats for which deputies and senators were to be elected on April 25, 1954, would not become vacant for another year, or until after another complete session of Congress had been held. In the interim, the country would have the novel experience of having two sets of congressmen on the scene, the incumbents and the designates, both enjoying parliamentary immunities.[43]

Whether or not to contest the Peronists in this election was an issue that deeply troubled the Radicals, Democrats, and other opposition parties. In the end, the participationist element won out in both the above-named parties, but only after bitter disputes that saw the

[42] *La Nación,* Dec. 24–31, 1953; Feb. 2, 4, 8, 15, 17, 1954.
[43] For the electoral convocation, see *La Nación,* Jan. 15, 1954.

Radical Party convention boycotted by its Unionist and Sabattinista sectors and the Democratic Party convention adjourned without being able to make a decision. The Socialist Party conditioned its participation on the lifting of the state of internal warfare, and when this was not done by March 15, withdrew the names of its candidates. The fact that the government allowed the dissident Dickmann group to run its candidates under the Socialist Party (National Revolution) label probably influenced the decision of the regular leadership.[44]

The electoral campaign itself was somewhat less marred by the kinds of excesses that had accompanied the previous elections in 1951, although once again radio facilities were not available to the opposition. A noteworthy aspect this time was the open partisanship shown by certain high-ranking Army officers. For example, two weeks before the election, Army Minister Lucero gave a luncheon at his official Campo de Mayo residence to which he invited the Peronist Party vice-presidential candidate, Senator Alberto Teisaire, and leading members of the administration together with the top Army brass and commanders of all Army units in the Greater Buenos Aires area. Neither this nor other comparable expressions of partiality had any visible influence on the results of the voting, but they did demonstrate the extent to which the party and the state, even in the sphere of the Army, had become intertwined. In the election, Teisaire won over his leading opponent, UCR candidate Crisólogo Larralde, by almost a two-to-one margin, receiving almost the exact percentage of the vote that Perón received in 1951. Once again it was clear that Perón's power could not be challenged via the electoral route.[45]

The lowering of tensions that characterized the Argentine political scene after June 1953 and that lasted well into 1954 coincided with new policy initiatives designed to create an economic union with neighboring countries, on the one hand, and, on the other, to attract foreign investment from the United States and Europe. The Perón

---

[44] Coverage of the internal conflict in the UCR may be found in *La Nación*, Feb. 1, 15, 1954; on the Socialist Party withdrawal, *ibid.*, March 15, 1954; for the Democratic Party's internal difficulties, *ibid.*, March 9–12, 17, 25. Some of its members even resorted to legal proceedings in an unsuccessful effort to impugn the legitimacy of the individual recognized by the Electoral Board as the Democratic Party candidate (*La Nación*, March 27, April 1, 1954).

[45] In the congressional elections the Peronists obtained 62.95 percent of the vote, the Radicals 31.64 percent (Cantón, *Materiales* [105], I, 153–55).

government gave great publicity to the economic union policy and to the series of treaties that were signed first with Chile, whose president, General Ibañez, visited Argentina in July 1953, and then with Paraguay, which Perón visited three months later. Acts of economic union were subsequently signed with Ecuador and Bolivia, but neither Brazil, Uruguay, nor Peru were willing to do so. Despite the fanfare that attended the launching of the economic union policy, it was to have little long-term impact either economically or politically.[46]

Of far greater importance on both scores was the decision by Perón and his economic advisors to seek foreign capital to develop basic industries. Implicit in this decision was a need for closer relations with the United States, a prospect that the recent change from the Democratic Truman to the Republican Eisenhower administration made mutually attractive. Indeed, in July 1953, Milton Eisenhower, sent by his brother on a Latin American fact-finding mission, was received with great cordiality by President Perón. His two-day visit enabled the State Department officials accompanying the mission to explore with their Argentine counterparts the issues outstanding between the countries and to take a hard look at the problems and prospects for U.S. investors in Argentina.[47]

Even before the arrival of the Eisenhower mission, the Perón administration was signaling its interest in new investments through a presidential interview given to a U.S. newsman and through the draft of a new investment law filed with the Congress on July 14, 1953.[48] As subsequently enacted by that body, the law guaranteed that foreign investors who brought new capital into the country under its provisions would be allowed to take out profits up to a maximum of 8 percent annually and after ten years of operations to withdraw their investment in a series of quotas. But of greater importance from the viewpoint of domestic political and economic interests was the

[46] *La Nación*, July 9, Aug. 15, 1953; for Perón's trip to Asunción, Sept. 4–6, 1953; also Conil Paz and Ferrari [230], pp. 174–76.

[47] For the Eisenhower visit, *La Nación*, July 18–21, 1953, and *New York Times*, July 19, 20, 1953. One by-product of the visit was the decision to lift the administrative restraints imposed two months before on the operations of the U.S.-owned news agencies (*ibid.*, July 29, 1953).

[48] Perón's July 15 interview with Clark Galloway of *U.S. News and World Report* (*La Nación*, July 16, 1953) was republished in *Hechos e Ideas*, XXV, No. 112–13 (July–Aug. 1953), pp. 377–84; for the July 14 message to Congress and the text of the proposed investment law, see *Diputados* [2], 1953, II, 671–75.

fact that the law gave the Executive Power broad discretionary authority, what Radical Party spokesmen called a blank check, in reaching agreements with potential investors.[49]

Of particular concern to both defenders and critics of the law during the debate in Congress were its implications for the petroleum industry. Radical deputies, in keeping with their party's traditional position, denounced the bill for its failure to exclude this industry as a field for potential private investment and taunted their Peronist colleagues by claiming that the bill marked the abandonment of the nationalist principles embodied in Article 40 of the 1947 constitution. The defenders of the measure, however, insisted that ways could be found for foreign capital to participate in the exploitation of petroleum without any sacrifice of those principles. In any event, whatever private doubts individual Peronist congressmen may have harbored, they voted overwhelmingly to adopt the measure in the precise terms requested by the administration.[50]

Although the enactment of the new investment law sent an encouraging signal to potential investors, it did not put an end to the domestic debate. Despite the expressions of blind confidence in his policy by his congressional adherents, Perón felt a continuing need to educate other sectors of opinion into accepting the necessity of that policy. This task was complicated by the exaggerated claims that had been made in the past about economic accomplishments. A case in point was the belief that existed in certain military circles about the state of the domestic petroleum industry. An authoritative article in the War Academy's prestigious *Revista de Informaciones* for May–June 1953, for example, noted that between 1946 and 1950, the physical volume of production in the oil industry, including public and private sectors, rose by 40 percent, "all this in accordance with the measures and resolutions of the First Five-Year Plan," when in fact total domestic output had grown by less than 13 percent. This same article, citing the increases projected by the Second Five-Year Plan, confidently expressed the view "that the day is not far off when our own industry will free us of supplies from abroad," but did not

[49] *Diputados* [2], 1953, II, 1010–44; Law 14,222 enacted Aug. 21, 1953.

[50] *Diputados* [2], 1953, II, 1010–44, 1047–87, 1096–1136. See especially remarks by Radical deputies Alende, Nudelman, and Perette; Peronist deputies Gomiz and Rumbo; also the July 30 statement of Minister of Economic Affairs Gómez Morales to the Budget and Finance Committee reproduced on page 1139.

examine the technical and financial obstacles that lay in the path of such an achievement.[51] The prevalence of such unrealism made it all the more difficult to justify allowing foreign capital into petroleum development.

President Perón himself, in various speeches over the latter part of 1953, tried to make the case for this, pointing to the ever-growing gap between domestic production and domestic consumption of oil and the huge outlays of foreign exchange that could be saved for other developmental needs by a rapid expansion of domestic output. Speaking to a group of labor leaders in September 1953, he addressed the issue of the great profits that foreign companies might make by noting that they would be working for the state oil company, YPF:

And so, if they work for YPF we lose absolutely nothing, because we even pay them with the same oil they take out. It is a good thing, then, that they come to give us all the petroleum we need. Before, no company would come if it weren't given the subsoil and all the oil it produced. Now for them to come, why shouldn't it be a business deal, a big one, if we are spending each year upwards of $350 million to buy the oil we need when we have it under the earth and it doesn't cost us a cent. How can we go on paying this? . . . That they will get profits? Of course they are not going to come to work for the love of the art. They will take their profit and we ours; that is just.[52]

To a group of Army officers whom he addressed at the conclusion of the large-scale maneuvers in Córdoba, also in September, Perón spoke not of petroleum specifically, but of the general thrust of his economic program and its significance for the conduct of foreign and defense policies:

I pledge my word that within a period of five years we will have gained (habremos conquistado) our industrial independence and consequently our political-international independence. Only then will we be able to carry out our own plans, our own hypotheses, and what is more, our own preparation. Until then we are in a holding pattern. It is difficult to pursue a suitably firm international political line. But numerous favorable circumstances may yet reduce the time period I have fixed.[53]

[51] Brig. General (Ret.) Julio Sanguinetti, "El problema nacional de los combustibles y las previsiones del 2° plan quinquenal" [211], pp. 240–41. For data on the domestic output of oil, see Díaz Alejandro [247], Table 42, pp. 451–52.

[52] *La Nación*, Sept. 17, 1953.

[53] *La Nación*, Sept. 11, 1953.

Self-sufficiency in petroleum was certainly an essential ingredient for what Perón called industrial independence, and presumably the favorable circumstances he referred to included the steps taken to accelerate the expansion of Argentina's oil production.

In his radio speech on Petroleum Day, December 13, an occasion commemorating the discovery of oil in Argentina and often utilized in the past for appeals to nationalistic feelings, Perón once again emphasized the benefits to be derived from rapid expansion of petroleum production and the contributions that foreign capital could make. "It is not strange," he observed, "that the government has a 'patriotic impatience' to achieve the goal of self-sufficiency in a short time and, given the transcendental consequences of such an objective, that we consider it useful to take advantage of everyone's effort, including that of the experience which may be brought to our country, together with capital, wealth, and material resources, under the protection of the investment law." Perón rejected, as unfounded, speculations about the nature of the foreign collaboration and assured his listeners that "my government is not going to be the one to renounce the principles of economic independence declared on July 9, 1947."[54]

The dilemma that confronted Perón and his administration, however, was how to live up to this commitment; how to satisfy the expectations that his prior nationalistic rhetoric had helped to create while at the same time providing the conditions and guarantees that would attract a foreign oil company. The initial strategy, at least as evidenced in statements made during the legislative consideration of the investment law, was to seek arrangements with independent operators rather than with the major international companies. Such a strategy rested on the assumption that the independents, unlike the majors, would not insist on concessions and would be willing to work for YPF under service contracts that the government could justify to Argentine opinion.[55]

[54] *La Nación*, Dec. 14, 1953.
[55] See the July 30 statement of Economic Affairs Minister Gómez Morales cited above in note 50. Gómez Morales later recalled that as early as 1949 he had discussed the possibility of further investments with Standard and Shell but had been told that they would not consider service-type contracts (interview, March 18, 1977).

The effort to implement this strategy proved more difficult than its formulation. The government received a score of proposals, and at one time seemed to be on the verge of signing with the Floyd Odlum interests. But as of October 1954, more than a year after the enactment of the investment law, no firm agreement existed with any company that could have a major impact on the exploration and exploitation of Argentine petroleum resources.[56]

In industries other than petroleum, the record for attracting foreign capital under the terms of the 1953 investment law was somewhat better. German and Italian companies were taking the initial steps to establish automotive and tractor manufacturing plants. United States firms, to be sure, were somewhat slower to act, especially the major automobile and farm machinery manufacturers, but by October 1954 the H. J. Kaiser interests were already committed to the formation of an Argentine corporation that would eventually manufacture jeeps and other vehicles in a plant near Córdoba.[57]

Even the integrated steel mill project, the military-controlled SOMISA works at San Nicolás in Buenos Aires province to which so much lip service had been paid in the past, but which had in fact been languishing for lack of funds, began to take life. The government finally funded a construction contract signed in 1952 with a French firm to build the deep-water port needed for the delivery of raw materials. Moreover, the government approved the purchase of the steel-plate finishing mill that had been constructed in the United States for a Czechoslovakian firm, but was placed under an embargo when that country went communist. This purchase was finally effected in May 1954, when the U.S. Treasury turned over to the SOMISA director,

---

[56] In June 1954, Floyd Odlum announced in a Buenos Aires press conference (*La Nación*, June 12, 1954) that he had reached an agreement on principle with the Argentine government for the formation of a company to drill wells and construct a pipeline to Bahía Blanca. Joining Odlum in a follow-up press conference was a Mr. O'Connor of Dresser Industries, which was also to participate in the new company (*La Nación*, June 13, 1954). In his March 18, 1977, interview, however, Dr. Gómez Morales insisted that no agreement had even been reached and that Odlum was trying to pressure the government into signing an undesirable contract. The negotiations with the California Argentina Oil Company, a subsidiary of Standard Oil of California, began in October 1954.

[57] The German firms of Deutz, Fahr, and Hanomag were committed to tractor production; Fiat of Italy was interested in manufacturing diesel engines for railway locomotives as well as in tractors (*La Nación*, Oct. 5, 23, 29, 1954).

Colonel Pedro Castiñeiras, the title to the mill in return for a payment of $9 million. Already in crates at the Port of New York, this steel-plate mill was soon on its way to the San Nicolás site.[58]

Still to be acquired, however, and the most expensive component of the integrated mill, was the blast furnace for producing cast iron. In March 1954, the SOMISA directors agreed in principle to award the contract for supplying, assembling, and installing the blast furnace to a United States firm, A. G. McKee and Company. The problem remained, however, how to finance this acquisition. Within the cabinet there was reluctance to have SOMISA approach the U.S. Export-Import Bank directly, and efforts were made, unsuccessfully, to have McKee and Company itself arrange the financing. Eventually, the SOMISA directors were authorized to make their own application to the Export-Import Bank, and in March 1955, they received the welcome news that the Bank was willing to provide $60 million toward the cost of the equipment and services that would be obtained in the United States. For the first time in several years, the steel plant that had been envisioned by General Savio and authorized by Congress in 1947 seemed really on the move toward completion.[59]

The changing economic orientation of the Perón administration with its emphasis on an increased role for foreign capital and for the private sector as a whole had implications of a social and political nature that were becoming visible after 1953. Organized labor continued to provide the core of Perón's support; yet the President now gave an increased role to the General Economic Confederation, or CGE, the businessmen's organization headed by José Gelbard. With encouragement from the government, the CGE sought to integrate all existing businessmen's associations into a network of local, regional, and national groups. The head of the CGE was invited to sit in cabinet meetings; and the CGE itself was treated as the authorized voice of the entire private sector, despite the resistance of certain groups, especially among cattlemen, to being absorbed by so progovernment a body.[60]

[58] Castiñeiras [138], pp. 56–61, 67, and annex 1.

[59] *Ibid.*, 67–71. The 1955 revolution that ousted Perón led to further delays, and it was not until May 5, 1961, that the General Savio plant at San Nicolás produced its first steel.

[60] For the origin and evolution of the CGE see Cuneo [246], pp. 191–214.

Another such body that made its appearance toward the end of 1953 was the General Confederation of Professionals, or CGP, which sought to link disparate associations such as teachers, lawyers, doctors, and agronomists into a national organization with direct links to the President.[61] Perón, in encouraging its formation, was presumably seeking to tie to the administration groups that did not belong in the CGE and did not feel comfortable in the CGT. The formation of the CGP, however, represented not only a further step toward achieving Perón's often-stated goal of having an organized society, but the creation of a potential counterweight that might be used at some future time to offset the power of the CGT.

For the present, however, Perón continued to maintain the closest of ties with organized labor, not only at the level of the CGT, but also with the country's individual unions. At least once a week, but often more frequently, he met personally with labor leaders. Every Wednesday he allocated time to address whatever union was holding a congress or meeting in the nation's capital. But the frequency of these personal contacts should not obscure the fact that Perón was looking to the labor leaders not so much to discuss social issues as to provide support for his economic policies. If Peronist trade union leaders had served in the past as the vehicle for acquiring benefits for their members, their present function was to return the favor by assuring worker cooperation with the government's economic goals.[62]

The emphasis now was increasingly on maintaining labor discipline, avoiding wage demands over and above the two-year industry-wide collective wage agreements, and preventing outsiders, whether communists or otherwise, from infiltrating the unions. Perón became very sensitive to the danger of such infiltration after an outbreak of violence in an intraunion dispute of metallurgical workers in June 1954; and frequently over the next several months his talks to union leaders stressed the necessity of vigilance to prevent the subversion

---

[61] *La Nación*, Sept. 30, 1953, reported the initial organizing steps of the CGP; its first public assembly, with President Perón in attendance, took place on April 22, 1954, on the eve of the national elections, when its officers announced the creation of an international prize to be known as the "Premio América Juan D. Perón" (*La Nación*, April 23, 1954).

[62] See especially his remarks to a national gathering of labor leaders at the Teatro Discépolo, *La Nación*, Nov. 13, 1953.

of their authority.[63] To all appearances, Perón's relations with the Argentine workers remained as cordial as ever, but behind the rhetoric of mutual support that continued to adorn his meetings with union leaders lay contradictions that an agile opposition might yet exploit.

As of the latter part of 1954, President Perón's relations with the military were also seemingly on a stable course, although here, too, behind the high-level statements of loyalty and support lay elements of strain. Some of this related to the manner in which the military ministers and other high-ranking officers demonstrated their political loyalties. Abandoning the restraint in public comment that was so much a part of military tradition, they indulged in words and deeds that amounted to a veritable cult of personality. Not only was this evidenced in the florid remarks addressed to the President on such occasions as Army Day, but in the new practice of designating military units or installations with the name "General Juan D. Perón." Military units frequently bore the name of heroes of independence, but this was the first time that the name of a living person was officially bestowed.[64]

Even the War Academy's staid official journal, the *Revista de Informaciones*, showed the effects of the trend toward personalism after the appointment of General Oscar Uriondo as director in early 1954. A longtime friend and supporter of the President, Uriondo, in the process of giving the journal a fresh appearance and a more appropriate title, *Revista de la Escuela Superior de Guerra*, yielded to the temptation of adorning each issue with quotations from President Perón. What had been a purely professional journal for over three decades now displayed overtones of a partisan political nature.[65]

[63] See his speeches to Education Ministry employees on June 24, textile workers on July 1, the CGT on Aug. 18, in *La Nación*, June 25, July 2, Aug. 19, 1954.

[64] For the 1953 Army Day speeches, see above at note 36; *Boletín Militar Reservado*, No. 3513, Dec. 1, 1954, for the resolution, dated Oct. 1, 1954, designating the Cavalry Instructional Center at Mercedes Corrientes with Perón's name. For both pro-Perón and anti-Perón officers this designation had a double meaning since it was this unit, then located at the Campo de Mayo, that had rebelled under Menéndez in 1951.

[65] Starting with No. 313 (May–June 1954) and continuing until No. 317 (April–June 1955), the last issue to appear before Perón's ouster, the *Revista* contained quotations from both Perón and Lucero. General Uriondo defended the inclusion of such materials as legitimate references to the men who were

To the professionally minded officer who preferred to remain aloof from political activity, such developments undoubtedly intensified the sense of uneasiness that had already been aroused by other measures adopted by the top military authorities. General Lucero's program of *adoctrinamiento,* now a standard part of military instruction, had proved counterproductive insofar as its effects on the outlook of many officers who resented its simplistic and artificial approach to Argentine realities. Such officers also resented another program close to the heart of the Army Secretary, his economic self-sufficiency policy. This program of *autoabastecimiento,* as it was called, had its origins in the idea that the Army, with the vast acres of land that it owned, could produce its own requirements for food and forage, and thus reduce its demands on the public budget. As early as 1951, General Lucero had committed himself enthusiastically to this goal, directing unit commanders throughout the country to organize and set up farms, making official inspections of such establishments, and eventually creating an overall command to administer the entire nationwide operation.[66]

To many Army officers, the autoabastecimiento program, whatever its economic logic, was in direct conflict with their sense of professionalism. Farming, after all, was a civilian pursuit, and as officers they wanted to be judged on their military skills, not on the ability of their unit to grow cereals or raise animals. General Lucero's practice of giving high priority on official visits to inspecting the farming operations of military bases left many an officer frustrated and with a lowered respect for his own superiors when he saw them bending every effort, including a resort to fakery, to show the Army Secretary what he wanted to see. A classic instance took place at a Mar del Plata antiaircraft base in late 1951 where, two days before General Lucero's anticipated visit, the commander ordered the construction

---

functioning as Commander-in-Chief of the Armed Forces and Minister of the Army (interview, Aug. 5, 1973).

[66] Ing. Carlos Emery, who served as Minister of Agriculture, 1947–52, claims to have originated the idea of having the Army exploit its properties to produce agricultural products (interview, July 22, 1971). For legislation relevant to the autoabastecimiento program see Law 14,147 of 1952 and Decrees 24,176 of 1948, 13,656 of 1952, 20,176 of 1954, and 5411 of 1954. For a press conference in which General Lucero announced the appointment of General Arnaldo Sosa Molina as Administrator of the program, see *La Nación,* April 10, 1954.

of an impressive-looking marketplace and stocked it with items ostensibly produced on the base, but in fact borrowed from civilian sources. The disillusionment among the junior officers of this antiaircraft unit was increased by General Lucero's insistence upon his arrival on first visiting the unit's farm and by his total indifference to what they regarded as their great professional achievement in mastering the use of the new equipment with its unfamiliar electronic controls that had recently been acquired from the United States.[67]

As of 1954, those Army officers who were alienated by the policies of the administration had additional personal reasons for concern in the increasing evidence that only individuals who made a positive show of political loyalty to the government were likely to reach the highest ranks. In the last round of promotions, at least one highly recommended colonel, an engineering officer serving as production director for the DGFM, was denied advancement to brigadier general because he was not *adoctrinado*.[68] That it was Perón's intention to apply this policy rigorously in the future was evident from his remarks to the recently promoted brigadier generals, who met with him in January 1954 to receive the curved sword (*sable corvo*) symbolic of their new estate:

We have seen how, by degrees, national indoctrination is progressing within the armed forces with a rapid and sure step. National indoctrination represents for us the point of departure of a New Argentina that thinks in the same manner, feels the same way, and will work unanimously in the same form. For that reason we give extraordinary importance to this indoctrination. I observe, especially in the Army, that this indoctrination progresses, and progresses constructively. I must assign the merit for this personally to the Minister and, in a general way, to the generals who are carrying out a true leadership in the Army within that national doctrine.

I take satisfaction as a citizen and as a soldier that this indoctrination is progressing, that it is taking effective shape in the sincerity and loyalty of those who command.[69]

[67] Interviews with Generals (Ret.) Emilio Forcher, July 4–7, 1971, and July 26, 1973; Juan José Uranga, July 24, 1971; and José T. Goyret, March 24, 1977. Goyret as a junior officer served with the Antiaircraft Artillery at Mar del Plata in 1951.

[68] Interview with General (Ret.) Pedro Castiñeiras, July 26, 1973. Castiñeiras, who never hid his criticism of Perón's policies, was retired as a colonel in February 1954. After Perón's fall, he was reincorporated into active service, was named president of SOMISA, and was reappointed to that post by five different Argentine presidents.

[69] *La Nación*, Jan. 5, 1954.

The impact of such a clear demand for political conformity naturally varied with the individual Army officer. For an undetermined number, it was simply a matter of accepting their role as members of a military establishment that was both professional and political, one that in their view was linked to the mass of the population and their chosen leader. For many others, however, the trend toward an overtly politicized force, one that in their view was increasingly identified with a single man rather than with a system that could exist apart from that man, was a source of grave discomfort. For the moment, however, the latter had little choice but to dissemble their feelings or go into retirement.[70]

As of October 1954, then, the Army was not seething with such discontent as to pose a direct threat to the stability of the government. A number of Army officers, to be sure, were sufficiently alienated to make them a potential source of danger, but it would require something outside the military institutions to translate that potential into reality. What was needed was a sharp change in the political atmosphere, a collapse of the conciliatory approach, with all its limitations, that the government had been following for the past year. Who would have anticipated that Perón himself would create that atmosphere and precipitate the events that would lead to his downfall?

[70] For a view that ascribes to the adoctrinamiento program the chief responsibility for spreading anti-Peronism among younger Army officers, see an unsigned article in *Extra*, No. 10 (May 1966). The author was Lieut. Colonel Alberto Garasino.

Chapter 6

End of an Era: The Fall of Perón, 1954–1955

In the ten months that elapsed between November 1954 and September 1955, the political structure that had kept Juan Perón in power for almost ten years came unstuck; the manipulative skills and forceful rhetoric he had used so often to rally his supporters, while keeping his opponents divided and off balance, no longer proved effective. Disaffection with Perón and his entourage was growing steadily with each passing month as onetime passive observers turned into political activists and former supporters joined with diehard opponents in a common search for a means of terminating the Perón experience.

What had happened? Why should the leader of a popular movement that as recently as April 1954 had demonstrated an overwhelming hold on the electorate now find himself unable to halt the erosion of his power? The answers must be sought in the highly politicized and emotional atmosphere that Perón, through acts of commission and omission, allowed to develop, rather than in the operation of such general factors as the economic situation.

Indeed, the Argentine economy, while not without its problems, was in a much improved state compared to the crisis-ridden years of 1951–52. The annual inflation rate, which had then exceeded 35 percent, had been brought down to single-digit levels in 1953 and 1954; unfavorable trade balances had been reversed; and the general level of economic activity was again on the upswing. The government, moreover, had decided to attack the obstacles to more rapid economic growth and by March of 1955 had reached agreements with a foreign petroleum company for investments that would reduce Argentine dependence on imported fuels and with the U.S. Export-Import Bank for a $60 million credit for the long-delayed steel mill. In addition, the government was encouraging worker and management groups to explore ways of increasing productivity. The economic situation, to be sure, was not without its weaknesses; the agricultural sector, after a dramatic recovery in 1953, was failing to produce any significant increase in exportable surpluses, and inflationary factors were still very much present, their effects temporarily disguised by government food subsidies, artificially low public service rates, and vigorously enforced price controls. Nevertheless, when all is said and done, the economy was not in a state of imminent crisis such as to provoke by itself a demand for revolutionary change.[1]

A more direct cause for the emergence of revolutionary tensions is to be found in the strained relations that developed between Perón's government and the Catholic church in November 1954 and in Perón's crucial decision to mount an open campaign against certain members of the clergy. Prior to this time, relations between the church hierarchy and the government, though not without occasional frictions, had remained harmonious. After all, the Peronist-dominated Congress of 1947 had voted to give permanent status to a previously temporary decree that made religious education a compulsory feature of the public school curriculum; and the Peronist-dominated Constitutional Convention in 1949 had retained the special status of Roman Catholicism as an established religion. In keeping with this principle, the Peronist government had been providing annual subsidies for the maintenance of Catholic institutions, including their extensive system of parochial schools. In turn, the Catholic hierarchy had been generally supportive of the Perón administration, or perhaps more accurately, had refrained from anything resembling open criticism.[2]

The issue that apparently precipitated the cooling of relations between church and government was Perón's decision to extend the

[1] For a brief review of economic policies and trends in this period see Mallon and Sourville [263], pp. 9–14.
[2] Perón's changing relations with the Catholic church are treated in considerable detail in Santos Martínez [115], II, 161–238; for Perón's venture into spiritualism and the friction this raised with Catholics, see Embassy BA Dispatches 617, Oct. 24, 1950, 735.00/10-2450, and 656, Oct. 31, 1950, 735.00/10-3150.

network of Peronist organizations to include the country's secondary-school youth. Justifying this action on the grounds that whoever ignores the youth forfeits the future, Perón authorized his Minister of Education, Armando Méndez San Martín, to proceed with the formation of two branches of a national organization, one for girls, the other for boys, to be known as the Union of Secondary School Students (UES). Membership in the UES brought with it not only exposure to Peronist concepts but a variety of benefits, including access to sports and recreational facilities and free vacations. Perón saw that properties belonging to the government were assigned to the UES for their activities. He opened the facilities of the presidential residence at Olivos for the use of the girls' branch of the UES. There these adolescents could take advantage of the swimming pool and other amenities, while the President, as he later described it, could "share with the young people my own family table and my repose, and sit down there as the father of a great family."[3]

The Catholic clergy, and a good many others, took a less benign view of the President's activities. Not only did they question privately the appropriateness of his behavior in surrounding himself with adolescent girls, but they undertook to counteract what they saw as the threat of the UES to parental and religious influence. In various parts of the country, but especially in Córdoba province, Catholic youth groups, affiliated with the lay organization, Catholic Action, competed with the UES for student support. In other spheres of activity, Catholic professional organizations apparently also made their presence felt in resisting Peronist influence.[4]

Whatever the true significance of these activities, Perón was urged by certain members of his cabinet, party officials, and provincial governors to take countermeasures. Influenced by allegations that Catholic priests were not only behind the anti-UES activities but also trying to infiltrate the trade unions, Perón used the occasion of a governors' conference on November 10 to deliver a public attack. In a speech broadcast to the entire country, he denounced Catholic Action as an international organization hostile to Peronism and sin-

[3] The quotation is from Perón's May 1, 1955, address to Congress as printed in *Hechos e Ideas*, XXVIII, No. 133 (May 1955), p. 398. See also his remarks at the inauguration of the UES facilities at Olivos as reported in *La Nación*, Jan. 17, 1954, and his speech to the legislators-elect, *ibid.*, March 30, 1955.

[4] Santos Martínez [115], II, 184–85.

gled out by name three bishops and several other priests as guilty of antigovernment action.[5]

From this point on, despite denials of the charges by the clergy concerned and despite efforts by the church hierarchy to compose the differences, the breach between the Peronist administration and the Catholic church grew wider. The arrest in Córdoba of several priests and the warning issued by the Peronist Party to its members to maintain vigilance against "those clerical elements" capable of causing disturbances served only to inflame Catholic opinion. So did the aggressive speeches of three Peronist leaders at a Luna Park rally called in support of the government on November 25, even though Perón's own remarks had a conciliatory tone.[6]

With his alienation of a growing part of Catholic opinion, Perón gratuitously provided his traditional opponents, many of them either anticlerical or lukewarm Catholics, with a potential new ally. Radical and Conservative Party leaders promptly expressed their solidarity with Catholics suffering from persecution, and the opportunity now existed for longtime rival sectors of the Argentine middle and upper classes to join in a common front of opposition to the Perón administration.

How far this process of realignment had reached by December 8 is not clear, but on that day, the celebration of Immaculate Conception at the Buenos Aires cathedral attracted a huge crowd that filled the adjacent Plaza de Mayo, exceeding by 50 times the size of the crowd that accepted the government's invitation to join with the President at the intown airport to greet Argentina's world champion boxer, Pascual Pérez, whose earlier arrival had been deliberately postponed to coincide with the religious ceremony. The presence of perhaps 200,000 people outside the cathedral in what could be interpreted as a political as well as a religious demonstration undoubtedly gave a lift to those who had long opposed Perón even as it served as a challenge to the prestige and authority of the administration.[7]

[5] Perón's November 10 speech to the governors is printed in *Hechos e Ideas,* XXVII, No. 126–27 (Oct.–Nov. 1954), pp. 387–97.

[6] Perón's November 25 speech is printed, *ibid.,* pp. 397–403; for the public aspects of the controversy including speeches, episcopal pronouncements, and reports of arrests, see *La Nación,* Nov. 11–25, 1954.

[7] *La Nación,* Dec. 9, 1954; Santos Martínez [115], II, 193–94. *Esto Es,* No. 55 (1954), p. 9, has a photograph of the crowd outside the cathedral.

Perón was not long in answering this challenge. The government closed down the Catholic daily, *El Pueblo*, which had given extensive coverage to the event; and Congress shortly thereafter enacted a bill, under the guise of regulating the constitutional right of assembly, that forbade political parties and other organizations from holding outdoor meetings. As if to guarantee against any possible composition of the differences with the Catholic church, the Peronist-dominated Congress enacted a law that broke with tradition in authorizing divorce with right of remarriage. Introduced as a rider to a bill under debate in the early hours of one morning, this far-reaching change in the civil code was effected without any public discussion or prior warning. Perón, in turn, despite the pleas of the bishops for a veto, signed it into law on December 22. As further demonstration that church opinion no longer counted, the administration ended the year by issuing a decree that authorized provincial and territorial governors and the Mayor of Buenos Aires to legalize houses of prostitution.[8]

How can Perón's decision to challenge the clergy and accept a conflict of unpredictable consequences be explained? Perón, after all, was a lifelong Catholic. He had had few differences with the church in the past and had never manifested an interest in redefining its place in the Argentine scheme of things. Was it a manifestation of megalomania? Did he believe that his power was so great that he could do anything he wanted with impunity? This is the implication of one explanation that ascribes the decision to launch the anticlerical campaign to Perón's desire to put an end to a struggle among several Peronist leaders for the presidential succession. Other explanations, however, see in the campaign the logical consequence of a political philosophy that could not accept the existence of any powerful independent institution and that saw in the church the last obstacle to total control of Argentine society.[9]

Still another approach to understanding the anticlerical campaign

[8] Santos Martínez [115], II, 194–97; on the bill to ban public meetings, *Senadores* [3], 1954, II, 1238–39, and *Diputados* [2], 1954, IV, 3162; on the divorce bill and its treatment, *Diputados* [2], 1954, IV, 2721–29, 2798–2811; on the unsuccessful episcopal appeal for a Perón veto, *La Nación*, Dec. 16, 18, 23, 1954.

[9] For the alleged linkage between the anticlerical campaign and the presidential succession, see Méndez San Martín's remarks as reported in Martínez [67], pp. 174–75; for an interpretation that emphasizes Perón's totalitarian aims, Whitaker, *Argentina* [116], pp. 141–43.

is to ascribe it to the pernicious influence of certain advisors, in particular the Minister of Education, Méndez San Martín, the Minister of Interior and Justice, Angel Borlenghi, and the head of the Superior Council of the Peronist Party, Vice-President Alberto Teisaire. There can be little doubt that Méndez San Martín actively urged Perón to adopt an anticlerical stance and helped plan many of the specific measures that were subsequently taken. It was he, of course, who was responsible for organizing the UES, but more important, it was he who pushed through a succession of steps designed to eliminate Catholic influence in education. Very early in the campaign he abolished the directorate and inspectorate of religious education within his own Ministry. Subsequently, he publicly denounced Catholic parochial schools for misusing their public subsidies and ordered these withdrawn. Still later, he suspended by decree the 1947 legislation requiring religious education in the public schools, a step that the Congress itself subsequently ratified. Whether or not he was an atheist as some have alleged, Méndez San Martín was undoubtedly moved by a deep-seated animus toward the position and prerogatives of the Catholic church.[10]

Less fanatical, but equally willing to encourage Perón in his challenge to the clergy, was Vice-President Teisaire, a retired admiral and said by some to have been a Mason. Teisaire was apparently convinced that the Argentine public was only nominally Catholic and would not react strongly to anticlerical measures. He even told the President at one point that he should not be worried, that the people no longer were attached to their local priest, and that many of them had replaced the image of the Virgin in their homes with pictures of Perón and Evita.[11]

The case of Interior and Justice Minister Borlenghi is less clear-cut, and the perceptions of his role as an advisor in the anticlerical campaign may well reflect the prejudices of his critics. Borlenghi, a one-time Socialist trade union leader, was married to a Jew and had appointed his wife's brother as his undersecretary. Ignoring Borlenghi's own Catholicism, his critics contend that he was moved by his Jewish ties to take an active role in the antichurch campaign. The truth

---

[10] *La Nación*, Dec. 3, 17, 1954, April 1, 15, 1955; *Diputados* [2], 1955, I, 213–44; interview with Dr. Alfredo Gómez Morales, March 18, 1977. In 1954, Dr. Gómez Morales was Secretary of Economic Affairs in the Perón government.
[11] Interview with Gómez Morales.

would seem to be quite different. As a shrewd politician who had held onto the delicate Interior Ministry post since 1946, one would expect him to be a pragmatic individual with a realistic view of public feelings, and of the dangers inherent in stirring up religious sensibilities. And in fact evidence exists that this was his view. The very day after the November 10 governors' meeting where Perón made his radio attack on members of the clergy, Borlenghi paid a visit to a fellow cabinet member who had not been present, Dr. Gómez Morales, to talk about the meeting. Borlenghi deplored what had taken place and took issue with the view presented there that most Argentines were hardly Catholic. As Gómez Morales recalls it, Borlenghi labeled this "global attitude" as completely in error and lamented that "Perón really has confronted the church without any necessity and this in the best of cases doesn't help, it hurts."[12] Despite his own misgivings, Borlenghi was not one to resign over tactical differences, and he accompanied Perón throughout the subsequent stages of the anticlerical campaign.[13]

But even if Perón received dangerous advice from men like Méndez San Martín and Teisaire, he was a skilled politician and surely astute enough to calculate the possible consequences of his actions. Why, then, was he willing to accept that advice? Here one must enter, with a certain amount of trepidation, into an examination of the man's mental and emotional state. Perón was now in his sixtieth year of age and his ninth year as President. He was, as those who saw him close up knew, a tired man, who was having difficulty concentrating on matters of state.[14] In addition, it was over two years since Evita had died. Whatever the nature of their relationship, and this is still more a matter of conjecture than of knowledge, her death deprived him of an anchor as well as of a fearless critic. Had she been alive, it is unlikely that he would have been so receptive to Méndez San Martín's influence. Evita would hardly have allowed the Olivos residence to take on the appearance of a presidential harem, what-

---

[12] *Ibid.*

[13] For the view of another cabinet minister who saw Borlenghi as one of the prime movers of the anti-Catholic church campaign, see Olivieri [68], pp. 98–99. Olivieri was Navy Minister from September 1951 to June 1955.

[14] Gómez Morales recalls that, after only a half hour of listening to an economic problem, Perón would show signs of restlessness and nervousness (interview, March 19, 1977).

ever her feelings might have been about the usefulness of the UES.[15]

But Perón in November 1954 did not have Evita to strengthen his will; and having associated himself in a personal way with the UES, he was very sensitive to criticisms about himself or the organization. This, in turn, increased Méndez San Martín's ability to influence him by exaggerating the importance of scattered episodes involving Catholic Action or individual members of the clergy. In responding as he did with a public denunciation, Perón allowed a minor issue to escalate to the point where his own prestige became involved. It was this that prevented any hope for compromise and drew him into supporting the ever more radical measures urged by his anticlerical advisors. Thus, what started out in November 1954 as a public denunciation of a few priests was transformed by May 1955 into an all-out assault on the constitutional status of the Catholic church in Argentina. Congress on May 20, 1955, adopted a law providing for the holding of elections within six months for a convention to reform the constitution "in everything that was related to the church and its relations with the state in order to assure effective freedom and equality of religions, as regards the law."[16]

As Perón's continued support for anticlerical measures became evident, his hold on the loyalties of military officers began to weaken. As Borlenghi had correctly anticipated, a global assault on an institution that was so much a part of the country's tradition could not but affect the attitudes of many Argentines, however nominal their Catholicism, and this was equally true in the armed forces. Religious ceremonies were a standard component of the military experience, from the blessing of the swords issued to graduates of the military academies to the field masses conducted on military bases. Catholic chaplains formed a part of the overall officer corps, and each of the armed services as well as many of their subordinate branches had its own patron saint.

But equally, if not more, important in shaping the attitudes of mili-

[15] Olivieri claims that Evita on her deathbed warned Perón to get rid of Méndez San Martín ([68], p. 91). For an indication of the stormy nature of the Perón-Evita relationship, see Embassy BA Dispatch 1319, March 6, 1951, 735.00/3-651.

[16] Law 14,404; for the Chamber debate on this measure, see *Diputados* [2], 1955, I, 256-97, 300-350.

tary men were the pressures exerted upon them by close relatives, especially wives, mothers, and sisters. Often more faithful church-goers than their male relatives, these women were frequently in contact with the clergy and in a position to reflect and transmit the passions aroused by the anticlerical campaign as its full dimensions were revealed.[17]

Also contributing to the weakening of military loyalties was the propaganda barrage directed to the armed forces from several sources. Catholic groups, including nationalist writers and activists who had once supported Perón, prepared and distributed leaflets designed to erode respect for the President. Military men were the initial targets of these subversive mimeographed leaflets, which, eventually in printed form and numbering in the tens of thousands, were distributed to other sectors of the populace despite everything the police tried to do to halt their production and dissemination.[18]

While Catholic activists sought thus to precipitate a crisis of conscience among members of the armed forces, Radicals, Socialists, Conservatives, and other long-standing opponents of Perón intensified their efforts to alienate military men from the regime. All of these opposition sectors found a common issue to exploit when Perón, early in 1955, announced that an agreement was reached with a United States company to invest in petroleum production in Argentina. The formal contract, which was signed by O. J. Haynes of the Standard Oil Company of California and Industry Minister Orlando Santos, approved by Perón on May 6, and submitted to Congress for ratification on the same day, provided a convenient target for those seeking to turn the military against the President.[19]

The petroleum contract assigned to the California company the exclusive right to explore for, extract, and exploit oil in an area of some 50,000 square kilometers in southern Patagonia. The oil and other hydrocarbons that were discovered were to be delivered to the State oil agency, YPF, until domestic demand was entirely met, at which time exports would be allowed. YPF was to pay the California company for the oil delivered to it in Argentine pesos at 5

17 Interview with Lieut. General (Ret.) Julio A. Lagos, Aug. 3, 1967.
18 Santos Martínez [115], II, 198–250; for a collection of these materials see Lafiandra [86].
19 The complete text of the contract is reproduced in *Diputados* [2], 1955, I, 122–58.

percent below the East Texas price for equivalent grades. In turn, YPF was to receive 50 percent of the profits earned by the company during the 40-year life of the contract.[20]

The critics who pounced upon the contract ranged across the spectrum of Peronist opponents from Catholics to communists and included not only spokesmen for the Radical, Socialist, Conservative, and Progressive Democrat parties and newly formed Christian Democratic groups, but also, one must presume, those with an economic interest in Argentina's continued dependence on petroleum imports. The nature of the criticism varied with the source, but much of it, playing upon nationalist feelings, denounced the contract as the surrender of Argentine sovereignty over a huge part of the national terrain. Radical Party leaders, traditional proponents of a YPF monopoly over oil production, denounced the contract as a move toward the destruction of this agency, which Army leadership in the person of General Enrique Mosconi had first helped to develop.[21]

Perón opponents were quick to insist that the contract represented a reversal of his earlier stand in defense of economic independence and charged that there was a direct contradiction between the contract and the provisions of Article 40 of the constitution, which prohibited the alienation of petroleum deposits. A Catholic nationalist leaflet even linked the contract with the church question:

We can state before public opinion that the *religious question which the Presidency of the Republic has so surprisingly promoted is only a smoke screen*. They want to hide the true purpose of the constitutional reform: it was demanded by the Yankee plutocracy as the price for assistance to the Argentine government which is desperately trying to overcome the disaster caused by its own tremendous errors.[22]

Contrary to such highly charged allegations, the administration did not consider the reform of Article 40 necessary. It was the view of the cabinet ministers concerned with economic policy that the California agreement was a service contract that did not involve the transfer of ownership of the petroleum in the ground and, more-

[20] *Ibid.*

[21] For statements by Arturo Frondizi and Federico Monjardin, respectively President and Secretary of the National Committee of the Radical Party, see Mazo, *El radicalismo: El movimiento de intransigencia y renovación, 1945–1957* [264], pp. 363–71.

[22] Lafiandra [86], p. 461.

over, that this contract could serve as a model for additional agreements, some of which were already in the preliminary negotiation stage, with other international oil companies. Nevertheless, the uneasiness created in military circles by the attacks on the California contract gave concern at the cabinet level. Even before the President signed and submitted the contract to the Congress, Army Secretary Lucero and General Ernesto Fatigatti visited Dr. Gómez Morales, Secretary of Economic Affairs and the head of the cabinet economic council, to voice the reactions of military circles. Gómez Morales expressed a willingness to give a lecture to officers to explain the contract, although he, too, agreed that certain provisions irritating to national pride should be changed.[23]

The contract as submitted to Congress, however, retained these controversial provisions; but after it became apparent that even Peronist congressmen were unwilling to approve it, the President agreed to have his economic team meet with a congressional delegation to hear recommendations for changes. On the basis of these discussions, the Secretariat of Economic Affairs drafted a series of revisions to the original contract, and sometime thereafter Gómez Morales and Orlando Santos reopened negotiations with the representatives of the California petroleum company.[24] This was the situation as known to administration insiders, but it did little to slow the disaffection that had been spreading within the armed forces, and nothing to reverse the determination of certain officers to attempt Perón's overthrow at the earliest possible moment.

To pinpoint the origins of the conspiratorial movement that culminated in the two-stage revolutionary uprising of June and Septem-

[23] Interview with Dr. Gómez Morales.

[24] Dr. Gómez Morales in his interview stated that his Ministry prepared the text of a revised contract for consideration by the California oil company representatives; it was for this reason, he insists, that the President put no pressure on the Congress to approve the original contract. Gómez Morales further states that the California spokesmen were quite willing to accept changes to the contract that did not affect its economic aspects. I have tried to corroborate these statements with the company. The papers of the California Argentina Oil Company are currently in the custody of Chevron Overseas Petroleum, Inc., of San Francisco. A search of the files made at my request did not turn up a copy of a revised draft of the entire contract but did reveal that "revisions to certain portions had been made and were being discussed during the period June 16–September 16, 1955" (letter from D. O. Nelson, Chevron Overseas Petroleum, Inc., San Francisco, California, July 26, 1977, to the author).

ber 1955 is a complicated task. Ever since the double failures of Menéndez in September 1951 and Suárez in February 1952, a number of Army officers had been in a state of latent conspiracy. Most of these, such as General Eduardo Lonardi or Colonel Arturo Ossorio Arana, were in retired status; a few, including General Pedro E. Aramburu, were on active service but usually in administrative posts that did not involve command of troops. Starting late in 1954, however, the belief that the military might have to act to oust Perón began to spread among active duty officers, especially among those with strong Catholic and nationalist ties. The process whereby loyal professionals were converted into potential or active conspirators was a gradual one, but over the course of eight months, a number of officers in the Army General Staff as well as in field commands convinced themselves of the need for military action to bring about a change. Among these, to name two of the principal ones, were Brigadier General León Bengoa, commander of the Third Infantry Division with headquarters in Paraná, Entre Ríos province, and Colonel Eduardo Señorans, deputy chief of the Army General Staff located in the Army Ministry building a block from Government House.

The specific initiative that led to the organization of a revolutionary movement early in 1955, however, came not from such Army officers, but from members of the Argentine Navy. Since the Navy has not been examined hitherto in this volume, a brief review of its relations with the Perón administration is in order here.

From the very beginning of his rise to power, Perón had few genuine supporters in the Navy, and even some of these were to turn against him. Navy officers by and large tended to identify with the social classes that he continually denounced as the oligarchy and to view his social programs as well as his person with ill-disguised hostility. But because of the technical requirements of the Navy, especially its need for highly trained officers to operate its vessels, Perón had been unable to carry out a thoroughgoing purge of disaffected elements. Thus, it was possible for officers of questionable loyalty to receive key assignments and to use their posts to obstruct Perón's wishes. A case in point was the Naval Intelligence Service (SIN), which, unlike its Army and Air Force counterparts, concentrated on external intelligence rather than on reporting on the political loyalties of naval officers. The SIN was of little help to the government in detecting the conspiracies of 1951 and 1952 even though naval officers were involved.[25]

The atmosphere in the Navy after 1952 continued to reflect a deep-seated hostility to Perón and the movement he led. A clear indication of the prevailing mood was the Navy's response to the nationwide campaign of October 1952 to finance the huge monument to Evita. At Puerto Belgrano, more than 90 percent of ships' crews refused to authorize the deduction of one day's pay that the sponsors of the collection were requesting, and on some vessels not a single crew member was willing to do so.[26]

In 1953, in the aftermath of the April violence that saw the Jockey Club and other buildings burned by Perón supporters, naval plotting took on new life. A group of officers worked on a plan to seize the President in July, when he would be visiting the flagship of the fleet during Independence Day ceremonies, to steam out of port, and proclaim a revolution. This wild scheme, which was discussed with General Lonardi and with Air Force officers, was eventually abandoned for lack of support. It reveals, nevertheless, the existence in 1953 of an incipient revolutionary state of mind among officers of a service that in the past had played only a minor role in Argentine politics.[27]

This state of mind during 1954 led officers at the Puerto Belgrano naval base to develop and test the strategy for a future uprising. Their concept envisaged a major role for the Navy, although with some support from the Army and Air Force. The Puerto Belgrano base would have to be strong enough to withstand counterattacks until the ocean fleet could place the Río de la Plata under blockade and weaken the government's will to resist by naval bombardment of sensitive coastal points. During the course of the year, with the

[25] Interviews with Admiral (Ret.) Samuel Toranzo Calderón, March 31 and April 6, 1970; also Memoirs of Admiral (Ret.) Jorge Perren, MS, pp. 28–36. I am deeply grateful to Admiral Perren for giving me access to this nearly 400-page manuscript which is a mine of information on Navy activities from 1943 to 1966. In 1950–51 Perren was deputy chief of Naval Intelligence.

[26] Perren Memoirs, p. 36. It is a further indication of Navy sentiment that in the April 1954 vice-presidential election, when military personnel stationed in the Antarctic had to vote openly by radio, Navy personnel without exception, in contrast to their Army colleagues, voted 100 percent against the Peronist candidate (Olivieri [68], pp. 77–78).

[27] Perren Memoirs, p. 42. Interviews with Admiral (Ret.) Adolfo Estévez, March 24, 1970, and Admiral (Ret.) Carlos A. Sánchez Sañudo, March 20, 1970.

consent of an unsuspecting superior, the officer in charge of base defense labored to improve its defensive capabilities. Specific defense plans were worked out that involved the deployment of marine units, naval aviation, and base personnel. At the close of the year, under the code name Álcazar, a 48-hour training exercise tested the defenses of the base against simulated attacks from land, sea, and air. As the base defense chief was later to recall, everything possible was done to prepare the base for revolution without revealing the ulterior objective.[28]

In an atmosphere of increasing political tension, early in 1955, a group of Navy commanders (*capitanes de fragata*) and lieutenant commanders (*capitanes de corbeta*) stationed near Buenos Aires, plus two Air Force captains, initiated a new effort to oust Perón. Their immediate task was to find a senior naval officer ready and willing to head the revolutionary movement. Unable to detect interest among any of the regular Navy admirals on active service, they finally found their leader in a Marine infantry officer, Rear Admiral Samuel Toranzo Calderón.[29]

Despite his rank, Toranzo Calderón was not the typical Navy officer. He was not a graduate of the Naval Academy, having started his career in the Army before transferring in the 1930's into the Marine Infantry Corps. Moreover, unlike most Navy officers, he had been an early Perón supporter and still retained much of his enthusiasm for Perón's social programs, even though totally alienated from the man. For an officer of Toranzo Calderón's views to emerge as the leader of an essentially Navy-based revolutionary movement reveals something of the movement's contradictory nature, as well as of the willingness of men of differing outlook to join in the common objective of ousting Perón.

With the designation of the leader settled, the next step for the plotters was a search for Army support. According to the then Navy Commander Antonio Rivolta, they reviewed the names of retired officers and made contact with General (Ret.) Eduardo Lonardi, only to be told that he thought the movement premature. Toranzo Calderón himself made contact with General Aramburu, who was in

[28] Perren Memoirs, pp. 43–44.
[29] Interview with Navy Captain (Ret.) Antonio Rivolta, April 20, 1970, and Admiral (Ret.) Samuel Toranzo Calderón.

agreement with the need for action, but as head of the Army's Sanitary Bureau, had no force at his disposal. It was after this that the name of General León Bengoa came up as one who was reported to be sympathetic to their goal and also had command of troops, howbeit in Paraná, far removed from Buenos Aires. Through the services of a mutual friend, the well-known nationalist Luis María de Pablo Pardo, contact was established between Toranzo Calderón and Bengoa and arrangements made for a face-to-face meeting in Buenos Aires. The resulting conversation, which took place in an automobile on April 23, produced an understanding that Bengoa would continue as he had already been doing to sound out fellow generals, but with great circumspection, given the close surveillance that the government maintained through its intelligence services, and that the two should meet again in another two or three months.[30]

Paralleling the efforts to put together sufficient military support was the task of defining the nature and character of the future government should the revolution succeed. The plotters were in contact with a broad spectrum of civilian political forces from Catholic nationalists at one extreme to Socialists at the other, but beyond the ouster of Perón, there seems to have been little agreement on a specific program to follow. All that was understood was that the military leader of the revolution would take over as head of a civil-military regime and that he would govern with a three-man civilian junta consisting of Miguel Angel Zavala Ortiz, a Radical, Adolfo Vicchi, a Conservative, and Américo Ghioldi, a Socialist.[31]

All three of these men were long-standing Perón opponents who had participated in past conspiracies and who had suffered incarceration or exile for their activities. But it should be noted that their ties were with the groups that had been dominant in their respective parties prior to 1945 and that they had little connection with the newer forces that had been emerging in recent years. Absent from the trio was any figure identified with the nascent Catholic political groupings, and even the Radical Party man, Zavala Ortiz, came from the Unionist sector that had recently lost control of the party's national committee to the rival intransigent sector headed by Arturo

[30] *Ibid.*; Amadeo [45], pp. 37–41.
[31] Interviews with Toranzo Calderón; Captain (Ret.) Rivolta; Américo Ghioldi, March 20, 1970; and Miguel A. Zavala Ortiz, July 22, 1971.

Frondizi. A civilian junta so narrowly constituted was bound to have problems in marshaling support from the fragmented elements that comprised the non-Peronist political universe.

But perhaps even more serious was the apparent failure of the civilian and military components of the proposed successor regime to define their respective spheres of authority and to agree on specific courses of action. With a strong-willed figure like Toranzo Calderón as chief of state, the junta of civilian politicians could well have anticipated a stormy relationship. Even so, this must have seemed of secondary importance to them compared to the prospect of putting an end to the Perón nightmare. Moreover, in the atmosphere of constant surveillance in which the conspirators had to work, frequent meetings among the principals to work out details were a dangerous luxury. As it was, Admiral Toranzo Calderón had only one face-to-face contact with Vicchi and Zavala Ortiz, the three of them together in an automobile, and none at all with Ghioldi, who was in exile in Montevideo.[32]

Although the conspirators had as yet no fixed date for their *golpe*, and in fact still lacked sufficient military force, events were creating a climate of tension that bordered on the explosive. The controversy generated by the government's anticlerical campaign had moved from the halls of Congress to the streets of Buenos Aires. There on Saturday, June 11, a massive demonstration took place in defiance of government orders. The occasion was Corpus Christi Day, which should have been celebrated two days earlier, but had been postponed to Saturday to permit greater participation. The Interior Ministry, which had authorized an outdoor procession for Thursday, refused to allow one for Saturday. Nevertheless, following conclusion of the rites held within the cathedral, which looks out on the Plaza de Mayo, thousands of Argentines, including many who had not seen the inside of a church since their youth, joined in the march that led along the main thoroughfare to the Congress, waving their handkerchiefs as an expression of solidarity with one another and repudiation of the government.[33]

Its response was not long in coming. The Interior Ministry denounced the demonstrators for their illegal actions and for a series

[32] Interviews with Toranzo Calderón and Américo Ghioldi.
[33] *La Nación*, June 10–12, 1955.

of alleged depredations including removing plaques honoring Evita's memory from the exterior of the Congress, raising the Vatican flag on a congressional staff, and, what was more heinous, burning an Argentine flag. The newspapers were furnished pictures of the President and Interior Minister viewing with distress the charred remains of a flag supposedly burned on the steps of Congress. Only later was the public to learn that the true authors of the deed were policemen carrying out the orders of the Interior Minister.[34]

With this ruse, Perón and his anticlerical advisors hoped to fix an anti-Argentine stigma on the church and to stir up the nationalistic feelings of his own supporters. Tensions rose to new heights as Perón supporters attacked the cathedral on Sunday, June 12, only to be fought off by Catholic defenders. Perón took to the radio to denounce the clergy in a nationwide address on June 13, and at a mass rally held on the 14th, ostensibly to wipe out the insult to the flag, he warned the clergy that if disturbances continued, harsh countermeasures would follow. That same day, in a dubious exercise of authority, he relieved two church dignitaries of their ecclesiastical positions and ordered their expulsion from the country.[35]

With passions raised by recent events, it is understandable that Toranzo Calderón and his fellow conspirators wished to strike as soon as possible. Unfortunately, they still had not solved their major problem: the guarantee of sufficient Army support. On June 12, the Admiral, accompanied by the nationalist Pablo Pardo, paid a secret visit to General Bengoa in Paraná to discuss Army participation. Bengoa persuaded him that it would be best to wait until July after the Independence Day celebration. This would give Bengoa time to win over other elements, especially since he would have an opportunity to talk to other generals at a Campo de Mayo *asado* to which he and all active duty generals had been invited for June 17 by the Army Minister himself. This invitation would allow him to leave his Paraná command without arousing suspicion and spend the period June 15–19 in the Buenos Aires area. It was Toranzo Calderón's understand-

---

[34] *La Nación*, June 13, 1955; Olivieri [68], pp. 110–16.

[35] *La Nación*, June 13–15, 1955; for a reproduction of Perón s June 14 speech and the text of the decree expelling Bishops Tato and Novoa, see *Hechos e Ideas*, XXVIII, No. 134–35 (June–July 1955), pp. 556–67.

ing, however, that if he had to launch the movement before July, Bengoa would support him from Paraná.[36]

The day of decision for the movement came much sooner than anyone expected and under circumstances that limited its chances for success. On Tuesday, June 14, Admiral Toranzo Calderón learned via a naval intelligence contact that the Air Force Intelligence Service had run off a film taken with a telephoto lens that showed the doorway to his house and a number of individuals exiting from a meeting. It was clear to him that his conspiratorial role had been discovered and that it was only a matter of time before he would be arrested and probably subjected to torture to reveal the identities of his fellow conspirators. In these circumstances, Toranzo Calderón made the fateful decision to act rather than wait to be taken and ordered the revolt to start on Thursday, June 16, at 10:00 A.M.[37]

The general plan of the revolutionaries called for an aerial assault by Navy and Air Force planes on Government House, with the aim of killing Perón. A Marine battalion stationed on the docks would make a ground attack on the structure aided by armed civilians, while other bands of armed civilians would assault the various radio stations. The plan anticipated that the revolt would then be supported by Army units in the Littoral under General Bengoa, by the Artillery and Aviation Schools in Córdoba, and by the naval base at Puerto Belgrano. There, it was expected, revolutionary officers would take over the fleet and order it to sea, as well as deploy the naval aviation and Marine units of the big base.[38]

Unfortunate for its promoters, the very timing of the revolution militated against its effectiveness. On June 16, General Bengoa was no longer at his divisional headquarters in Paraná, but in his Buenos Aires apartment preparing to attend the next day's asado. He was unaware that morning that the revolt was imminent and even if he were, he could hardly return to Paraná without arousing suspicion.

[36] Interviews with Admiral (Ret.) Toranzo Calderón and Navy Captain (Ret.) Rivolta. According to Rivolta, the Admiral offered to yield the leadership of the movement to General Bengoa, but the latter refused.

[37] Interviews with Admirals (Ret.) Toranzo Calderón and Sánchez Sañudo and Navy Captain (Ret.) Rivolta.

[38] Interview with Admiral (Ret.) Toranzo Calderón; Perren Memoirs, pp. 50–59.

At Puerto Belgrano, where word of the decision to act was received only two hours before the designated time, the situation was equally unpropitious. The vessels of the fleet were tied up with many of their personnel on leave; no specific directives had been issued for the revolutionary sympathizers; and the officer designated by Toranzo Calderón to take over as fleet commander was a Navy captain whose professional qualities and political outlook were viewed with suspicion by fellow officers. The lack of coordination between the revolutionary leadership in Buenos Aires and the forces in the Littoral and Puerto Belgrano largely limited the movement to elements available in or near the Federal Capital.[39]

The events of June 16, 1955, constitute a bloody chapter in Argentina's domestic history, as weapons of war, acquired ostensibly to defend the nation against external attack, were employed by members of its armed forces and by armed civilians against one another. The casualties of that day in dead and wounded numbered almost 1,000, most of them civilians caught in the hail of bullets and shrapnel that fell in the Plaza de Mayo and in the few blocks that separated it from the Navy Ministry building.[40]

In deciding to bombard Government House from the air, the revolutionary leadership deliberately adopted a tactic that could have bloody consequences. They did so in part because of the nature of the forces available to them. These consisted chiefly of the naval aviation units of Punta Indio, Air Force jets based at Morón, and Marine infantry stationed in the Buenos Aires port area. But the decision to employ an aerial attack also reflected the conviction, presumably reinforced by the memory of the 1951 failure in which only leaflets were dropped from the air, that only through a willingness to inflict and accept casualties could the government be toppled. So great was the anger generated by recent events among Perón's foes, so great the eagerness to see his fall, that they were prepared

[39] *Ibid.* It was known that General Bengoa would be driving from Paraná to Buenos Aires on June 15, but the men sent out to intercept his car and urge him to return to his command in Paraná missed him completely.

[40] *La Nación,* June 17, 1955, published an estimate of 350 dead and 600 wounded. Later references scaled down the fatalities to around 200. According to Admiral Toranzo Calderón, the planes were to drop demolition bombs first and then fragmentation bombs, but the demolition bombs that were expected from Puerto Belgrano never arrived. The high number of casualties may be related to the exclusive use of fragmentation bombs.

to injure or even kill innocent bystanders to achieve a goal for which they in turn were prepared to risk their own lives.

The revolt of June 16 failed in almost every respect to go according to plan. Not only was there no echo of support from Army units in the interior, but a heavy fog over the capital prevented the Navy planes from carrying out their 10:00 A.M. attack on Government House. Not until 12:30 P.M. did the first planes, now based at Ezeiza Airport, appear over the Plaza de Mayo to drop their projectiles. By this time the civilian groups waiting in nearby streets had received the order to disperse; but, more important, the delay had revealed the existence of the movement, and Perón, acting on General Lucero's advice, had moved from the Casa Rosada to the safety of the Army Ministry a block away. From the subbasement of this massive structure, the President was able to follow the course of events while General Lucero, designated by him to take charge of repressing the movement, directed Army units in the defense of Government House and the recapture of the areas held by the rebels. By late afternoon, despite repeated bombings and strafings by Navy and Air Force planes, all rebel-held bases had fallen, including the Navy Ministry that served as Toranzo Calderón's headquarters.[41]

There the Navy Minister, Rear Admiral Aníbal Olivieri, and the Marine Commandant, Vice Admiral Benjamín Gargiulo, although not parties to the original conspiracy, associated themselves with the doomed rebellion in an act of moral identification that was to produce the ouster and court-martial of the former and lead the latter to take his own life.[42]

Despite its failure as a military operation, the June 16 uprising sent a shock wave through the Argentine political system that affected the Perón administration, the opposition, and the armed forces. The violent actions of June 16, it should be noted, were not limited to men in uniform. Civilian activists were involved on both sides, and indeed it was the threat that armed civilians might break in and burn the

[41] Interview with Admiral (Ret.) Toranzo Calderón; Olivieri [68], pp. 120–32; Lucero [65], pp. 79–100; Amadeo [45], pp. 47–50.

[42] Perón's aide, Major Vicente, visited each of the three admirals, Toranzo Calderón, Olivieri, and Gargiulo, in the early morning hours of June 17, notifying them that they faced execution under martial law and offering each man a pistol to take his own life. Only Gargiulo acted upon what turned out to be misinformation, for the other two, declining the pistol, were given only prison sentences (Olivieri [68], p. 132; interview with Toranzo Calderón).

Navy Ministry that led the Minister to initiate its surrender to Army troops.[43] Even after the termination of hostilities, however, civilian elements, unrestrained by the police, burned and looted various churches, including the metropolitan curia and the historic structures of San Domingo and San Francisco. Although Perón denied responsibility for these depredations, and there is some evidence that he approved an effort to forestall them, the very fact they took place further tarnished his image in the eyes of many citizens.[44]

The response of the Perón administration to the failed revolt was a series of moves and countermoves that reflected uncertainty over the course to follow. The initial reaction was to show the iron fist. The police arrested scores of civilians, including Radical Party Deputy Oscar Alende and other oppositionist luminaries, while the Peronist-dominated Congress rushed through legislation establishing a nationwide state of siege. Perón announced that the participants in the revolt would suffer the full penalties of the law, which seemed to imply executions. In fact, except for Admiral Gargiulo, who took his own life, no one suffered the extreme penalty, and the most severe sentence was that of life imprisonment for Admiral Toranzo Calderón. The naval and Air Force aviators who had carried out the bombings and strafings had flown to safety in Uruguay and suffered only dishonorable discharges.[45]

But even though Perón directed that the uniformed participants be tried in the military courts and that the conduct of all military personnel during the crisis be the subject of inquiry by special boards in each of the services, he was sufficiently shocked by the events of June 16 to consider the need for major changes in his government.

[43] Olivieri [68], pp. 128–29. The assault on the Navy building was carried out by workers with weapons supplied presumably by the CGT and by members of the nationalist paramilitary group, the Nationalist Liberation Alliance (ALN).

[44] General (Ret.) José Embrioni, Undersecretary of the Army at this time, claims that Perón instructed him to order the Chief of Police to protect the churches (interview, May 19, 1970). For Perón's disclaimer of responsibility see his speech of June 17, 1955, in *Hechos e Ideas*, XXVIII, No. 134–35 (June–July 1955), p. 520.

[45] *Diputados* [2], 1955, I, 604 and 614, on the arrests: Law 14,409, enacted on June 17, established the state of siege; for Perón's June 16 speech in which he stated: "They will feel the full force of the law; I won't take any step to mitigate their guilt or ease the penalty they deserve," see *La Nación*, June 17, 1955, and also *Diputados*, 1955, I, 597–98, where it was reproduced. For a list of the Navy and Air Force personnel who fled to Uruguay and were dropped for rebellion, see *La Nación*, July 8, 1955.

At a cabinet meeting the very next day, according to one of those present, he even proposed his own resignation. None of the ministers supported the idea, as he might well have anticipated. What did emerge from this meeting was a seeming consensus that the entire cabinet be replaced.[46]

Within the cabinet a major proponent both of Perón's continuation in the presidency and of the need for sweeping personnel changes was Army Minister General Lucero. Lucero's views carried the added weight of the man who had personally directed the defeat of the rebels and who could claim, moreover, in contrast to the Navy and Air Force, that not a single member of his force from general to private had taken part in the revolt. It was the Army's loyalty, which Perón publicly and repeatedly recognized, that had saved the day. General Lucero, however, did not use his enhanced position to try to impose military control over the administration; he was far too loyal a subordinate to Perón for that. But he did try to influence Perón to adopt a conciliatory course toward the regime's critics. Not only did he urge a total cabinet change, for which he submitted his own resignation, but he recommended the relaxation of restrictions on the use of the media by opposition parties and other steps that could lower tensions and bring about an accommodation.[47]

The influence of these proposals on Perón may be seen in his retreat from the tough-fisted approach of the first week after the abortive coup. In a matter of days, beginning June 29, the state of siege was lifted, and many of those arrested in connection with the revolt were released. Perón, moreover, replaced the more controversial members of his government, including the Ministers of Interior and Education, although not the entire cabinet as Lucero had recommended. In other moves, the government's press and propaganda chief, Raul Apold, resigned, as did Secretary-General Vuletich of the

[46] Lucero [65], p. 116; the military shakeup was authorized by Law 14,410 and implemented by the appointment of special review boards, the formation of which was reported in *La Nación*, July 1, 1955.

[47] Lucero [65], p. 116; interview with General (Ret.) José Embrioni, May 19, 1970. Perón in exile claimed that "to put down the June 1955 Navy rebellion they imposed tough conditions which in fact were the equivalent of extortion on a large scale" (Pavon Pereyra [70], p. 145), but there is no independent evidence to support this claim insofar as the Army hierarchy was concerned. No meeting of generals was ever held on June 16 or on the following days to discuss political matters (interview with Lieut. General (Ret.) Emilio Forcher, July 4–7, 1971).

CGT. But, more important, on July 5, Perón, in a nationwide radio address, committed himself to a policy of national pacification. Explicitly exonerating the opposition parties for any responsibility for the "criminal events of the 16th," he invited their leaders to an exchange of ideas for establishing domestic peace and to enter into a political truce.[48]

Perón's conception of the meaning of pacification and of the significance for him of the new orientation of public policy was set forth on July 15 in an address to legislators of his own party:

The Peronist revolution has ended; now begins a new constitutional stage without revolution, since revolution cannot be the permanent state of a country.

What does this imply for me? The answer, gentlemen, is very simple: I cease to be the head of a revolution and become the president of all Argentines, friends and adversaries.

My situation has changed completely; this being the case, I must give up all the restrictions placed on our adversaries by the need to promote our revolutionary program and allow them to act freely, within the law, with all guarantees, rights, and liberties.[49]

What was Perón's aim in calling thus for a political truce and announcing his determination to govern as a constitutional executive? Apparently he hoped to win the cooperation of the legalistic elements within the Radical and other opposition parties while isolating and undermining those who still sought his forcible overthrow. He did not succeed. The latter continued to work for a revolutionary uprising, as shall be seen below, finding new converts in the military services. The former, though intrigued by government promises of equal treatment for all political parties, were not content with words alone. They could well recall that Perón, in his first inaugural of June 4, 1946, had proclaimed himself to be "the president of all Argentines, of my friends, and of my adversaries," only to ignore this pledge, as he himself now acknowledged. It was not enough for the administration to relax its controls over indoor party meetings or to allow opposition leaders to speak over the radio for the first time since 1946.

---

[48] *La Nación*, June 29–July 6, 1955. The cabinet replacements were: Oscar Albriu for Borlenghi in Interior and Justice; Francisco M. Angalada for Méndez San Martín in Education; Alberto Iturbe for J. E. Maggi in Transportation; and J. M. Castiglione for Carlos Hogan in Agriculture. Perón's July 5 speech is reproduced in *Hechos e Ideas*, XXVIII, No. 134–35 (June–July 1955), pp. 532–35.

[49] *Hechos e Ideas*, XXVIII, No. 134–35 (June–July 1955), p. 538.

Whatever their other differences, opposition party spokesmen were now agreed that a minimal condition for entering into a political truce was the immediate dismantling of the structure of laws and decrees, starting with the state-of-internal-warfare legislation, that enabled the government to operate as a police state.[50]

Perón, however, was not prepared to take such steps. As a result, the pacification policy was stalemated, and by late August it was clear that his call for a political truce had served only to give opposition spokesmen new opportunities for denouncing his administration. Pamphlets and rumors designed to discredit it continued to circulate; the streets of Buenos Aires were again the scene of demonstrations and disturbances; and violent incidents, often directed at individual policemen, were multiplying. Under such circumstances, it was not surprising that the President would move forcefully in a new direction.[51]

That move was initiated dramatically the morning of August 31, when the Argentine public learned that the President had addressed a note to the leaders of the three sectors of the Peronist Party setting forth in detail the reasons why he should step down from office and requesting their permission to do so. Their unanimous reaction was to reject the proposal and to accompany the CGT leadership in its decision to order an immediate general strike and to summon the workers to the Plaza de Mayo to remain there indefinitely until Perón withdrew his note. A huge crowd did in fact begin to assemble there starting at 10:00 A.M. and remaining until nightfall, when the President finally emerged on the Casa Rosada balcony to address them.[52]

Although many of those present in the Plaza de Mayo, and in similar concentrations in other cities, believed their leader to be sincere in offering to resign, the evidence is clear that this was a carefully staged maneuver designed to arouse the emotions of the working

---

[50] Cf. the radio addresses of the Radical Party leader Arturo Frondizi, Conservative Party leader Vicente Solano Lima, and Progressive Party head Luciano Molina as reproduced in *La Nación*, July 28, Aug. 10, and Aug. 23, respectively. Socialist Party leaders Alfredo Palacios and Nicolás Repetto were denied radio time, but the texts of their statements were released to the press and may be consulted in *La Nación*, Aug. 13, 1955.

[51] The abandonment of the pacification policy, despite denials to the contrary, dated from August 15, when numerous arrests were made of oppositionists and the new Interior Minister Albriu denounced the existence of a terrorist plot (*La Nación*, Aug. 16, 17, 1955).

[52] *La Nación*, Sept. 1, 1955.

class, to demonstrate the President's continuing massive support, and to provide a dramatic opportunity, as in 1945, for intimidating those in opposition. The evidence lies in part in the chronolgy of events.

Although the general public was not aware of the resignation until the morning of August 31, and indeed it was not until 10:30 A.M. that the full text of Perón's note was made available, CGT leaders had the text the night before and had made their decision to mobilize their supporters shortly after midnight. Before 2:00 A.M., long before the public learned of the resignation offer, it was presumably known in the intimacy of the cabinet that the resignation was not seriously intended. For at about that hour, the Chief of Naval Operations, acting on reliable information, telephoned the Maritime Area Commandant at Puerto Belgrano advising that the President would resign on the 31st, that the Commandant should not be alarmed, since it was a maneuver to make a demonstration of force, and that at midmorning when the CGT requested it, the civilian personnel should be released.[53]

But perhaps the best proof of the insincerity of the resignation offer is the fact that Perón chose to submit it not to the Congress, which had the legal authority to act on it and where opposition deputies could take part in the debate, but to functionaries of the Peronist movement. As in the past, these individuals could be counted on to carry out his wishes and to cooperate in staging a massive audience for Perón to address.

Perón's announcement the night of August 31 that he would withdraw his resignation note should have come as no surprise then, except, perhaps, to the näive. But the wildly irresponsible nature of his accompanying remarks was not anticipated. Denouncing his opponents as criminals who had rejected his offers of pardon and reconciliation, he not only proclaimed that any violence on their part would be met by greater violence, but he authorized his followers to take the law into their own hands:

With our exaggerated tolerance, we have won the right to repress them violently. And from now on we establish as a permanent rule for our movement: Whoever in any place tries to disturb order against the constituted

[53] Perren Memoirs. A tap on the Area Commandant's telephone line provided Captain Perren with the information.

authorities or against the law or the Constitution may be killed by any Argentine.

This rule which every Peronist is to follow is directed not only against those who carry out violence, but also against those who conspire and incite.

. . . The watchword for every Peronist, whether alone or within an organization, is to answer a violent act with another more violent. And whenever one of us falls, five of them will fall.[54]

Whether Perón originally intended to utter such inflammatory statements, or whether he was carried away by a feeling of power on seeing the crowd, cannot be readily established. What is clear is that coming from a head of state sworn to uphold the laws, his words caused deep alarm among opponents, while raising concern for his mental balance even among supporters. Within the armed forces, moreover, his statements came as a shock, giving new impetus to plotting that in any event was already under way.[55]

Within the Navy the spirit of rebellion against Perón had remained very much alive despite the June 16 fiasco, and despite, or, in part, because of, the punitive measures ordered by the government against the institution. Indeed, the dissolution of the Naval Air and Marine headquarters and of two of their component units, the withdrawal from Navy jurisdiction of the territorial administrations of Tierro del Fuego and Martín García, and the sequestering of naval ordnance including the fuses for aerial bombs, served both to reinforce the determination of existing conspirators and to win new recruits for their cause.[56]

The management of the conspiracy also came into new and abler hands. In Buenos Aires, Captain Arturo Rial, an officer who had graduated first in his academy class and was now director of naval schools, took over as general coordinator, while in Puerto Belgrano, the deputy base commander, Captain Jorge Perren, took charge of the conspiratorial effort. What was equally important, a flag rank

---

[54] *La Nación*, Sept. 1, 1955.

[55] Interviews with Dr. Arturo Frondizi, April 14, 1970, and Lieut. General (Ret.) Forcher; letter from General (Ret.) Francisco A. Imaz to the author, May 26, 1977. An indication that Perón's working-class listeners may themselves have been shocked by his remarks is to be seen in the fact that the Plaza de Mayo crowd dispersed without incident and in complete order.

[56] Perren Memoirs, pp. 72ff.; Plater [76], p. 216.

officer in the person of Rear Admiral Isaac Rojas agreed to assume the naval leadership of the forthcoming rebellion. Rojas, director of the Naval Academy at Río Santiago, had had no prior involvement in anti-Perón conspiracies, but as a result of his experiences in serving as defense counsel for ex-Minister Olivieri in his military trial, he came to the attention of the conspirators, whose offer of leadership he accepted.[57]

Thus, even before Perón's August 31 speech, the naval conspiracy had achieved unified leadership and solved its principal organizational problems. Indeed, on August 27, a group of leaders representing the various regional components of the conspiracy met near Bahía Blanca to work out specific tactical details, agree on the selection of a Navy Minister for the future government, and examine possible dates for the uprising. From their viewpoint, the ideal time would be during the next cycle of sea exercises that was to begin on September 8, when personnel on leave would return to their posts and tied up vessels were again ready for open water.[58]

The main deterrent to fixing a date, however, was the belief held by some, but not all, of the naval conspirators that Army participation in the rebellion was an absolute necessity. It was essential, they felt, to have Army units come out in open rebellion, to avoid a repetition of June 16, when the Army remained loyal and the conflict took on an interservice character. The fact of Army participation, even if limited at first to a single regiment, would, it was believed, weaken the willingness of other Army units to crush the rebellion.[59]

The conspiratorial movement within the Army was much more scattered and less well organized than that in the Navy. The close surveillance maintained by the government's intelligence services, as well as personal rivalries and suspicions, were contributing factors to this situation. Moreover, in a service where demonstrations of loyalty to Perón had been a prerequisite for advancement to senior grades, the number of high-ranking officers prepared to take part in a rebel-

[57] Plater [76], p. 216; also interviews with Admirals (Ret.) Arturo Rial, May 4, 1970, Isaac F. Rojas, May 29, 1970, and Jorge Palma, April 3, 1970.

[58] See Aug. 27, 1955, entry in Perren Memoirs. Present at this meeting were the then Navy Captains Jorge Perren and Mario Robbio and Commander Patrón Laplacette. Their agreed-upon choice for future Navy Minister was retired Admiral Teodoro Hartung.

[59] *Ibid.;* also interview with Admiral (Ret.) Arturo Rial.

lion was relatively small. As of late August, only three or four of the 90-odd generals on active duty could be described as actively committed to the ouster of Perón.

The highest-ranking of these was Major General Pedro Aramburu, until recently Director of the Army's Sanitary Bureau and now Director of the National War College. Neither of these posts involved command of troops, but his new assignment at the College gave Aramburu legitimate reason for meeting with officers of the other services. One of these was the above-mentioned Navy Captain Arturo Rial, a graduate of the War College and secretary of its alumni group. Rial, as general coordinator of the naval conspiracy, asked Aramburu, in view of his rank, to assume overall command of the gestating conspiracy and to provide the Army cooperation that was essential to success.[60]

As chief of the conspiracy, General Aramburu was naturally concerned with both avoiding premature disclosure of its existence and protecting his leadership position from possible rivals. He was well aware that a conflict over leadership had contributed to the failure of the 1951 movement. The potential rival whom Aramburu apparently regarded with most suspicion was General (Ret.) Eduardo Lonardi, whom Aramburu had helped select to lead the 1951 movement, but with whom relations had cooled in subsequent years. This coolness presumably explains Aramburu's curious behavior in denying flatly to Lonardi that he was conspiring when the latter sought him out sometime in August.[61]

The greatest threat to his plans arose, however, not from the retired Lonardi, but from an unanticipated quarter in the person of a freewheeling, active duty general. On September 1, in reaction to President Perón's speech of a few hours before, the Commandant of the Fourth Military Region at Río Cuarto, Córdoba, Brigadier General Dalmiro Videla Balaguer, tried unsuccessfully to mount a revolt. Videla Balaguer, who once had a reputation as a Perón crony, acted on his own initiative. But the danger now existed that an investigation into the Río Cuarto episode would uncover the existence of other conspirators and result in the destruction of the entire movement.

[60] Interview with Rial; Guevara [153], p. 75. General Aramburu's appointment as Director of the National War College dated from July 29, 1955.
[61] The episode is described in Lonardi [161], p. 23.

In these circumstances, Aramburu had to make a difficult choice between ordering an early uprising or lying low. The prospects for success, however, insofar as the Army was concerned, appeared dubious. Only in the Córdoba area was there reasonable assurance of support in the Artillery School, the Paratroop School, and nearby Air Force units; but in the Buenos Aires area nothing was prepared, and elsewhere only individual officers rather than units could be counted on. To make matters worse, the War Ministry had advanced the date of the year-end field exercises, making it difficult to contact the officers of the Entre Ríos cavalry regiments on which great hope for support had rested. In terms, then, of the number of Army units that could be relied on, the prospects for an uprising were indeed dim. General Aramburu, therefore, fearful of another failure like June 16 and the dire consequences that could be anticipated from an enraged President and his working-class supporters, suspended his own conspiratorial activity and advised postponement of the revolution for a more opportune time.[62]

In the light of what was to follow, it has been fashionable in certain quarters to condemn Aramburu for lack of courage. In his defense, it might be argued that as head of the conspiracy in Buenos Aires, he had little direct contact with the young and enthusiastic revolutionary officers in Córdoba and other areas. He commanded no troops of his own and had no special links to the artillery and cavalry regiments where anti-Peronist sentiment was supposed to be strongest. Indeed, he might well have experienced a sense of isolation since most of his peers from the infantry were arrayed on the side of the government. Unable, therefore, to judge the psychological factors that favored the revolutionary cause, he chose what seemed to be the path of prudence.

It was this decision, however, that led to the emergence of General Lonardi as the major figure of the impending revolution. Lonardi had already been invited by an old artillery colleague and co-conspirator of 1951, Colonel (Ret.) Arturo Ossorio Arana, to join him in the

---

[62] On Aramburu's decision to postpone the revolution, interviews with Admiral (Ret.) Arturo Rial and with General (Ret.) "Y", March 10, 1977; see also Lonardi [161], pp. 37–38, for a conversation between General Lonardi and the then Colonel Eduardo Señorans. Señorans had been acting as General Aramburu's revolutionary chief of staff.

Córdoban sector of the general movement. Now that Aramburu had withdrawn, Ossorio and other officers urged Lonardi to take charge of the overall revolutionary effort and launch it from the Artillery School in Córdoba. Although living in Buenos Aires, Lonardi was able to determine through members of his family the intensity of the revolutionary spirit that characterized both the younger officers and organized civilians in that Catholic center. Accordingly, on September 11 he accepted the invitation and immediately began planning for a revolt that would break out there, and hopefully elsewhere, at midnight of September 15–16.[63]

A certain irony surrounds General Aramburu's decision to suspend his leadership of the conspiratorial movement. The fear that the War Minister would conduct a vigorous investigation of the Río Cuarto affair and proceed through arrests, transfers, and retirements to destroy the conspiratorial apparatus proved erroneous. The War Minister, General Lucero, was loath to believe in the existence of a widespread conspiracy. To be sure, he sent a military judge to investigate the Río Cuarto episode and even sent the Commanding General of the Interior, Lieut. General Forcher, to assess the situation. But when Forcher reported on September 7 or 8 that he suspected the existence of a widespread conspiracy involving elements of many garrisons, Lucero refused to believe it. What is more, on September 12 and 13, Lucero himself was in Córdoba to witness an artillery demonstration at the Pampa de Olaen and used the occasion to talk to the key officials of the Córdoba garrison. Yet on September 15 at a 7:00 A.M. Army Ministry meeting attended by General Forcher and other generals to hear a report of his trip, the recently returned General Lucero asserted that "those who suppose there is a conspiracy under way are completely mistaken." Seventeen hours later the War Minister realized it was he himself who was in error.[64]

General Lonardi's decision to lead the revolution regardless of the state of Army support outside of Córdoba was an act of courage that is in no way diminished by the fact that he was a sick man and perhaps aware that he had only a few months to live. But to conclude

[63] Lonardi [161], pp. 24–25, 36–41.
[64] Interview with Lieut. General (Ret.) Forcher; on the Lucero visit to Córdoba and his return, *La Nación*, Sept. 13–15, 1955

that had it not been for Lonardi there would have been no revolution is to ignore the pent-up pressures that existed elsewhere.[65] It is perhaps more than a coincidence that on September 11, the very day General Lonardi made up his mind to lead the revolt, several hundred miles away, in Puerto Belgrano, Navy Captain Jorge Perren made the independent decision that if there were no word of Army units prepared to rebel by September 20, he would launch the base in revolt together with the adjacent air and marine forces. On September 14, however, Perren received the welcome news that the Navy would not have to go it alone.[66]

General Lonardi's decision to launch the revolution from Córdoba at zero hour of the 16th reflected not only a desire to anticipate possible government countermeasures, but also an awareness that the Artillery School in Córdoba on which he based his strategy would be turning in its weapons for maintenance the very next day. Accordingly, he had only a little time before he himself had to leave Buenos Aires for Córdoba.[67] Unable because of the close surveillance to convoke a meeting of the key figures who had been part of the existing conspiracy, he was nevertheless able to make individual contact with many of them, largely through the indefatigable assistance of a member of the Señorans staff, Major Juan Guevara. In this manner, he obtained assurance from a representative of Navy Captain Rial that the Navy would also revolt on the 16th; he also secured promises of collaboration from several senior Army officers who offered to try to revolutionize units in the Littoral and the Cuyo.[68]

The precipitousness of these arrangements, however, precluded the holding of any serious discussion about the political problems

[65] For an expression of such a view see Guevara [153], p. 82. In 1955 the then Major Guevara served as a key aide to Lonardi.

[66] Perren Memoirs, pp. 135ff.

[67] General (Ret.) Lonardi in civilian clothes left Buenos Aires at 5:00 P.M., September 13, by public bus and arrived in Córdoba the next morning at 10:00 A.M.

[68] General Julio A. Lagos, who had recently stepped down as commander of the Second Army in the Cuyo area, agreed to go out to San Luis to win over its officers to the revolutionary cause; General Aramburu accepted Colonel Señorans's invitation to take control of the armored units based at Curuzú Cuatiá in Corrientes; General Uranga, unable to carry out Lonardi's directive to organize a rebel unit to move on Rosario, attached himself to the Navy rebels at Río Santiago (Lonardi [161], pp. 47–60; Carril [51], pp. 55–68).

that would confront the revolutionaries should they be successful. Not only was there no agreement among the major participants on their political goals apart from eliminating Perón, but the very make-up of the future government was left to conjecture and assumption rather than to specific understanding.[69] No lesson had been learned from the 1943 experience. Thus, while General Lonardi took it for granted that as leader of a successful revolution he would take over the presidency, the Navy conspirators did not even recognize Lonardi as the overall chief of the revolution. Neither, for that matter, did General Aramburu. The issues left unresolved before the launching of the revolution were to plague the victors long after its success.[70]

That success, however, was far from assured when the revolt broke out on September 16. General Lonardi's forces managed, although only after a hard battle with the Infantry School, to take control of all Army and Air Force units in the outskirts of Córdoba; but at the Curuzú Cuatiá armored troop base, the revolutionary effort in which General Aramburu played a role was totally suppressed; and at the Río Santiago naval base the rebels, after several hours of fighting, had to be evacuated to vessels of the river squadron. The next day, although rebel officers under General (Ret.) Julio Lagos succeeded in taking control in the Cuyo, numerically superior government forces were converging on General Lonardi's position in Córdoba and on the Puerto Belgrano naval base. To all appearances, the government's confidence in its ability to suppress the rebellion, as reflected in press and radio announcements, was not misplaced.[71]

[69] Interview with Admiral (Ret.) Isaac F. Rojas, May 29, 1970. Rojas's words are worth quoting: "I did not know General Lonardi personally, I knew him through his activities . . . we had no political understanding whatsoever [no hubo ningún acuerdo político]."

[70] Interviews with Admirals (Ret.) Arturo Rial and Jorge Palma. Palma denies the accuracy of Luis Lonardi's account ([161], pp. 52–53) of the General Lonardi–Captain Palma conversation in which the latter is supposed to have asked who the chief of the revolution was and to have said "Understand, sir," when Lonardi identified himself as the chief. Palma recalls that it was Lonardi who asked about the identity of the Navy revolutionary chieftain.

[71] The military aspects of the rebellion are treated in various printed accounts, all of which reflect a particular bias and must be used with care. On the action around Córdoba, Lonardi [161], pp. 63–118; on the events in the Cuyo, Carril [51], pp. 59–123; on the naval aspects, Rear Admiral (Ret.) Carlos Sánchez Sañudo, "La Revolución Libertadora," *Gaceta Marinera*, VII, No. 51 (Sept.

But superior numbers alone did not hold the final key to a situation that was as much psychological and political as it was military. Many Army officers in supposedly loyal units lacked the will and conviction to fight vigorously in defense of the Perón government. This in turn gave the Navy the opportunity to play a decisive role. For rebel officers, having successfully taken over the entire Navy would attack the oil storage facilities at Dock Sud in Buenos achieve their goal. The contrast in outlook may be seen in the military operations around Puerto Belgrano, where inferior naval forces employing air power harassed approaching Army troops and, by September 19, secured the surrender of two Army generals and their entire commands.[72]

It was in Buenos Aires, however, that the Navy hoped to gain the final victory by breaking Perón's own will to resist. With the vessels of the sea fleet finally arriving in the Río de la Plata after a hasty two-day voyage from Puerto Madryn, Admiral Rojas on September 18 officially proclaimed a blockade of the coast and warned that the Navy would attack the oil storage facilities at Dock Sud in Buenos Aires and the YPF refinery at La Plata. The next day before noon the Navy broadcast warnings to the civilian population to clear away from the La Plata facility because it would be attacked at 1:00 P.M. Earlier that morning the Navy had given convincing proof of its seriousness when a cruiser with a few accurate salvos destroyed the oil storage tanks at Mar del Plata. The bombardment of the La Plata targets never took place, however, for just prior to the designated hour, Army Minister Lucero went on government radio to call for a parley between the opposing sides and an immediate cessation of hostilities. Shortly thereafter he read a letter from President Perón

---

16, 1967); for the events as seen by the loyalist commander, Lucero [65], pp. 132–57.

[72] Army officer attitudes may have been influenced by efforts of the CGT to obtain government consent to form worker militias. Although Army Minister Lucero refused to go along, the idea was in the air and could have served to further weaken military enthusiasm for defending Perón. For an example of a unit whose officers decided to remain on the fence, see Lonardi [161], pp. 92–93. For the operations around Puerto Belgrano that resulted in the surrender of Generals E. Molinuevo of the Third Cavalry Division and Jorge Boucherie of the Sixth Mountain Infantry Division, see Perren Memoirs, chapters 12–13. A defense of Molinuevo's conduct is given by Lucero [65], pp. 145–51.

offering to turn his authority over to the Army in order to facilitate a negotiated settlement. Victory for the revolutionaries seemed close at hand.[73]

Perón's letter, nevertheless, was not a clear-cut resignation, and his action was to raise problems not only for the rebels, but for the Military Junta of senior generals that was formed to conduct the negotiations. The former had to consider whether Perón's move was not a ruse to avoid the threatened bombardment while gaining time for the forces converging on Córdoba to attack Lonardi. The Junta, on the other hand, was confronted with the need to define the scope of its own authority. Was it serving simply as an intermediary for the President, or was it acting as a de facto successor with full authority to seek a settlement on whatever terms it thought best?

This issue was to perplex the Junta even as it assumed responsibility for preventing disorders in the city of Buenos Aires and took its first steps to find out with whom on the revolutionary side it would have to deal. From 1:00 P.M. on September 19 until almost 6:00 P.M., the seventeen generals who comprised the Junta debated this question.[74] In part the debate revolved around a semantic issue, for Perón in his letter calling on the Army to negotiate a settlement described his action as a "renunciation" (*renunciamiento*), a more ambiguous term than "resignation" (*renuncia*). This was interpreted by some to mean that he was not in fact abandoning his powers. Constitutional issues were also raised, for a president normally submits a resignation for consideration by Congress. Finally, however, after hearing Army legal experts argue on both sides of these issues, the seventeen generals, who included several officers formerly very close to the Peronist government, voted unanimously that the letter should be inter-

[73] Sánchez Sañudo, "La Revolución Libertadora"; Perren Memoirs, chapter 13; for a photocopy of Perón's handwritten note, see *Clarín* (Buenos Aires), Sept. 20, 1955.

[74] Convoked by Army Minister Lucero, the Junta consisted originally of all the generals serving in the Greater Buenos Aires region. It was later decided to form an executive junta limited to those of major general grade or higher but to allow brigadier generals to attend its sessions with the right to speak but not to vote. Air Force and Navy observers also attended the sessions. The nominal presiding officer was Lieut. General José D. Molina, the Army Commander-in-Chief, but given his close identification with Perón, Lieut. General Emilio Forcher, Commanding General of the Interior, emerged as the dominant figure in the Junta's proceedings.

preted as a resignation and that the Junta Militar had full freedom of action to negotiate with the revolutionary command.[75]

The Junta Militar did not assume the powers of a government, however, except for those of maintaining order; it did not, contrary to the expectations of some, proceed to appoint a cabinet. Rather, it conceived its function as the narrow one of negotiating a peace agreement with the revolutionaries. To this end, it appointed a four-man committee to study the issues involved and to prepare a negotiating position for the approval of the Junta. That committee, under the chairmanship of General Forcher, began its labors around 7:00 P.M. and around midnight was ready to present its recommendations to the full Junta.[76]

At this point, however, it became evident that Perón had either never intended to resign when he presented his letter early in the day or had subsequently changed his mind. For he summoned the Junta Militar to come to the presidential residence and at the same time requested the General Staff operations section to bring the latest data on the military situation. Some members of the Junta felt that Perón's intervention was now inadmissible, but the prevailing view was to send a delegation of the six most senior generals to hear what he had to say. At the presidential residence, Perón denied that he had resigned the power given him by the electorate to a group of generals and insisted that if he were to resign, he would do so to the Congress. The delegation took its leave and returned to the Army Ministry building to report to the full Junta. Once again, after some discussion, the Junta voted unanimously to confirm its earlier decision. Moreover, it designated one of their number, General Angel J. Manni, to advise Perón that the Junta Militar had ratified its interpretation of his note as a resignation and that it was acting in complete independence. Manni conveyed the message by telephone to one of Perón's aides and added the personal advice that if Perón wanted to save his life, he should *"ponga distancia cuanto antes."*

[75] Interview with Lieut. General (Ret.) Forcher. Contributing to the decision to regard Perón's act as a resignation may have been General Lonardi's insistence on this as a prior condition for accepting a truce. The text of the revolutionary general's message is given in Lonardi [161], pp. 125–26.

[76] Interview with General (Ret.) Forcher.

The former President, heeding the advice, shortly thereafter sought refuge at the Paraguayan embassy.[77]

Why Perón conducted himself as he did on September 19–20 is a subject of unresolved controversy. His critics have insisted that lack of personal courage underlay his behavior; his supporters, in contrast, have contended that Perón sacrificed his position to avoid further bloodshed and loss to his fellow citizens. The available evidence is contradictory. It is true that in his letter of renunciation, Perón made reference to the loss of life and the material damage that could be expected from continued fighting:

I am convinced that the people and the Army could crush the uprising, but that would be too bloody and harmful to the country's permanent interests. . . .

In the face of the threat to bombard the nation's wealth and its innocent people, I think nobody can fail to put aside his other interests and passions. I blindly believe that this should be my conduct. I am not afraid to follow that road.[78]

But if these were his motives on the morning of September 19, what had changed by midnight when he tried to reassert his authority? Certainly the capacity of the Navy to destroy the petroleum installations and cut off Buenos Aires from its fuel sources was in no way diminished by the twelve-hour delay. Perhaps he contemplated summoning his civilian supporters; but as of 6:00 P.M. on the 19th, the CGT Secretary-General had issued a radio appeal to the workers to remain calm, and there was no evidence of spontaneous action on the part of the workers. One other possibility existed, at least theoretically. Through General Lucero, who still occupied his Army Ministry office despite his own announced resignation, Perón might have ordered loyal troops to arrest those members of the Junta Militar who had been most adamant in insisting that he was through. But by this time, the early morning hours of September 20, with the Junta Militar making no move to stop him, personal escape seemed the wisest course of action.[79]

[77] *Ibid.*

[78] See *Clarín*, Sept. 20, 1955, for the text of the letter.

[79] *Clarín*, Sept. 20, 1955, published the exhortation of the Secretary-General of the CGT, Hugo Di Pietro, for worker calm on the front page; on the Junta's actions vis-à-vis Perón, interview with General (Ret.) Forcher.

The involved events of September 19–20 reveal that, unwilling to play the role of a simple emissary, the Junta Militar, in effect, ousted Perón prior to the opening of negotiations with the revolutionaries. The significance of their contribution to a peaceful conclusion to the conflict has, however, been obscured, in part because of the subsequent reluctance of General Lonardi to make any distinction between Perón and the Junta Militar, in part because of the interpretation given to a controversial episode that occurred with the Junta Militar in the early hours of September 20.[80]

The agreed-upon facts of that episode are these: Some time after the Junta Militar reassembled in its conference room to hear the report of the delegation that went out to the President's residence, and while the Junta members were again discussing the appropriate course of action, a group of officers carrying weapons burst into the room. The leader of the group was Brigadier General Francisco A. Imaz, the deputy chief of the Army General Staff and until recently a key aide of the Army Minister in directing the operations of loyal troops. Imaz was now an advocate of prompt negotiations with the rebel side. After an exchange of words with members of the Junta, the Imaz group withdrew. Shortly thereafter, Perón was notified that despite his disagreement with their interpretation, the Junta Militar regarded him as having resigned.

The controversy revolves around the motives of General Imaz and his associates, on what actually was said during their intrusion in the conference room, and on the relevance of all this for the Junta's subsequent actions and reputation.

According to General Imaz, with the resignations earlier in the day of General Perón and Minister Lucero, everything indicated that a patriotic solution would be found. But various developments, including General Lucero's continued presence in the Army Ministry, the Junta's acceptance of Perón's summons to a meeting at his residence, and the resumption of the debate within the Junta over the meaning of his resignation letter, led General Imaz to conclude that a maneuver was under way that would only discredit the Army and, if fighting resumed, lead to civil war. Leaving the conference room where he had been listening to the debate, he gathered a group of

---

[80] On Lonardi's attitude toward the Junta, Lonardi [161], pp. 144–45, 159–61.

younger staff officers, explained his concerns, and won their support for a bold move to end the Junta's vacillation. Breaking into the conference room with this group of officers, all of them carrying weapons, General Imaz notified the Junta members that they had fifteen minutes to let General Perón and General Lucero know that their resignations were accepted and to adopt the measures necessary to reach an agreement with the rebel side. The Imaz group then retired to await the results in an antechamber; shortly thereafter, they learned that the Junta had indeed decided to advise Perón and Lucero that they were out.[81]

This version of events, with its assertion of double-dealing on the part of at least some Junta members and its implication that the seventeen generals who voted for Perón's resignation did so under coercion from the Imaz group, is one that gained credence in anti-Peronist circles. Apparently, as a result, General Imaz and his associates were able to survive the purge of Army officers that followed the change of government and to retain their active duty status. It is a version of events, however, that has been sharply challenged by several members of the Junta, and especially by Lieut. General Forcher. Forcher, who served as the moving force on the Junta and who chaired the committee that drafted its negotiating document, flatly denies that the Imaz intervention had the character or consequences ascribed to it.

The Forcher account of the controversial episode agrees that General Imaz, accompanied by a group of weapons-carrying staff officers, interrupted the Junta, proceeding to express impatience with delay and a demand to know what had been decided. Since Imaz, as a general, had free access to the conference room, his behavior now came as a great surprise. Forcher insists, however, that the Junta did not bow to any threat. Rather, on hearing one of the officers accompanying General Imaz shout "Long live the fatherland," he, Forcher, launched into a vigorous reply. He pointed out that everyone present was sensitive to the invocation of the fatherland, but under certain conditions and with a minimum respect for the hierarchy and order that should characterize military conduct. Noting the concern that

[81] Letter from General (Ret.) Francisco A. Imaz to the author, May 26, 1977. He enclosed a nine-page memorandum replying to a set of questions that will be referred to hereafter as the Imaz Memorandum.

had moved the staff officers, he stated that "this Junta Militar has adopted the measures that best suit the national interest." He then ordered the officers to withdraw, an order Lieut. General Molina repeated, and they did so without another word.[82]

It is General Forcher's view that the Junta Militar acted without coercion from any quarter; that it reached its conclusion to accept Perón's resignation and to enter into a pact with the revolutionary side not as the result of any fifteen-minute ultimatum by a group of armed officers, but as the result of a process of orderly deliberation over many hours. It is a view that a military honor court made up of retired generals without personal or political interest in the matter later found to accord with the facts.[83]

While the Junta Militar was engaged in establishing its independence of Perón prior to entering into negotiations, the revolutionary leaders had to set their own house in order. With basic political decisions to be made they needed to settle the postponed issue of who was the head of the revolution. Among Army leaders the logic of the battlefield simplified the solution. General Lonardi's success in creating a revolutionary focus in Córdoba and holding out against great odds gave convincing legitimacy to his claim. In the Cuyo, General Lagos was quick to place himself under Lonardi's orders, while General Aramburu, in hiding after his failure in Corrientes, was in no position at this time to raise any dispute. The crucial question, however, was the relationship between the naval revolutionaries and General Lonardi. It was here that Admiral Rojas, now commander of the revolutionary fleet, made the key decision. Without consulting Captains Rial or Perren, who were directing the revolutionary effort in the Puerto Belgrano area, Rojas recognized General Lonardi as Chief of the Revolution and as Provisional President. Had Rojas consulted those officers, he would have encountered a lack of en-

---

[82] The Imaz version is reproduced practically verbatim by Lonardi [161], pp. 135–36, and is accepted by Bonifacio del Carril [51], p. 118; the Forcher version, set forth in our interviews, is supported by the Air Force observer at the Junta sessions, Brigadier Mayor Horacio Apicella (interview, July 12, 1971).

[83] The Tribunal Superior de Honor consisting of Major Generals (Ret.) Pertiné, Rodrigo, Rossi, Fosbery, and Brig. General (Ret.) Nougés reported their decision on November 7, 1957, but it was never published. For efforts of General Forcher and others to have it made public, see their letter to the editor of *Clarín*, Sept. 12, 1965.

thusiasm, not only for this decision, but for the very idea of acceding to a truce. Once the decisions were made, however, they were loyally accepted. Navy discipline, even among revolutionaries, remained firm.[84]

With the truce holding fast in the Buenos Aires area, actual negotiations between the Revolutionary Command of the Armed Forces and the Junta Militar began at 6:00 P.M. on September 20 aboard Admiral Roja's flagship, a cruiser anchored in the roadstead off La Plata.[85] The choice of site had been imposed by the Navy under threat of renewed hostilities; but despite this flexing of military muscle, when the Junta's emissaries reached the cruiser, they were escorted aboard with full military honors. Indeed, throughout the eight hours they were aboard ship, the delegation, consisting of Lieut. General Forcher, Major Generals Manni and José Sampayo, and the legal officer, Brigadier General Oscar Sacheri, were treated with the dignity befitting their status. Moreover, at the conclusion of the lengthy negotiations, the atmosphere was such that Admiral Rojas invited the delegation to join him and his staff in a meal, and even insisted that General Forcher should preside over the table. At least for the moment, the spirit of military camaraderie obscured the depth of political differences.[86]

Those differences had emerged, however, in the course of six hours of continuous discussion, not only in the specific points advanced by each side, but in the concept each held of the nature and purpose of the negotiation. The Junta Militar delegates, representing the loyal Army that was still intact in the Buenos Aires area, saw themselves not as the representatives of a defeated party, but as the arbiters of the Argentine situation. They had come to the talks with the idea of participating, together with the military on the other side, in a caretaker regime that would move promptly to hold elections. To this

[84] Interview with Admiral (Ret.) Arturo Rial; on the actions of General Lagos, Carril [51], pp. 105–6.

[85] There is a certain irony in the fact that the Navy cruiser bore the partisan Peronist name *17 de Octubre* recalling Perón's triumphant return to the political stage in 1945. The cruiser was quickly renamed the General Belgrano after the hero of independence.

[86] Interviews with Generals (Ret.) Forcher and Juan J. Uranga, July 24, 1971. Photographs of the Junta's negotiators aboard the cruiser were published by *Clarín*, Sept. 24, 1955, pp. 2–3.

end they came prepared with a list of seventeen proposals, both of a general and a specific nature, based on the premise that the guiding principle for future actions should be that "between the parties there are not, nor should there be, winners or losers."[87]

The Revolutionary Command, as represented by Admiral Rojas and General Uranga, viewed the negotiations from a far different perspective.[88] They saw themselves as military victors dealing with an Army that had been too closely associated with the fallen regime to have any share in the future government. The main purpose of the negotiations was to effect the transfer of loyal troops to revolutionary control and to gain acquiescence in the designation of General Lonardi as Provisional President. Their basic approach was reflected in the draft document prepared by General Uranga before the opening of the talks. Under the heading "Conditions Imposed by the Chief of the Revolution," its seven points dealt with the resignation of Perón and other national authorities, the arrival of General Lonardi in Buenos Aires to assume the presidency, the handing over of Perón and a number of other officials to revolutionary control, the return of troop units to their normal garrisons, and the surrender of all loyal aircraft at a naval air base.[89]

In the lengthy negotiations, the spokesmen of the Revolutionary Command, backed up by the implicit threat to bombard key installations should the talks break down, imposed acceptance of most of their points. Only on the issues relating to the handing over of ex-officials did the Junta Militar delegation get Rojas and Uranga to

[87] These seventeen proposals comprise the second part of the *acta* that was drawn up and signed by all the negotiators aboard the cruiser. I am indebted to Admiral (Ret.) Rojas for providing me with a photocopy of the signed original, Acta Nro. 1 de la Marina de Guerra en Operaciones, and to Admiral (Ret.) Palma for another copy that differs only in its lack of signatures. The phrase "neither winners nor losers" is a historic one in Argentina and was originally ascribed to General Urquiza after his defeat of the dictator Juan Manuel de Rosas in 1852. In 1955 both General Forcher and General Lonardi adopted the concept but with differing interpretations.

[88] General Uranga served as the Army representative in the negotiations when General Lonardi declined Admiral Rojas's invitation to have a Navy plane fly him in from Córdoba. Lonardi did send a representative, Major Juan F. Guevara, but Guevara arrived aboard the cruiser after the signing of the acta.

[89] I am indebted to General (Ret.) Uranga for providing me with a photocopy of this four-page document, written in his handwriting with a few corrections by Admiral Rojas. It was drafted on the stationery of the cruiser *La Argentina* where Admiral Rojas and his staff were located prior to transferring to the *17 de Octubre*.

1. The electoral campaign of 1946. Perón with his vice-presidential running mate, Hortensio Quijano (to his left), and his future foreign minister, Dr. Juan Bramuglia (to his right), February 12, 1946.

2. Presidential candidate Perón casts his ballot, February 24, 1946.

3. Perón and Evita at their country house in San Vincente, 1946.

4. Mrs. Perón receiving a gift from an association of retired women, September 1947.

5. Evita Perón speaks to her people.

6. President Perón and key supporters, July 1947. Left to right: Interior Minister Borlenghi, Buenos Aires Governor Mercante, War Minister Sosa Molina, Foreign Minister Bramuglia, Industry and Commerce Secretary Lagomarsino, Finance Minister Cereijo.

7. President Perón, in the safety of the Army Ministry, reads about the attempt to overthrow him, June 16, 1955. General Franklin Lucero, Minister of the Army, is to his right.

8. Perón embraces Army Minister Lucero after Lucero reports the defeat of the rebels, June 16, 1955.

9. A tense Perón addresses the nation after the abortive revolt of June 16, 1955.

10. General (Ret.) Eduardo Lonardi's assumption of the provisional presidency following Perón's ouster is greeted by huge crowd, September 23, 1955.

11. General Lonardi receives civilian political leaders, September 27, 1955.
From left to right: Carlos Perette and Miguel Zavala Ortiz of the Radical Party;
Alfredo Palacios, Socialist; General Lonardi; and Américo Ghioldi, Socialist.

12. General Pedro E. Aramburu assumes the office of provisional president,
November 13, 1955.

13. President Aramburu reviewing troops at inaugural of monument to the flag, Rosario, June 1957.

14. Vice-President Rojas (left) and Admiral Arturo Rial, two powerful Navy figures, November 1957.

15. President Arturo Frondizi receiving a visit in his office from his brother, Dr. Risieri Frondizi, rector of the National University of Buenos Aires, August 1961.

16. Two Presidents meet in New York. Frondizi and Kennedy are accompanied by Secretary of State Dean Rusk and Foreign Minister Miguel Cárcano, September 1961.

17. Dr. José M. Guido, successor to Frondizi, surrounded by the press.

18. Dr. Arturo Illia, President of Argentina, 1963–66.

19. General Juan C. Onganía, President of Argentina, 1966–70.

back down. But the emissaries were unable, despite prolonged discussions, to gain acceptance for their view that the future government should be in the hands of a new military junta, or at least that General Lonardi should share power with a military triumvirate. The most the Junta Militar emissaries were able to achieve was the incorporation into the final agreement of their seventeen points, but without any binding obligation that the future government would follow them.[90]

Yet the friendly atmosphere in which the talks were conducted gave General Forcher and his associates the feeling that at least some of their proposals would be implemented. There is evidence, moreover, to suggest that Admiral Rojas and General Uranga encouraged this feeling. In a September 22 reply to a Buenos Aires newspaper asking for information about the negotiations, Admiral Rojas radioed:

Points of agreement which resolved cessation of hostilities were: Cessation national and provincial authorities General Lonardi assuming provisional government Nation, neither winners nor losers, solidarity armed forces and people, constitutional rule within broadest concept of liberty and order, operation of Saenz Peña Law, new registration lists controlled by political parties. All social and worker conquests will be maintained intact, intervention for judiciary.[91]

All of the items cited above as points of agreement, with the exception of the first, came directly from the paragraph introduced into the jointly signed document by General Forcher and his delegation.

The acceptance by the full Junta Militar on the morning of September 21 of the conditions imposed by Admiral Rojas and General Uranga put a formal end to hostilities throughout Argentina. Two days later, with General Lonardi's arrival in Buenos Aires to take the oath of office, the Junta Militar disappeared. In serving as a transitional authority after Perón's resignation, it had performed a

[90] Letter from General (Ret.) Emilio Forcher to the author, May 24, 1973; letter from Admiral (Ret.) Isaac Rojas to the author, Aug. 28, 1974; Acta Nro. 1 de la Marina de Guerra en Operaciones, MS cited above in note 87.

[91] Comandante en Jefe Fuerzas Marina de Guerra en Operaciones, Mensaje Naval 22/ix/1955 12.00 hs al Diario El Clarin-Capital via Radio Pacheco. I am indebted to Admiral Rojas for providing me with a photocopy of the original, especially since the published version in *Clarín*, Sept. 24, 1955, p. 5, differs in several respects from the original.

useful role, despite its negative image in the eyes of the revolutionaries. It had kept order in the capital, discouraged worker demonstrations, and repressed a diehard nationalist group that was still loyal to Perón. If the tense situation produced by Perón's maneuvers did not deteriorate into civil war, some part of the credit is owed to the senior Army officers who made up the Junta Militar.[92]

General Lonardi, however, with the pride of a leader who had successfully defied the military power of a repressive regime, was little inclined to give any credit to Army officers whose repudiation of the President dated only from September 19. Lonardi's outlook was not vindictive, as he demonstrated in Córdoba in honoring the soldiers of the Infantry School who had fought against him and in proclaiming his own adherence to the slogan "neither winners nor losers." But it was as chief of a successful revolution that he rested his claim to the presidency, and he was unwilling to accept the limitations to his authority that might arise from acknowledging the role of the Junta Militar. Thus, despite the events of the preceding days and the agreement signed aboard the cruiser, Lonardi began his administration by refusing to recognize the Junta Militar and deepening the divisions in an already divided Army.[93]

In the atmosphere of exhilaration and optimism that surrounded his inauguration before a huge crowd in the Plaza de Mayo that September 23, General Lonardi might well be forgiven if he thought that a government committed to honesty, decency, and a respect for law would find a solution to the problem of a divided army, as well

[92] Interview with General (Ret.) Forcher. He points out that the Junta asked for and obtained the cooperation of the CGT leadership in preventing worker disorders by promising to press for the maintenance of labor gains in the negotiations. This goal was included in the Junta's seventeen-point proposal and was cited in Admiral Rojas's radiogram to *Clarín* cited above. For a CGT communiqué issued at 0510 of September 20 calling on the workers to keep calm in view of the negotiations, see the Sept. 21, 1955, issue of the Buenos Aires daily *El Mundo*. This would seem to corroborate General Forcher's account.

[93] For Lonardi's attitude toward the Junta Militar, see note 80 above. General Forcher tried unsuccessfully to have General Lonardi make a brief allusion to the Junta Militar in his inaugural address so as to indicate continuity within the Army. Lonardi's refusal was viewed by Forcher as a retreat from his announced commitment to a policy of neither winners nor losers. Forcher and the other generals who made up the Junta Militar submitted their written requests for retirement the day Lonardi arrived in Buenos Aires to take over the government (interviews with General Forcher).

as to other problems that would confront it. But the passions, ambitions, and conflicting interests unleashed by his "Liberating Revolution" proved to be far less manageable than this ailing, retired general, elevated in one week from relative obscurity to political power, would ever anticipate.

Chapter 7

The Military in Power:
The Liberating Revolution, 1955–1958

The ouster of Perón in September 1955 marked the return of Argentina to direct military control after nine years of quasi-legal rule. The dissolution of the Congress, the provincial governments, and elected municipal bodies concentrated all power in the hands of the new authorities and their appointees. For the next 33 months, first under General Lonardi and then under General Aramburu, the self-styled government of the Liberating Revolution had to confront the problems that arose from the very nature of its origin. It had to define its own orientation, domestic and foreign, in the absence of any prerevolutionary understandings and to develop policies amid the competing pressures of rival groups, each seeking to fill the vacuum left by the departure of Perón. But it was not only with civilian groups that it had to be concerned. As a government that derived its power from the exercise of force, it had to be sure of its control over a military establishment that was itself severely affected by the events of September.

For in the aftermath of the revolution, each of the armed forces undertook to review the situation of its personnel, deciding on the future of those who had not demonstrated loyalty to the victorious side and studying, with a view to reincorporation, the cases of those officers who had been dropped or retired for political reasons in the past. This utilization of a political criterion to make decisions affecting the officer corps could not but affect hierarchical control and the quality of discipline in all three services.

The Navy, because of its nearly unanimous support of the September uprising, was less affected than the Army except at the highest levels. The special revolutionary advisory board created on October 7 saw fit to recommend the retirement of only 114 officers, but these included every admiral save Isaac Rojas and 45 Navy captains. To fill their posts, younger officers were assigned who normally would not have acquired such responsibilities until they were older and had greater experience.[1]

In the Army, the purge of questionable personnel was initiated by President Lonardi's first appointee to the War Ministry, General León Bengoa. In consultation with the President, but without the participation of an advisory board, General Bengoa concentrated his attention on the highest ranks. It was his view that generals, by virtue of their high responsibility, should have reacted opportunely to the excesses of Perón and that those who did not no longer deserved to remain in active service. The result of this policy was that 63 of the 86 generals serving at the outbreak of the revolution saw their careers terminated. The purge of officers at lesser grades, begun in a limited fashion by General Bengoa, became more extensive under his successor in the War Ministry, General Ossorio Arana, who was responsible for placing another twelve generals on the retired list. Reliable totals are not available, but it is clear that as of early 1956 hundreds of officers were affected and possibly over 1,000 were forced into retirement. Noncommissioned officers, whose loyalty to Perón had been demonstrated in the past, were also forced out of the service in a wholesale manner.[2]

Although the ousting of Army personnel in such large numbers raised the possibility of counterrevolutionary movements, a more immediate threat to the unity and discipline of the Army came from the reincorporation of military personnel who had lost their careers as a result of the abortive movements against Perón of 1951 and 1952. As one who had been directly involved in those early conspiracies, President Lonardi was anxious to compensate his former comrades for the years spent in jail, exile, or premature retirement by restoring them to full military status with back pay and promotions. The re-

---

[1] Perren Memoirs, p. 314.
[2] *Escalafón del ejército argentino . . . hasta 31 de diciembre de 1954* [18], first part; *Boletín Militar Reservado*, Nos. 3562–76, Oct. 1955–Jan. 1956; Decree-Law Nos. 2545, 2546, 2757, 3758–60, dated Feb. 10 and 17, 1956; Decree-Law Nos. 6616–18, 6655, all of April 13, 1956.

turn of these approximately 170 officers, most of them at field and superior grades, meant that individuals who had been out of service for three or four years were now eligible for choice assignments and further promotions in competition with officers who had remained in the profession without interruption.[3] It was perhaps inevitable that the latter should resent the advantages given to individuals with less professional experience, or that the returnees should regard political correctness as more important in personnel decisions than seniority. In any event, the ensuing struggle among rival officers materially affected discipline within the Army and at times threatened the very stability of the government.

The struggles within the Army were also to a certain degree a reflection of the political, economic, and ideological controversies that affected the Argentine community as a whole in the aftermath of Perón's fall. The great issue of the day was how to dispose of Perón's legacy: the mass support, the institutions, the policies that had developed over the past decade. What was to be done with the Peronist Party? With the powerful labor movement centralized in the CGT? With the newspapers and radios that were in the hands of Peronist supporters? With the universities? What was to be done with the economy? With the controls and subsidies that favored certain groups at the expense of others? With the state-owned enterprises and their padded payrolls? What international orientation should the country now adopt? Questions such as these aroused sharp differences within the Argentine community and subjected General Lonardi to contradictory pressures from the very start of his government.

The new President, a man of generous impulses but limited political experience, began his administration by appointing to office friends and participants in the anti-Perón struggle without apparent concern for their political views. The result was a government that was predominantly civilian at the cabinet level, but did not share a common approach to the issues of the day. At one extreme were self-styled democrats, men who identified with Argentina's liberal tradi-

[3] *Boletín Militar Público*, No. 2728, 2729, 2734, 2741–49; also *Boletín Militar Reservado*, 3570 for the amended *escalafón* of the returnees. Twenty of these officers were reincorporated as generals, 25 as colonels, 16 as lieutenant colonels, and 43 as majors.

tions, most of whom had been pro-Allied during World War II, and who had opposed Perón's rise from the very beginning. From moderate to conservative in their socioeconomic views, they wanted to dismantle the Peronist political apparatus, reduce the power of the CGT, and reconstruct Argentine political life on the basis of the anti-Peronist political parties.

At the other extreme were Catholic nationalists, men who viewed both Argentine liberalism and the traditional parties as betrayers of true national values. Neutralist if not clearly pro-Axis during the war, they had welcomed Perón's election in 1946 and found much that was praiseworthy in his first administration. It was only later that they turned against him, alienated by his hostility toward the Catholic church, by his turnabout in petroleum policy, and by the corruption and excesses that characterized his final years. Now with Perón gone, they hoped to attract his supporters by maintaining the structure of the Peronist Party and by coming to terms with the leaders of the CGT. Looking ahead to future elections, they apparently hoped to reorganize Argentine political life on the basis of a Peronism without Perón and thus to assure victory for nationalist candidates.

The key exponents of the nationalist viewpoint in the cabinet were Foreign Minister Mario Amadeo, Labor and Welfare Minister Luis Cerruti Costa, and two Army generals, Transportation Minister Uranga and War Minister Bengoa. An equally, if not more important figure, however, was Dr. Clemente Villada Achaval, the President's brother-in-law, who served as a principal advisor in the Casa Rosada. A militant Catholic who had helped organize the Córdoba rebellion, Villada Achaval was in a strategic position to influence appointments and shape the policies of the administration.[4]

The rival group had its principal cabinet-level focus in the Ministry of Interior and Justice, to which the President had appointed his longtime friend and legal advisor, Dr. Eduardo Busso. A distinguished professor of civil law, Dr. Busso relied heavily in political matters on his Undersecretary of the Interior, a former student activist, Dr. Carlos Muñiz. Muñiz and his associates devoted their energies to strengthening the influence of like-minded elements and

[4] Zuleta Álvarez [119], II, 548–49; also interview with General Juan J. Uranga, July 24, 1971.

halting what they saw as a threat of the nationalists to dominate the government.[5]

Sharing this concern, although for reasons that transcended the civilian milieu, were Admiral Rojas, now Vice-President of the nation, and the Navy leadership headed by Admiral (Ret.) Teodoro Hartung, now serving as Navy Minister, and Captain Arturo Rial, the Navy Undersecretary. Convinced that the Navy had been responsible for Perón's overthrow, these men were determined that their institution should have a strong voice in government appointments and policy decisions. Traditionally suspicious of the nationalists in the Army, whom they regarded as little better than Perón, the Navy leaders were sensitive to any moves that would strengthen nationalist influence within the government.[6]

Still another focus of antinationalist concern was to be found in the Casa Militar, the office concerned with presidential security, official audiences, and protocol. To the post of Chief of the Casa Militar, President Lonardi named Colonel Bernardino Labayru, an old friend and associate in the abortive conspiracy of 1951. Reincorporated now into active service, Labayru worked to counteract the influence of the nationalists with the Amy. It was partly through Labayru's influence over the President that other reincorporated officers of similar outlook obtained key appointments in the Buenos Aires area.[7]

With nationalists and liberals jockeying for positions of influence, each ready to interpret any move of the other as an attempt to dominate the administration, a major blowup was only a matter of time. It was to come in the second week of November. Preliminary

[5] For example, they saw to it that men of the liberal left were appointed as directors of the daily newspapers seized from the Peronists, and they used the press to denounce their rivals within the government.

[6] Diary of Admiral Hartung, MS. This manuscript diary kept by the late Navy Minister covers the period November 1955 to April 30, 1958. I am grateful to an anonymous individual for enabling me to examine a copy of this authoritative source, which contains various appended documents in addition to the individual entries.

[7] "Relatos de los acontecimientos que motivaron el cambio del excmo. señor Presidente de la República, General de División don Eduardo Lonardi," Hartung Diary, 8. Among the officers so placed were Colonel Emilio Bonnecarrère as *jefe de despacho* in Government House; and Major (later Lieut. Colonel) Alejandro A. Lanusse as chief of the presidential guard regiment, the San Martín Horse Grenadiers. *Boletín Militar Reservado*, No. 3565, Oct. 26, 1955, gives the assignments of most of the reincorporated officers.

skirmishing over a proposed governmental reorganization plan and over the designation of a presidential press secretary was meanwhile hardening the lines between the rival groups. The proposed reorganization plan would elevate the authority of Dr. Villada Achaval, by giving him ministerial status and placing him between the cabinet and the President. As head of a proposed office of presidential advisor, he would be able to control policy by deciding which decrees initiated by the ministries should be submitted to the President for signature and by drafting decrees on his own initiative. Equally ominous to the liberal camp, the advisor was to serve as the "interpreter of the revolutionary spirit," the ideological guardian, as it were, of what was so obviously a heterogeneous movement.[8]

Although President Lonardi, physically worn down by the demands of his office and by illness, saw in Dr. Villada Achaval an able individual who could relieve him of many of his burdens, he abandoned the reorganization plan and tore up the draft decree in the face of the strenuous opposition of Interior and Justice Minister Eduardo Busso. Interested parties, however, pieced the decree together and circulated copies among liberal Army and Navy officers to serve as a warning against other nationalist moves. Little wonder, then, at the storm of reaction that greeted the President's designation, at Villada Achaval's suggestion, of Juan C. Goyeneche to head the press secretariat. The prospect that Goyeneche, an experienced writer but ultranationalist, would take control of the intervened newspapers and radios, currently in the hands of men designated by the Interior Ministry, alarmed liberal opinion both in and out of government. As a result of protests that directed attention to Goyeneche's record as a wartime Nazi collaborator, the new secretary offered and the President accepted his resignation.[9]

More crucial posts than that of press secretary were now at stake, however. Concerned by reports of a meeting between Army minister Bengoa, Dr. Villada Achaval, and Foreign Minister Amadeo, and by rumors of a plot to establish a "neofascist" regime, the head of the Casa Militar, Colonel Labayru, together with other reincorporated

[8] Interview with Dr. Carlos M. Muñiz, March 29, 1977; for the arguments for and against the proposed reorganization see Lonardi [161], pp. 265–66, 269–70.

[9] Interview with Dr. Carlos Muñiz; Lonardi [161], pp. 253–54, 271–72, 302–3. On Goyeneche's wartime activities, see the allegations in the Argentine Blue Book, pp. 43–44.

officers, mounted a campaign to discredit the Army Minister. Hard-line anti-Peronist officers in various regiments charged Bengoa with delays in replacing Peronist regimental commanders and with retaining Peronist officers in key ministerial posts. Senior officers, echoing these charges, urged President Lonardi of the need to replace the Army Minister to conserve order. General Bengoa, for his part, tried to justify his personnel decisions as consistent with the President's own policy that there should be "neither winners nor losers," but the pressure on Lonardi was so great that on November 8, when Bengoa offered to resign rather than approve certain transfers, the President promptly accepted the offer. When, hours later, it appeared that Bengoa's friends were trying to reverse the decision, young officers with weapons in their briefcases crowded the antechamber of the presidency to make sure that the resignation was a fact.[10]

The President's choice of a replacement for Bengoa went to Colonel (Ret.) Arturo Ossorio Arana. Lonardi insisted on Ossorio despite the declared preference of the senior Army officers that he name General Pedro Aramburu, and despite the warnings of nationalist General Uranga that Ossorio could not be relied on to defend the President against those who would soon be pressing for his own ouster. Lonardi, however, preferred to place his trust in his fellow artilleryman, the man who had invited him to take over the revolution in Córdoba and who had been his comrade-in-arms in the dangerous days of the September rebellion. To enhance Ossorio's status, moreover, Lonardi did not hesitate to ask General Bengoa as his last official act prior to the swearing in of his successor to sign a decree that restored Ossorio to active duty status and that promoted him, despite his lack of general staff training, to the grade of brigadier general.[11]

A certain irony attaches to President Lonardi's refusal to consider General Aramburu for the War Ministry. Although Ossorio Arana's revolutionary record and general orientation made him acceptable to

[10] Hartung Diary, pp. 8–9; interview with General Uranga. Additional details on the steps that led to Bengoa's resignation are given in a twenty-page mimeographed document that circulated in late 1957 under the title "La verdad sobre los relevos de los altos mandos del ejército," p. 2. I am indebted to Lieut. General (Ret.) Benjamín Rattenbach for furnishing me with a copy of this document.
[11] Interview with General Uranga; Hartung Diary, pp. 9–11.

the anti-Peronist officers in the Army, he was not a distinguished professional. Aramburu, on the other hand, was the senior major general in the Army, a man with unbroken military service as well as anti-Peronist credentials. Lonardi, however, in the view of the shabby treatment he had received from Aramburu in August and of the long-standing coolness that had characterized their relations, was not disposed to reward him with any cabinet position, and least of all with the Army Ministry. Yet had he done so, under the curious military etiquette that governs such matters, Aramburu would have been ineligible to succeed Lonardi in the presidency when the military leaders finally decided to oust him on November 13. As it was, Lonardi had to swallow the double humiliation of being forced out by his military colleagues and seeing his archrival sworn in to replace him.

The crisis that produced the ouster of the Liberating Revolution's first president was the unintended consequence of the nationalists' effort to redress their loss of the Army Ministry by taking over that of the Interior. For some time, consideration had been given in government circles to the idea of dividing the Ministry of Interior and Justice so as to separate the essential political functions of the one from the tasks of rehabilitating the judicial system. It nevertheless came as a surprise when on November 10, President Lonardi signed decrees that had been prepared, not by that Ministry, but by Villada Achaval, calling for the creation of two separate cabinet posts and designating as the new head of Interior the well-known nationalist figure Dr. Luis María de Pablo Pardo.[12]

Although Pablo Pardo had taken an active part in the June 16 revolt and had cooperated with Navy officers in its preparation, his reputation as a nationalist militant and contributor to fascist publications in the 1930's and 1940's made him unacceptable as an Interior Minister to Navy leaders as well as other liberal circles. Their response was to try to bring pressure on the President to withdraw the appointment, but despite their efforts, he was urged by his immediate circle of advisors, including his son, Captain Luis Lonardi, and his aide, Major Juan Guevara, to assert his authority and not to yield. After a two-day delay, the president finally decided to go

[12] Hartung Diary, p. 12; also Lonardi [161], pp. 258–60, 323–28; and Guevara [153], pp. 97–98.

ahead and swore in his new Minister of Interior on Saturday, November 12, at 1:30 P.M., fully aware of the powerful opposition the appointment had generated. Indeed, just prior to the ceremony, the Navy Minister, yielding to the President's request for his signature on the decree of appointment, warned: "Mr. President, at this moment that I sign, the rebellion against you begins."[13]

Not all military men by any means, including the Navy leadership, wished to see President Lonardi ousted from office. They hoped to reach an understanding whereby he would agree to eliminate both Villada Achaval and Pablo Pardo from their respective posts, adopt firmer policies toward labor and the Peronist Party, and allow a revolutionary military junta to control appointments and policy pronouncements. The 24 hours that followed Pablo Pardo's swearing in witnessed an attempt to reach such an understanding.[14]

During the night of November 12–13, the three military ministers talked with the President, and then a large group of senior officers from all three services met with him at the Olivos residence. This meeting, which lasted until 4:00 A.M., produced no firm understanding. The President indicated his willingness to do without the services of Villada Achaval and to accept Pablo Pardo's resignation if he offered it voluntarily; he was adamant, however, in insisting on retaining Major Guevara at his side as his personal aide; and he refused to share his authority with a junta, although willing to meet weekly with the military ministers to exchange ideas. On more than one occasion during the long, drawn-out session, General Lonardi, visibly tired and showing signs of nervous exhaustion, offered to step aside, but was turned down.[15]

Atlhough a few of the military participants at the Olivos meeting came away hopeful that a compromise could still be worked out, others felt, on reviewing the tenor of the President's statements later that morning, that it would have been better to accept his offer to resign. Encouraged by General Aramburu, these officers summoned a new conclave of revolutionary Army, Navy, and Air Force officers

[13] Hartung Diary, pp. 12–14; also interview with Navy Captain (Ret.) Antonio Rivolta, April 20, 1970. For Pablo Pardo's association in the 1930's with fascism and anti-Semitism, see Zuleta Alvarez [119], I, 284–88.

[14] Hartung Diary, p. 14; interviews with Admiral (Ret.) Adolfo Estévez, March 21, 1970, and General (Ret.) Carlos S. Toranzo Montero, March 26, 1970.

[15] Hartung Diary, pp. 14–15; Lonardi [161], pp. 233–41.

later that morning at the Army Ministry, where it was unanimously decided to request Lonardi to formalize his resignation offer and to install General Aramburu as his successor. Acting as delegates of the assembled officers, the three military ministers, General Ossorio Arana, Admiral Hartung, and Air Force Vice Commodore Ramón A. Abrahin, went out to Olivos to inform Lonardi that he had lost the confidence of the armed forces and to ask for his written resignation.[16]

What took place thereafter was an uncomfortable experience for all concerned. Lonardi's first response was to inform his visitors that after the conclusion of the previous night's meeting, he had himself decided to present his resignation and was in the process of drafting a statement setting forth his reasons. At his suggestion, word of this decision was telephoned to the officers assembled at the Army Ministry. After further conversation and when the three ministers were about to take their departure, leaving Admiral Hartung's aide behind to wait for the resignation statement, the President's son, Luis, pushed his father into an adjacent room where Dr. Villada Achaval was waiting. After an interlude in which angry voices could be overheard, Lonardi emerged a changed man. Accompanying the ministers to their waiting automobiles, he angrily announced that they could proceed as they saw fit, but that he would neither write anything nor send anything. All that the departing ministers obtained from their visit was Lonardi's consent to their request that he issue no statements to the press in the interests of conserving the public peace.[17]

The lack of a signed resignation did not prevent the installation of General Aramburu later that day as the Liberating Revolution's second president. It did mean that contrary to the information issued to the public, Lonardi did not ask to resign for reasons of health. A victim in a direct sense of a military ouster, he was also a victim of his countrymen's inability to subordinate ideological differences, political passion, and the quest for partisan advantage to the general interest. Lonardi's lack of political experience, his indecisiveness,

[16] Hartung Diary, p. 15–16.

[17] *Ibid.*, pp. 17–18; Lonardi [161], pp. 241–47. A sworn account of the events of November 13 is embodied in the "Acta de Relación de Hechos" which the three military ministers signed before the Escribano General de la Nación. A copy of this document is included with the Hartung Diary.

and, indeed, the very decency that prevented him from acting ruthlessly, probably also contributed to the brevity of his presidency. Had he identified clearly with either of the contending factions, or had he possessed the skill to manipulate both for his own advantage, he might have been able to remain in office until his health finally failed. As it was, his death in March 1956 removed the embarrassment of his presence for his successors and enabled him to receive, at least among the non-Peronist part of the community, the universal acclaim that had been denied him in office.

The choice of General Aramburu to succeed General Lonardi was not a spur-of-the moment decision made by the Army and Navy officers who assembled in the Army Ministry the morning of November 13. Five days earlier, when a group of Army generals had visited the Navy Ministry to discuss their intention of pressing for the ouster of Army Minister Bengoa, the question had been raised of what would happen if President Lonardi insisted on his own resignation rather than abandon Bengoa. The ensuing discussion made it clear that, even though Admiral Rojas was Vice-President, the Navy would accept a general as Lonardi's successor in order to avoid a possible confrontation between the services. It was at this meeting also that the Army Commander-in-Chief, Lieut. General Julio Lagos, disqualified himself as a possible candidate, noting that he had once been a Peronist, and proposed that General Aramburu, who stood next on the rank list, should be the successor if it proved necessary to find a replacement for Lonardi.[18]

While the Navy leaders thus acquiesced in the elevation of General Aramburu, they were determined to ensure that all three military services would henceforth exercise a direct control over the policies and appointments of the administration. Accordingly, at the November 13 conclave, even as the military ministers went off to secure Lonardi's resignation, Navy Undersecretary Arturo Rial drafted a document to serve as a basic accord among the three armed forces. Subsequently approved when the ministers returned from Olivos, this agreement was signed by twenty military notables, including Generals Aramburu and Lagos, Admirals Rojas and Hartung, and Air Force Vice Commodore Ramón Abrahín.[19]

[18] Hartung Diary, p. 19; interview with Admiral (Ret.) Estévez.
[19] Interview with Admiral (Ret.) Rial, May 4, 1970. The November 13 ac-

The text of this accord dealt with both the organization of the new government and specific policy measures to be adopted in the future. In the latter category were agreements to dissolve the Peronist Party, disqualify its leaders from further political activity, and push investigations already initiated into the corruption and excesses of the Perón years. It was also agreed, looking ahead, to have the new government issue a declaration of principles and, as part of a commitment to the restoration of democracy, to declare military men ineligible to run for office in the next elections.[20]

The Navy's concern to guarantee its own role in the decision-making process is most evident in the organizational provisions of the accord. The agreement provided not only that Aramburu should replace Lonardi as Provisional President, but that the Navy should choose the Provisional Vice-President. In effect, this meant the continuation of Admiral Rojas, who had earlier submitted his own resignation. But, more important, the accord called for the establishment of a Revolutionary Military Council with the structure and powers set forth in a document to be signed separately.[21] That document was made public a few hours later in the form of a decree-law, the first to be signed by General Aramburu after his installation as Provisional President. As spelled out in that measure, the Revolutionary Military Council was to serve as a check on the Executive Power in the absence of an elected congress. The approval of the Military Council was required for all decree-laws issued by the government in the exercise of legislative faculties; its consent was necessary for the appointment of cabinet ministers and provincial interventors; and it was to participate, together with the Executive Power, in the is-

---

cord consisted of nine lettered provisions and was typed on two pages of Ministry of Army stationery under the heading "ACUERDO." I am grateful to General (Ret.) Juan E. Guglialmelli for giving me a photographic copy of the signed original. The signatories include: Admirals Rojas, Hartung, Toranzo Calderón, Rial, and Estévez; Navy Captains Robbio and Vago; Generals Aramburu, Lagos, Huergo, Videla Balaguer, Solanas Pacheco, Carlos Salinas, Tassi, and Zerda; Air Force Vice Commodore Abrahín. Four other signatories remain to be deciphered.

20 "ACUERDO," paragraphs e, g, h, i.

21 *Ibid.*, paragraphs a, b, c. Paragraph d called for the restructuring of the nonmilitary ministries with the participation of the Revolutionary Military Council; paragraph f called for the reestablishment of the National Consultative Board (Junta Consultiva Nacional) and the rejection of resignations by members of the Supreme Court if any had been submitted.

suance of "plans, declarations, and measures of importance designed to fulfill the goals pursued by the Liberating Revolution." Given the fact that the Military Council was to consist of the Vice-President and the ministers of each of the three armed services, the Navy, with half the membership of this body, seemed to have assured itself of a major voice in the post-Lonardi administration.[22]

The administration of General Aramburu thus began as one of shared authority between the Provisional President, on the one hand, and the armed forces, represented by their respective ministers and the Vice-President, on the other. Civilian presence within the government was exercised primarily in the cabinet, whose membership underwent a considerable turnover with the change in the presidency. Even so, as under Lonardi, only the Transportation post, now assigned to a retired Navy captain, was placed in military hands. Civilian input of an advisorial nature was also provided for in the National Consultative Board (Junta Consultiva Nacional), a twenty-man body that had been set up in the final days of the Lonardi presidency to give the various non-Peronist political parties a sense of participation in the government. In the crisis that had led to his separation, all but two members, both affiliated with a small Catholic nationalist party, gave moral support to the antinationalist forces. With these two men replaced by Christian Democrats, the Junta Consultiva Nacional, which met under the chairmanship of Vice-President Rojas, served as a sounding board for major policy issues confronting the Aramburu government. Over the long run, however, its partisan makeup and the practice of opening its sessions to the public made the Junta more a forum of debate among increasingly competitive political parties than an effective instrument for influencing the policies of a military administration.[23]

President Aramburu was not insensitive to anti-Peronist civilian opinion, especially where it suited his purposes; and in one notable instance, a single individual, not even a member of the Junta Consultiva, was able to effect a vital change. Dr. Alfredo Palacios, veteran

[22] Decree-Law No. 2908, Nov. 13, 1955. This degree like the "ACUERDO" was drafted by Admiral Rial (Hartung Diary, p. 288).

[23] Interview with Américo Ghioldi, March 20, 1970; for contradictory views of the origins of the Junta Consultiva, see Lonardi [161], pp. 254–55, 273–74; see also Decree No. 3153 of Nov. 17, 1955.

Socialist leader, prestigious public personality, and currently Argentine Ambassador to Uruguay, took sharp exception to the November 13 decree-law that created the Revolutionary Military Council. In an interview with the President, attended by Vice-President Rojas, Palacios took the position that the decree-law made the President a prisoner of the armed forces, that this was intolerable in a democratic regime, and that, if the situation continued, he would have to resign his ambassadorial post. General Aramburu understandably agreed to a move that would strengthen his own powers and proposed the transformation of the Council into an advisory junta, a solution the Ambassador found acceptable.[24]

Vice-President Rojas was not at all happy with the proposal, but in the face of assurances by Aramburu that nothing in fact would change, that he would always act by agreement with the military, he went along. Accordingly, a new decree-law was issued that changed the name of the council to Junta Militar Consultiva (Military Advisory Board) and gave it consultative rather than mandatory powers. President Aramburu assured his military colleagues when they countersigned the new decree-law on November 22 that it was done simply for appearances, that nothing was changed.[25] But in fact, a legal basis had been established whereby the President could eventually escape from the armed forces' tutelage, a tutelage that the Navy especially was anxious to maintain. That time was to come some thirteen months later at the end of 1956.

In the meantime, the final months of 1955 and the early months of 1956 were to witness a series of measures that defined the orientation of the provisional government. On December 7 it issued a declaration of basic objectives that originated in a document prepared by the Navy. This declaration committed the government to the suppression of all vestiges of totalitarianism and to the creation of conditions that would permit the restoration of a democratically elected constitutional government. To this end, the declaration pledged the members of the provisional government not to seek office themselves in the next election and to maintain a position of

[24] Hartung Diary, p. 287; *La Vanguardia*, Nov. 24, 1955, carries an exchange of letters between Palacios and Rojas and the text of a press release by Palacios after his interview with the President.

[25] Decree-Law No. 3440, Nov. 22, 1955; Hartung Diary, pp. 382–83.

neutrality and independence vis-à-vis the differing tendencies and the democratic political parties.[26]

The term "democratic political party" did not include the Peronist Party, which had been declared illegal and its assets seized within a few days after General Aramburu took over as President. Indeed, a major concern of the authorities was to discredit all those who had held leadership positions with the Peronist movement and to destroy any possibility for the recreation of a mass movement with its characteristics. At the political level, this went so far as to include the outlawing of the publication of Perón's name or any symbol, word, or image that was synonymous with his movement. Moreover, individuals who held elective or high appointive posts in the Peronist government after 1946, or who had been Peronist party leaders, were now declared ineligible to run for elective office, hold government jobs, or serve in political party posts until a date to be decided by the next constitutional government.[27]

The effort to destroy the Peronist political apparatus extended also to the labor movement. Abandoning the temporizing tactics of its predecessor, the Aramburu administration, within two days of taking power and confronted with a general strike ordered by the Peronist leadership of the CGT, declared this an illegal stoppage and called for the intervention of that national trade union body. Authority over the CGT was entrusted to a military interventor, Navy Captain Alberto Patrón, who in turn was empowered to designate military interventors for its affiliated unions. The government's policy was to encourage the emergence of an anti-Peronist trade union leadership, while reducing the political power of the labor movement as a whole.[28]

To these ends it welcomed Socialist, syndicalist, and other independent leaders who had been forced out of union posts during the Perón regime to serve as advisors to military interventors. Moreover,

---

[26] The text of the declaration was issued by the presidential office in the form of a pamphlet, *Carta Republicana de la Revolución. Declaraciones de Principios, República Argentina,* 1955. The text was also appended to the April 27, 1956, proclamation that voided the 1949 constitutional amendments and declared the 1853 constitution in effect. See *Anales* [1], XVI-A, 1–4.

[27] Decree-Law Nos. 3855, Nov. 24, 1955; 4161, March 5, 1956; 4258, March 6, 1956.

[28] Decree-Law Nos. 3032, Nov. 16, 1955; 6295, April 16, 1956.

in an April 1956 decree, it banned anyone who had served in a leadership post in the CGT or its affiliated unions between February 1952 and September 16, 1955, from holding any trade union post until such time as a future constitutional government would decide otherwise. Further, in May 1956, it ordered the suspension of the existing trade union statute, replacing it with a decree-law that not only banned unions from engaging in political activities, but authorized the existence of plural unions in any industry and at the level of national confederations. The depoliticization of the labor movement was the hoped-for objective of these reforms.[29]

The economic policies of the provisional government also had the effect, intended or not, of lowering the real income of the working class. Following the advice of a U.N. consultant team headed by the Argentine economist Raúl Prebisch, the government devalued the peso, denationalized bank deposits, and ended quantitative controls over trade, hoping thereby to stimulate exports, especially in the field of agriculture. The results in terms of the balance of payments were less than expected. Declining international prices reduced anticipated earnings, while, in the absence of quantitative controls, imports of consumer goods shot up, causing a continuing drain on exchange reserves. Domestic prices also spiraled above intended levels as businessmen, unrestrained by price controls, sought to compensate themselves for the reduced profit margins of the past. The overall result was to produce a redistribution of income away from the wage earners to other sectors, a process that, taken together with its trade union policies, could hardly enhance the popularity of the government in the eyes of the working class and especially of the Peronist sectors.[30]

In adopting its harsh anti-Peronist policies, the Aramburu government had to confront the possibilty of counterrevolutionary violence. This was especially so in view of the punitive measures it was taking

[29] Decree-Law Nos. 7107, April 19, 1956; 9270, May 23, 1956.
[30] Mallon and Sourroille [263], pp. 14–19; *Anales* [1], XVI-A, 308–25, has the texts of the Prebisch policy recommendations. The government's failure to resolve inherited disputes with overseas investors discouraged substantial new foreign investment; moreover, its domestic policies shifted income to the well-to-do and failed to produce increased investment. The investment share of the GNP actually declined from 1955 to 1957.

against those it regarded as immoral beneficiaries of the Peronist regime. The detention of once prominent personalities, the investigations of persons and companies believed to have made illicit profits, and the widespread purges that affected the status of government officeholders, teachers, labor leaders, and military men, all served to create a pool of alienated individuals. It was only logical to expect that some of them, especially those with a military background, would resort to direct action to harass the government or to bring about its overthrow.

Although incidents of worker sabotage were common in the months that followed the Aramburu takeover, it was only in March 1956, following the decrees that banned the public reference to Peronist symbols and that instituted the political disqualifications mentioned above, that serious plotting actually began. A contributing, although ultimately misleading, factor may have been the government's decision, announced in February, to remove from the code of military justice the death penalty for promoters of military rebellion. This penalty, which had been enacted by the Perón-led Congress after the Menéndez revolt in 1951, was now eliminated from the military code on grounds that it "violated our constitutional traditions which have suppressed forever the penalty of death for political causes." Events were to prove this statement premature.[31]

The leading figure in the anti-Aramburu conspiratorial effort was Juan José Valle, a major general who had retired voluntarily after Perón was overthrown. A Military Academy classmate of Aramburu, he sought to attract other officers disillusioned by the government's actions. One of those who chose to join him was General Miguel Iñíguez, a highly regarded professional who was still on active duty, although in an unassigned status, awaiting the results of an inquiry into his conduct as a commander of loyal forces in the Córdoba area in September. An essentially nonpolitical officer prior to the fall of Perón, but with an intense nationalistic outlook, General Iñíguez joined General Valle in reaction to the policies of the Aramburu government. Iñíguez agreed in late March 1956 to serve as the chief of staff for the revolution, but a few days later he was arrested, de-

---

[31] Decree-Law No. 8313, Dec. 30, 1955 (which was published in the *Boletín Oficial* of Feb. 21, 1956), lifted the death penalty. For a list of sabotage acts, see *Qué*, March 7, 1956, p. 11.

nounced by an informer. Kept under detention for the next five months, he thus escaped the fate that awaited his fellow revolutionaries.[32]

The Valle conspiracy was essentially a military movement that sought to exploit the resentment of retired Army personnel, officer and noncommissioned, as well as the uneasiness in the active ranks. Although it had the cooperation of numerous civilian Peronists and anticipated the backing of working-class elements, the movement did not have the personal blessing of Juan Perón, then in exile in Panama.[33] Indeed, in its preliminary stages, the movement sought to attract such alienated nationalist officers as the recently retired Generals Bengoa and Uranga, but apparently disagreement over who would assume power once it succeeded put an end to their participation. In the final analysis, Generals (Ret.) Juan José Valle and Raúl Tanco assumed the leadership of what they called the "Movement for National Recovery," and they, rather than Perón, whose name never appeared in the proclamation prepared for the June 9 revolution, expected to be its direct political beneficiaries.[34]

The conspiratorial plan called for commando groups of military men, chiefly noncommissioned, and civilians, to take over Army units in various cities and garrisons, seize communication facilities, and distribute weapons from military deposits to those who would respond to their proclamation of a popular uprising. The plan also apparently envisaged terrorist assaults on known government supporters and the kidnapping of government leaders and prominent political party personalities. To this end, red crosses were painted on the houses of certain of the intended victims, the Socialist Party leader Américo Ghioldi for one, to indicate their location for the assault groups.[35]

The Aramburu government had been aware for some time that a

[32] Interview with General (Ret.) Miguel Iñíguez, Aug. 21, 1973.

[33] For Perón's views toward the military conspirators, see his two letters of June 12, 1956, in *Perón-Cooke correspondencia* [72], I, 7–15; see also Martínez [67], p. 61.

[34] Martínez [67], p. 73. The text of the proclamation is reproduced in Ferla [143], pp. 307–12.

[35] Ferla [143], pp. 51ff.; interview with Américo Ghioldi; President Aramburu press conference, *La Prensa*, June 12, 1956. Documents and materials allegedly seized from the conspirators are reproduced or summarized in a slender volume by Cerro Fernández [138].

conspiracy was in the making, although without precise knowledge of its scope or timing. Early in June, various indications, including the appearance of the painted crosses, made it seem likely that an uprising was near at hand. Accordingly, before President Aramburu left on June 8 in the company of the Army and Navy Ministers for a scheduled visit to Santa Fe and Rosario, arrangements were made to sign undated decrees and leave them behind with Vice-President Rojas for the proclamation of martial law should the circumstances warrant. On June 8, the police detained hundreds of Peronist labor militants to discourage any large-scale worker participation in the anticipated movement.[36]

The rebels launched their uprising between 11:00 P.M. and midnight on Saturday, June 9, seizing control of the Seventh Infantry Regiment in the city of La Plata and gaining temporary possession of radio stations in a number of interior cities. In Santa Rosa in La Pampa province, the rebels quickly took over the military district headquarters, the police station, and the center of the city. In the area of the Federal Capital, however, loyal officers, alerted hours ahead to the impending blow, were able within a short time to frustrate rebel attempts to take over the Army Mechanics School and its adjacent arsenal, the regiments at Palermo, and the NCO School at Campo de Mayo. Only in La Plata were the rebels able to exploit their initial success, and, with the aid of civilian supporters, to mount an attack on the headquarters of the provincial police and that of the Second Infantry Division. Here, however, with Army and Marine reinforcements brought in to supplement the police, the rebels were forced back to the regimental barracks, where, after undergoing attacks from Air Force and Navy planes, they surrendered at 9:00 A.M. the morning of June 10. Aerial attacks in Santa Rosa also resulted in the surrender or dispersal of the rebels at about the same time.[37]

The June 9 uprising was put down with a harshness that was unprecedented in recent Argentine history. For the first time in the twentieth century a government resorted to executions when con-

[36] "Proceso de la revolución del 9 al 10 de junio de 1956," Hartung Diary, pp. 34–37; for the arrest of trade unionists including the former Communist Party activist, Juan José Real, see his *Treinta años de historia argentina* [78], p. 178 and note 2.

[37] *La Prensa*, June 10–12, 1956, provides an account of the events as seen by government officials and supporters.

fronted with an attempted rebellion. Under the provisions of martial law, proclaimed shortly after the first rebel assaults, the government decreed that anyone disrupting public order, whether bearing arms or not, would be subject to summary justice. Over the next three days, despite the removal of the death penalty from the code of military justice, 27 individuals, eighteen military and nine civilians, were shot by firing squads.[38]

What accounts for this unusual bloodletting? One critic sees it as a deliberate move, instigated by the oligarchy, to drive a wedge "between the armed forces and Peronism, between the armed forces and the people. Before June 9 the Liberating Revolution was cancelable; after June 9, it will appear as an irreversible event, especially in the eyes of officers who performed or consented to the executions."[39] This same writer, an ardent critic of the Aramburu government, denounced the episode as premeditated crime.[40]

The facts support a somewhat different, though hardly more benign, interpretation. During the night of June 9–10, when all nine civilians and two officers were shot, the rebels still held a part of La Plata, and the possibility of worker uprisings in Greater Buenos Aires and elsewhere could not be discounted. These first executions were an emergency response designed to create shock and to prevent the rebellion from escalating into civil war. This would explain the government's hastiness in authorizing and publicizing the executions, a hastiness that was reflected in the absence of anything like orderly hearings, in the inclusion among those who faced the firing squads of men who had been captured prior to the public proclamation of martial law, and in the confusions of the official communiqués issued during the night of June 9–10 that exaggerated the number of civilian rebels shot and gave erroneous identifications for the two executed officers.[41]

[38] Ferla [143], pp. 67–200, provides a passionate account that sympathizes with the victims; Hartung Diary, pp. 37–40, gives an insider's view that was written on June 13, 1956.

[39] Ferla [143], p. 40.

[40] *Ibid.*, pp. 258–71.

[41] Fear of civil war was the chief consideration behind the decision to order executions, according to Admiral (Ret.) Carlos Sánchez Sañudo (interview March 20, 1970). As a Navy Captain, Sánchez Sañudo was a member of Rojas's immediate staff and was with him the night of June 9–10, 1956. Years later in a television interview Admiral (Ret.) Rojas stated: "We had the feeling that the counterrevolutionary movement was very powerful and that it had to be stopped

But if the first day's executions may thus be ascribed to the government's determination to halt the rebellion in its tracks, the same cannot be said for those that were carried out on June 11 and 12, when it was clear that the rebellion had already collapsed. Here it was not a question of an emergency measure, but of imposing punishment on those military men, mostly retired Army officers and NCOs, who had been captured during the course of the rebellion or while trying to escape after its collapse. Moreover, it was not just Vice-President Rojas, but the entire Military Junta, Aramburu, Rojas, and the three military ministers, who made the fateful decision about the prisoners in a meeting held the afternoon of June 10. This meeting took place amid scenes of exhilaration and relief as anti-Peronist crowds thronged to the Plaza de Mayo to cheer the recently returned President Aramburu and Vice-President Rojas and to demand heavy penalties for the rebels. Similar scenes, but with the roles reversed, had occurred in the past when Peronist crowds had demanded vengeance against anti-Peronist rebels in September 1951 and June 1955. Now, however, the military government paid greater heed to the demand for blood than had Perón.[42]

Despite the advice of certain civilian political figures, including members of the Consultative Board, to put an end to the executions, and despite the recommendations of Army courts-martial officers that the rebels be subjected to ordinary military justice, the Military Junta decided to continue applying the penalties of martial law. In so deciding, they persuaded themselves that they were setting an example that would strengthen the government's authority and discourage future rebellions, thereby preventing the loss of other lives.[43]

---

in a drastic manner. And so we, General Aramburu, the military ministers, and I, collectively assumed the historic responsibility for those lamentable sentences" (*La Nación* [international edition], Dec. 4, 1972).

[42] Hartung Diary, p. 37; *La Prensa*, June 11, 1956.

[43] Interviews with Américo Ghioldi, March 20, 1970, and General (Ret.) Juan E. Guglialmelli, March 13, 1970. Ghioldi, a member of the Junta Consultiva, states that this body was not consulted about the executions but that on learning of them over the radio he and other members of the Junta went to Government House on Sunday, June 10, to urge clemency and an end to the executions. Guglialmelli, then a staff officer in the War Ministry, recalls that he and others in the Ministry opposed the executions and that he personally telephoned Arturo Frondizi to urge that he try to bring pressure on the authorities to stop them. At Campo de Mayo the court-martial had voted four to two against the death penalty for those seized in the rebellion (Hartung Diary, p. 38).

It is not known whether the Military Junta in its June 10 meeting gave any consideration to the fact that most of those already executed were civilians and that if the executions stopped, the military leaders of the rebellion would have suffered lesser penalties than these civilians. What is known is that the Military Junta rejected a suggestion from the Campo de Mayo commander, Colonel Lorio, to limit further executions to one or two junior officers. Admiral Rojas vehemently opposed the exemption of the more senior officers as a violation of ethics that "History" would not forgive; he preferred no further executions at all to adopting a course that would allow the rebel military leaders to escape the penalty imposed on their followers. Ultimately, the Military Junta assumed direct responsibility for ordering the execution over the next two days of nine Army officers and seven NCOs.[44]

With the capture and execution of General Valle, the leader of the rebellion, on June 12, the government suspended martial law, yielding to increasing civilian and military pressure to put an end to further executions. Nevertheless, the punitive measures already taken put a stamp on the government that affected its future. The June executions were to become a political issue that was exploited against the Aramburu government. Resistance to its efforts to wean the working class from its Peronist orientation was strengthened by the memory of the "martyrs of June 9." The long-term effects were even more serious. A precedent for political harshness was set that affected Argentine society as a whole. The brutal behavior of young Argentine guerillas in the 1970's owes something to the manner in which the Aramburu government, itself the product of a successful revolution, treated those who rebelled against it in 1956.[45]

Nevertheless, whatever the long-run cost in political terms, the Aramburu government did succeed in freeing itself from the threat of further Peronist revolts. To be sure, an underground resistance movement of various strands was able to operate, performing acts of sabotage, circulating subversive materials, but never endangering the government's hold on power.

[44] Hartung Diary, pp. 38–39.
[45] Aramburu himself fell victim to that brutality when a guerilla group known as the "Montoneros" kidnapped him on May 29, 1970, and subsequently after a "trial" shot him to death. The episode had great reverberations on the Argentine political scene.

Of far greater concern to the Aramburu administration were its internal military problems, the product of dissensions within the Army and of interservice jealousies. Even before the June 9 uprising, the efforts by a group of reincorporated officers known as "gorillas," of whom Colonels Bernardino Labayru and Víctor Arribau were the most prominent, to force the ouster of a number of Army generals whom they denounced as undemocratic created an atmosphere of continuing tension. The subsequent removal of both Labayru and a principal "gorilla" target, Chief of Staff General Roberto Dalton, through the elegant device of diplomatic assignments, proved only a palliative. Unable to satisfy the rival groups or to impose a much-needed sense of discipline in the institution, Army Minister Ossorio Arana found himself the object of such severe attack that President Aramburu early in June asked Navy Minister Hartung to request his colleague's resignation. The reaction to this unusual procedure, involving the Navy Minister in an Army matter, was so sharp that the President, insisting lamely that he had been misunderstood by Hartung, restored Ossorio Arana to his ministerial post a day later. Needless to say, Aramburu's reputation was not enhanced in the eyes of any of those involved, and especially the two military ministers.[46]

The Peronist revolt a few days later produced a temporary unity within the armed forces, but over the next several months, the tensions again increased, leading ultimately to a confrontation of unprecedented proportions in November 1956. Once again, the crisis revolved around the person of Ossorio Arana, but the underlying causes were more complex than in the past. To the personal frictions, ideological differences, and policy disagreements that had underlain the earlier internal Army crises were added factors deriving from increased interservice tensions and the intensified maneuvering of civilian politicians, parties, and factions.

Although a certain degree of interservice friction was inevitable, that which developed in the latter half of 1956 reflected the special

[46] "Acontecimientos del 21 de mayo con relación al ejército," Hartung Diary, pp. 20–28; "Episodio de la renuncia del general Ossorio Arana como ministro de ejército," *ibid.*, pp. 29–33. General Dalton was appointed Ambassador to Peru (*La Prensa*, June 7, 1956); Colonel Labayru was shifted from his post as secretary-aide to the War Minister and named military attaché to Belgium. Another victim of the infighting was General Julio Lagos, the Army Commander-in-Chief, whom President Aramburu asked to retire and who was succeeded on June 5 by General Francisco Zerda (*La Prensa*, June 6, 1956).

circumstances of a country under the control of an avowedly provisional regime looking ahead to the restoration via elections of a constitutional government. In July 1956, President Aramburu, on behalf of his colleagues, announced that such elections would take place before the end of 1957; he also reaffirmed the pledge, set forth in the December 1955 declaration of basic objectives and embodied in the decree banning military candidates, that the government would not seek to influence the election results.[47] None of the armed services, however, could be totally immune to efforts by civilian politicians to secure preelectoral measures that would benefit their respective interests. Moreover, it was evident that government inaction as well as action could be a form of political favoritism.

This was well illustrated in the heated discussions that arose in military as well as civilian circles over the scope of a proposed new political party statute. The most controversial issue was whether or not to require political parties that were split into rival factions to undergo a process of reorganization and unification through new internal elections. The proposed requirement affected in the first instance the country's largest non-Peronist party, the UCR, several of whose provincial and local committees had been challenging the legitimacy of Arturo Frondizi's control over the party's national organization.[48]

In the National Consultative Board, only the two anti-Frondizi Radical figures of its twenty members favored the idea. Within the cabinet, however, the Navy representatives pressed for the adoption of a draft statute prepared by Navy Undersecretary Admiral Rial that would force the Radical Party to unify. After a lengthy debate in which the Army and Air Force joined forces against the Navy, the government finally adopted a law in October 1956 that permitted rival factions of any party to present separate candidates in the

---

[47] Mensaje del Presidente Provisional de la Nación en la comida de camaraderia de las Fuerzas Armadas, July 6, 1956.

[48] The challenge to Dr. Frondizi's leadership dated from early 1954 when his bloc, the Movement of Intransigence and Renovation (MIR) took control of the UCR national committee after a heated party convention. Opposed to MIR control were the Unionists led by Miguel A. Zavala Ortiz and the National Intransigents led by Dr. Amadeo Sabattini. Moreover, even within the MIR, Frondizi's aspiration to be the party's presidential nominee in the next election was alienating elements attached to Ricardo Balbín, who had been the UCR standard-bearer in the 1951 election.

forthcoming elections if they could not resolve their own differences. In effect this guaranteed that the UCR would approach those elections not as a unified organization, but as two rival parties of roughly equal strength competing for Peronist votes to swing the balance.[49]

Although the Navy leadership accepted the defeat of its proposal, the struggle over the political party statute left its scars. Navy Minister Hartung felt that the Navy's intentions had been deliberately misrepresented by elements sympathetic to Frondizi to make it appear that it was trying to veto a Frondizi candidacy, when its real objective was to assure the existence of a strong, well-organized centrist party capable of winning an election and taking over as a successor government. Hartung was also concerned that the Navy's initiative in the matter of the statute had resulted in its isolation from the other two military services and a weakening of its overall position in the government. A determination to avoid new friction with the Army and Air Force and a sensitivity to any further loss of power became major preoccupations of the Navy Minister.[50]

Within the Army, the debate over the statute also had repercussions. Many Army officers, including a majority of the current generals, viewed with concern the role of the Navy in the government. Their attitude was due in part to differences in political and economic outlook. These Army officers tended to be more nationalistic than their Navy counterparts, and therefore more inclined to sympathize with the kind of program that Arturo Frondizi was associated with. But the attitudes of these Army officers also reflected a historic bias, a reluctance to accept the Navy as anything but a junior partner. The facts that the Navy had been acquiring new equipment to beef up its air and marine components, that Navy officers held

[49] For the text of the political party statute as finally accepted by all members of the Junta Militar, see Decree-Law No. 19,044, Oct. 16, 1956. On the internal controversy that preceded the agreement, for the Navy viewpoint, "Suceso del estatuto de los partidos políticos," Hartung Diary, pp. 41–43. For the successful Army effort to shape the final result, I am indebted to General (Ret.) Juan E. Guglialmelli for providing me copies of the following documents: "Antecedentes a los proyectos de estatuto partidos políticos," which was circulated among senior officers prior to their September 3, 1956, meeting; and "Informe a S.E. El Señor Ministro Secretario de Estado de Ejército," dated September 6 and presented by Army Commander-in-Chief, General Francisco Zerda.

[50] Hartung Diary, pp. 41–46. See especially the Sept. 15 entry entitled "Apreciación de la situación."

key positions in the police and other agencies, and that it now had pressed for its own version of a political party statute raised fears about its ultimate aims. To these Army officers, it seemed that the Navy was planning to grow at the Army's expense and take over its place in the scheme of things.[51]

The contrast between this perception, which viewed the Navy as an aggressive force seeking to dominate the government, and the self-image of Navy leaders, who saw themselves in a defensive posture trying to retain a hard-won share in the decision-making process, was a notable feature of the confused and confusing situation that preceded and accompanied the military crisis that burst out in November 1956.

A major political development that contributed to that crisis was the government's decision, announced by President Aramburu in a speech given at Tucumán on October 26, that elections to a constituent assembly utilizing a proportional representation system would be held prior to the general elections already promised for the end of 1957. This announcement brought sharp protests from the UCR; from the Frondizi supporters, who saw it as a move to renege on the promise of general elections on the very eve of the party convention that was expected to nominate Frondizi; and also from the rival Radical forces, who opposed any deviation from the Sáenz Peña electoral system as giving too much voice to the smaller parties. Some critics saw the constituent assembly decision as a device to hold a trial run that might convince the government to prolong itself in power indefinitely, rather than run the risk of the general election.[52]

The announcement of the decision to hold the constituent assembly elections had repercussions within the military. A group of nationalist staff officers in the Army Ministry, apparently without the knowledge of Ossorio Arana, tried to blame the Navy for the decision in an effort to stir up officers in interior garrisons and thus generate pressure for a renewed government commitment to the original

[51] This is very much the concern reflected in the anonymously prepared twenty-page mimeographed pamphlet, "La verdad sobre los relevos de los altos mandos del ejército," pp. 3–4. This pamphlet circulated late in 1956 and from internal evidence was prepared by (or with the assistance of) General Francisco Zerda, Army Commander-in-Chief until his ouster on November 22.

[52] The weekly magazine *Qué*, now supporting Dr. Frondizi's presidential aspirations, frequently voiced such complaints. See the issues of Oct. 30, 1956, pp. 4–5; Nov. 6, 1956, p. 4; and Feb. 5, 1957, p. 4.

timetable.[53] At about the same time, attempts were made to exploit anti-Navy feelings in both the Army and Air Force through the circulation of apocryphal documents said to be secret Navy plans for establishing its political hegemony. A so-called "Plan Cangallo" that surfaced around October 27 presented as Navy objectives the abolition of the Junta Militar, the appointment of Admiral Rial as Interior Minister, the ouster of Ossorio Arana and Julio Krause as Army and Air Force Ministers, and the "prevention at all costs of the Radical convention scheduled for November 9 where Frondizzi [sic] expects to consecrate his candidacy."[54] In reality, the Navy Minister placed great importance on the strengthening of the Junta Militar as the key to Navy influence; he was in no way anxious to see Rial play a greater political role; and, as shall be shown below, he would throw his weight behind Ossorio Arana rather than against him.[55]

Although the generally conservative Navy leaders had no liking for what Arturo Frondizi stood for, their role in the decision to hold the constituent assembly elections before the general elections was greatly exaggerated, if not deliberately misrepresented, by nationalist Army officers. When the idea of a constitutional reform was first brought up in the Junta Militar, Navy Minister Hartung, as well as Army Minister Ossorio Arana, both opposed it. It was President Aramburu who introduced the idea early in July and it was he, together with Vice-President Rojas, who was its most consistent supporter. The Tucumán announcement of October 26, including the provision for proportional representation, was, as far as can be de-

[53] Hartung Diary, p. 48; interview with General Guglialmelli. I am indebted to the latter for furnishing me with copies of controversial telegrams that were sent via the Army Intelligence Service (SIE) communications network to interior garrisons. The author of the telegrams, a Lieut. Colonel Pasqual Ypoliti, disclaimed any intention to create division within the armed forces, but President Aramburu thought otherwise and ordered a shakeup in the Army Ministry staff.

[54] General Guglialmelli, who kindly furnished me with a typed copy of the Plan Cangallo, stated that he received his copy from Luis Pablo Pardo on October 27, 1956, at 2300 hours (interview, May 14, 1970). Admiral (Ret.) Rojas, on the other hand, stated that Ossorio Arana, shortly prior to his death, told him "that the author of the Plan Cangallo was the present General Guglialmelli" (interview, May 29, 1970).

[55] Hartung Diary, p. 45. In his Sept. 15, 1956, entry entitled "Apreciación de la situación," the Navy Minister listed as one of the measures to reduce interservice friction "to avoid having Rial deal directly with the Military Cabinet [evitar la intervención directa de Rial en tratos con el Gabinete militar]." Hartung's concern with preserving the Junta Militar is reflected throughout the diary.

termined, Aramburu's personal decision, to which the Junta Militar, consulted a few days before, made no objection.[56]

Having made the decision to move in a political direction that nationalist Army officers found disquieting, President Aramburu now addressed himself to the task of asserting firm control over the Army. The final months of a year were a normal time for effecting retirements and reassignments; yet this year, because of the heated political atmosphere, Army officers were more than normally apprehensive about what to expect and more sensitive than ever to rumors about impending changes. And rumors there were. Civilians with contacts in the Casa Rosada, and even Navy officers, seemed to know more about what was to happen than the highest-ranking Army generals, including the Commander-in-Chief, General Francisco Zerda. Despite personal denials from the President that he had made any decisions, General Zerda continued to be bombarded by rumors that heads were to roll, his own included. The assurances of the Army Minister, Ossorio Arana, that he would not agree to such changes did little to assuage the malaise that swept the ranks of the generals, a malaise that reached new heights when they learned on November 21 that at an open-air rally the night before, Dr. Arturo Mathov, the Unionist Radical, had publicly labeled a number of generals as Nazis and neofascists.[57]

What followed has been variously described, depending on the viewpoint, as a "gorilla plot" to liquidate the nationalist officers in the Army, or a "nationalist plot" to terminate liberal influence in the government and restore the Army to its traditional hegemonic role.[58] In view of the confusing events of previous days and weeks, events that are hard to explain when viewed as separate happenings—as, for example, the exaggerated attacks on the Navy and the surfacing of documents, on the one hand, or the public denunciations of Army traditions, the campaign of rumors, and the attacks on the generals, on the other—a case can be made for the simultaneous existence of

[56] Hartung Diary, pp. 332–33. The Navy Ministry's opposition to having the constitution reformed prior to the general elections was later acknowledged by the pro-Frondizi magazine, *Qué*, Feb. 5, 1957, p. 4.

[57] "La verdad sobre los relevos de los altos mandos del ejército," pp. 19–14.

[58] For the "gorilla plot" interpretation, see *ibid.*, *passim*; for the "nationalist plot" explanation, see "Crisis en Ejército en Noviembre de 1956," Hartung Diary, pp. 47–49.

both plots. What is more likely, however, is that the internal struggle for power and predominance that had been wracking the Army and affecting the government of the Liberating Revolution since its inception could no longer be contained with minor adjustments.

The night of November 21 saw military tensions erupt into open confrontation between Army Minister Ossorio Arana, supported by President Aramburu and the Navy leadership, on the one hand, and the principal Army commanders led by their Commander-in-Chief, General Francisco Zerda, on the other. The confrontation arose when the generals comprising the Army promotion board abandoned their assigned tasks to talk about the Mathov attack and Ossorio Arana's weakness in defending the Army's interest. After hearing from General Zerda and Chief of Staff Guillermo Alonso that the Army Minister that very day had complained of the tremendous pressures on him and expressed his intention to resign, the assembled generals agreed unanimously that he had been a failure. They thereupon adopted a resolution, with only two of the twenty senior officers present dissenting, to inform Ossorio Arana that the "high command of the Army had lost confidence in him" and to request that if he had not already done so, he should submit his resignation to the President. General Zerda, who was not present at this phase of the meeting, endorsed the resolution and undertook to deliver the request himself.[59]

What followed certainly did not conform to the anticipation of the commanders. Instead of meekly accepting their request, Ossorio Arana struck back. With the explicit encouragement of the President, with the support of loyal troop commanders including Lieut. Colonel Alejandro Lanusse of the Grenadier Regiment, and with the cooperation of the Navy, which put on a show of strength by placing its units on alert and moving the fleet toward Buenos Aires, Ossorio Arana notified General Zerda that he was relieved of his post. Taking over as Commander-in-Chief in addition to his ministerial duties, Ossorio Arana then proceeded to summon, one by one, the superior officers who had requested his resignation, relieve them of their military assignments, and send them to their respective homes.[60]

[59] "La verdad sobre los relevos de los altos mandos del ejército," pp. 14–17.
[60] *Ibid.*, p. 18; Hartung Diary, pp. 50–55.

The vigor with which Ossorio Arana reacted to their collective demarche apparently caught these generals by surprise, for they made no immediate move to resist. Later, however, meeting in a private dwelling, the ousted generals put together a hasty plan for restoring General Zerda to the post of Commander-in-Chief and getting rid of Ossorio Arana. The plan called for each of the ex-commanders to return to his former command and seize control; General Zerda, meanwhile, would establish a command post at the Colegio Militar and from there send telegrams to all Army units advising them that "General Aramburu and his Commander-in-Chief General Zerda are taking charge of the Army." Apparently they counted on the resulting confusion to enable them to gain physical control of enough of the Army to confront Aramburu with the choice of appointing a new Army Minister or facing something worse.[61]

Fortunately for the President, the plan was revealed before it went into action. On November 23, two of the generals, Jorge Nocetti Campos and Imaz, paid a visit to the Air Minister, Julio Krause, to request the neutrality of the Air Force in the impending crunch. Krause, despite his sympathy for the generals' nationalist outlook, and despite a personal feeling that the Navy somehow was behind the whole crisis, remained loyal to Aramburu and informed him of the plot. The ousted generals were now placed under arrest pending an investigation of the plot, and a kind of calm descended on the Army.[62] It is perhaps worthy of note that as a result of a nationwide printers' strike that began on November 13, no newspapers or magazines appeared throughout the crisis and only on November 24 was the general public made aware of its existence.

The November 1956 confrontation put an end to the series of intra-Army clashes that had had their principal roots in political or ideological differences. The ouster of the most prominent nationalist generals—seventeen were placed in retirement—and the relegation to remote interior garrisons of other officers who had used their assignments in Buenos Aires to pressure for their political viewpoint

---

[61] "Fin de la crisis de Noviembre en el Ejército," Hartung Diary, pp. 60–61.

[62] *Ibid.*, pp. 61–62. Coincident with the ouster of seventeen active duty generals, two retired nationalist generals, Leon Bengoa and Juan J. Uranga, former members of the Lonardi government, were detained on suspicion of plotting. They were to remain under arrest for almost a year.

left the Army largely in the hands of officers who were content to play a more passive role vis-à-vis the policy-making process.[63]

This did not mean that the Army was completely free of political intrigue or that a high level of professional discipline was restored. It did mean that the new squabbles that ruffled the calm of the officer corps derived primarily from personal rivalries and ambitions. A contributory factor was the existence of cliques based on prior experiences, as, for example, among the reincorporated field grade officers, many of whom were cavalrymen.[64] The task of creating an esprit de corps in an Army that had undergone so many shocks in the last several years was not an easy one to accomplish. Neither was the restoration of patterns of behavior based on Army regulations. On more than one occasion in the next several months, Army Minister Ossorio Arana was forced to remind the officers of their obligation to respect hierarchy and the chain of command and to refrain from going over the heads of superiors. In the final analysis, however, Ossorio Arana was not an effective disciplinarian, and he was later to complain of his unhappiness at having to be the *verdugo* (hangman) of so many colleagues.[65]

With the appointment in December 1956 of a new Commander-in-Chief in the person of General Luis Bussetti, a cavalry veteran of the 1951 Menéndez coup and an officer with ties to some of the same circles as Ossorio Arana, it might be expected that the Army would finally achieve a degree of stability. The fact is that the relations between the Army Minister and the Army Commander-in-Chief were to deteriorate after only a few months. Eventually, in May 1957, a clash between them over Ossorio's manner of disciplining a cavalry general persuaded President Aramburu that the time had come to

---

[63] Actual retirement of the seventeen generals took place in batches of five, one, and eleven over the three-month period January to March 1957 (*Boletín Militar Reservado*, Nos. 3639, Jan. 24, 1957; 3642, Feb. 14, 1957; 3648, March 22, 1957). Eleven of these officers were experiencing forced retirement for the second time in their careers.

[64] Of the 24 field grade officers who were awarded general staff officer status at the close of 1956, fourteen were cavalry and all were reincorporated officers (*ibid.*, No. 3635, Dec. 1956).

[65] *Ibid.*, Nos. 3641, Feb. 7, 1957, and 3651, April 12, 1957, for the texts of general orders issued by Ossorio Arana; see also "Crisis General de Brigada Dn. Arturo Ossorio Arana," Hartung Diary, pp. 214, 217.

choose a new minister. Ignoring General Bussetti's obvious desire to fill the post himself, as well as the ambitions of the Army Undersecretary, General Luis Leguizamón Martínez, the President turned to a distinguished retired professional, the 66-year-old Lieut. General (Ret.) Víctor J. Majó, in the hope that he could restore discipline.[66] It was a good choice.

Ironically, one of the first victims of the new Army Minister's determination to discipline officers who violated regulations was General Bussetti himself. Relieved as Commander-in-Chief on May 22 for holding an unauthorized assembly of officers, he was forced into retirement a few weeks later.[67] In a further ironic twist, General Majó, with the President's approval, if not at his instigation, turned to Ossorio Arana to be the next Army Commander-in-Chief.[68] With this combination of General Majó, the man of experience and seniority as Minister, and General Ossorio Arana, the chief living symbol of the 1955 Córdoba uprising against Perón as Commander-in-Chief, President Aramburu at long last had a team capable of keeping the Army in order until the government turned over its powers to an elected successor.

While the Junta Militar continued to discuss major policy issues in the months that followed the November 1956 military crisis, it is evident that a subtle shift was taking place in the internal political balance. The collective decision-making process that had characterized General Aramburu's first year as President was giving way to a situation in which he was increasingly becoming the dominant force. On issues of importance, Aramburu did not hesitate to follow the advice of his immediate staff or his civilian ministers rather than that of his military colleagues. Undoubtedly, the experience acquired from a year in office had increased his confidence in his own judgment; but his growing independence of the Junta Militar may also be ascribed to the changed situation within the Army, where he now

[66] Hartung Diary, pp. 215–27.

[67] "Consecuencias de la renuncia del señor general dn. Arturo Ossorio Arana," Hartung Diary, pp. 226–28, entry dated May 23, 1957. General Majó assumed the post of Army Commander-in-Chief as well as Army Minister on May 22, and Bussetti was formally retired on June 4 (*Boletín Militar Reservado*, Nos. 3657, May 22, 1957; and 3659, June 7, 1957).

[68] Ossorio was named Army Commander-in-Chief on July 17 (*Boletín Militar Reservado*, No. 3666, July 18, 1957).

enjoyed far greater ascendancy than when he was elevated to the presidency in 1955.

As a consequence of his increased control over the Army, President Aramburu's relations with the Navy also underwent change. Ironically, the Navy leaders, especially Vice-President Rojas and Admiral Hartung, by assisting the President in coping with the November 1956 Army crisis, contributed unintentionally to a weakening of their own influence. For, as noted earlier in this chapter, it was through the functions of the Junta Militar that the Navy exercised its main political influence, and any diminution in the authority of that body meant a corresponding lessening in the Navy's ability to shape policy.

The evidence that the Navy was no longer in a position to assert the influence that it had enjoyed in the first year of Aramburu's presidency may be seen in a series of developments that took place at the close of 1956 and the beginning of 1957. The first, which was itself a symptom of the changing situation, was Admiral Rojas's sudden decision to resign from the vice-presidency. Never made public, this decision was communicated in a long letter of December 16 to Admiral Hartung. A firm believer in the concept of shared leadership, Rojas was sensitive to the fact that the President did not seek out his collaboration or make use of the work that his staff produced; proud but strong-willed, Rojas felt uncomfortable in a role in which he appeared to have greater influence than he actually had. Believing that there were personal factors that explained what he regarded as Aramburu's lack of confidence in him, Rojas asked the Navy, which had named him to the vice-presidency, to accept his resignation and allow him to serve in a nonpolitical post.[69]

Whether Admiral Rojas seriously intended his resignation to be accepted or was simply giving vent to the periodic sense of frustration that all vice-presidents must feel at one time or another is not clear. In any case, Admiral Hartung made no move to accept the resignation. Rather, he urged Rojas not to abandon his post but instead to concentrate on eliminating sources of friction through ministerial and staff changes and on working to strengthen the influence of the Junta Militar. Hartung stressed that there could be only one visible head of the government, but he was confident that the Pres-

[69] "Carta a S.E. el señor Ministro de Marina, Buenos Aires, 16 de diciembre de 1956," Hartung Diary, pp. 63–68.

ident wanted and needed the collaboration of the Vice-President and the three armed forces.[70]

The Navy Minister's confidence was itself shaken by the manner in which President Aramburu carried out the sweeping cabinet changes that were initiated on January 25, 1957. Although it had been a matter of general understanding that ministerial shifts were in the offing, the President did not bring the issue before a meeting of the Junta Militar. It was the President himself who decided which ministers to replace and it was he, in consultation with certain advisors, who took the initiative in choosing their successors. To be sure, he discussed the proposed changes with Admirals Rojas and Hartung, but not with Air Minister Krause and only in part with the Army Minister. Quite possibly, the President was hoping to provoke the Air Minister into resigning, but the Navy leaders, despite their own differences with Krause, were quite sensitive to the fact that if he were to go and Aramburu were to name his replacement, the power of the Junta Militar would be further weakened. Admirals Rojas and Hartung accordingly reminded the President of his obligations to share power under the accord of November 13, 1955, and obtained his promise to have the Junta Militar participate in all future designations of cabinet ministers and undersecretaries. The Navy leaders, however, continued to believe that the President's promise was not sincere. They realized now that they would have to "keep their antennas raised and their hands on the valves" to prevent further debilitation of the Junta Militar.[71]

Although the Aramburu government could not ignore economic and social questions, especially in view of the greater-than-anticipated inflation, the continuing drainage of foreign reserves, and the intensification of labor unrest, the principal issues absorbing the attention of the highest authorities of the government, the political parties, and the public at large were political. These issues related to the manner in which the government proposed to implement its stated political plan. As of early 1957, it was understood that it planned to hold two elections, one for an assembly to reform the

[70] "Analisis de la carta del Almirante Rojas de fecha 16/12/56," Hartung Diary, pp. 69–75.
[71] "Apreciación al 1° de febrero de 1957 luego de la crisis ministerial de enero," *ibid.*, pp. 81–89; Decrees No. 1086–88, Jan. 26, 1957; No. 1115 and 1155, Jan. 30, 1957; and 1277, Feb. 1957.

constitution, the other, a general election, for the civilian authorities to whom power would eventually be transferred. What remained unclear was the timing of these events: When would the constituent assembly elections take place? Would the government fulfill its pledge, made in the name of all the armed forces, to call the general elections before the end of 1957? When would the new authorities take office? Equally unclear was whether the government's frequently repeated promise to remain politically neutral would in fact be honored in view of the political realities.

One of these realities was the persistence, despite government efforts to redirect it, of a mass of Argentine voters still loyal to Perón and responsive to directives issued by him through his clandestine organization. In advance of an actual election, the extent of this loyal mass could not be defined, but a realistic assessment of the impact of government policies would have had to conclude that the workers, who comprised the bulk of this mass, had little reason to feel sympathy for the government or any politicians identified with it. A second political reality was the emergence of a formidable opposition movement that sought to capitalize on Peronist discontent to promote the candidacy of Arturo Frondizi.

Although the Frondizi wing of the Radical Party had originally accepted the elevation of General Aramburu in place of the ousted General Lonardi and continued to maintain its representation in the National Consultative Board, even after the executions in June 1956, that wing began to transform itself into a vigorous critic of the Liberating Revolution. Contributing to this evolution was the political alliance that was established between Arturo Frondizi and the economist-journalist-industrialist Rogelio Frigerio.[72] As director of the influential weekly *Qué*, which welcomed to its pages the contributions of former Perón supporters, Frigerio mounted a systematic attack on the policies of the government, depicting it as a retrograde instrument of the oligarchy and of international interests. Attacking the government for its punitive actions against Peronists, for economic measures that favored agriculture over industry, and for intended

[72] Frigerio met Frondizi for the first time in January 1956; shortly thereafter the former took over the editorship of the weekly *Qué* and in his first issue featured Frondizi on the cover (interview with Rogelio Frigerio, March 23, 1977; also Díaz, [55], pp. 31–32; *Qué*, Feb. 29, 1956).

sellouts of Argentine control over natural energy resources, Frigerio sought to exploit the concerns of industrialists and workers, of nationalists and Catholics, and of members of the armed forces, to create a constituency for Frondizi. This constituency was intended to transcend Radical Party loyalists and comprise a multiclass movement committed to a program of national development through industrialization.[73]

The efforts to create this constituency, including calls on the government to release political and labor prisoners, denunciations of its intelligence agents for torturing prisoners, and criticism for the executions of the previous June, were a challenge that President Aramburu could not, or would not, ignore. Encouraged by his close advisors, of whom the most important at this time was the recently promoted General Leguizamón Martínez, a man with close links to anti-Frondizi Radical leaders, Aramburu entrusted key cabinet posts in the January 25 shuffle to men who would work to defeat the Frondizi-led forces. Dr. Carlos Alconada Aramburú, the new Interior Minister, and Dr. Acdeel Salas, the new Education and Justice Minister, were both associates of Ricardo Balbín, Frondizi's principal rival at the Tucumán convention; and there is good reason to believe that the President had specifically asked Balbín to suggest the candidates for these posts. The Ministry of Communications, with its control of the postal service, was given to Dr. Angel Cabral, an affiliate of the equally anti-Frondizi Sabattinista wing of the Radical party, while Dr. Tristan Guevara, a Progressive Democrat, was appointed Minister of Labor.[74]

In appointing anti-Frondizi politicians to take charge of these ministries that controlled vital state functions, and with their extensive opportunities for patronage, President Aramburu gave to

[73] Frigerio and his group of associates came to be known as the *desarrollistas* (developmentalists). Their criticisms of the Aramburu government and the presentation of their views on political, social, economic, and international issues filled the pages of *Qué* and of the special monthly supplements that began to appear in anticipation of the elections in February 1957. The authors of these supplements included Arturo Frondizi, Raúl Scalabrini Ortiz, and Arturo Jauretche, the latter two, well-known nationalist writers who had supported Perón.

[74] Hartung Diary, pp. 83–84. General Leguizamón Martínez, at this time serving as Undersecretary of the Army, was son-in-law of a Radical Party veteran of the Unionist wing, Eduardo Laurencena. Leguizamón was a former commander of the La Plata-based Second Infantry Division and had ample opportunity to get to know the Radical Party leaders in Buenos Aires province.

his earlier pledge of political neutrality a new meaning that was not lost on those most directly concerned. While Frondizi supporters intensified their charges of political favoritism, the various anti-Frondizi Radical Party factions, Unionists, Balbinistas, Sabattinistas, and Rabanalistas, overcame their mutual differences to form a new political party, the Unión Cívica Radical del Pueblo (UCRP) which would henceforth compete with the Frondizi-led Unión Cívica Radical Intransigente (UCRI) in the forthcoming elections.[75]

But even before the dates for such elections could be fixed, President Aramburu was confronted with two crises, one involving the Navy, the other the Air Force, that revealed that his new policy was looked upon with deep suspicion among military officers in both these services. The Navy crisis arose early in March when a series of private letters to the President written by Admiral Arturo Rial was published in the pages of a political weekly. Rial, who had been the moving force in organizing the anti-Perón revolution in the Navy, had assumed the self-appointed role of watchdog over the revolutionary government. From his post as Navy Undersecretary, he maintained a network of observers in the various ministries and provincial governments, a situation that was neither hidden from nor unresented by their designated heads, but his personal prestige and the general support of the Navy had hitherto insured him against removal.[76]

Now, however, with the publication of the letters, President Aramburu demanded Rial's ouster. For whereas four of the letters criticized acts of commission or omission by the Minister of Commerce and Industry and the Minister of Public Works, both of them holdovers incidentally from the previous cabinet, the fifth letter denounced violations of the pledge of political neutrality. "The acts of the components of this Revolutionary Government," wrote Admiral Rial, "have to be adjusted inevitably to the Basic Directives of December 7, 1955. It is not even permitted 'to be indifferent' to the point where the confidence which it should merit in fulfilling its pledge to neutrality is compromised."[77] Although the specific target

---

[75] *Qué*, Feb. 5, 1957, pp. 3 and 6; Feb. 19, 1957, p. 6.

[76] "Posición del Señor Almirante Rial," Hartung Diary, pp. 90–92.

[77] Letter of Feb. 12, 1957. The texts of all five letters are given in Hartung Diary, pp. 133–37. The political weekly that published them was Raúl Damonte Taborda's *Resistencia Popular*, an antigovernment organ.

of Rial's epistolary criticism was the interventor-governor of Buenos Aires province, the fact that the Minister of Interior was his immediate superior implied that the criticism also embraced that official, if not the President himself, who was responsible for appointing him.[78]

Aramburu's insistence, once the letters got into the public domain on March 5, that Rial would have to go, and that unless he did, he himself would resign from the presidency raised the crisis to major proportions. At a meeting of the Junta Militar and again in direct discussion with the President, Admirals Rojas and Hartung flatly opposed the ouster of Rial, offering instead a compromise in the form of a temporary leave of absence from his post, a 30-day house arrest for having shown the letters to friends, and a press release announcing an investigation into how the letters got into the press. Aramburu, however, was adamant in insisting on Rial's resignation, arguing that anything less would leave him "without prestige" in the eyes of the Army.[79] For three days from March 8 to 10, the Navy's senior officers, admirals, and captains met to consider alternatives that ranged from having Admiral Rojas, as Vice-President, assume the presidency if Aramburu insisted on resigning, to having the Navy withdraw from the government and limit itself to military functions. Finally, after President Aramburu talked personally with a number of admirals, support for Rial's continuation in his post weakened. The majority concluded that the Navy was in no position, should Aramburu resign, to support Rojas's claim to the presidency in the face of anticipated Army and Air Force opposition; that Aramburu's continuation in office was to be preferred to any of the generals whose names were being mentioned as possible successors; and that the issues at stake did not justify the risks of taking the country into civil war.[80] The crisis was resolved when the senior Navy officers voted that Rial should resign as Undersecretary, but with the understanding that the President should be urged to take steps to restore

[78] Rial's specific charge was that the interventor, General Emilio Bonnecarrère, had requested the resignation of all municipal interventor-mayors and was asking Balbinista Radicals for names of individuals to replace the politically neutral incumbents.

[79] "Asunto Almirante Rial," Hartung Diary, pp. 138–39.

[80] *Ibid.*, pp. 139–43; Perren Memoirs, pp. 321–23. The generals who were mentioned as possible successors were Benjamín Menéndez, Luis Bussetti, and José Francisco Suárez.

the appearance and reality of the government's political neutrality and move as promptly as possible to hold elections.[81] The resolution of the crisis for all of its crosscurrents left Aramburu in a stronger position than before, for he had gotten rid of a burr that had annoyed members of his administration and in the process had demonstrated to Admirals Rojas and Hartung that they could not always count on the unified support of their own senior officers.[82]

The Air Force crisis that confronted the Aramburu government from March 30 to April 2 was directly linked to the task of defining the political calendar and fixing the dates for the two elections. In view of the President's desire to announce the calendar in a nationwide speech scheduled for March 30, the Junta Militar, in a series of sessions that began on March 28, explored the issue on the basis of an initial proposal made by the Minister of Interior. Dr. Alconada's proposal called for holding the constituent assembly elections on July 28, 1957, the general election on March 2, 1958, and the transfer of power by June 20, 1958. His rationale was that technical reasons made it impossible to hold the first election prior to July 28, that the constituent assembly, if it began its sessions on September 1, would need until mid-November to complete its work, and that a general election in December would be inconvenient both because it was the harvest and tourist seasons and because the political parties needed a three-month period in which to campaign.[83] Air Minister Julio Krause alone of the military ministers objected strenuously to the proposed calendar as a violation of the July 6, 1956, pledge made by President Aramburu on behalf of all the armed forces to call the general elections for the last quarter of 1957. Not even a compromise solution, which General Aramburu, Admiral Rojas, and the Army and Navy Ministers accepted, to have the general election on February 23, 1958, and the transfer of power on

[81] Hartung Diary, pp. 129–30, 143–44.

[82] Admiral Rial, after serving out his 30-day detention, was rewarded with a prestigious assignment, Commander of the Plata Naval Area. Ironically, during the period of his arrest, Rial was depicted by the Frondicista *Qué* (issues of March 5, 12, 19, 1957) as a champion of electoral fair play and an opponent of foreign economic interests, while nationalist generals, smarting over their own ouster the previous November, hoped to find in him an ally for a conspiratorial movement to oust President Aramburu (Hartung Diary, p. 144).

[83] "Reuniones realizadas entre el 28 de marzo al 2 de abril de 1957," Hartung Diary, p. 168.

May 1, 1958, could overcome the refusal of Krause to give his assent. Whether the Air Minister was acting as the instrument of the Frondicistas, as the Minister of Interior seemed to believe, or was reflecting the influence of civilian nationalists, as the Navy Minister thought, or was, as he claimed, only bespeaking the feelings of his fellow Air Force officers that their sense of honor did not permit them to endorse a violation of the pledged word, the Air Force position threatened the unity of the armed forces. No amount of persuasion by the Navy and Army Ministers that the honor of their forces was not affected by a 50-day delay in the holding of the general election could overcome Krause's determination to dissent from the decision.[84]

Whatever the Air Force officers hoped to accomplish, and possibly it was to delay any firm commitment to specific dates, President Aramburu went ahead with his March 30 radio address announcing the political calendar as agreed to by the Army and Navy. The Air Ministry, for its part, issued a remarkable manifesto explaining the position of the Air Force and announcing that henceforth Minister Krause would no longer participate in the Junta Militar, but would confine himself to his ministerial duties. The Air Force, the manifesto pointed out, would no longer share the responsibility of governing the nation, but this did not "signify withdrawal of its support from the provisional government in every other order, particularly in the permanent vigilance against the danger of the rise of any totalitarianism."[85]

This situation, in which the Air Force was in open dissidence with a major policy pronouncement of the government, was one that the latter could ill afford to permit. President Aramburu ordered the withdrawal of the manifesto, an order that was only partially complied with, and asked for Krause's resignation. The problem, however, was to find a successor. Air Force brigadiers urged the retention of Krause, something that the President was determined not to do. An offer of the post to the Air Force Commander-in-Chief, Brigadier Guillermo Zinny, was initially accepted, and a time for his swearing-in ceremony publicly announced, only to have him subsequently decline on the grounds that the Air Force officers would not obey his

[84] *Ibid.*, pp. 169–74.
[85] The text is reproduced, *ibid.*, pp. 174–76.

orders. The President asked the Air Force brigadiers to select their own minister, but again and again they put forth Krause. Finally, after Aramburu had to postpone an announced swearing-in ceremony three different times, and amid rumors that junior officers at the various air bases were about to revolt, Commodore Eduardo McLoughlin, a close friend of ex-Minister Krause, took over the post on April 2. The entire episode revealed that within the Air Force there were sizable elements quite prepared to discredit the Aramburu government, but that without cooperation from the other services they lacked the capacity to effect its ouster or even a change in its basic policies.[86]

The elections for the constituent assembly went off as scheduled, under military supervision, on July 28, 1957. The preceding campaign, however, was characterized by denunciations from Frondicista and nationalist circles that the government was fabricating directives in Perón's name to advise his followers to cast blank ballots. The purpose of this alleged activity was to take away votes from those parties, especially the Frondizi-led UCRI, which had proclaimed their opposition to the constituent assembly and were demanding the immediate holding of the general elections. The Frondicista magazine *Qué,* for its part, embarked on a campaign to persuade Peronist voters that the way to oppose the government was to vote for the UCRI. Intellectuals of considerable prestige in Peronist circles, Raúl Scalabrini Ortiz and Arturo Jauretche, published statements in *Qué* denouncing blank balloting as a vote for the oligarchy.[87] Such statements, however, were made without authorization from Perón himself. The exiled leader was in fact urging his followers through his own clandestine channels to show their resistance to the "tyranny" by either abstaining, spoiling ballots, or voting blank. But when Perón's operations chief, John W. Cooke, wrote letters to *Qué* and to the nationalist weekly *Azul y Blanco* affirming the authenticity of Perón's directives, their respective editors refused to publish them.[88] Little wonder, then, at the confusion

[86] *Ibid.,* pp. 176–86.

[87] For the allegations by Frondicista and nationalist circles and for the articles of Scalabrini Ortiz and Jauretche, see the issues of *Qué,* July 9, 16, 23, 26 (special issue), 1957.

[88] On Perón's directives and Cooke's efforts to reaffirm them, *Perón-Cooke correspondencia* [72], I, 210–20.

surrounding the July 28 elections or at the varying interpretations given to the results.

Those results showed that, although no party received an absolute majority, the pro-government Radicals, the UCRP, received the largest number cast for any single party, 2,107,000, or 24.2 percent of the total; in second place was the UCRI, which received 1,848,000, or 21.2 percent. The controversial blank vote category was the largest of all, however, with 2,116,000 votes, or 24.3 percent. The remaining 2,600,000 votes were scattered among a large number of smaller parties headed by the Socialists with 6 percent and the Christian Democrats with 4.8 percent. In the distribution of seats in the constituent assembly, the parties that favored the constitutional reform received 120 seats; those that were opposed won 85.[89]

The Aramburu government saw the July election as a success because the parties supporting its political plan, provided they could agree with one another, would hold a working majority in the forthcoming assembly. Moreover, since the three great factions into which the electorate divided, the UCRP, the UCRI, and the Peronists as measured by the blank votes, were all roughly equal, none was in a position to impose its will on the provisional government.[90] To Juan Perón in his Caracas exile, however, who considered not only the blank ballots, but the abstentions, the spoiled ballots, and those votes that in the confusion had gone to other parties, the results were evidence "that the Peronist electorate is today as firm as in its best times" and "a very satisfactory proof for us which demonstrates our cohesion, discipline, and organization, as well as the firmness of the intransigent position we are maintaining."[91] To Arturo Frondizi and Rogelio Frigerio, on the other hand, the results were proof that it was not sufficient to campaign for the support of Peronist voters, but would be necessary to reach an understanding with Juan Perón.[92]

[89] Zalduendo [301], pp. 31–32; *Qué*, Aug. 6, 1957, p. 3.

[90] "Comentarios sobre las elecciones del 28 de julio de 1957," Hartung Diary, pp. 248–51.

[91] Letter, Juan Perón to John W. Cooke, Caracas, Aug. 5, 1957, *Perón-Cooke correspondencia* [72], I, 236.

[92] On August 28, 1957, a month after the election, Cooke wrote to Perón: "Alicia will inform you of the visits we are receiving from friends of Frondizi. He is anxious for me to become enthusiastic over his proposals because he wants me to be an enthusiastic intermediary" (*ibid.*, I, 247). For an account of the initial overtures by Frondizi supporters to Cooke, see Prieto [77], pp. 71–73. Américo Ghioldi, a member of the National Consultative Board at that time,

Within the miliary, the election results had no perceptible impact save in the Air Force, where ex-Minister Krause and other pro-Frondizi or nationalist officers still exercised considerable influence through the new Minister McLoughlin and the Air Commander-in-Chief Brigadier Angel Peluffo. Encouraged apparently by the evidence that the Frondizi-led forces did not constitute a majority, a group of rival Air Force senior officers took the offensive, precipitating an internal crisis that enabled President Aramburu, backed by the Army and Navy Ministers, to intervene. McLoughlin was asked to submit his resignation, and the President named Commodore Jorge Landaburu, one of the anti-Krause officers, as the new Air Minister. The resulting personnel changes placed members of this group in other key Air Force posts, reducing the possibility for Frondicistas, on the one hand, and nationalist political groups, on the other, to exercise influence on government decisions through allies in the Air Force.[93]

With only seven months remaining before the general election promised for February 23, 1958, the provisional government found it increasingly difficult to disassociate the policy-making process from electoral considerations. This was especially evident in the handling of labor problems. Although its original goal had been to destroy Peronist control of the trade unions through the intervention of the CGT and its affiliates and through the disqualification of pre-1955 labor leaders from holding trade union posts, the process of normalizing the unions through internal elections in 1957 proved that goal difficult if not impossible to achieve. Peronist-oriented leaders gained direct control of the key national industrial unions, and even in the commercial, transportation, and government service sectors where independents were elected to the top posts, the rank and file were often responsive to Peronist influence. That influence, which was exercised through a shadow organization of "disqualified" CGT leaders, exploited legitimate labor grievances to provoke work-

---

recalls that a fellow member, López Serrot of the UCRI, told him privately that the very night of the election Frondizi, calculating the number of his own votes and those in blank, declared: "I have the next elections won." Ghioldi interpreted this to mean that Frondizi decided that very night to enter into a pact with Perón (interview, March 20, 1970).

[93] "Crisis de aeronautica entre los días 3 y 7 de agosto de 1957," Hartung Diary, pp. 252–59.

er unrest as preparation for the eventual revolutionary insurrection that Perón and his chief aides were working for. In the short term, they sought to rebuild their ascendancy over the labor movement and to harass the government through various demands backed up by strikes and acts of sabotage. Even the independent labor leaders were not immune to their tactics, and in order to maintain their own prestige in the eyes of the rank and file, they, too, adopted hardline positions in demanding the repeal of restrictive labor legislation and changes in economic and social policy. In September and October, the government found itself confronted with a rash of work stoppages culminating in two general strikes, the second of which found the independent leaders joining with the rival Peronist and other trade unionists in demanding wage increases to cope with the inflation.[94]

Within the government, a sharp division existed on how to respond to the labor pressure. President Aramburu and the civilian ministers tended to favor a soft policy, including the granting of some wage increases and the avoidance of actions that might exacerbate feelings. Vice-President Rojas, on the other hand, supported by Navy Minister Hartung, favored a hardline policy opposing wage increases not based on productivity increases as inflationary and urging the arrest of the "Peronist and Communist agitators" they felt were responsible for the labor unrest.[95]

The differing approaches to the labor problem were part of a broader disagreement in outlook, motivated by the impending general election, that threatened to produce an open split between the President and Vice-President early in October. To Vice-President Rojas, the President seemed to be evading the policy suggestions of the Junta Militar and relying more on the advice of his civilian ministers. On two occasions, one in connection with a proposal to outlaw the Communist Party, the other in connection with the issuance of

[94] For Peronist efforts to recover control of the trade unions see *Perón-Cooke correspondencia* [72], II, 15–19; for the views of government officials toward labor unrest, see "Crisis de Octubre" and "Problema Gremial," Hartung Diary, pp. 292–310.

[95] Hartung Diary, pp. 303–10. The justification for arrest was the violation of the provisions of Decree-Law No. 10,956 issued on Sept. 9, 1957. This law banned strikes in public service industries and stipulated that a majority of rank-and-file union affiliates had to give their approval to validate a strike in any other industry.

an arrest order for Peronist labor leaders, the President refused to issue decree-laws that had been prepared with his initial consent by the Junta Militar. In each case it was the Minister of Interior who had objected to the measures, and in each case the Vice-President suspected that political considerations had led Aramburu to repudiate the recommendations of the Junta Militar.[96]

Relations between the President and Vice-President approached the breaking point on October 6, when at a meeting at Olivos attended by the three military ministers and their undersecretaries, the general and the admiral angrily charged each other with actions that could impair the government's commitment to political neutrality in the holding of the general elections. Aramburu complained that the Rojas-initiated decision to arrest labor leaders was deliberately intended to provoke worker disturbances. Although Aramburu was apparently not more specific, he was alluding to the charges circulating in various quarters that the Vice-President was part of a movement to use worker unrest to justify the abandonment of the elections and the creation of a dictatorial regime that would hold onto power indefinitely. Rojas hotly denied this, and in turn charged the President with relying on civilian ministers who were openly using their offices to promote the political prospects of the UCRP and take away votes from Arturo Frondizi. Rojas urged the ouster of the Interior Minister, a move that President Aramburu was not willing to make.[97]

The President and Vice-President, despite the angry exchanges of this meeting, managed to maintain a public appearance of cordiality, but it is evident that they viewed one another's intentions with more

[96] *Ibid.*, pp. 292–95. The Junta Militar wanted to act on the basis of its power as a revolutionary body; the Interior Minister took the view that the government should respect constitutional limitations in ordering arrests. A compromise was reached in the issuance of a decree-law establishing a 30-day state of siege in the capital and Buenos Aires province and backdating it to cover arrests that had already been made.

[97] *Ibid.*, pp. 296–98. At this time rumors began to circulate in various circles that Admiral Rojas wanted to postpone the elections to remain in power. Rojas publicly and privately denied the allegations at the time (Hartung Diary, pp. 285, 308–9) and subsequently (interview, May 29, 1970). No firm evidence, moreover, has even been produced that he did in fact want to postpone the elections. Even Admiral Adolfo Estévez, who served directly under Admiral Rojas as Fleet Commander in 1957–58 and then was selected by President Frondizi as Navy Minister, insists that contrary to the general impression Rojas never sought to prevent Frondizi's election (interview, March 24, 1970).

than a little suspicion and that they had differing concepts of how to conduct the government in the months remaining before the election.[98]

These differences extended not only to specific policy measures, but to the legal character of the provisional government once the constituent assembly met in Santa Fe and voted to recognize the validity of the 1853 constitution and its various amendments, excluding those of 1949.[99] In effect, the assembly was ratifying the April 27, 1956, manifesto of the provisional government, but that manifesto had stipulated that the provisional government would adhere to the 1853 charter "insofar as it was not opposed to the goals of the revolution enunciated in the basic directives of December 7, 1955, and the necessities of the organization and conservation of the provisional government."[100] The question raised by the assembly's action was whether the provisional government still exercised revolutionary authority or had to conform to constitutional restraints.

President Aramburu, encouraged by his Minister of Interior, tended to the view that a "state of law" (*estado de derecho*) now prevailed. Vice-President Rojas, on the other hand, insisted that the provisional government owed its origins to revolutionary action and had not lost its character because of the vote of the constituent assembly. Underlying Rojas's opposition to the "state of law" was his fear that the accord of November 13, 1955, providing for government by the armed forces would no longer have any validity, that Aramburu would be free to act without any restraints by the Junta Militar, and that the Navy, which in Rojas's view had won the 1955 revolution, would lose its political role.[101]

Vice-President Rojas's apprehension about the possible change in the government's legal status was heightened by the plan of some members of the constituent assembly to conclude its session with a "spectacular ceremony" in which Aramburu and Rojas would appear

[98] Hartung Diary, pp. 382–84. The tensions between the two top leaders of the government could not be hidden from the public, especially after Vice-President Rojas, angered by the President's failure to consult the Junta Militar on certain judicial appointments, decided on Jan. 5, 1958, not to attend Government House ceremonies (*Qué*, Jan. 15, 1958, p. 5).

[99] This vote was taken on Sept. 23, 1957. For the extensive debates leading up to this action, see Convención Nacional Constituyente [4], I, 259–722.

[100] *Anales* [1], XVI-A, 2.

[101] Hartung Diary, pp. 344, 353.

before that body to swear allegiance to the reformed constitution and the assembly would designate them as *de jure* President and Vice-President. General Aramburu was attracted to this plan, apparently seeing in it a means of ratifying the acts of the provisional government, and thus obviating a future review by the next constitutional authorities. Admiral Rojas, however, was willing to go along with the plan only if the role and authority of the Junta Militar were also protected.[102]

The collapse of the constituent assembly itself, through its inability to form a quorum after October 25, made the *de jure* issue academic. From the very beginning, the assembly had suffered from the repudiation of the UCRI, whose 77 delegates, the largest single bloc, walked out on August 20, and from the inability of those who remained to overcome personal, partisan, and ideological differences. Unable to escape the pressures generated within and among the political parties by the forthcoming general election, the assembly managed to enact only one constitutional change, a declaration of labor and trade union rights, before the withdrawal of other members broke the quorum and reduced the body to impotence.[103]

The experience of the constituent assembly demonstrated the impracticality of trying to get agreement on fundamental political changes in an atmosphere characterized by the outlawing of what had been the country's majority party and by a bitter competition among the other parties to attract the votes of its followers. The hopes of those, like Vice-President Rojas, that the powers of the president could be weakened in favor of the legislature and judiciary and that provincial and municipal autonomy could be strengthened at the expense of the central government proved illusory in the face of the inability or unwillingness of the anti-Peronist and non-Peronist forces to overcome their own differences.[104]

With the issuance on November 15 of the official decree calling for

---

[102] *Ibid.*, pp. 353–57.

[103] For the text of this declaration, Convención Nacional Constituyente [4], II, 1668. The quorum needed to keep the convention going was broken by the successive withdrawals of National Intransigent Radical (Sabattinista) and Conservative delegates.

[104] Admiral Rojas's expectations from the constitutional reform are set forth in Hartung Diary, p. 331.

general elections on February 23, 1958, doubts held in certain quarters that elections would ever take place began to dissipate, and the country entered in earnest into the heated atmosphere of a presidential campaign. Although over a dozen parties proceeded to nominate candidates, it was generally recognized that the choice of the next president lay between the two men who had jointly comprised the Radical Party ticket in 1951, Ricardo Balbín, now the nominee of the UCRP, and Arturo Frondizi, the candidate of the UCRI.

Balbín, with close personal allies in the national government as well as in several provincial administrations, obviously counted on the advantages that would accrue to one who enjoyed the *calor oficial*. But as the official candidate, he had to bear the burden of identification with the controversial record of the Liberating Revolution. To his opponents he represented *continuismo*, the indefinite prolongation of the anti-Peronist measures of the military government and of its economic and social policies, policies that left the country with a higher inflation rate and lower foreign reserves than when Perón was overthrown, and with a working class that was resentful at the deterioration of its real wages and at the proscription of the political movement that had catered to its interests in the past.[105]

In these circumstances, it was not illogical that Arturo Frondizi should fashion his campaign so as to depict himself as the opponent of what the Liberating Revolution stood for. Calling for an end to ideological and political persecution and promising a broad amnesty for those charged with politically related offenses, Frondizi announced his intention to give a "national and popular" character to the economy and to integrate the working class into active participation in national life. His declared intention to govern with the most capable regardless of party, his carefully worked-out program of economic priorities with emphasis on the development of heavy industry, his responsiveness to Catholic concerns in the areas of family life and education, all served to broaden his appeal and to generate enthusiasm for his candidacy across traditional divisions and especially among the young. The crowds that turned out for his public appearances and the endorsements he received from national-

[105] "Solo hay dos caminos," *Qué*, Jan. 21, 1958, pp. 8–9.

ists, Catholics, former Peronists, and even the Argentine Communist Party demonstrated the effectiveness of his campaign.[106]

In view of the growing momentum of the Frondizi movement, pro-Balbín elements within the government gave serious thought to allowing Peronist candidates to run for election as a means of splitting Frondizi supporters. Early in January 1958, President Aramburu himself broached the idea of lifting the proscription on the Peronist Party to a meeting of naval officers at the Puerto Belgrano base. The reaction was almost uniformly negative, with only two of the senior officers present willing to consider the idea.[107]

Although nothing came of this, the government did permit a group of neo-Peronist parties, including the Unión Popular, Partido Blanco, Partido Populista, and Partido de los Trabajadores, to register with the electoral courts and to obtain the right to present candidates. Here again it might be noted the Navy was not at all in agreement, and, acting behind the scenes, protested sharply at the situation. Navy Minister Hartung, labeling these parties as simply the Peronist Party under other names, denounced their participation as a contradiction of the "Basic Directives" adopted by the Liberating Revolution. In a lengthy letter to President Aramburu, he set forth the Navy's view that the issues involved were moral and ethical as well as political and asked for an urgent meeting of the Junta Militar to decree the outright dissolution of those parties.[108] The Navy's hope that the Army and Air Force might share its position proved illusory, however, when the Junta Militar took up the question at its meetings on January 24 and 29. President Aramburu, supported by War Minister Majó and Air Minister Landaburu, rejected the Navy's proposal, expressing confidence that the Peronists were themselves divided and had no chance of winning.[109]

[106] For a typical Frondizi campaign statement see the interview published in the newly created UCRI weekly *País Unido,* Año I, No. 1, Nov. 26, 1957. Directed by Celestino Gelsi, *País Unido* was used to appeal to Radical Party affiliates, whereas Frigerio's *Qué* directed itself to nonparty sectors, especially Peronists, Nationalists, and Catholics.

[107] Perren Memoirs, p. 334; interview with Admiral (Ret.) Adolfo Estévez, March 24, 1970. The two naval officers who saw merit in the idea were Captain Francisco Manrique, Aramburu's chief of the Casa Militar, and Arturo Rial.

[108] Hartung Diary, pp. 385–91.

[109] *Ibid.,* pp. 392–93; also "Reunión del 24 de enero relativo a intervención partidos neo-peronistas en acto eleccionario del 23 de febrero," *ibid.,* pp. 395–97.

The basic differences within the Junta toward the election were never more clearly revealed than when its members responded to the Navy's concern that the blank voters of the July election might unite at Perón's instruction to support a common slate under a neo-Peronist label. President Aramburu, War Minister Majó, and Air Minister Landaburu took a pragmatic approach. They were prepared to accept a neo-Peronist victory in one or two provinces if the presidency and the general result were democratic; if, however, the neo-Peronists won a major victory, the election should be annulled. The Navy position, in contrast, was based on a consistent principle: No Peronists under any label should be allowed to run. Admirals Rojas and Hartung took the view that "it was immoral to allow the neo-Peronists to run, and then to rob them of the election if they won; that it was more decent to run the risk that they would cement their unity under proscription, and to hold a clean election with the democratic parties."[110]

President Aramburu's refusal to cut off the neo-Peronist parties a month before the election was linked to the belief that, by dividing former Peronist votes, they would contribute to a victory for the UCRP. Indeed, a general survey carried out at his request by SIDE, the presidential intelligence service, indicated at the end of January that Balbín's UCRP would win the election with 35 percent of the votes as against 20 percent for the UCRI; the rest of the votes would be scattered among the remaining parties with only 8 percent going to the neo-Peronists.[111]

The confidence that existed in and out of government circles in a Balbín victory began to wither early in February with the indications that Perón, now in Santo Domingo, was calling on Peronists who had accepted candidacies in the neo-Peronist parties to renounce them and was urging his followers "to prevent with their votes the continuista plans of the tyranny."[112] What could be read as an endorse-

---

[110] *Ibid.*, p. 392.

[111] *Ibid.*

[112] Quoted from a lengthy statement Perón released to the press on February 4. Neither the *New York Times* which carried the story on February 5 under the title "Perón Drops Plan for Blank Ballots" nor *La Prensa* in Buenos Aires which entitled its back-page account of the same day "Habría Trasmitido una Orden a sus Parciales El ex Tirano Prófugo" treated this Perón announcement as explicit support for Frondizi. The same is true of the translated radio news item

ment of Arturo Frondizi, but equally well as support for the Popular Conservative candidate Vicente Solano Lima, was clarified a week later when members of the Peronist Tactical Command in Buenos Aires displayed photostatic copies of a Perón order received from Santo Domingo expressly instructing his supporters to vote for Dr. Arturo Frondizi.[113] What had happened between February 4, when Perón ordered his followers to vote against continuismo, and February 10, when he told them to vote for Frondizi? The answer is to be found in the history of the secret understanding usually referred to as the Perón-Frondizi pact.

That the UCRI candidate and the exiled leader were involved in a political agreement had been a matter of speculation in press and political circles for a number of weeks. It was one thing to allege such an agreement, however, and another to prove it. Within the government, the highest military leaders could not bring themselves to believe that Frondizi would ever enter into a deal with Perón, and on more than one occasion they chose to ignore the evidence that civilian cabinet ministers presented to them.

The first of these occasions occurred in early 1958, when the Foreign Minister, Dr. Alfonso Laferrère, urgently requested a meeting with the President. In the presence of both General Aramburu and Vice-President Rojas, Dr. Laferrère displayed affidavits and other documents collected by Argentine diplomatic personnel attesting to contacts between Frondizi representatives and Perón and alleging the existence of a political pact between them. Admiral Rojas, according to his later recollection, proposed that the President summon Dr. Frondizi to confirm or deny the allegations, but no action was taken, for neither Aramburu nor Rojas "believed that Dr. Frondizi could have made promises of that sort to Perón." The only consequence was that the Foreign Minister, feeling his efforts rebuffed, chose to submit his resignation.[114]

---

reproduced in the Foreign Broadcast Information Service (hereafter FBIS) No. 26, Feb. 6, 1958.

[113] According to Chapter XXIV of "De Perón a Ongania," a historical series published in *Panorama Semanal*, April 15, 1969, p. 69, Adolfo Cavalli, a labor leader, carried Perón's order from Ciudad Trujillo to Buenos Aires on February 10. This is consistent with contemporary news accounts reported in FBIS, No. 30, Feb. 12, 1958, and *La Prensa*, Feb. 14, 1958, which refer to a handwritten Perón instruction to support Frondizi.

[114] The quoted words are from Admiral (Ret.) Rojas, interview May 29, 1970.

The Junta Militar apparently never met formally to discuss the possible existence of a Perón-Frondizi agreement; at least there is no reference to any such discussion in the accounts of its sessions maintained by the Navy Minister. Even after Perón's February 4 announcement, when Interior Minister Alconada claimed to have proof that UCRI members and Peronists had made agreements to present joint slates in the congressional elections, the Navy Minister dismissed this as a ploy by the pro-Balbín Minister to have the UCRI proscribed. As of February 9, Admiral Hartung still did not believe in the inevitability of a Frondizi victory.[115]

But while the military leaders of the provisional government apparently found it difficult to conceive that Frondizi, who had opposed Perón before 1955, would commit himself to the total reversal of the Liberating Revolution, the groundwork for an electoral alliance between the UCRI and the Peronists was in fact being laid. The key figure in this effort was Frondizi's political ally, Rogelio Frigerio. Committed to a "developmentalist" economic and social program that envisaged the transformation of the country through the expansion of the national industrial sector and the weakening of traditional agricultural and import interests, Frigerio had been seeking for months to win Perón's support. His idea was to fashion an electoral alliance that would make possible the eventual integration of Peronists, intransigent Radicals, and other groups into a multiclass movement that would support the structural changes envisaged by the developmentalist program. It was Frigerio's contention that this program would promote the very goals of political sovereignty and social justice with which Perón himself was identified.[116]

Despite Frigerio's overtures, Perón placed little confidence in

---

Rojas places the episode in December 1957, but it seems more likely that it occurred after Rogelio Frigerio's visit to Caracas to see Perón on January 3. Lafarrère submitted his resignation on January 13 (*La Prensa*, Jan. 14, 1958).

[115] Hartung Diary, p. 394. The Admiral believed that the decision of the Argentine Communist Party to support Frondizi would cost him votes among Peronists and anti-Peronists.

[116] Frigerio's *Qué* had been setting forth a program for Frondizi in the form of relentless criticism of the Liberating Revolution's policies and the elaboration of his own developmentalist economic and social ideas. For the early steps that led to the electoral alliance and his own role in them, see Prieto [77], pp. 71–77, 101–13; and also his more recent edited work, *Correspondencia Perón-Frigerio* [54], pp. 11–15. Prieto, who began as a Peronist and ended up a Frigerista, provides a partisan and not always accurate account.

Frondizi's purposes until late 1957 and was unalterably opposed to endorsing any candidate in the February election. "To intervene in it indirectly," he wrote to his delegate in Chile, "by supporting any candidate is to give the dictatorship a political out that it does not have, and to give an appearance of legality to an election we all know to be fraudulent." "The experience of these two years, he went on, "shows us that absolute intransigence is the only position compatible with our cause and with our movement; it is the only one that keeps the insurrectional state alert."[117]

But from a position of totally disdaining a deal with Frondizi, Perón proceeded at the close of 1957 to change his mind. Apparently it was the legalization of the neo-Peronist parties that moved him to do so, for he now faced the prospect that in the forthcoming general election his followers would be less willing than in the constituent assembly election the previous July to obey his orders to cast blank ballots. His status as the unquestioned leader of the Peronist movement would thus be undermined. A political deal with the Frondizi forces, on the other hand, could serve Perón's interest in preventing divisions and reasserting his control over his Argentine followers.[118]

That Rogelio Frigerio, on behalf of Frondizi's candidacy, and Juan Perón, for his own political goals, negotiated an agreement prior to the February 23 election is now an accepted fact. What needs to be clarified is the exact chronology of the negotiations, the extent of Arturo Frondizi's involvement, and the specific terms of the agreement.

The negotiations that looked forward to the electoral pact took place in Caracas, where Frigerio, at Perón's invitation, arrived January 3, 1958.[119] After a preliminary discussion, Frigerio left Caracas, probably to talk the matter over with Frondizi, and then returned to Caracas on January 18.[120] The intention of both parties to draw up a

[117] Perón to John W. Cooke, Caracas, Nov. 22, 1957, in *Perón-Cooke correspondencia* [72], II, 46. For Perón's observations about Frondizi, see his Sept. 1, 1957, letter, *ibid.*, I, 320–22.

[118] For an explanation that ascribes Perón's decision to support Frondizi's election to pressure from labor leaders, see Domínguez [56], pp. 70–71.

[119] Díaz [55], p. 42; Prieto, [77], pp. 110–11; see also *Panorama Semanal*, April 15, 1969, p. 68, and Perina [71], pp. 133–34, all of which deal with the Frigerio-Perón meeting.

[120] None of the sources cited in the previous note, not even the recent Fanor Díaz interview volume, mention two Frigerio trips to Caracas. Yet Prieto and

written agreement at this time was interrupted, however, by the outbreak of the revolt that toppled the Venezuelan dictator Marcos Pérez Jiménez on January 21. Fearful of his safety now that his Venezuelan protector was overthrown, Perón took refuge in Santo Domingo while Frigerio returned to Buenos Aires.[121] It was there that the document embodying the details of the agreements reached at Caracas was prepared and dispatched via a special messenger, Ramón Prieto, to Santo Domingo on February 5.[122] Perón's receipt of this document, which seemingly bore the signatures of Arturo Frondizi and Rogelio Frigerio, was the prerequisite for his issuance of the instructions, delivered to Buenos Aires on February 10, that expressly called on his supporters to vote for Frondizi for President of the Republic.[123]

But what did the document that Prieto delivered to Perón contain? And did Frondizi, despite his consistent denials over the years that he had ever agreed to any pact, actually sign that document? According to information supplied by Frigerio, he and Frondizi signed the two copies of the document that Prieto carried.[124] But Frigerio also insists that "*it did not establish concrete measures* but rather the necessity of utilizing the electoral process as a battlefield to oppose the CONTINUATION OF THE LIBERTADOR VIA THE RADICALISM OF BALBIN and the maneuvers of neo-Peronism of the Partido Blanco de los Tra-

---

Perina both state that Frigerio was in that city when the Venezuelan dictator, Marcos Pérez Jiménez, was overthrown on January 21, 1958. Unless one assumes that Frigerio remained in Caracas continuously from January 3 to 21, he had to have made two separate trips. In fact, by examining the issues of *Qué*, Jan. 14, 21, and Feb. 4, 1958, it is clear that Frigerio was back in Buenos Aires sometime after his early January trip and departed again after the middle of the month, probably reaching Caracas the second time on January 18, three days before Pérez Jiménez's overthrow. The importance of establishing that Frigerio returned to Buenos Aires after his January 3 meeting with Perón lies in the opportunity it provided for Frondizi and Frigerio to discuss Perón's conditions.

[121] *Correspondencia Perón-Frigerio* [54], p. 15. Prieto again erroneously places the interruption of the talks, Perón's departure for Santo Domingo, and Frigerio's return to Buenos Aires in early January. For contemporary press accounts of the Pérez Jiménez overthrow and Perón's seeking refuge in the Dominican Embassy, see *La Prensa*, Jan. 22–26, 1958.

[122] Letter, Rogelio Frigerio to the author, April 6, 1977. This letter enclosed a ten-page statement responding to questions I left with Sr. Frigerio during an interview in Buenos Aires on March 23, 1977. This statement is hereafter referred to as Frigerio Memorandum.

[123] See note 113 above.

[124] Frigerio Memorandum, p. 4.

bajadores. Likewise, the points of coincidence on the goals to be achieved were set forth."[125]

Frigerio's contention that the document did not provide for "concrete measures" is at variance with the text that Perón released in June 1959, after he had turned against the Frondizi administration. Were there, then, two separate documents: an authentic one, embodying simply a general understanding on goals, which Frigerio and Frondizi had signed; and an apocryphal one, with specific commitments and forged signatures that Perón concocted to try to undermine Frondizi in 1959? The most effective way of resolving this question would be if Frigerio or someone could produce the original of the document he says he sent to Santo Domingo. But no such document has ever appeared, and the only text available for analysis is the one that Perón distributed in 1959.[126]

Although Frondizi denied ever having signed it, and although his Interior Minister denounced it as a deliberate fraud designed to create unrest, evidence exists to indicate that at least some of its provisions were in fact part of the preelectoral agreement.[127] That evidence is to be found in the letters Perón wrote to a trusted aide in April and June 1958 when the exiled leader still had expectations for the new administration. On April 26, for example, Perón observed that "Frondizi is well disposed to comply" and mentioned the ouster of the Supreme Court and the reinstitution of the 1946 banking law, both points mentioned in the text made available in 1959.[128] Later, on June 7, 1958, the exiled leader, less confident now of Frondizi's intentions, wrote: "I continue to believe that we must take various steps designed to compel Frondizi to fulfill his promises. . . . He must learn that if by August 1 he has not clearly complied on all the things promised, we will deliver a mortal blow against him."[129] The docu-

[125] *Ibid.*, p. 3. The italicization and capitalization are as in the original.

[126] For a United Press dispatch from Ciudad Trujillo that describes the physical aspects as well as the contents of the Perón-released document, see *La Prensa*, June 12, 1959. The text is also given in Guardo [60], pp. 109–11.

[127] For Frondizi's denial, see his letter to Interior Minister Vítolo, *La Prensa*, June 15, 1959: "I have not signed any political pact. The signature attributed to me has been falsified. You may pledge in this statement my honor before God and before history. The only obligations I have acquired are those I assumed publicly before the people of the nation."

[128] Perón to John W. Cooke, Ciudad Trujillo, April 26, 1958, *Perón-Cooke correspondencia* [72], II, 52–53.

[129] Perón to Cooke, June 7, 1959, *ibid.*, II, 58. Other references to Frondizi's

ment released by Perón, it should be noted, stipulated a maximum of 90 days after Frondizi assumed the presidency for the adoption of seven specific measures, a period that would expire on August 1, 1958.

The consistency between the references to Frondizi's commitments in Perón's private correspondence and the text of the agreement as later released is persuasive evidence that the latter is at least partially accurate. Until such time, then, as the Frigerio version of the Perón-Frondizi pact can be substantiated by documentary evidence, the Perón-released text cannot be dismissed.[130]

What, then, were the terms of the agreement according to that text? The pact set forth as general goals the promotion of domestic harmony and the revision of the policies of the Liberating Revolution that in their view had increased Argentina's international dependence and lowered the living conditions of the people. To achieve these goals, Perón and Frondizi agreed to a political plan whereby the former committed himself to issue electoral instructions that would result in a Peronist vote for Frondizi on February 23, while the latter pledged himself once in office to "reestablish the conquests obtained by the people in the social, economic, and political spheres." Nine numbered paragraphs specified the measures Frondizi would adopt. Among these were policies of a long-term nature as well as the steps to be taken within the first 90 days in office. The latter included the abrogation of all measures adopted since September 16, 1955, that persecuted the Peronists; the cessation of all interdictions and the restitution of properties, including those sequestered from the Eva Perón Foundation; the lifting of trade union disqualification and the normalization of trade unions and the CGT via elections that jointly named officials would supervise; the replacement of the entire

---

commitments to Perón are to be found in the latter's second letter to Cooke of June 7, 1958 (*ibid.*, II, 60–61); the third letter of the same date (*ibid.*, II, 63); the letter of June 18, 1958 (*ibid.*, II, 68. 70); the letter of Sept. 30, 1958 (*ibid.*, II, 105–6); the letter of Dec. 20, 1958 (*ibid.*, II, 128–29); and the letter of Dec. 26, 1958 (*ibid.*, II, 131).

[130] Frondizi at the time and ever since has denied that he *signed* an agreement with Perón (interview, April 14, 1970). The possibility cannot be excluded that he did not in fact sign the document Perón issued but that someone else copied his name, thus allowing him to deny its authenticity. Supporting this hypothesis is the fact that Navy officers familiar with his signature questioned the authenticity of the signature that appeared on the Perón-released document (interview with Admiral (Ret.) Adolfo Estévez, March 13, 1970).

Supreme Court and of other judges who had engaged in acts of political persecution; and the restoration to full legal status of the Peronist Party under officials to be named by General Perón. Finally, within a period not to exceed two years, a constituent assembly was to be summoned that would totally revise the constitution, declare all elected offices vacant, and call for new general elections.[131]

In the light of these terms, it is understandable why Frondizi repeatedly denied that he had entered into any agreement with Perón or any other group. It is also understandable why neither General Aramburu nor Admiral Rojas, nor anti-Peronist elements in the UCRI, were prepared to believe before the January 1958 elections that an agreement of this nature could possibly exist. Even after the passage of many years, it is hard to believe that the UCRI candidate in February 1958 regarded the pact, if indeed this text is authentic, as anything but a temporary deal that he intended to implement only in part. It was not in keeping with the political ambition that had brought Frondizi this far to accept for himself a presidential role that would cease after only two years and would serve primarily as a legal nexus to a Peronist restoration.

Whatever the specific terms of the pact that Frigerio negotiated with Perón, there can be no doubt that it gave to Arturo Frondizi and the UCRI an overwhelming victory in the February 23 elections. With 4,070,000 votes, over 2,000,000 more than his party had received in the constituent assembly elections seven months before, Frondizi easily defeated Ricardo Balbín. The UCRI, moreover, captured 133 of the 187 seats in the Chamber of Deputies, took control of the governments of every province, and gained every seat in the national Senate. What would have happened had there been no pact can only be a matter of speculation. It is possible that Frondizi would have won the presidency anyway, but by a narrow margin and with reduced representation at national and provincial levels. Frondizi, however, wanted to enter office with as broad a base as possible, one that, as Frigerio saw it, would better enable the government to withstand the pressures of those who would "try to undermine its revolutionary transforming character."[132]

But in deliberately seeking Peronist support, openly through his

131 Guardo [60], pp. 109–11.
132 Frigerio Memorandum, p. 4.

campaign rhetoric and secretly through negotiations with the exiled Perón, and in also receiving the support of the Communist Party, Frondizi was to enter the presidency with a dual liability: on the one hand, the heightened suspicion of the anti-Peronist military, chagrined almost as much by their own political ineptitude as by the manner of Frondizi's victory; and on the other, the determination of Juan Domingo Perón to demand full political payment for the borrowed votes.

Chapter 8

The Shadowed Presidency:
Frondizi and the Military, 1958–1961

The 1958 elections and subsequent transfer of power marked a number of firsts in Argentina's recent political history: it was the first time in 30 years that a presidential candidate who had campaigned against an incumbent administration was declared the winner; it was the first time since 1930 that a military regime voluntarily proscribed the candidacies of military men and committed itself to turning over power to a civilian successor; and it was the first time since 1943 that the Argentine armed forces would have as their new commander-in-chief a man who had never worn a military uniform. In these circumstances, the great challenge that confronted both President-elect Frondizi and the members of the military was to work out a viable relationship that would overcome the mutual suspicion and distrust that were the inevitable legacy of the recent past. On the success of this effort would depend not only the survival of Dr. Frondizi's administration but the future of constitutional government in Argentina. The completion of a full six-year term, whatever the accommodations and compromises that might be required from all the parties concerned, could set a useful precedent for post-Perón Argentina.

The President-elect brought to his new post an austerity of person, an analytical mind, and a gift for reasoned expression that gave him a special appeal among the young and the well-educated. Tall, thin, with horn-rimmed glasses perched on a nose that was a cartoonist's delight, Frondizi projected an image of aloofness and coldness, of a man almost without emotions. Years of experience in the rough-and-tumble of politics had left him with a reputation for total dedication to public issues, but with a lesser commitment to friendship and personal loyalties.[1]

As President-elect, Frondizi was well aware of his need to bring tranquillity to the armed forces. His "military problem" was not a simple one, however. During the campaign, his supporters had assailed the members of the Aramburu government for a variety of actions, going back to the ouster of Lonardi and including the harsh repression of the June 9 revolt.[2] Frondizi, moreover, had committed himself to a broad amnesty for political offenders, and this raised the possibility that officers who had been ousted either for Peronist or for nationalist proclivities might now be restored to active duty. Such a prospect, which would mean shaking up the existing officer corps, was of great concern within the Army and Air Force, which had undergone the most extensive purges, but of less importance to the Navy. All three services, however, were exercised by the possibility that their decisions and actions since 1955 might be subjected to critical review under the new government.

Despite the urgings of retired Peronist and nationalist officers that he act in their behalf, Frondizi was well aware that the greatest threat to his political future lay not in the ranks of the retired, but among officers high and low within the existing cadres, officers so hostile to the manner of his electoral victory that they might try to prevent his installation as President on May 1.[3] What was needed at once, therefore, was to guarantee the cooperation of General Aramburu and his colleagues of the Military Junta. Accordingly, from the day after the election to the eve of his inauguration, Frondizi gave repeated assurances to Aramburu, Rojas, and the top military leaders that he had no intention of authorizing any reincorporations, that the present cadres would continue intact, and that he did not propose to

---

[1] On Dr. Frondizi's earlier career, life style, and personality, see Pandolfi [228], pp. 9–60; and Casas [224]. Both these works are highly sympathetic to their subject, and the Casas volume even carries a personal endorsement as to its accuracy from Dr. Frondizi.

[2] The Junta Militar members were especially incensed with such Frondicista organs as *Qué* and *Resistencia Popular* (Hartung Diary, p. 434).

[3] For efforts to prevent the transfer of power, interview with General (Ret.) Carlos S. Toranzo Montero, March 26, 1970; for the views and hopes of retired Peronist and nationalist officers, see Gómez [59], pp. 149–50; Hartung Diary, p. 488; interview with General (Ret.) Miguel Iñiguez, Aug. 21, 1973.

review anything carried out by the armed forces since the revolution. Frondizi even extended a blank check to the military services in stating that the ministries should draft all the decree-laws they felt necessary prior to 11:30 P.M. on April 30, that he would accept them, and that there would be no reexamination.[4]

Although it is evident that the military ministers were by no means convinced of Frondizi's sincerity, they did take advantage of the "blank check" as evidenced by the various decree-laws that were issued in the final days of the Aramburu government. One of these was a new organic military statute replacing the Peronist legislation of 1950. Among its novelties was the flat prohibition on those enjoying military status (*estado militar*) from accepting or serving in an elective post. Even retired officers under this new law were required to wait two years after leaving active service before engaging in political careers.[5] But if the Aramburu government sought, thus, to reverse the permissiveness of the past toward officers aspiring to public office, it did not hesitate to use the final weeks of its authority to improve the pecuniary rewards of a military career. Encouraged, apparently, by Frondizi's promises, it decreed an entirely new salary scale for the officer corps effective April 1. Coming only five months after a previously handsome increase, the new scale practically doubled existing salaries. For officers at the grade of major and above, the new salaries represented an increment of more than 300 percent over what they had been receiving prior to November 1, 1957, this in a period when the rate of inflation did not exceed 25 percent (see Table 6).

But salary increases, however gratifying to the beneficiaries, could not, and did not, eliminate the uneasiness that pervaded military circles. Widespread concern was felt that Frondizi might appoint Peronists or communists to high positions in his administration. General Aramburu, himself, in one of his first meetings with Frondizi after the election, had voiced this concern, warning him that the armed forces would be watching out against any such appointments. The President-elect, however, unwilling to yield any of his prerogatives to outside control, did little to assuage the military on this score in the weeks before his inauguration. His appointment to his

[4] Hartung Diary, pp. 428, 488.
[5] Decree-Law No. 6301, April 29, 1958.

TABLE 6.—MONTHLY BASE SALARIES FOR ARMY OFFICERS,
1956–58

Grade	Prior to Nov. 1957	1 Nov. 1957– March 30, 1958	April 1, 1958
Lieutenant General	5,000	9,800	18,500
Major General	4,300	8,500	15,700
Brigadier General	3,800	7,400	13,200
Colonel	3,100	6,100	10,500
Lieutenant Colonel	2,500	4,800	7,900
Major	2,000	3,920	6,100
Captain	1,700	3,200	4,700
First Lieutenant	1,300	2,440	3,500
Lieutenant	1,000	1,810	2,500
Sublieutenant	850	1,540	2,100

Sources: *Boletín Militar Reservado*, No. 3628, Nov. 29, 1956; No. 3677, Sept. 20, 1957; No. 3721, Apr. 30, 1958. Decree-Law No. 3810, dated Mar. 30, 1958, authorized the last increase.

transitional staff of men who had worked hard for his election included individuals regarded as communists in military circles. In the one case where the Army and Air Force Ministers actually challenged Frondizi's decision to include a controversial individual in the official party that was to accompany him on a preinaugural visit to Uruguay and Brazil, the President-elect chose to retain that individual, even though it meant the withdrawal of the military aides who were supposed to accompany him.[6]

In the transitional period between the election and the inauguration, Frondizi sounded out the military men on the creation of the post of Minister of Defense. Apparently he had hoped that the Aramburu government would create such a post by decree so that he could begin his administration by assigning only one of the eight cabinet posts allowed by the constitution to the military. The existing three military ministers, redesignated as secretaries, would continue to sit with the cabinet, and each would handle his own budget, but the Minister of Defense would sign decrees. The Navy leadership in the persons of Admiral Rojas and Admiral Hartung were adamantly opposed to the idea, fearful that the Defense Minis-

[6] Hartung Diary, pp. 434, 476–81. Rogelio Frigerio, Isidro Odena, and Dardo Cuneo were all looked upon with suspicion in military circles. The individual Frondizi insisted on including in his official party to Uruguay was the editor of *Resistencia Popular*, Raúl Damonte Taborda.

try in the hands of a general would result in the Navy's loss of its independence. Even though Frondizi insisted that it was his intention to appoint a distinguished civilian to the post, the Navy leaders refused to approve any decree-law that would bring the post into immediate existence and warned the President-elect against creating it in the future.[7]

Of all the military-related questions Frondizi had to face before his inauguration, the one that aroused the greatest interest among officers was his choice of future collaborators. Would he select retired officers to serve in his cabinet, or would he appoint men from the active ranks? What kind of person would he choose? In the weeks preceding May 1, Frondizi met with numerous officers in the three services, both active and retired, listening to suggestions although without committing himself. In the case of the Navy, the advice he received was fairly consistent: to appoint as Secretary a retired admiral of acknowledged prestige for his professional capacity, democratic ideals, and identification with the Liberating Revolution. The admirals on active duty, it was argued, were all to one degree or another personal rivals: they had been promoted to their grade prematurely because of the revolution, and it was useful to have as Secretary an admiral who would inspire respect, if only for reasons of age, and who would be obeyed without discussion.[8]

Frondizi chose not to follow this advice. He decided, rather, to name active duty officers to the military secretariats. Moreover, against the recommendation received from experienced officers, he decided not to appoint a separate Army Commander-in-Chief, but to combine this post with that of the cabinet Secretary in a single person. Similarly, in the Navy, his appointee as Secretary was to serve simultaneously as Chief of Naval Operations. In theory, this combination of functions avoided the friction that might develop between a cabinet Secretary and a strong-willed service commander; but it also meant that each military service was deprived of a full-time military chief and that the traditional balance between the political interests of the administration, as represented by the cabinet Secretary, and the interests of the Army or Navy, as represented by its top commander, was upset. Moreover, it meant that a pres-

[7] Hartung Diary, pp. 428, 430–32, 438, 442.
[8] Perren Memoirs, pp. 336–37.

tigious post, to which a senior officer could aspire, was in effect removed from the *escalafón*.[9]

Not until after his inauguration did Frondizi announce publicly his choices for the military cabinet posts. Behind the scenes, however, especially among a group of Army generals, a concerted effort was made to influence his selection of Army Secretary. Their candidate was Major General Carlos Toranzo Montero, currently Inspector General of Instruction and the ranking officer behind Army Commander-in-Chief Ossorio Arana. A cavalry officer with family links to the Radical Party, Toranzo Montero was known for his adamant opposition to Peronism, communism, and ultranationalism. More relevant perhaps, in the immediate aftermath of the February election, he was one of those officers who tried unsuccessfully to persuade Aramburu to void the election on the grounds of the alleged Perón-Frondizi pact.[10]

The President-elect understandably preferred another officer with whom he had developed a close relationship, Major General Héctor Solanas Pacheco, currently commander of the Second Army. Possessed of equally good anti-Peronist credentials, although lacking general staff training, Solanas Pacheco was a more flexible individual than Toranzo Montero and, moreover, had good rapport with nationalist officers. In mid-March, Frondizi quietly offered the combined posts of Army Secretary and Commander-in-Chief to Solanas Pacheco, and although the latter expressed preference to have someone else as Secretary, under Frondizi's insistence, he accepted.[11] The arrangement would give the President a reliable cabinet Secretary while preempting the Army Commander-in-Chief post from the officer most entitled by seniority to receive it, the ambitious and independent General Toranzo Montero.

Unaware that Frondizi had made a firm decision, and believing that the choice for Army Secretary still lay between Solanas Pacheco and Toranzo Montero, the proponents of the latter's candidacy con-

[9] Dr. Frondizi's explanation of his appointment of active duty officers to the military ministries is that he was requested to do so by the Junta Militar (interview, April 14, 1970). The Hartung Diary, which reports in detail the discussions between the Junta Militar and the President-elect, makes no mention of this. It is possible that General Aramburu advised him privately to follow this course, but the Navy's viewpoint was clearly in favor of a retired admiral.

[10] See note 3 above; Hartung Diary, pp. 482–85, 491.

[11] Interview with General (Ret.) Héctor Solanas Pacheco, May 28, 1970.

tinued their efforts until practically the eve of the inauguration. In a specially arranged meeting to discuss military matters between Frondizi and the Junta Militar at Olivos on April 27, General Aramburu joined his voice to that of Ossorio Arana and Army Undersecretary Martín Cabanillas in denigrating Solanas Pacheco's personal qualifications for command. Frondizi deftly countered their arguments by pointing out that those who were speaking against him had retained Solanas Pacheco on active service and, moreover, had recently promoted him to be a major general. The President-elect could not believe that if Solanas Pacheco were lacking in character and easily managed by others, as they alleged, he could be holding down that high a military post. Toranzo's supporters, although not told explicitly by Frondizi that he had made his choice, were left with the impression that they had argued in vain. Two days later, April 29, the mystery was over. Solanas Pacheco as incoming Minister and Commander-in-Chief and Ossorio Arana as outgoing Commander-in-Chief met and agreed that the latter's responsibilities would extend to 4:00 P.M. on May 1, when Solanas would take over.[12]

It was at this same April 27 meeting that Frondizi, on hearing from the Navy members of the Junta, Admirals Rojas and Hartung, that they had no particular problem to discuss, gave them advance notice of his choice for Navy Secretary: Admiral Adolfo Estévez. These two admirals were prompt to voice approval.[13] Estévez, the senior admiral below Rojas, was currently serving as Fleet Commander. Like General Solanas Pacheco, he had been involved in the abortive anti-Perón conspiracies of 1951–52; both had suffered forced retirement and joint imprisonment on Martín García Island. Moreover, it was through Estévez that Solanas Pacheco first met Frondizi, then a national deputy, and joined his political circle.[14] Now, five years later, President-elect Frondizi was calling on these two military friends to take on the difficult task of directing the Army and Navy at a time of political transition.[15]

[12] Hartung Diary, pp. 490–93; interview with General (Ret.) Solanas Pacheco.

[13] Hartung Diary, p. 492.

[14] Interviews with Admiral (Ret.) Adolfo Estévez and General (Ret.) Solanas Pacheco.

[15] To head the Air Force Frondizi chose Commodore Roberto Huerta, an active duty officer who had close ties to the nationalist sector identified with the former minister, Julio Krause. This was a controversial appointment that was to produce a serious crisis in a matter of months.

The inauguration of Dr. Arturo Frondizi on May 1 marked the end of almost 32 months of military government and the transfer of political authority to civilian hands. Before examining the ways in which the new administration exercised its authority, it is appropriate to recognize the major role that General Aramburu played in making that transfer possible. As noted in the previous chapter, he had not wanted to see Frondizi elected president and had allowed the latter's political rivals to work from within the administration to combat his candidacy. Once the election results became clear, however, General Aramburu did everything possible to ensure the safe installation of the winner. Despite his own misgivings about Frondizi, he refused to yield to the pressures of fellow officers to prolong the life of the military government. To do so, he felt, would be to go back on his word and to discredit both the revolution and the Army. On the other hand, to respect the popular will would strengthen the democratic and antimilitarist forces within the Army.[16]

This was the argument that General Aramburu used to counter pressures from fellow officers. Moreover, in his last public address as President, he contrasted the errors of past military regimes in 1930 and 1943 with the performance of his own government in restoring the country to the people "with liberties and institutions reestablished in the path of democracy and on the prefixed date." In urging his comrades in arms to return to their professional duties proud of their accomplishment but without expectation of gratitude, he warned them against the false politicians of the future who might try to persuade them that they were "the nation's reserve and the new solution to new problems." "Be careful," he went on, "of the intriguers and imposters who still yearn for strong governments and submissive peoples, because in their sweet venom and warm promises are concealed destruction, hate, slavery, and misery."[17]

Coming from an Army general, these words were received by military listeners with far more grace than those which President Frondizi delivered in his inaugural two days later. Although he did little more than state certain truisms, that henceforth the elected representatives and not the armed forces would make the decisions,

[16] These were Aramburu's views as recalled by General (Ret.) Carlos Toranzo Montero, one of the proponents of denying the presidency to Frondizi (interview, March 26, 1970).

[17] The full text of this address is given in *La Prensa*, April 30, 1958.

that the duty of the armed forces was to respect the mandate of Congress, the courts, and the orders of the constitutional president, that he, Frondizi, wanted the military as "servitors of the nation and not as a praetorian guard of the President of the Republic," and that hierarchy, discipline, and unity must prevail, Frondizi's remarks were deeply wounding to many in uniform. Even officers who loyally supported the transfer of authority saw in the President's words a gratuitous reminder of their changed estate and an insult that he probably never intended.[18]

Dr. Frondizi's inaugural address was, of course, much more than a message to the military; it was a carefully prepared statement outlining the overall aims of his administration and specifying steps by which he hoped to move the country on the path toward national development. The principal focus was on the economy, especially the need to develop heavy industries and achieve self-sufficiency in petroleum production. Frondizi announced his intention to assume direct charge of YPF; he also indicated that foreign capital would be needed to accelerate economic growth. Noting that social tensions could affect development, Frondizi committed his government to raising wages and to restoring control over the labor movement, including the CGT, to whatever leaders the workers themselves chose without official interference. Stressing the need for domestic political harmony, the new President announced that he would try to eliminate hatred and fear from the hearts of all Argentines. He proposed lowering a curtain over the past, granting an amnesty for all political offenses, and ending all political discrimination. Henceforth, he stated, no one would be persecuted for his ideas or his political acts, everyone would be free to vote and run for office, and all political parties would be allowed to function freely.[19]

Throughout his address, Frondizi emphasized that he would govern within the framework of law and with respect for the other branches of government. He also committed himself to a policy of openness, promising to consult with all political parties and interest groups on the great national problems. More specifically, in the use

[18] Perren Memoirs, p. 336. The full text of Frondizi's May 1, 1958, message to the joint session of Congress is reproduced in the appendix of Casas [224], pp. 407–34.
[19] Casas [224], pp. 407–34.

of its economic powers, he promised that the government would not act arbitrarily. "It will submit programs of action and practical measures to public discussion. . . . The various interested social sectors will participate actively in the plans for national economic development."[20] The reality would turn out to be something short of this categorical promise.

Indeed, it was one thing for Frondizi to announce his program and quite another to implement it. The obstacles lay not in the existence of congressional opposition—his supporters dominated both Houses—but in the divisiveness and hostility that characterized the society as a whole. To many an Argentine, Frondizi's appeal for an end to political hatreds was premature. The anti-Peronists, heavily represented in the armed forces, were reluctant to see the restraints imposed by the recent military government undone; the Peronists, their control over the bulk of the workers confirmed, were impatient for full restoration of their former power, including the return of their exiled leader. Even within the ranks of Frondizi's immediate supporters there was rivalry between the so-called integrationists, the non-UCRI elements associated with Rogelio Frigerio on the one hand, and UCRI leaders like Vice-President Alejandro Gómez on the other; the latter resented the former's influence over the President and would like to have excluded them from key posts in the government.[21]

The first eight months of his administration provided a test of President Frondizi's ability to advance his program within his announced framework of openness and the rule of law. From the very first, he showed a capacity for making concessions in order to balance pressure groups and retain control over the decision-making process. The appointments to his cabinet are an illustration. Although he might have preferred to name Rogelio Frigerio, his closest advisor, as Minister of Economy, he was well aware of the negative reverberations such an appointment would produce in the armed forces, where Frigerio was widely detested, as well as in the UCRI. Accordingly, Frondizi named a party eminence, Emilio Donato del Carril, as Finance Minister, but created a new post in the Office of

20 *Ibid.*, p. 418.
21 Gómez [59], pp. 171–75, 185–88; for the integrationist viewpoint, see *Qué,* June 17, 1958, p. 8.

the Presidency for Rogelio Frigerio. As Secretary of Socio-Economic Relations in the Casa Rosada, Frigerio had direct jurisdiction over all negotiations with foreign investors and immediate access to the President. In similar fashion, Frondizi named party figures to most of the other cabinet positions, but assigned key functions in the Office of the Presidency to members of the integrationist group. It is not surprising, then, that critics of Frigerio complained that a dual system of authority existed in the administration, one leading through the cabinet ministers, the other through the Secretary of Socio-Economic Relations.[22]

Frondizi's readiness to balance concessions in order to advance his own goals was also illustrated in his handling of his promises to wipe out the anti-Peronist measures of the Liberating Revolution. Frondizi had originally made these promises during his electoral campaign; he had also incorporated them, it will be recalled, in the electoral pact reached with Perón. Their fulfillment now was a key to retaining the latter's cooperation. Accordingly, as one of the first acts of his administration, Frondizi submitted to Congress the draft of a broad amnesty bill, one that would wipe out all political offenses, including related common or military crimes, and put an end to any investigation of, or judicial process against, anyone accused of committing such offenses. At the same time, Frondizi submitted to Congress a bill to render homage to the armed forces of the nation and another to promote General Aramburu and Admiral Rojas to the highest military rank in recognition of their responsibility for having carried out the pledge of the armed forces to restore constitutional government. All three bills were enacted by the UCRI congressional majorities,

[22] In addition to Dr. Carril and the three military ministers, Dr. Frondizi's first cabinet consisted of the following: Héctor V. Noblía and Luis Mackay, both Intrasigent Radicals, in the Health and Welfare and Education and Justice Ministries; Alfredo Vítolo, a onetime Unionist Radical from Mendoza as Interior Minister; and Carlos Florit, a young man in his twenties with links to Frigerio as Minister of Foreign Affairs and Worship. A new ministerial law enacted in June redesignated the military posts as State Secretariats, thus permitting the creation of the Ministry of Defense, to which the Radical Party veteran Gabriel del Mazo was appointed, and the Ministry of Labor and Social Security, which was entrusted to a labor leader, the head of the insurance workers union, Alfredo Allende. Though not an original member of the Frigerio circle, Allende came under its influence. In the Office of the Presidency the key officials apart from Frigerio were: Colonel Juan E. Guglialmelli, Secretary of Liaison and Coordination; Samuel Schmuckler, Executive Secretary; and Nicolás Babini, Technical Secretary.

but not without creating the sensation in both Peronist and anti-Peronist camps that the President was cynically playing with their deeply held feelings.[23]

The amnesty bill, however, for all of its breadth, did not explicitly pave the way for Perón's return. Nor did the legislation enacted a few days later to abrogate the bans on Peronist political activity imposed by the Liberating Revolution extend to the legalization of the Peronist Party. Henceforth, it was perfectly legal to utilize Peronist symbols and carry on Peronist propaganda; outlawed Peronist political and labor leaders were again allowed to hold public or trade union offices; but the Peronist Party, as such, ordered into dissolution in 1955, was allowed to remain in a legal limbo. Little wonder that the exiled Perón began to complain in his private correspondence about Frondizi's unreliability.[24]

Perón, of course, was not the only one to question the sincerity of the President's commitment to his preelectoral promises. Among a good many of Frondizi's non-Peronist supporters, especially those with nationalist or socialist inclinations, a sense of disillusionment spread as the new administration revealed the details of its economic policies. For although Frondizi had mentioned in his campaign the need to call on foreign capital to accelerate industrial development, he had carefully refrained from spelling out his plan. Many who voted for him had done so in the belief that as President he would be loyal to the UCR's Avellaneda program; that he would never make concessions to the international companies that had exploited Argentina's energy market in the past; and that in the petroleum sector, especially, he would continue to champion the idea of a complete state monopoly of production, refining, and distribution.[25]

As President, however, Frondizi had no intention of adhering to

[23] Law 14,436 (General Amnesty), May 22, 1958; Law 14,441 (Promotion of Aramburu and Rojas), June 23, 1958; see also Casas [224], pp. 62–63.

[24] Law 14,444, July 1, 1958. Letters, Juan Perón to John W. Cooke, June 7, Sept. 30, 1958, *Perón-Cooke correspondencia* [72], II, 58–64, 105–9.

[25] Frondizi's views on petroleum were widely known as a result of his book *Petróleo y política* [256], and his congressional speeches attacking Perón's oil policies prior to 1955. During the electoral campaign he gave no inkling that he had changed his mind as evidenced in the following exchange with a radio interviewer on the eve of the election: "Question—Dr. Frondizi, do you have any concrete solutions for a formula for nat'onal sovereignty in regard to national resources? Answer—Our position on petroleum is well known. It has not changed" (FBIS, No. 36, Feb. 21, 1958).

positions that could delay the rapid expansion of energy production. Long before his election, he had come to share Rogelio Frigerio's "realistic" approach to the role of foreign capital in a developing society: that it was the purpose of the investment, not the source of the capital, that determined whether it strengthened or weakened a country's economic independence. Investments in heavy industry, in steel, petroleum, electricity, petrochemicals, and cellulose were needed. Given the impoverished state of the treasury, the initial objective should be the rapid expansion of petroleum production. With foreign capital and expertise, the country would be able to achieve self-sufficiency in a few years, reducing its dependence on imported fuels and releasing up to $300 million annually in foreign exchange for use in developing other sectors of the economy. Such a policy would do more to promote Argentina's economic independence than continued insistence on nationalist rhetoric that only prolonged the existing state of affairs.[26]

President Frondizi was acutely aware of the wave of protest that would follow public announcement of his petroleum policy, but he was apparently confident that through his loyal followers in the UCRI and through Frigerio's contacts in the Peronist movement, he would be able to withstand the pressures. Until preliminary agreements could be reached with prospective investors, however, he shrouded his intentions from the public eye. His inaugural day promise to consult with interested sectors before adopting specific economic measures and his pledge not to use the economic powers of the state arbitrarily were conveniently ignored in the effort to negotiate favorable contracts with foreign companies and present the public with a fait accompli. Only on July 24, in a televised message to the country, did Dr. Frondizi take the wraps off his petroleum program.[27]

A central feature of this program was to be a series of drilling

[26] For the developmentalist view of the role of foreign capital see Rogelio Frigerio's 1959 essay, "Introducción a la política económica," in his *Los cuatro años (1958–1962)* [254], pp. 33–51. Exactly when Frondizi shifted his traditional opposition to foreign investment in petroleum development is not clear. Pandolfi [228], pp. 82–84, makes a persuasive case for 1957.

[27] Casas in her "authorized" study writes of Frondizi's decision not to consult the interested parties: "But it was not part of his plan to submit the issue for discussion either at the bureaucratic level or in the Congress because he knew very well that the issue would get hung up in proceedings and time was short. He decided therefore to move in secret [actuar por sorpresa]" ([224], pp. 39–40).

contracts awarded directly (to avoid the delays of public bidding) to a number of private companies. Some of these companies received areas where YPF teams had already established the existence of oil; others had to assume the risks of exploration; but in every case, they were to deliver the oil they produced to YPF at prices stipulated in their respective contracts. Government spokesmen labeled these agreements as service contracts, denied that they were concessions, and insisted that they involved no sacrifice of Argentine sovereignty. Even so, anxious to avoid anything that could delay the march toward self-sufficiency, Frondizi refused to submit the contracts to congressional ratification, insisting that he already had adequate legal powers to proceed. This approach undoubtedly permitted him to bypass congressional opposition, and thus accelerate the implementation of his program, but it left the President exposed to charges that he was violating the very rule of law he had promised to uphold.[28]

It was not just in the petroleum sector that Frondizi was prepared to challenge nationalist shibboleths. Convinced that foreign investors needed clear evidence of a favorable investment climate, he was anxious to come to terms with those foreign companies that had had assets expropriated in the past, but for which final payment or settlement was still in abeyance. Because several of these companies, especially the ANSEC and CADE electric utilities, were so unpopular, previous governments had been hesitant to act since any settlement acceptable to the foreign owners was likely to be denounced as a sellout by nationalist opinion.[29]

As President-elect, Frondizi had tried to persuade the lame-duck Aramburu government to resolve the disputes, partly to give a quick start to his own economic program, but also, it would appear, to reduce the political costs to himself. Three days after the election, he had urged the Minister of Industry to settle the ANSEC claims at whatever price the company insisted on; but when asked by the Minister whether he would sign a document authorizing the settle-

---

[28] The text of the July 24 message entitled "La Batalla del Petróleo" is reproduced in Frondizi, *Petróleo y nación* [84], pp. 61–79.

[29] See the interesting letter of Raúl Scalabrini Ortiz to Rogelio Frigerio of April 1, 1958, reproduced in the appendix of Merchensky [292]. Scalabrini Ortiz, who had just learned of the Frondizi-Frigerio ideas for solving the CADE, ANSEC, and petroleum problems warned of the political dangers.

ment, the President-elect flatly refused.[30] The Aramburu government declined to take the responsibility for solving this claim and bequeathed the issue to its successor. As President, Frondizi moved decisively to create the favorable investment climate that was essential to his economic program. In May, he returned to private German hands a number of companies that had been seized from their compatriots in 1945; in September, he submitted to Congress an agreement reached with CADE to create with its assets a mixed enterprise to furnish electricity in the area of Buenos Aires. The ANSEC problem was also resolved by an agreement that called on the American owners to reinvest at least part of the sum to be paid them for their expropriated properties in a new 300,000 kilowatt plant in the Greater Buenos Aires area.[31]

If his policies toward foreign investors aroused bitter criticism, so did Frondizi's labor policies, although here it could not be said that he was going back on electoral pledges. Within a few days of taking office, he decreed a 60 percent wage increase for all public and private workers, restored six intervened unions to Peronist leadership, initiated moves to reestablish the autonomy of the CGT, and, a few weeks later, sent to Congress a trade union statute that would reverse the post-1955 effort to promote plural unionism. Through the efforts of his Minister of Labor, Alfredo Allende, himself a trade union official, and through Rogelio Frigerio's contacts with Peronist labor leaders, the administration was obviously seeking trade union support for its overall policies in return for favors. But in many other sectors of the public, including the opposition political parties, business interests, and anti-Peronist trade union leaders, the administration's labor policies conjured up the vision of a vertically dominated labor movement once again serving as the powerful instrument of an authoritarian government. In military circles, diehard opponents of

[30] Hartung Diary, p. 429. At this February 26 meeting with Dr. Cueto Rúa, according to Hartung's entry, Frondizi used the following analogy: "The A.N. S.E.C. case is very similar to that of a Cadillac stuck in the field; a farmer passes by and offers to haul it out for 300 pesos. The owner has no choice but to pay the 300; and we have no choice but to pay A.N.S.E.C. Do so, you have my approval." Cueto Rúa in a press conference eight months later confirmed that Frondizi had discussed with him the need to find friendly solutions to the ANSEC, CADE, and other issues (*La Prensa*, Oct. 17, 1958, p. 4).

[31] Law 14,793 of Jan. 13, 1959. The sums to be paid for their expropriated assets were to be fixed by the President of the Argentine Supreme Court.

Frondizi tried to exploit the proposed trade union statute to whip up fears about the administration's alleged totalitarian tendencies.[32]

The attitudes of military personnel, especially of high-ranking officers, were naturally of concern to Frondizi. As an elected president, however, he was unwilling to tailor his policies, political, social, or economic, to the demands made upon him by military critics; on the other hand, he was equally unwilling to follow the advice of those like his Vice-President who urged the prompt ouster of officers known to have opposed his election. Rather, he preferred to follow a cautious policy, avoiding steps that might inflame opinion or precipitate an early crisis. The apparent premise of his military policy, at least in the early months of the administration, was that the bulk of the officer corps were supporters of constitutional government and that the way to strengthen that support while isolating the diehard opponents was to respect the autonomy of the armed forces. Recalling perhaps the unfortunate consequences of President Yrigoyen's military meddling, Frondizi decided to follow an opposite course, not interfering with his military ministers, endorsing their budgetary requests, and giving them a free hand in personnel decisions.[33]

General Solanas Pacheco, the Army Secretary, used the confidence extended by the President to try to assert his own control over the Army establishment. While refraining from forcing any number of officers into retirement, he effected a major shakeup of key posts in order to dismantle what he later described as "la máquina bien preparada" left behind by his predecessor, Ossorio Arana.[34] The transfers he ordered embraced practically the entire high command, and in some instances, namely, the armored and motorized units in the vicinity of the capital, reached down to regimental and battalion levels. Indeed, the transfers of officers at the grade of colonel were so extensive that the opening date of the advanced course for colonels at the War Academy had to be postponed. As a result of this shakeup, anti-Frondizi officers were by no means eliminated from the

[32] Law 14,455 (Statute for Professional Associations of Workers) was enacted August 8, 1958. For military reaction, interview with Admiral (Ret.) Arturo Rial, May 4, 1970. The trade union statute was a source of military criticism throughout Frondizi's presidency.

[33] Gómez [59], pp. 149–52; interviews with General (Ret.) Solanas Pacheco and Admiral (Ret.) Adolfo Estévez.

[34] Interview with General (Ret.) Solanas Pacheco.

Army, but were placed in less sensitive positions than they had formerly enjoyed. In some instances this meant assignment to provincial locations, but in the case of two prominent officers of uncertain loyalty, Generals Carlos Toranzo Montero and Emilio Bonnecarrère, the solution was found in an elegant form of diplomatic exile. Both were assigned in military capacities to Washington, D.C. Not until the following year when both returned to Argentina were they in a position to create serious problems for the administration.[35]

The President's caution in dealing with his military opponents seemed to work most successfully in his relations with the Navy. Here his Secretary, Admiral Estévez, made very few transfers, at most eight or nine at the senior level. The President, moreover, adhered to the practice begun in 1955 of ensuring a Navy role in domestic security activities by placing the Federal Police under the control of Navy rather than Army officers. In a further move to seal Navy support, Frondizi approved the purchase of an aircraft carrier, long a goal of the Navy, but never implemented until now. The decision did not fail to arouse criticism in the other services, and even in the Navy, anti-Frondizi elements chose to see in it a hidden goal of ending the Navy's possession of land-based planes.[36]

Despite such rumors and their own misgivings about Frondizi's appointments and policies, the majority of Navy admirals were opposed to any break with constitutional order. Their determination to support the government, however, was put to its first real test in the Rial affair that climaxed in July 1958. Taking issue with his colleagues, Admiral Arturo Rial, the ranking admiral in the service below Admiral Estévez, was a violent critic of Frondizi as well as a personal rival of the Navy Secretary. Exploiting the discontent with both officials that existed in many quarters, Rial presented his candidacy for the head of the Centro Naval, the social organization to which most officers, retired and active, belonged. In an election that revealed through its heavy turnout the politicized atmosphere that existed in Navy circles, Rial and his associates won out. This gave

[35] *Boletín Militar Reservado*, Nos. 3720–23, May 1958; *Boletín Militar Público*, Nos. 2992 and 2995, June 1958.

[36] Interviews with Admirals (Ret.) Adolfo Estévez and Jorge Palma. Palma, who was no friend of Frondizi, confirms that Estévez as Navy Secretary always accepted the recommendations of the Navy boards and did not allow political considerations to influence promotions and assignments.

him a platform for opposing the President, especially since Frondizi was expected to attend the annual armed forces banquet scheduled for July 7, and Admiral Rial, as Centro Naval head, was to be the principal spokesman for the armed forces.[37]

Rial had earlier met privately with President Frondizi to express concern about the administration's trade union policies and his appointment of "extreme leftists" to government posts, but without result. Now, however, the Admiral proposed to use the text of his banquet speech as a lever to get the President to make concessions or face revolt. A day or so before the banquet, he submitted the text to Frondizi, expecting that the latter would summon him to resolve their differences and that he in turn would alter the violent tone of his speech. The President, however, did nothing of the kind. Acting with a deftness he did not always display in military crises, he ordered the cancellation of the dinner and placed Rial under eight days' disciplinary arrest. If the Admiral expected his colleagues to rise up in protest, he was mistaken.[38]

Although the Rial episode sent shock waves through naval ranks, most senior officers, as noted above, were opposed to a military takeover. Rial himself was forced to retire from active duty a few months after the July episode. Even here it should be noted that the President acted with great caution and that, in the last analysis, it was the forthright Admiral Rial who made his own retirement inescapable. As the senior officer next in rank to Admiral Estévez, he would have been the natural candidate to take over as acting Chief of Naval Operations when Estévez was invited in September for an official visit to the United States. President Frondizi, however, was understandably reluctant to name an avowed enemy to this sensitive post; but if he named another admiral, Rial would automatically have to retire.[39] A senior officer, Navy General Staff Chief Jorge Perren, who disagreed with Rial's policies, but did not want to lose his services, proposed a solution which the President accepted: to appoint Rial as acting Chief of Naval Operations provided that he give a formal pledge not to use the post to upset the government. Rial, however, refused to give Admiral Perren such a pledge and revealed his in-

[37] Perren Memoirs, pp. 338–39.
[38] Luna, *Diálogos con Frondizi* [66], p. 84; interview with Admiral (Ret.) Rial.
[39] Military custom rather than law compelled such retirements.

tention, if appointed, to launch a revolution at the first opportunity. In these circumstances, there was no alternative but to ask him to request retirement and appoint another admiral to the acting post.[40]

Frondizi's prestige was if anything strengthened by his handling of the Rial affair, but he was less fortunate in dealing with his first Air Force crisis. Here the challenge was more than that of removing an outspoken military critic; it involved coping with the refusal of nearly all senior Air Force commanders to obey his Air Force Secretary, Commodore Roberto Huerta. Frondizi's initial appointment of Huerta on May 1 had aroused the anxiety of these senior officers, but this anxiety was temporarily allayed by the repeated promises from both the President and Secretary Huerta that they would no nothing to alter the existing command structure. Of particular concern to these officers was the possibility that the government might recall to active service either men who had been ousted in 1955 for support of Perón or others like ex-Air Minister Krause, who was himself eased out in 1957.[41]

It was precisely the President's decision, communicated by a September 1 decree signed by Frondizi and Huerta, to summon the controversial Commodore Krause from retirement and restore him to the active duty list that precipitated the crisis in the Air Force. Practically all senior officers from the Commander-in-Chief down showed their opposition to this move, resigning from their posts or refusing to follow the Air Secretary's orders. Secretary Huerta was reduced to appointing majors (*comandantes*) and lieutenant colonels (vice-commodores) to cover posts that by law called for brigadiers and colonels (commodores). The rebellious officers, moreover, took control of the Air Force communications network, forcing the Secretary to rely on an improvised system to maintain contact with interior bases and units.[42]

Why the President ordered Krause's recall and whether it was his own or Secretary Huerta's idea are questions that cannot be definitively answered. Some Frondizi critics saw in the move a deliberate

[40] Perren Memoirs, pp. 338–41; *La Prensa*, Sept. 9, 11, 13, 1958. Because of his political activities Rial was later forced to resign as president of the Centro Naval.

[41] On the initial unhappiness of anti-Krause officers with the appointment of Huerta as Air Force Secretary, see Hartung Diary, p. 491.

[42] *La Prensa*, Sept. 3–9, 1958, provides detailed coverage of the crisis.

effort to weaken the Air Force by intensifying internal rivalries; others saw in it an initial step toward the goal of transforming the Air Force into a presidential instrument. Krause, after all, had the reputation of having worked to advance Frondizi's presidential aspirations when he was Air Force Minister. But whether the President had even initiated the Krause recall is subject to question. Given his generally cautious approach to military problems and the free hand he gave to the Army and Navy Secretaries, it seems more likely that he went along with a proposal of the Air Force Secretary. Huerta's motives may have been partly to strengthen his own control, partly a gesture of friendship to allow Krause to earn time in grade to merit promotion to the coveted brigadier's grade. In any event, the senior Air Force officers were taking no chances.[43]

The result was an impasse that lasted a week. At first President Frondizi gave full support to his Secretary, but the list of officers requesting retirement or submitting resignations grew with each passing day. According to press accounts, in one Córdoba-based unit 66 officers took such action, leaving only two on duty. In the face of such developments, and confronted by demands that he rescind the Krause recall and replace Colonel Huerta, the President finally yielded.[44]

Whether or not his original intention had been to gain control over the Air Force, Frondizi emerged from the crisis with less influence than before it began. Even his choice of a replacement for Air Secretary had to be negotiated with the senior commanders. They rejected his first selection, an active duty commodore who had sided with Huerta, and only when the President turned to a retired brigadier, Ramón Abráhin, did the crisis fade away.[45] The entire episode demonstrated to the President that any effort to enhance his authority over the military would have to avoid the reincorporation of ousted officers;[46] at the same time, it taught a lesson to dissident officers.

[43] On Huerta's possible motivations see Commodore Pizarro's interview in *La Prensa,* Sept. 7, 1958.

[44] *Ibid.,* Sept. 10, 11, 1958.

[45] President Frondizi's first choice, Commodore Gallina, was unable to take the oath of office at the announced time on September 11. The next day Abráhin's appointment was announced (*La Prensa,* Sept. 12–14, 1958).

[46] As an indication of the sensitivity of this issue, in the midst of the Air Force crisis the Army Secretary radioed all his units that there would be no reincorporations in the Army (*La Prensa,* Sept. 5, 1958).

They learned that the President would sacrifice his own appointees when confronted by determined resistance on the part of their subordinates. The principle of respect for hierarchy was bent if not broken, and an unfortunate precedent was established for the future.[47]

In agreeing to abandon his Air Force Secretary, President Frondizi was apparently moved by fear that the Air Force confrontation, if allowed to continue, might ignite an insurrection against his government. Indeed, reports of meetings between opposition political party leaders and military men had been circulating for weeks. Moreover, the atmosphere was already strained by politically motivated strikes and protests against the administration's labor, energy, and education policies. The possibility that military dissidents might seek to overturn his government was sufficiently real to Frondizi that even as he sought a solution to the Air Force crisis, he asked General Aramburu to use his influence in military circles to discourage any break with legality. The ex-Provisional President, in a radio address on September 10, spoke out strongly against any military takeover, while at the same time criticizing the Frondizi administration for its murky policies and for entrusting key positions to nonparty figures of dubious antecedents.[48]

The principal target of this attack was, of course, the President's key aide, Rogelio Frigerio. General Aramburu's criticism simply echoed the view held by many in the armed forces that Frigerio was the evil genius of the administration. So widespread was the belief that he was a communist, a belief deliberately encouraged by political opponents of the administration, that the Secretaries of the Navy and Army, Admiral Estévez and General Solanas Pacheco, despite

[47] To restore some semblance of discipline the Air Force subjected the officers who had rebelled against Huerta to courts-martial. None of these officers suffered anything more than a few months' detention; all were restored to active duty, many in their former assignments. The new Air Secretary did, however, appoint a new Air Force Commander-in-Chief in the person of Brigadier Mayor (Major General) Manuel Alemán, who by virtue of his assignment as Air Attaché in Washington had managed to escape involvement in the ruckus (*La Prensa*, Sept. 20, 25, Oct. 1, 7, 1958).

[48] On Frondizi's apprehensions about allowing the Air Force crisis to continue, see Luna, *Diálogos con Frondizi* [66], p. 84; for the role of Vice-President Gómez in securing Aramburu's assistance, Gómez [59], pp. 348–54. For the text of the ex-President's address to a group of radio station owners, *La Prensa*, Sept. 11, 1958.

their own high regard for the importance of his services, urged the President to remove Frigerio as a means of improving the administration's image in the eyes of the military. Frondizi, on November 10, did in fact relieve Frigerio from his Casa Rosada post as Secretary of Socio-Economic Relations but he promptly installed him in the Olivos residence as a personal advisor, a transparent move that did little to reduce attacks on the administration.[49]

It was not the threat of military intervention, however, but a politically motivated labor protest that led Frondizi to take the most drastic step of his six months in the presidency, the declaration on November 11 of a 30-day nationwide state of siege. The immediate excuse was the continued defiance by workers in the state-owned (YPF) petroleum facilities in Mendoza province of a presidential exhortation to end an illegal strike they had initiated eleven days before. Called by the Peronist-led State Oil Workers Union (SUPE), this strike was not an ordinary labor dispute, for its principal objective was to force the government to nullify the contracts it had recently signed with two American companies to produce oil in areas where YPF had already proved the existence of reserves.[50]

The oil workers' strike was certainly political in intention, but whether it was part of an insurrectional movement, as the decree proclaiming the state of siege intimated, is not all clear. The available evidence indicates that Perón himself, although annoyed by Frondizi's failure to live up to his preelectoral promises, had still not reached the point of authorizing his followers to attempt Frondizi's ouster. Only a few weeks before the strike, Perón's representative, John William Cooke, was cautioning against playing into the hands of Frondizi's "gorilla" opponents. "The Peronists, save for a small extremist sector, understand that the fall of Frondizi will not mean

---

[49] Interviews with General (Ret.) Solanas Pacheco and Admiral (Ret.) Estévez. Frigerio was the special target of a Navy Intelligence Service (SIN) report on communist infiltration into the government that was a mixture of fact and exaggeration. Frigerio's transfer to Olivos after the Navy had pressed for his removal as being too dangerous to be in the Casa Rosada left a bitter taste in Navy circles (interview with Admiral (Ret.) Jorge Perren, April 30, 1970).

[50] On the origins and evolution of the strike, see *Qué*, Nov. 11, 1958, and *La Prensa*, Nov. 2–10, 1958; see also the full-page advertisement taken out by three unions including SUPE (Sindicato Único Petroleros del Estado) and FASP (Federación Argentina Sindical de Petroleros) in *La Prensa*, Sept. 5, 1958; for Decree 9764, Nov. 11, 1958, establishing a nationwide state of siege, see *Anales* [1] XVIII-B, 1223–24.

improvement of their problems, but the worsening of the ills they now suffer."[51]

It is true that on November 10 the Peronist-led union group, the "62" bloc, reversing an earlier position, gave support to the Mendoza strike; but it is also true that the SUPE leadership offered that day to call it off if the government would listen to its objections to the petroleum contracts and not take reprisals against the strikers. The Undersecretary of Labor, Ruben Virue, accepting these terms, even signed an agreement with the SUPE leaders that called for the creation of an ad hoc committee to examine their objections to the contracts. President Frondizi, however, repudiated the agreement and, with the support of his entire cabinet, decreed a state of siege. In the early morning hours of November 11, the police carried out raids in the Federal Capital and in several provinces, arresting hundreds of individuals, mostly Peronists and communists but including members of the UCRP.[52]

In resorting to the state of siege, Frondizi stretched to its limit the concept of the rule of law he had announced as the guiding principle of his administration six months before. Although the constitution certainly provided for the suspension of individual guarantees in a time of domestic insurrection, it was not at all clear that the existing circumstances in the oil fields, or even the threats of other groups to call a general strike in support of the petroleum workers, added up to the conditions that would justify so extreme a measure. Moreover, even if the administration felt that it had no other weapon with which to cope with the SUPE strike, its decision to declare a nationwide state of siege rather than one limited to Mendoza raised doubts about its real intentions. Equally troubling was the administration's thinly disguised violation of the constitutional precepts governing the establishment of a state of siege. Alleging that the Congress was in recess, the President resorted to a decree to put it into effect rather than request authorization from that body as stipulated by the constitution. The Congress, in fact, was in session, even if not meeting, in the early morning hours of November 11; and its

[51] Anales [1], XVIII-B, 1223–24; Cooke to Perón, undated [Oct. 1958], *Perón-Cooke correspondencia* [72], II, 117.

[52] *La Prensa*, Nov. 11–12, 1958; *Qué*, Nov. 25, 1958, p. 8. The press reported 250 arrests but Ricardo Guardo, a Peronist writer, gives the number as 1,000 ([60], p. 120).

approval after the fact was sought and obtained from the UCRI-dominated chambers later that very day.[53]

The administration's justification for employing such measures was its determination to uphold the principle of authority in the face of threats of anarchy and subversion. In setting forth the government's position to the Congress, Interior Minister Alfredo Vítolo cited the actions of various groups, labor and political, who were exploiting the petroleum issue as a rallying cry. Vítolo, however, was unable to produce concrete evidence of an imminent threat to its authority.[54]

Indeed, the closest thing to a specific plot that the Frondizi administration would be able to point to in the next few days was the embarrassing behavior of its own Vice-President, Dr. Alejandro Gómez. Gómez had been unhappy for months with the influence Rogelio Frigerio exerted over the President and with the specific policies Frondizi had adopted in regard to the electric power contracts, higher education, and the petroleum contracts. In direct conversations with the President, and in meetings with party leaders, he had made no secret of his discontent and periodically spoke of the possibility of resigning. Most recently, on November 10, he had warned the President that if he did not agree to the legal necessity of submitting the petroleum contracts for congressional approval, he, Gómez, would definitely resign.[55]

What happened over the next several days is still shrouded in controversy. According to Gómez, on learning from an Army officer friendly to Frondizi that military men were deeply unhappy with the government's orientation and were in a state of incipient revolt, the Vice-President, in good faith, proposed on November 12 to Interior Minister Vítolo and to the President himself that he, Gómez, might serve as an instrument for carrying on discussions with civilian leaders outside the administration with a view to broadening its popular support and discouraging a military takeover. Gómez's personal goal was to bring about the unification of the intransigent Radicals, currently split between the UCRI and UCRP, and his hope was that the President would agree to reorient his policies so as to make this possible. According to his account, he had no intention whatsoever

[53] *Diputados* [2], 1958, VIII, 6095–6126; *Senadores* [3], 1958, IV, 2737–42.
[54] *Diputados* [2], 1958, VIII, 6103ff.
[55] Gómez [59], pp. 295–98, 337–38.

of trying to use the threat of a military coup to coerce Frondizi into forming a coalition government, nor was he aspiring to replace him at the head of such a government.[56]

This, however, was the interpretation that Frondizi chose to place upon Gómez's actions. Summoned to attend a meeting of the military cabinet presided over by Frondizi that very afternoon, the Vice-President heard himself depicted by the President as trying to drive a wedge between the military and the civil administration. Moreover, when asked by the Army Secretary to identify the officer who had informed him about an impending military revolt, the Vice-President refused and stalked out of the meeting. Within the hour, rumors were circulating in government circles, in the military, and in the press that Gómez had been discovered in a plot to supplant Frondizi with a coalition government. Demands for his resignation from the vice-presidency mounted over the next several days, and on November 18, after an exchange of letters with the President in which the latter assured Gómez of his complete confidence in his integrity, the Vice-President submitted his resignation to the UCRI-dominated Congress.[57]

A Gómez apologia, published five years after the events, reveals the ex-Vice-President to have been more a victim of his own ingenuousness than an ambitious plotter. In refusing to reveal the name of his military source, and thus accepting the onus of appearing to cover up for a possible conspiracy, Gómez claims that he was fulfilling a pledge of honor, not to the officer in question, but to Frondizi, who had extracted it from him in a friendly meeting shortly before the tense confrontation with the military cabinet. The subsequent attacks on Gómez, until he consented to give up the vice-presidential post, also appear to have been orchestrated by Frondizi, or at least carried out with his knowledge and consent.[58]

Why did the President treat his running mate in so callous a fashion? One hypothesis relates to the timing. Because of his rigid

[56] *Ibid.*, pp. 357–62.

[57] *Ibid.*, pp. 362–79; "Transcripción del Acta de la reunión efectuada el día 12 de noviembre de 1958 en la Presidencia de la Nación," communicated to the Army via *Boletín Militar Público*, No. 3034, Nov. 21, 1958; *Qué*, Nov. 18, 1958, pp. 4–6; *Diputados* [2], 1958, VIII, 6169–94.

[58] Gómez [59], pp. 361–365, 373–79.

adherence to the electoral program enunciated by the UCRI, because of his open antipathy to Frigerio and other nonparty men holding high posts, because of his criticism of specific administration policies, Gómez was both a thorn in the side of the President and a problem that had to be handled with finesse. Should Dr. Gómez make good his threat of November 10 to resign in protest over the handling of the oil contracts, he could well divide the party and weaken the administration's support in the Congress. On the other hand, if the Vice-President could be made to appear as a traitor, participating in a plot masterminded by elements from other political sectors, Frondizi could achieve his elimination from office with minimal risks to party unity.

In moving swiftly on November 12 to discredit Gómez in the eyes of the party, the public and the military, President Frondizi managed to achieve several objectives with one maneuver. He got rid of an associate who was becoming more of a liability with each passing month and with each administration departure from its campaign platform. Moreover, with a vacancy in the vice-presidency, the possibility that the office might be used in a legal maneuver against the President at any time in the future was ruled out. Frondizi carefully refrained from summoning an election to fill the vacancy as long as he himself remained in office. Finally, the discovery by Frondizi and Interior Minister Vítolo of the "Gómez plot" a day after they proclaimed the state of siege lent added credibility to the argument for its necessity.

The full purpose of the state of siege declaration, however, was to be revealed only with the passage of time. When the 30-day limit of the original enactment was replaced in December by an indefinite extension, one that in fact was to last as long as the Frondizi government itself survived, it became clear that the motive was not so much the threat of an existing conspiracy as the anticipation of future resistance to unpopular economic policies. The original November 11 decree was thus a tacit admission that Frondizi's efforts to retain Perón's cooperation had broken down, as well as a public declaration that the President would not be deterred by political or trade union opposition, whether anti-Peronist or Peronist, from implementing his economic program. But that decree embodied still another implicit message: that whenever labor unions engaged in direct action to oppose his policies, President Frondizi would not hesitate to turn to the military to enforce acceptance.[59]

The first test of this determination, after the ending of the SUPE strike,[60] came in a matter of weeks, when on November 27, the President ordered the mobilization of the nation's railway workers to break a strike that was paralyzing transport. In so doing, Frondizi relied on the powers provided by a Peronist law of 1948 that he and other Radical Party leaders had denounced as totalitarian at the time of its enactment. Now, however, under President Frondizi's direction, Army chiefs took over the operation of the six state-owned railway lines, while military courts were empowered to pass sentences on workers who refused the summons to report to their jobs.[61] But the President's dependence on the military to enable him to proceed with his economic policies was to grow even greater in subsequent months, especially after the announcement on December 29 that his government was embarking on a stabilization program that required major changes in existing economic practices and would affect all sectors of Argentine society.

This stabilization program was, in fact, the price required of Argentina by the International Monetary Fund (IMF) and the United States Treasury for providing the financial assistance needed to cope with a balance-of-payments crisis. The Frondizi administration, in its eight months in office, had been unable to reverse the deteriorating trade and payments situation inherited from the previous administration. Faced now with the prospect of suspending payments

[59] The presidential message requesting an unlimited extension of the state of siege was submitted to Congress on December 4 and enacted as Law 14,785 of Dec. 11, 1958. For Interior Minister Vítolo's justification, see *Senadores* [3], 1958, IV, 2825ff.; for criticism by the Chamber of Deputies UCRP block that walked out in protest when the vote came up, see *Diputados* [2], 1958, IX, 6558–92.

[60] The Mendoza affiliate of SUPE voted to lift the strike on November 17 on the basis of a government promise to give their national union representation on YPF's board of directors (*Qué*, Nov. 25, 1958, p. 15). This promise was fulfilled when the new organic statute for YPF, embodied in Decree No. 10,612 of Nov. 28, assigned two of the fourteen seats on the YPF board of directors to representatives of the petroleum workers. In a sense this decision gave the workers the voice they had sought in the Nov. 10 agreement with Undersecretary of Labor Virue that the President had refused to approve.

[61] Decrees 10,394 and 10,395, Nov. 27, 1958; the names of the six colonels designated as mobilization chiefs for the railways are given in *Boletín Militar Público*, No. 3042.

unless external assistance could be secured, Frondizi agreed to make economic stabilization as well as development the aim of his policy. The reward was a financial package from the IMF and from public and private United States banks amounting to $329 million. The stabilization program called for an assortment of measures: the elimination of multiple exchange rates, consumer subsidies, and price controls that had artificially distorted domestic prices; the limitation of wage increases to those justified by productivity increases; restrictions on credit and its channeling to productive purposes; and the reduction of the fiscal deficits, generated in large part by state-owned enterprises, that were the principal source of currency inflation.[62]

As has often been the case in Latin America, the economic medicine prescribed by the IMF produced a bitter reaction among working-class and other low-income groups. It was not only the resulting sharp increases in consumer prices—increases that were to double the cost of living by year's end—that generated discontent, but the government's announced intention of divesting itself of deficit-ridden enterprises that had been acquired in the Perón era. To the workers in these companies and to many other Argentines, these enterprises represented part of the national patrimony that should be preserved and not surrendered to private hands whatever the deficits they incurred.

It was in fact the congressional enactment in January 1959 of a bill authorizing the sale of one of those enterprises, the Frigorífico Nacional, the stockyards and meat-packing plant in the Mataderos district of Buenos Aires, that touched off a spontaneous worker protest that soon mushroomed into a major confrontation between the government and labor. The Frigorífico workers, hoping to pressure the President into vetoing the bill, barricaded themselves inside the plant. Frondizi, about to depart on his first official visit to the United States, refused to be coerced in this manner, and ordered the plant retaken. A massive police operation, aided by Army tanks used as battering rams, carried out the task apparently without inflicting fatalities; but the courage and defiance shown by the Frigorífico workers and their friends in the Mataderos district stimulated other sectors of the labor movement into action. The Peronist "62" bloc de-

[62] Peterson [232], pp. 511–12; Potash, "Argentina's Quest for Stability" [187], p. 72.

clared an indefinite strike while even the non-Peronist labor blocs, their members angered by both the police measures and the recent price rises, also took part. For two days, the Argentine economy was at a standstill as industries shut down, public transportation in the capital came to a halt, and newspapers failed to appear.[63]

With President Frondizi in the United States, Acting President José M. Guido, advised by Interior Minister Vítolo and the military service secretaries, responded to the strike with firm measures. Orders were issued placing the employees of the capital transport system under military mobilization. Now both the national railway workers, mobilized since the previous November, and the Buenos Aires transport workers were under military discipline. The government also mobilized all YPF personnel and, fearful of sabotage attempts, declared the Dock Sud area of Buenos Aires, the city of La Plata, and the neighboring areas of Berisso and Ensenada, to be military zones. Troop reinforcements were summoned from interior provinces, and, with military guards posted in trains, buses, and at strategic sites, the Federal Capital took on the appearance of an occupied city. The counterpart of these security measures was the government effort to arrest those whom it regarded as responsible for an insurrectional strike. Acting under the standard procedures for combating domestic insurrection, known as the Plan Conintes, the police and military shut down Peronist and communist offices and detained scores of labor leaders. Radio comment on the strike, other than official releases, was banned and violations punished.[64]

The firmness of the government's response to the general strike restored the economy to near normalcy in a matter of days. But the episode of the strike, with its background of the austerity measures ordered to implement the stabilization program, marked a turning point in the administration's labor relations. The original Frigerio-Frondizi policy of seeking Perón's cooperation while courting Peronist union leaders through a process of restoring control of the union movement to their hands, was in a shambles. It was, after all, these selfsame leaders, urged on by Perón's representative, J. W. Cooke,

[63] *La Prensa*, Jan. 15–18, 21–22, 1959; *New York Times*, Jan. 18–20, 1959.

[64] *New York Times*, Jan. 18–20, 1959; *La Prensa*, Jan. 22, 1959; *Boletín Militar Público*, No. 3048, Jan. 21, 1959, No. 3051, Jan. 30, 1959. Radio Rivadavia, which was often used to voice antiadministration views, was shut down by the government for 30 days.

who made the decision to launch the general strike. From their view-point, the Perón-Frondizi understanding was now all but dead.[65]

Within the administration itself, while Frigerio and his adherents still hoped to resurrect that understanding,[66] Interior Minister Vítolo, on the one hand, and the military ministers, on the other, inevitably exercised a greater voice in the decision-making process. The military, having been asked to suppress the strike, could not be expected to accept without protest the renewal of a policy designed to turn the CGT over to Peronist hands. And, indeed, in the weeks following the January confrontation, it became clear that the earlier policy of nor-malizing the labor movement through elections that favored Peronist leaders had come to a standstill. Government interventors, in the persons of retired military officers, once again took control of the major unions that had been turned over to Peronist control in Fron-dizi's first weeks in office; elections that had been scheduled in vari-ous unions were postponed; and Labor Minister Allende, a trade union leader himself and Frigerio follower, resigned to be replaced by a longtime Radical Party confidant of the President, Dr. David Bléjer. Bléjer's policy of dealing firmly with the trade unions ap-pealed in general to the military, but raised the danger that hard-pressed Peronist labor leaders might join in another antigovernment venture.[67]

In this connection, a source of concern to President Frondizi and the focus of considerable political speculation were the political am-bitions of the Army Undersecretary, Colonel Manuel Reimúndez. Colonel Reimúndez had been appointed in July 1958 at the urging of Army Secretary Solanas Pacheco, who saw in his energy and organizational skills qualities useful in an assistant. But Colonel Reimúndez did not hesitate to use his position to place friends in

[65] Perón's increasing hostility toward Frondizi can be seen in his December 20, 1958, letter to Cooke, *Perón-Cooke correspondencia* [72], II, 127. On Cooke's plan to create disturbances to coincide with Frondizi's trip to the United States, see *ibid.*, p. 138; on his support for the general strike and the waffling of other Peronist politicians, see his letter to Perón dated Feb. 5, 1959, *ibid.*, pp. 139ff.

[66] The Frigerista effort to promote the renewal of ties between the govern-ment and the Peronist labor leadership is reflected in the treatment of labor news presented by the weekly *Qué*. See, for example, the issue of March 3, 1959, p. 10.

[67] Bléjer, the first Argentine Jew to serve as a cabinet minister, was careful to consult the armed forces secretaries and to obtain their assurances of support before accepting the post of Labor Minister (interview with Dr. David Bléjer, May 12, 1970).

strategic places. Moreover, he maintained ties, or so it was believed, with Andrés Framini, a hardline Peronist labor leader whom he had gotten to know in 1955 when he, Reimúndez, was attached to the Labor Ministry during the short-lived Lonardi presidency. Reimúndez was also widely reported to be the creator of a secret military lodge, the Dragón Verde (Green Dragon), through which he was said to be organizing support for his political future. The parallel between the alleged activities of Colonel Reimúndez and those of another Undersecretary of War in 1943, Colonel Perón, was not lost upon observers of the Argentine political scene. Even Juan Perón, in his Dominican exile, was intrigued by Reimúndez, although he shrewdly observed that "second helpings were never as good, and the situation of the Argentine people in 1958 is nothing like what it was in 1943."[68]

The Dragón Verde lodge, insofar as can be determined, never did in fact exist; it seems to have been, rather, the astutely publicized invention of Reimúndez's enemies. These included not only civilians, but a number of high-ranking Army officers who resented Colonel Reimúndez's treatment of them in his official capacities. Generals rarely find it comfortable to receive directives from a colonel, and Reimúndez's harsh personality did not make it any easier.[69]

But, if professional reasons explain part of the negative reaction to him, there was still the unresolved question of his ambition for power. The Colonel's potential for organizing a nationalist-Peronist military and labor bloc, in short, for reviving the political alignment attempted by Lonardi, made him a marked man both to anti-Peronist, anti-Frondizi political sectors and to President Frondizi himself. According to one source, who cites General Aramburu as his authority, the President was sufficiently concerned to have kept a close watch on Colonel Reimúndez through a special intelligence office.[70]

It was a group of anti-Peronists in civilian and military ranks, however, men with links to extremist factions in the UCRP, conservative,

[68] Juan Perón to Dr. John W. Cooke (Very Confidential), Ciudad Trujillo, December 26, 1958, in *Perón-Cooke correspondencia* [72], II, 134; interview with General (Ret.) Solanas Pacheco. Reimúndez replaced in the Undersecretariat Colonel D'Andrea Mohr, a Frondizi choice, who proceeded to show a lack of good sense by attending a dinner in honor of Admiral Rial after his release from disciplinary arrest imposed by the President.

[69] Interviews with Generals (Ret.) Solanas Pacheo and Juan E. Guglialmelli.
[70] Toryho [79], pp. 62ff.

and socialist parties, who were the most consistent enemies of Frondizi. Using as a cover the legitimate activities of their respective parties, these men sought to arouse military opinion by charging the administration with extensive corruption, by denouncing the President for surrounding himself with communists, and by insisting that he was deliberately promoting chaos so as to foster a communist takeover. Unsuccessful in their efforts to mount a coup in Frondizi's first eight months in office, they intensified their efforts in the Argentine autumn of 1959.[71]

Actual plotting for a military coup, as distinct from armchair conversation, seems to have begun in late March or early April. The principal military leaders were retired officers, former members of the Liberating Revolution, including adherents of both General (Ret.) Aramburu and Admiral (Ret.) Rojas. Aramburu himself, who left for Europe in late April, later warned against any disruption of the constitutional order. Rojas, on the other hand, in remarks published at home and abroad, denounced the Frondizi administration in such blunt terms as to leave little doubt that he favored its overturn. Such, indeed, was the interpretation made thousands of miles away in Mexico by Argentina's military attaché and onetime political ally of Rojas, Colonel Alejandro Lanusse, who felt moved to write a personal letter to the Admiral taking issue with his stand.[72]

Army Secretary Solanas Pacheco, and presumably his Navy and Air Force counterparts also, were well aware of the efforts to subvert the minds of impressionable officers. Through general orders, visits to garrisons, and personal contacts, they worked hard and successfully to maintain the loyalty of their respective services.[73] At the same time, together with other ministers, they were apparently urging the

[71] Interior Minister Vítolo once labeled these perennial conspirators the "elenco estable del golpismo [permanent plotters corps]." They included among others Dr. Arturo Mathov of the UCRP; Adolfo Zinny, head of the Movimiento Cívico Revolucionario, a civil commando group that had originated in the anti-Perón resistance of the 1950's; and a retired Army general, Fortunato Giovannoni.

[72] General (Ret.) Aramburu's admonition, issued in Paris, was printed in *La Prensa*, June 7, 1959; for Admiral Rojas's declaration to the Associated Press, which began with the words "the political situation could not be more deplorable," see *La Nación*, March 24, 1959, front page; for Colonel Lanusse's letter to Rojas, see excerpts printed in Lanusse [63], pp. 193–94.

[73] For the Army Secretary's talks to groups of commanders and his visits to interior garrisons, see *Qué*, March 24, 1959, p. 6; and *La Prensa*, April 23–25, 1959.

President to take firm measures to improve the administration's public image. To what extent their advice was decisive is not clear, but in April, following street disturbances in Buenos Aires, the government adopted an increasingly anticommunist stance, ordering the departure of several Soviet-bloc diplomats and placing a ban on all communist activities throughout the country.[74] Moreover, in a major housecleaning move, Frondizi began to replace government officials most closely identified with Rogelio Frigerio. Frigerio himself, in a letter made public on May 13, resigned as the President's *asesor personal* in economic matters, but, in fact, continued to make secret visits at night and on weekends to the Olivos residence.[75]

Despite the elimination from the national government of controversial officials and their replacement by others more acceptable to traditional political and economic interest groups, political tensions in Argentina remained high. Even the evidence that the Frondizi administration was respectful of legitimate forms of political activity and that opposition parties were able to participate in and win provincial elections did little to reduce the zeal of the plotters to effect the ouster of the President.[76] Indeed, the month of June was to find Frondizi confronted by one of the most severe politico-military crises he had to face since assuming the presidency.

Contributing to the onset of the crisis were not only the anti-Frondizi conspirators, but ex-President Juan Perón from his Dominican exile, and, as it would appear, even President Frondizi himself. In Perón's case, the critical move was his release to the press of the

---

[74] Details of the April 3 street disorders, the expulsion of Soviet-bloc diplomats, and Minister Vítolo's statements labeling the disorders as communist-inspired may be found in *La Prensa*, April 4–8, 1959. Decree No. 4965, issued on April 27, banned all activities by the Argentine Communist Party and front groups and ordered the closing of their offices and the suspension of all publications.

[75] On Frigerio's secret visits, see Díaz [55]. The list of those who were eased out of their posts in the administration included Dardo Cuneo in the presidential press office, Isidro Odena in the Radio and Television Broadcasting Interventorship, Carlos Florit as Foreign Minister, Bernardino Horne as Minister of Agriculture, and General (Ret.) Juan J. Uranga as head of the State Coal Board (YCF). A respected conservative, Dr. Diógenes Taboada, took over as Foreign Minister, and Dr. Angel Lagomarsino became Minister of Commerce, Finance, and Transportation. See *La Prensa*, April 25–May 6, May 14–16, 1959.

[76] On the elections and their results in San Luis, Corrientes, Catamarca, and Mendoza provinces, see *La Prensa*, March 9, 30, 31; April 1, 5, 27, 1959. Only in San Luis did the UCRI win the majority of seats at stake.

document containing the alleged text of his secret 1958 pact with Frondizi. On June 11, Perón's agents in Buenos Aires distributed photocopies of the text and issued a manifesto in which the exiled dictator denounced the Frondizi administration for violations of the constitution and the laws. When asked by reporters on Santo Domingo, to whom he showed the original document, why he was releasing it at this time, he replied: "Because the situation in Argentina has turned so dramatic for national popular ideals that it has become impossible to keep secret the solemn promises undertaken and broken by Frondizi. In short, I am revealing it for patriotic reasons."[77]

Politics rather than patriotism, however, would seem to have motivated Perón's decision. With the Peronist trade unions under severe restraints, with the elimination of Frigerio's influence over administration labor policy, and with little to be gained from further behind-the-scenes contacts with the government, he was now trying, in paradoxical combination with his own enemies, to bring Frondizi to his knees.

The revelation of the document inevitably intensified pressure on Frondizi. Although he firmly denied, as he had done in the past, that he had even made an agreement with Perón, and although he labeled the signature ascribed to him on the document as a forgery, he was placed on the defensive.[78] Demands for an investigation into the authenticity of the document were now being sounded not only in the halls of Congress, but in military circles as well. The anti-Frondizi, anti-Peronist groups had received a boost from an unexpected source and had a new weapon for conducting their psychological warfare against the loyalties of the military to the constituted authorities.

In these circumstances, Frondizi took defensive measures that may have included a risky attempt to promote a diversionary movement. Information about the President's actions in this crisis is incomplete and rests on more or less partisan accounts rather than on reliable documentation. On the basis of one such account, it would appear that Frondizi tried to focus attention on the controversial Army Un-

[77] *La Prensa*, June 12, 1959, provides full coverage of the revelation of the document over Radio Rivadavia by Perón's henchmen and of his press conference at Ciudad Trujillo.

[78] Frondizi's denial took the form of a letter to Interior Minister Vítolo. See above, Chapter 7, note 127.

dersecretary, Colonel Reimúndez. Rumors to the effect that Reimúndez was linked in a political pact with hardline Peronist labor leader Andrés Framini began to circulate among military men in the days before June 15. It is just possible that the President, utilizing secret channels available to him, sought to give credibility to such rumors as a device to divert attention from the now dead Perón-Frondizi pact to a Reimúndez-Framini deal that could have serious implications for the future.[79]

Whether, as one source contends, the President deliberately had information leaked to those military men most critical of his administration so as to provoke them into action against Reimúndez cannot be established.[80] What is clear is that on June 15, amid signs of uneasiness in various garrisons, two of the highest-ranking troop commanders in Buenos Aires, Generals Raúl Poggi and Florencio Yornet, claiming to speak for their subordinates, presented the Secretary of the Army with a three-point request that included the ouster of Colonel Reimúndez, an investigation into the authenticity of the Perón-Frondizi pact, and the ending of the military mobilization of the railway workers. General Solanas Pacheco immediately relieved the two generals from their posts, but the ground under the Army establishment was already beginning to quake.[81]

The very next day, the fourth anniversary of the June 16, 1955, anti-Perón revolt, an attempt was made to incite a military rebellion against President Frondizi. Ex-Army Commander-in-Chief Lieut. General (Ret.) Ossorio Arana, accompanied by Admiral (Ret.) Toranzo Calderon and two other generals, flew to Córdoba at dawn hoping to win over the local garrison. In the Buenos Aires area,

[79] The hypothesis of a Frondizi diversionary move is my own and is admittedly based on two slender bits of evidence: the Aramburu assertion that Frondizi decided to "quemar" Reimúndez by spreading word of the latter's secret negotiations with Framini (Toryho [79], p. 72); and the statement in Perren's Memoirs (p. 346) that the story of the Reimúndez-Framini contact surfaced just before the military unrest of June 15. Given the sequence of events—first the Perón disclosure of his pact with Frondizi on June 11 and then the circulation among military men of the alleged Reimúndez-Framini deal—the idea of a deliberate attempt to divert attention from the former seems plausible.

[80] The main thrust of the Aramburu account is that Frondizi used the golpistas to get rid of Reimúndez (Toryho [79], p. 72).

[81] *La Prensa*, June 16, 17, 1959. Poggi, Commander of the Third Army, and Yornet, Commander of the First Motorized Division, were replaced by Generals Angel Peluffo and Colonel Carlos Muzzio, respectively.

meanwhile, Admiral (Ret.) Rial and other plotters sought to win over Army unit commanders by conveying the impression that the Navy stood squarely behind the rebellion.[82]

Neither in Córdoba nor in Buenos Aires, however, did any Army unit move. During the night of June 15–16 and over the next 36 hours, loyal officers worked to prevent any outbreak. The Navy Ministry for its part sent representatives to all Army regiments in the vicinity of the capital and to the Córdoba garrison advising their officers that the Navy was not taking part. The upshot was that the rebellion never got off the ground, not even to the extent of issuing a proclamation. The Army and Navy Ministries ordered the arrest of the leading participants, but the Federal Police, possibly under orders from President Frondizi, allowed Ossorio Arana to escape into Uruguay. The entire episode revealed that although many officers disliked the personalities and practices of the Frondizi administration, the spirit of loyalty to the constitutional order was still strong. As Admiral Rial, a leader of the plot, later recalled, the time was not ripe; but he and others who shared his view of the Frondizi administration were impatient to halt what they saw as a slide into communism.[83]

The failure of the June 16 attempted coup did not resolve the atmosphere of crisis that surrounded the government. Within military circles, it was evident that discipline, order, and the esprit de corps were suffering from the immersion of officers in political discussions. As a conciliatory gesture to the most disaffected, and as a move to strengthen the sense of unity at the Córdoba garrison, its Chief of Staff, Colonel Osiris Villegas, proposed to the Army Secretary that the controversial Colonel Reimúndez be replaced as Undersecretary. Army Secretary Solanos Pacheco, seeing this as a challenge to his authority, offered his own resignation, but the President refused it. Frondizi did, however, move promptly to replace Reimúndez, thus

[82] Interviews with General (Ret.) Solanas Pacheco and Admiral (Ret.) Arturo Rial; Perren Memoirs, p. 346. The generals who accompanied Ossorio Arana to Córdoba were Emilio Bonnecarrère, an active duty officer, and Bernardino Labayru, who was in retired status. Also involved was Admiral (Ret.) Pedro Favarón, former head of the Marine Corps.

[83] On the Navy efforts to discourage the revolt, see Perren Memoirs, pp. 346ff.; interviews with General (Ret.) Solanas Pacheco and Admiral (Ret.) Rial.

eliminating from a strategic post a man perceived as a threat both by members of the Frondizi administration and by its enemies.[84]

The June 1959 crisis was, of course, far more than a military matter. For many Argentines, the issues lay in the failure of the administration to halt the soaring inflation, achieve prosperity, and bring about labor peace. Viewed from within the administration, however, the problem was seen as the need to gain time to allow its economic policies to produce their full effect. Frondizi's political foes in the UCRP and other parties saw a simple solution to the crisis in a presidential resignation and the holding of new elections. The President, however, looked for the answer in a dramatic change of cabinet personnel that could overcome the administration's tarnished image, win support in both military and civilian circles, and yet not abandon the developmentalist orientation. That change was made on June 22–24, when Frondizi shook up his cabinet and invited a constant critic and political rival, Alvaro Alsogaray, to take control of the Economy and Labor portfolios.[85]

The Alsogaray appointment came both as a shock to Frondizi's UCRI supporters and as a surprise to his political foes. A businessman with little known sympathy for trade unions, a champion of private as against state-run enterprise, an admirer of Ludwig Erhardt and postwar German economic policies, Alsogaray seemed an unlikely choice for Frondizi to make. The President appointed him, however, at the urging of several advisors, including Rogelio Frigerio and General Solanas Pacheco. Frigerio saw in Alsogaray a man who would fight the inflation that preoccupied vast sectors of the middle class and one whose presence in the government would satisfy military groups that it was not pro-left. Frigerio also believed that Alsogaray, while carrying out the stabilization measures, would work to promote the existing developmentalist policy.[86] General Solanas Pacheco for his part saw in Alsogaray a man who could bring military support to the government.[87] A onetime junior Army officer, he en-

[84] Interview with General (Ret.) Solanas Pacheco; *La Prensa*, June 17, 18, 1959.

[85] On the Socialist Party position, *Afirmación*, June 30, 1959; for the UCRP position, see Azoategui [222], p. 135; for the cabinet changes, *La Prensa*, June 23–27, 1959.

[86] Díaz [55], pp. 64–66.

[87] Interview with General (Ret.) Solanas Pacheco.

joyed considerable prestige in Army circles in his own right as well as through his brother, Julio, a well-known colonel and Olympic Games equestrian. Given his contacts within the military, it is not surprising that one of Alvaro Alsogaray's first governmental acts was to end the military mobilizations that had put the armed forces in a conflict situation with Argentine transport and other workers.[88]

The sweeping cabinet changes that Frondizi carried out in June 1959 were not intended to affect the military ministries. Indeed, the President was anxious to retain the services of Army Secretary Solanas Pacheco, Navy Secretary Estévez, and Air Force Secretary Abrahín, who had shown both loyalty and efficiency in keeping their respective forces under control during the crisis. Their very success, however, especially in the case of Army and Navy Secretaries, was to work against their continued tenure, in view of the attitude which many Argentine military men had come to hold about the proper role of a military minister. Reacting against the kind of relationship that had existed under Perón, officers increasingly expected the minister to be their representative in the national administration rather than the President's agent. The minister was, in fact, both, but the difficulties of performing such a dual role increased over time, especially in an atmosphere in which most military men harbored reservations about the President's integrity.

General Solanas Pacheco, for his part, had tried through words to emphasize his own independence from partisan politics and his identification with Army aspirations. For example, in remarks delivered during a tour of interior garrisons, he asserted: "I am not a party man; I have never served nor will I ever serve any interests other than those of the nation and of the Army to which I have devoted my life passionately and to which I owe everything I am. The experience acquired through suffering and sacrifices during the Perón dictatorship should not be forgotten. Fifteen years ago, I saw clearly when others were confused."[89] Solanas Pacheco's advice to uneasy colleagues was to be patient with the elected government: "We are suffering and we will continue to suffer the pressures of an opinion that urges action without measuring the consequences. This singu-

---

[88] Decree No. 8197, June 30, 1959, in *Boletín Militar Público*, No. 3090, July 8, 1959.

[89] Statement issued at Salta, *La Prensa*, April 26, 1959.

lar historic opportunity should not be wasted through imprudence or impatience."[90]

As noted above, the Army Secretary did succeed in preventing any open outbreak, but he paid a price in the reduction of his authority and prestige in the eyes of fellow officers. As the superior of Colonel Reimúndez and, therefore, responsible for approving the latter's professional decisions, he felt his position undermined by the recent events; and indeed, in the Córdoba garrison especially, voices were raised demanding his ouster. On June 30, following the completion of the cabinet reorganization, Solanas Pacheco resubmitted his resignation, leaving to the President the delicate task of finding a new Army Commander-in-Chief, as well as a cabinet Secretary, both of which posts he had been filling since Frondizi's inaugural.[91]

The departure of General Solanas Pacheco was followed in a matter of weeks by that of the Navy Secretary, Admiral Estévez. But, whereas Solanas Pacheco had withdrawn voluntarily, amid growing signs of Army unrest but while still retaining a maximum of personal dignity, the Navy Secretary tried to cling to his post, underestimating the depth of feeling that had been building up against him. Frondizi persisted in retaining him despite the nearly unanimous advice of the flag officers to appoint a new minister. The result was that a problem that could have been resolved tactfully without a breakdown of hierarchical order was allowed to explode into a mutinous confrontation. In the face of a threat that could have extended to his own position, the President finally agreed to jettison Estévez, but too late to prevent seven admirals and various other officers from being dragged down in his wake. Unfortunately, in the long run, for Frondizi, the list of those who went into retirement at this time included outstanding professional officers who had been working to restrain adventurous elements and to maintain support for constitutional government. In March 1962, when his political future would be decided, they would not be present to express their views in the council of admirals.[92]

---

[90] Statement issued at Jujuy, *ibid.*

[91] Interview with General (Ret.) Solanas Pacheco; *La Prensa*, July 1, 1959.

[92] Those who voluntarily retired after the July 25, 1959, mutiny included: Admiral Helvio Guozden, Director of Naval Materiel; Admiral Jorge Perren, Chief of the Naval General Staff; Admiral Mario Robbio, Naval Attaché in Washington; Admiral Alberto Patrón Laplacette, Director General of Personnel;

Why, then, did the President allow the situation to develop as it did in 1959? The answer appears to lie, on the one hand, in his analysis of the nature of the opposition to Estévez and, on the other, in his reluctance as a civilian President to intervene in what he thought could be handled as an intramural quarrel. Frondizi apparently saw the opposition to Estévez as coming from a minority of golpistas, politicized officers who were linked to his civilian opponents in the UCRP and other parties; these officers, in his view, wanted to overthrow him and would make trouble for any minister identified with his administration. This judgment was correct insofar as it dealt with the original promoters of anti-Estévez feeling, but it failed to appreciate that broad sectors of the naval officer corps, men who were not moved by political ambitions, and who, though critical of government policies, were not golpistas, were becoming fed up with Estévez and his style of management. An intellectually gifted individual, Estévez was erratic in his contacts with senior officers, tactless and patronizing in dealing with people, and indifferent to the need to maintain good public relations. As both Navy Secretary and Chief of Naval Operations, he was held responsible for everything that went on in the Navy, a situation that made him the inevitable target of criticism for decisions that were, in fact, made by others.[93]

The rising discontent of the nongolpistas, added to the activities of the anti-Frondizi minority, required prompt remedies. A belated decision to appoint a separate Chief of Naval Operations in the person of Admiral Alberto Vago proved ineffective in halting the growing demands for Estévez's resignation. Even such loyal subordinates as Admiral Perren, the Chief of the Navy General Staff, felt that the only way to head off an open insurrection was for Estévez to resign, but the President would have none of it. Refusing the advice of practically all the admirals on active duty, who met with him at his request on July 14, Frondizi insisted that the issue was not the person of Estévez, but the principle of upholding discipline. They were re-

---

Admiral Carlos Kolungia, Commander of the Cruiser Force; and Admiral Renato Ares, Naval Attaché in London (Perren Memoirs, pp. 363–64).

[93] Perren Memoirs, pp. 341–45. As Chief of the General Staff, Admiral Perren estimates that he made 80 percent of the decisions issued over the signature of the Chief of Naval Operations, but, because he was not the most senior admiral, this only caused more unhappiness with Secretary Estévez.

sponsible for the situation, and they should have been punishing insubordination and not requesting the Secretary's resignation.[94]

Although theoretically he was correct, the President underestimated the sensitivity of the admirals to his rebuff and overestimated their capacity to defuse the situation. The admirals present at the July 14 meeting, their advice having been sought and rejected, presented individual requests for retirement; at the same time, nevertheless, they agreed with one another to prevent acts of indiscipline while continuing to press for Estévez's resignation. This unity of outlook, however, soon gave way under the pressures emanating from officers of lesser ranks. Such admirals as Perren and Mario Robbio, for whom a breakdown of discipline was anathema, remained loyal to Estévez as long as he was Navy Secretary, even while urging that he resign to forestall a mutiny, but others led by Admiral Vago put themselves at its head. On July 24, the Chief of Naval Operations and Admiral Eladio Váquez, the Navy Undersecretary, in contact with officers at various installations, declared themselves in open rebellion against the authority of Admiral Estévez. Frondizi, confronted now with the alternative of replacing his Navy Secretary or having the revolt directed against himself, set aside principles and made his choice.[95]

To replace Estévez, the President turned to a respected retired admiral, Gastón C. Clement. With Clement's appointment as Secretary of the Navy, Frondizi was to enjoy a period of relative ease in dealing with this branch of the armed forces. Indeed, down to March 1962, Admiral Clement was able to retain the confidence both of his Navy subordinates and of the President. Perhaps it was the new

---

[94] *Ibid.*, pp. 346–58; see also *La Prensa*, July 18, 1959, for the text of the July 15 letter of President Frondizi to Admiral Vago, the new Chief of Naval Operations, explaining his refusal to replace Estévez as Navy Secretary.

[95] Perren Memoirs, pp. 358–65. The final confrontation was both dramatic and depressing. President Frondizi himself rushed down to the Navy Ministry to find Admiral Vago surrounded by a group of Navy and Army officers. In front of this group the President ordered him to give up his attitude of disobedience to Secretary Estévez. The reply was blunt: "Me niego" (I refuse). Frondizi, apparently stunned, went into an office to confer with Admirals Estévez, Perren, and Robbio. Asked for their advice, Perren and Robbio told the President that if he did not announce within one minute that he was replacing Estévez, in another five minutes the Navy would oust him. This time the President accepted the advice (interview with Admiral (Ret.) Jorge Perren, April 1, 1970; Perren Memoirs, p. 363).

Secretary's personal qualities—his maturity, experience, and administrative skills—but perhaps also the realization of most officers, once the Estévez issue was resolved, that the Navy as an institution had a stake in the preservation of the status quo, that enabled Clement to satisfy his two constituencies. After all, if the military took power, the resulting regime would inevitably be Army-dominated, and the influence the Navy was currently enjoying within the civilian government might well deteriorate.[96]

But if President Frondizi's problems with the Navy were for the time being eased, his experience with the Army, especially after August 1959, was just the reverse. From that time until March 1962, he was exposed to a series of pressures, confrontations, and incipient revolts that aimed either at his transformation into a complete puppet or at his definite ouster from office. Indeed, only through his dogged determination to hold onto the presidency and his ability to outsmart and outmaneuver his Army opponents was he able to last as long as he did.

The most trying period in this struggle to survive, from August 1959 to March 1961, coincided with continuing severe economic difficulties. Fiscal deficits, cost-of-living increases, and foreign trade imbalances tended to obscure the administration's very real achievements in promoting petroleum and steel production. During this period, real wages remained at deteriorated levels, contributing to social tensions that found expression in acts of violence; at this time also, the administration's popular support, as measured by provincial and congressional elections, stood at an all-time low. To add to Frondizi's problems, these twenty months coincided with the entrenchment in the post of Army Commander-in-Chief of a headstrong and basically hostile officer, Major General Carlos S. Toranzo Montero.

The appointment of Toranzo Montero was an indirect consequence of the June 1959 crisis that saw Solanas Pacheco resign from his twin posts of Army Secretary and Commander-in-Chief. To fill the cabinet position, Frondizi turned to an elderly retired general, Elbio Anaya, whose anti-Peronist reputation, aloofness from recent quarrels, and

---

[96] Despite his ouster in March 1962 in which the Navy played a major role, Frondizi regards the Navy as having contributed significantly to the preservation of the constitutional government (interview with Dr. Arturo Frondizi, April 14, 1970).

military prestige, especially in the cavalry, gave promise that he might be able to restore unity and discipline to the Army. However, in getting General Anaya to accept the cabinet post, the President promised him a free hand in managing the Army, a promise he would soon have reason to regret; for the new Secretary, an Army traditionalist, insisted on appointing the senior major general on the active list to be Commander-in-Chief. That general, who as a cavalry captain years before had served Anaya as a loyal subordinate, was Carlos S. Toranzo Montero.[97]

Anticipating that General Toranzo Montero would create problems for both of them, the President tried to talk the Army Secretary out of making the appointment. When that failed, he proposed that the appointment be made for a probationary period, a condition that Toranzo Montero refused to accept. Finally, Frondizi went ahead with the appointment on the basis of an understanding reached with General Anaya, and seemingly also with Toranzo Montero, that the latter would make no key personnel changes.[98] The new Commander-in-Chief, however, was unwilling to accept a condition that required him to maintain in sensitive posts officers in whom he had little confidence. Indeed, the President's efforts to place limitations on his authority led him to conclude that Frondizi's real intention in appointing him was to have him fail. Unable to carry out his ideas for military reforms, he would be discredited in the eyes of the officers who looked up to him and would soon be replaced and sent into retirement. Frondizi, as he saw it, would thus have shown respect for the principle of military seniority and at the same time have gotten rid of a dangerous opponent.[99]

Whether or not this was the President's intention, the insistence of Toranzo Montero on replacing men identified with the Reimúndez circle and his desire to staff crucial posts with officers of his own

---

[97] Interview with Lieut. Colonel (Ret.) Alberto Garasino, March 11, 1970. Anaya made his choice from a list of possible candidates, the major generals on active duty. For one reason or another he disqualified all but Toranzo Montero. Apart from his personal experience with Toranzo Montero years before, Anaya may have been influenced by the strong endorsement of his candidacy received from Admirals Perren and Robbio (interview with Admiral (Ret.) Jorge Perren, April 30, 1970).

[98] Interview with General (Ret.) Carlos Toranzo Montero, March 26, 1970; Casas [224], pp. 110–11.

[99] Interview with General (Ret.) Carlos Toranzo Montero.

confidence paved the way for a clash that was to split the Army anew and raise the specter of civil war. The crisis was precipitated on September 2, when Army Secretary Anaya, unwilling to approve the changes insisted on by Toranzo Montero, proceeded to remove him as Commander-in-Chief and, with the consent of the President, to replace him with an interim appointee. Coming as it did only a few weeks after Toranzo Montero had assumed his duties, this action provoked those officers most closely identified with his view, and by the same token most suspicious of Frondizi, into open resistance.[100]

Fourteen generals of the Buenos Aires area, none of them with important troop commands, collectively radioed their repudiation of Toranzo Montero's ouster to all Army units and called on their officers to take a stand.[101] Although Secretary Anaya proceeded to have these generals placed under arrest, Toranzo Montero was encouraged by their support and by the information he received about Army attitudes from friends in the Army Intelligence Service to make a countermove against the Army Secretary. On the night of September 3, he established a headquarters in the Army Mechanics School, several blocks from the main Army building; and with communications equipment secretly removed from this building and set up at the Mechanics School, Toranzo Montero made radio contact with all Army units of the country announcing that he was resuming the post of Commander-in-Chief.[102]

Toranzo Montero's strategy was to utilize the favorable reactions of interior garrisons—the Córdoba division had already declared in

[100] General Toranzo Montero was most anxious to replace General Héctor Lambardi, the commander of the cavalry corps, and General Conesa, the Chief of the Army General Staff (*ibid.*).

[101] The fourteen generals were: Cordes, currently unassigned; Cordini, Director of the Army War Academy; Fraga, Director of the National War School; Hosking, Director of the Military Geographic Institute; Locatelli, Director of Motorized Materiel; Martijena, Director of Army Factories; Picca, Chief of the Coordinating General Staff; Pizzaro Jones, Director of Army Materiel; Poggi, unassigned; Sosa, head of Military Regions; Federico Toranzo Montero, Director of Remount Service; Villamil, Director of Engineers; Yornet, unassigned; and Zenarruza, Quartermaster General of the Army.

[102] Interview with General (Ret.) Carlos Toranzo Montero. General Fraga, the one signatory of the September 2 radiogram who escaped arrest, was asked by Toranzo Montero to go to Córdoba and take over the Fourth Infantry Division, which he had commanded earlier in the year. Another key aide was Lieut. Colonel Catán, who was responsible for disassembling the radio equipment in the Army Ministry and reassembling it at the Mechanics School, thus giving Toranzo Montero superior communications facilities with the entire Army.

his favor on September 2—to bring pressure on the officers of units in the Buenos Aires area that were under commanders loyal to the Army Secretary. The first such unit to repudiate its commander, the Third Regiment of the First Motorized Division, gave Toranzo Montero a force of regulars that enhanced his ability to defend his position against an expected tank attack. His battle plan called for leaving only a small number of troops in the Mechanics School, but surrounding it with barricades to give the impression that his main force was there. The bulk of his troops were to be hidden in buildings in the neighboring blocks where, with antitank weapons obtained from the Army arsenal that was adjacent to the Mechanics School, they could fire from all sides on the tanks once they entered the narrow streets.[103]

During the night of September 3–4, as tanks moved up from Campo de Mayo to the outskirts of the city, the stage was set for bloody combat. Throughout the country, Army garrisons were choosing sides, with the preponderance of forces in the interior swinging behind Toranzo Montero. In the Buenos Aires area, while the Campo de Mayo garrison, the Ciudadela artillery group, and the San Martín Grenadiers stayed loyal, the two remaining infantry regiments of the First Motorized Division were taken over by Toranzo Montero supporters. Meanwhile, the crisis was having its effect on the other services. The Air Force could be counted on, with certain defections, to assist the government in repressing the rebels, but the position of the Navy was, to say the least, ambivalent. Navy Secretary Clement offered the cooperation of the fleet, but Chief of Naval Operations Admiral Vago displayed a reluctance to have the Navy take part in the repression. Individual Navy and Marine officers, moreover, were visiting the Campo de Mayo and Grenadiers barracks trying to persuade their officers not to oppose Toranzo Montero.[104]

It was President Frondizi who had to make the painful and difficult choice: whether to order the tanks that had been halted at San Isidro to proceed with the repression of the rebels at the Mechanics School or to try to find a compromise that would avoid violence.

[103] *Ibid.*
[104] *Ibid.*, also interview with Dr. José R. Cáceres Monié, May 20, 1970. Dr. Cáceres Monié was Undersecretary of Defense at the time of these events and was in a position to receive reliable data on the stand taken by various troop commanders.

Amid contradictory advice from his closest military advisors, and unable to get assurances of a prompt and painless victory, Frondizi chose the latter course.[105] Utilizing as a mediator a mutual friend, General (Ret.) Rodolfo Larcher, Frondizi invited Toranzo Montero to the Casa Rosada and, after learning that the latter's aim was not to overthrow the government, agreed to a solution whereby Larcher would replace Anaya as Army Secretary and Toranza Montero would be reinstalled as Commander-in-Chief. By late afternoon of September 4, the respective swearing-in ceremonies had taken place, military units were returning to their bases, and the immediate crisis was over.[106]

But the resolution of this September crisis was itself to have serious consequences for both the President and the Army. Frondizi was now saddled with an Army commander whose authority derived from a successful act of defiance and with an Army Secretary not of his own free choice. In failing to uphold the authority of General Anaya when confronted with an act of open rebellion, he lowered his own prestige as constitutional Commander-in-Chief of the armed forces and invited further invasions of his own authority.

For the Army, the September crisis was also an unsettling experience. It brought to the surface the persistent divisions in the officer corps and demonstrated once again the tenuous nature of hierarchical control in the post-1955 Army. To be sure, the new Army Secretary, in his first general message to the force, sought to paper over the situation by presenting an optimistic view. In ponderous language he declared:

The events that took place from September 2–4, 1959, permitted the materialization of the essential purpose of reestablishing the principle of

[105] An example of the conflicting advice was that provided by the staff of the Liaison and Coordination Secretariat in the Casa Rosada. Colonel Guglialmelli, its head, warned the President not to let the tanks come into the city and recommended negotiation; Major Garasino, however, was of the belief that the War Ministry garrison itself could crush the 500 men at the Mechanics School (interview with Lieut. Colonel [Ret.] Alberto Garasino, March 11, 1970). For Frondizi's subsequent defense of his decision, see Luna, *Diálogos con Frondizi* [66], pp. 86–88.

[106] Interview with Carlos Toranzo Montero; *La Prensa*, Sept. 4–5, 1959. Larcher and Toranzo Montero had known each other since at least 1930 when as fellow lieutenants in the Eighth Cavalry Regiment under the command of Lieut. Colonel Francisco Bosch they had opposed the Uriburu overthrow of President Yrigoyen. I am indebted for this information to Dr. José Shaw, who,

authority, respect for hierarchy, and, in short, discipline. . . . The situation reveals the Argentine Army firmly in the fulfillment of its permanent mission: to defend the honor of the nation, to guard the rule of constitutional legality, and to guarantee the moral and material patrimony of the Argentine people.[107]

Such a view was hardly shared by those officers who had shown their loyalty to the constituted authorities. It was a bewildering, not to say disillusioning, experience to find themselves "sold out" by their chief civilian authority and subordinated to the man who was yesterday's rebel. The bitterness of some of these officers was to find expression in attacks on President Frondizi's character. Writing years after the event, Colonel Juan Guevara, the man who had commanded the loyal First Motorized Artillery Group, would assert:

Military order rests on command and on obedience. Without them the bases of discipline are undermined, and without this there are no military forces.

Few times does our history present a more serious error than that committed by President Frondizi. His first obligation was to repress the uprising, especially when he had forces to do so. But if he didn't feel himself capable of having his hierarchy respected and of having himself obeyed by all military sectors, he had no alternative but to resign and leave. . . .

On that bitter day, Frondizi showed that he did not possess these primary, essential concepts. *He believed that he could govern without authority* [italics in original] and he confused government with physical permanence in the presidency in which he wanted to remain at any price.[108]

Dr. Frondizi, as we have seen, saw the problem in a different light. As Chief Executive of the nation, he was anxious to prevent loss of life to his fellow citizens. Moreover, as a civilian statesman-politician committed to the idea that economic development held the key to future political and social stability, he did not regard the personalities or issues involved in the military disputes as of intrinsic importance. Consequently, he was prepared to make compromises, to make whatever sacrifices were called for in terms of persons or his own

---

as Bosch's brother-in-law, was a friend of both Larcher and Toranzo Montero and also known to President Frondizi.

[107] *Boletín Militar Público*, No. 3107, Sept. 21, 1959.

[108] Guevara [153], pp. 128–29.

prestige to ensure that he could continue to direct the country's affairs. The fact that his willingness to compromise would be seen by military men as a sign of weakness, not of statesmanship, of political self-interest, not of public service, made his remaining tenure in the presidency all the more difficult.

Contributing to those difficulties was the chief winner in the September 1959 crisis, General Toranzo Montero. A more powerful figure now than any previous Army Commander-in-Chief, he was in a position to implement his ideas for reorganizing the Army and at the same time to exercise a restraining influence over the Frondizi administration. To ensure his control within the Army, he carried out, with the cooperation of the new Army Secretary, far-reaching personnel changes, shuffling the key commands and appointing reliable allies to the strategic posts in the Buenos Aires area. All but one of the major generals serving in the country, as well as three brigadier generals, were placed on retirement, thus removing completely from top posts the friends of Colonel Reimúndez, who was himself compelled to retire.[109]

The year-end promotions within the Army were inevitably influenced by these events. Army Secretary Larcher appointed a new promotions board on which six of the seven members were generals who had signed the September 2 radiogram protesting Toranzo Montero's ouster. Their recommendations, which were routinely forwarded by the Executive Branch for Senate approval, resulted in the promotion of a group of senior officers who had been passed over by Solanas Pacheco the previous year, as well as of a long list of new candidates for senior grades. Four new major generals were created, all of them Toranzo Montero backers, but it was not possible, nor did the Commander-in-Chief desire, to limit the other promotions to identifiable supporters. In fact, at least one of the new

[109] For the personnel changes see *Boletín Militar Reservado*, Nos. 3818–21, 3827, and 3833, Sept. 16–Dec. 3, 1959. Retired were Major Generals Castiñeiras, Huergo, Solanas Pacheco, and Lambardi. Major General Julian García was placed on unassigned status (disponibilidad), and Major General Villaruel was assigned to a Washington post. The only other active duty major general, Videla Balaguer, was serving as ambassador to Italy. The three brigadier generals who voluntarily retired on September 22 were Eduardo Conesa, Julio Teglia, and E. P. Taquini, who had been serving as Chief of the General Staff, Second Army Commander, and Third Infantry Division Commander, respectively.

brigadier generals, Juan Carlos Onganía, and several of the new colonels were prominent Anaya supporters in the September crisis.[110]

Although General Toranzo Montero insisted that his aim was to
restore unity and discipline to Army ranks, he instituted a practice
that helped to politicize its upper spheres. This was the fortnightly
meeting of generals—they met every other Monday morning—to
take up issues of common concern. These meetings, held under the
chairmanship of the Commander-in-Chief, enabled him to explore
issues of political as well as of a strictly military nature and to work
up support for his program of redefining and expanding the functions of the Army.[111]

Toranzo Montero's goal as Commander-in-Chief was to prepare
the Argentine Army to fight against communist-inspired revolutionary movements. In his view, it was necessary to update traditional
military planning by developing an operational capacity based on
the hypothesis of revolutionary war.[112] This concept was not new to
the Argentine Army—actually the idea had been introduced by visiting French officers in 1957 and had been the subject of lectures and
discussions in military circles.[113] Toranzo Montero, however, fresh
from his experience on the Inter-American Defense Board, was
anxious to use his post to press for the restructuring and reequipping
of the Army in keeping with the hypothesis of a possible insurrection.
His hostility to communism and his view of Peronism as a "con-

[110] For the new promotion board, see the Army Secretary Resolution of September 15 in *Boletín Militar Reservado*, No. 3819 of Sept. 16, 1959; for the promotion list that advanced four colonels to the grade of brigadier general with
date of rank Dec. 31, 1958, thirteen to brigadier general with date of rank Dec.
31, 1959, and promoted Raúl Poggi, Eduardo Sosa, Juan B. Picca, and Octavio
Zenarruza to major general, see *Boletín Militar Público*, No. 3128, Dec. 29, 1959,
and *Senadores* [3], 1959, IV, 3680–81. Among the Anaya supporters who received promotion to colonel were Jorge F. von Stecher, Jorge E. Cáceres Monié,
and Manuel A. Laprida.

[111] For references to specific meetings see the Tuesday editions of *La Prensa*;
for an extremely negative view of the impact of these meetings and of Toranzo's
policies on Army discipline, see the unsigned article published by Lieut. Colonel
(Ret.) Garasino in the magazine *Extra*, No. 10 (May 1966).

[112] Interview with General (Ret.) Carlos Toranzo Montero.

[113] French influence may be seen in the presence of French Army officers who
served as advisors at the War Academy and in the publication of articles translated from French military journals in the Academy's house organ. See *Revista
de la Escuela Superior de Guerra*, Nos. 328, 329, 331, 334, 335 (Jan.–March
1958 to Oct.–Dec. 1959) for articles dealing with revolutionary war.

glomerate of delinquents" seeking "to restore a totalitarian state" provided an ideological underpinning for his military reforms.[114]

But Toranzo Montero was not content to direct his reforming fervor to intra-Army matters. The prevention of a Peronist revival, which he saw as a prelude to communism, or of an actual communist takeover, required that the civilian authorities at the national and provincial levels take appropriate actions. As Army Commander-in-Chief, he felt that he had a specific duty to guard against mistakes by civilian officials. He later recollected:

I believe that I had been reinstalled by the Army precisely because the government that was called constitutional had deviated from the objectives of the Liberating Revolution; and therefore I believed in the Army's need to exercise vigilance over the actions of President Frondizi's government. I was perfectly aware that this is in no way normal; but given the special situation of the Army and of the country's politics at that moment, there was no other power besides the armed forces that could watch over those objectives.[115]

This doctrine of vigilance, as it might be called, guided the actions of Toranzo Montero and his fellow generals for about a year from September 1959. It was based on the premise that President Frondizi could, when necessary, be pressured into adopting the policies they felt were essential and that his ouster from office was neither necessary nor desirable. It also reflected the widespread view in military circles that history had endowed the Army with a special responsibility for safeguarding the nation's interests. Stated in the baldest terms by Army Secretary Larcher on the occasion of the celebration of Army Day (May 29, 1960): "There is not a single transcendent act

[114] Quoted from Toranzo Montero's report to fellow generals at the March 14, 1960 (Monday), meeting as reproduced in *La Prensa*, June 28, 1960, p. 4. As Commander-in-Chief, Toranzo Montero promoted closer ties with the United States Army. In 1960, the Argentine Army accepted a U.S. military training mission (such missions already existed in the Air Force and Navy), and opportunities were increased for Argentine Army officers to become exposed to U.S. military doctrines. Relations between the U.S. and Argentine armies, however, never achieved the level of friendship and cooperation that characterized the U.S.–Brazilian military relationship in the 1960's.

[115] Interview with General (Ret.) Carlos Toranzo Montero. The idea that the Army had a moralizing function and that this was "without doubt the greatest contribution it makes to the Republic" was widely held among its officers. These words are from Leoni [159], p. 34.

in the life of the nation in which the Army has not played a principal role. . . . It is therefore very true that the Argentine fatherland
is not the child of political action, but of the sword. From Suipacha
to Caseros, from Ituzaingó to Tuyutí, war created it, developed it,
secured it, and protected it on the path of its destiny."[116]

The implementation by the Army of its policy of vigilance inevitably created a climate of intermittent jousting. President Frondizi, for
his part, was unwilling to accede to every request, but his fine sense
of political reality indicated when to make concessions. Thus, in
March 1960, in the face of a rising tide of terrorism that claimed its
first military victims, the President, while refusing a demand for
martial law, did agree to put in effect the Plan Conintes. This was a
state of emergency that assigned to the armed forces direct responsibility for repressing terrorism, subordinated provincial police forces
to their authority, and gave military courts jurisdiction over civilians
accused of participating in or fostering subversive acts.[117]

In still another move related to terrorism, the President asked
Congress to amend the provisions of the criminal code. In what
seemed to be a spirit of cooperation with military views, he proposed
an increase in penalties that included the institution of capital punishment. The Congress, however, while approving the stiffening of
lesser sanctions, refused to legalize the death penalty. Given the administration's control over both chambers, it was not too difficult to
conclude that Frondizi was insincere in calling for that penalty. A
longtime opponent of capital punishment, his aim seems to have been
to yield in appearance, but not in substance, to military views.[118]

Even before the amended criminal code was promulgated, however, the President found himself confronted with a military demand
he could not evade. Armed forces investigators had discovered that
members of the Córdoba provincial government, especially in its

[116] *Boletín Militar Público*, No. 3156, June 1, 1960, p. 511.

[117] Decrees No. 2628 and 2639 of March 13 and 15, 1960; *Boletín Militar
Público*, No. 3145, March 17, 1960; Casas [224], p. 118.

[118] The legislative history of the bill supports this conclusion. The Chamber
of Deputies committee that reported out the bill omitted the death penalty provision, and the Interior Minister made no effort to restore it. Indeed, the UCRI
spokesman for the committee, Deputy Bulet Goñi, justified the elimination of
the provision as "freeing the [Executive Power] of a great weight and responsibility." For these remarks, the original text of the bill, and its final form see
Diputados [2], 1960, I, 451–55, and Law 15,293.

police, had links to individuals accused of terrorism. Faced with the unyielding insistence that he oust the UCRI governor and other officials, Frondizi called on Congress to authorize the intervention of the province. For the UCRI majorities in both houses who voted the measure in the realization that failure to do so might precipitate the ouster of their President, this was a bitter exercise in political realism. For the military leadership, on the other hand, it was a major victory for their policy of vigilance.[119]

Not all Army officers by any means, however, were content with Toranzo Montero's doctrine of vigilance. A good many at regimental levels were distressed by what they saw as a departure from military professionalism, but a few others felt that it did not go far enough. Such officers, under the influence of civilian elements and of other retired anti-Peronist officers, entered into plots; but without support from the military hierarchy, these efforts rarely got beyond the talking stage. In June 1960, however, on the eve of President Frondizi's trip to Europe, a handful of officers led by a retired general, Fortunato Giovannoni, tried to launch a revolution in distant San Luis province. Although the commander of the Second Army, Brigadier General Mauricio Gómez, gave it his support, the movement was easily quashed and had few repercussions. Five months later, another plot, this time of Peronist inspiration and led by ex-general Miguel A. Iñíguez, produced an unsuccessful uprising at Rosario, where the attempt to seize the Eleventh Infantry Regiment was put down at the cost of several lives.[120]

Far more dangerous to President Frondizi than these abortive movements was the evolution of General Toranzo's attitude, and that of the generals who responded to him, on the issue of preserving the

[119] *La Prensa*, June 2–5, 1960, reports the situation in Córdoba, the military pressure for intervention, and President Frondizi's message to Congress. For the allegation that Governor Zanichelli was personally involved in protecting Peronist terrorists, see Toryho [79], pp. 90–91; for Frondizi's contention that a small group of Army officers deliberately plotted to provoke the intervention, see Luna, *Diálogos con Frondizi* [66], pp. 123–24.

[120] On the San Luis uprising and the punishments meted out to the participants, *La Prensa*, June 14, 1960, and *Boletín Militar Público*, No. 3163, July 11, 1960; on the Rosario insurrection, interview with General (Ret.) Miguel A. Iñíguez, Aug. 21, 1973. General Iñíguez claims that he had widespread support from officers in various interior garrisons as well as trade union leaders, but a seemingly well-informed contemporary account insists that his uprising was doomed before it began (*Usted*, Año I, No. 7 [Dec. 3, 1960], 8–9).

civilian government. Exactly what it was that decided them to abandon the policy of vigilance for one of outright control is still not clear. Undoubtedly the accumulated experience of the past months was a major factor. They realized that President Frondizi, despite grudging concessions on internal security matters, was still intent on pursuing his own objectives; he had refused to purge the national administration or to intervene in other provinces, to accommodate the loosely defined anti-Peronist, anticommunist criteria of the military intelligence agencies; he was still committed to the goal of a unified labor movement even under Peronist leaders; and he was still hoping to recover the support of Peronist voters once economic conditions improved. The generals' outlook was presumably also shaped by civilian opinion and by advice received from economic interest groups and from antiadministration political personalities. But one cannot exclude the element of personal ambition. If a new regime replaced the civilian administration, General Toranzo Montero would in all likelihood become the predominant figure.[121]

The shift in Army attitude toward the administration became manifest early in October when the Commander-in-Chief firmed up plans for a showdown with President Frondizi. Central to Toranzo Montero's planning was the need to develop a common stance within the armed forces, and especially in the Army, so as to avoid the danger of civil war. In preparing for the anticipated confrontation with the President, Toranzo Montero was counting heavily on the support of the Secretary of the Army, General Larcher, who had been cooperating with him over the past year. The adoption of a joint position by both the Army Secretary and the Commander-in-Chief would make it very difficult for Army officers not in sympathy with their plans to offer effective opposition.[122]

The scenario developed by Toranzo Montero called for the presentation to Dr. Frondizi of a demand for sweeping changes in the conduct of the administration. To this end a twelve-page memorandum was drawn up by officers in the Army General Staff. Depicting the

[121] A factor that deserves further exploration is the influence of the international situation on Toranzo Montero's decision. For his apparently accidental involvement in an internal dispute that divided the members of the Argentine delegation to the Sixth and Seventh Consultative Meetings of Foreign Ministers at San José in September 1959, see Conil Paz and Ferrari [230], pp. 188–90; and Casas [224], p. 133.

[122] Interview with General (Ret.) Carlos Toranzo Montero.

Army as a defender of Argentine democracy, the memorandum listed a series of complaints: the government's failure to root out communists, especially in the educational and cultural institutions; the presence in the national and certain provincial administrations of integrationists (Frigeristas) who were still playing with the Peronists and even condoning subversive acts so as to capitalize on the resentments felt by the Peronist masses against the military when the latter engaged in countermeasures; the corruption and inefficiencies in the operation of state enterprises including YPF; the weaknesses and mistakes made in the pursuit of economic policy objectives. The memorandum concluded by stating that the armed forces were not willing to be regarded as accomplices to mistaken national policies and called for prompt action to change policies and purge the administration of undesirable officials.[123]

The planned-for confrontation between the Army and President Frondizi took place the week of October 10–14. However, contrary to Toranzo Montero's expectation, Army Secretary Larcher, who had been out of the country for the past month and apparently not in close touch with the Commander-in-Chief, refused to endorse the memorandum of demands. Whatever his past relationship with Toranzo Montero, Larcher now identified himself fully with the Frondizi government. As a cabinet member, he was not disposed to collaborate in the government's ouster, and indeed worked hard to head it off.[124]

The split between Larcher and the Commander-in-Chief was an important factor in upsetting the latter's plans. The Army Secretary, a retired cavalryman himself, was able to win support of the cavalry officers. Toranzo Montero was thereby forced to choose between accepting responsibility for provoking an armed clash if he pressed ahead with his original intentions or retreating to a prepared posi-

[123] The original text of this memorandum has not come to light. For a summary of its contents, see *La Prensa*, Oct. 14, 1960, p. 4. Toranzo Montero in the previously cited interview downplayed its contents and stressed its tactical value: "A mi no me importaba tanto lo que estaba escrita en el memorandum como que el memorandum fuera, digamos, el ariete, el arma materializada con la cual llegar a chocar con Frondizi para producir ¿no es cierto? la acción de fuerza en caso que Frondizi no aceptara."

[124] Interview with Toranzo Montero; see also news accounts of the Larcher–Toranzo Montero differences in *La Prensa*, Oct. 11–15, 1960; on the Army Secretary's absence from the country from Sept. 9 to Oct. 8, see *Boletín Militar Público*, Nos. 3174 and 3178.

tion and waiting for another opportunity. He chose the latter course, announcing through a communiqué that the Army's goal was to direct attention to serious problems, not to disrupt the constitutional order.[125]

Contributing also, and in a major way, to frustrating Toranzo Montero's goal were the countermeasures taken by President Frondizi. Once again, as in past crises, he enlisted the support of ex-President Aramburu to speak with military personnel to discourage any interruption in the constitutional order. President Frondizi also managed to achieve a psychological coup that weakened the enthusiasm of the military plotters. At the very moment that he was receiving General Toranzo Montero at the Casa Rosada on October 12 to discuss the contents of the Army memorandum, a national radio hookup was carrying his prerecorded voice denouncing the existence of a "miniscule sector which is conspiring to assume power." In this radio address, the President defended the accomplishments of his administration, impugned the motives of the plotters, and proclaimed his determination not to resign whatever the pressure. The net effect of this timely speech was to place the military critics of Frondizi on the defensive. No one wished to admit openly that he favored the disruption of the constitutional order.[126]

The October 1960 crisis passed with President Frondizi still in office, his powers relatively intact. At a face-to-face meeting with a group of generals whom he invited to the Casa Rosada on October 14, he did concede that the armed forces had the right to make observations about any aspect of administration policy; and he even agreed to the creation of a special Ministry of Defense committee to examine complaints and forward recommendations. But he remained adamant in insisting that his was the constitutional authority to appoint his cabinet and determine policy, and he would not subordinate these decisions to an Army veto.[127]

[125] Interview with Toranzo Montero: see also Rauch [200], pp. 96–97. General Rauch, commander of the Second Cavalry Division, claims that he was the only general to voice opposition to the Commander-in-Chief's plans, which suggests that it was cavalry unit commanders at the regimental level that were decisive in forcing Toranzo Montero to back down.

[126] For Aramburu's intervention, see *La Prensa*, Oct. 12, 1960; for the text of Frondizi's radio address, *ibid.*, Oct. 13, 1960.

[127] Frondizi surprised the generals by having the proceedings recorded and later released to the press. This may explain the reticence with which Toranzo

President Frondizi refused to dismiss from his cabinet the civilian members singled out for criticism by the Army generals, but he did find it expedient to yield to their demand for the resignation of the Army Secretary. General Larcher, in fact, had voluntarily offered his resignation on October 10 after refusing to support the presentation of the memorandum, but Frondizi refused to accept it. Larcher's relations with the Commander-in-Chief and other generals were now so strained, however, that presidential insistence on retaining him in office could only prolong the atmosphere of crisis. Agreeing on October 14 to allow Larcher to resign, Dr. Frondizi's first choice for a successor was General (Ret.) Aramburu. The ex-President, despite his efforts to ward off a coup, was unwilling to become identified with the Frondizi administration. The President finally offered the post, after consultations with various officers including Toranzo Montero, to an active duty officer, the current chief of the Campo de Mayo garrison and director of the Colegio Militar, Brigadier General Rosendo Fraga.[128] For President Frondizi, the appointment of General Fraga proved to be a felicitous choice. Although he had been closely identified with Toranzo Montero in the September 1959 crisis and was an active participant in the generals' meetings that produced the October 10–14, 1960, confrontation, once appointed to Frondizi's cabinet he became a staunch supporter of the continuation of the civilian government. Moreover, as a member of a distinguished military family and a man of considerable personal appeal, he was the right individual to attempt to win over officers who had hitherto followed the lead of the Commander-in-Chief.

Montero and his fellow officers presented their views. The President, on the other hand, made his points with vigor. In particular, he placed Toranzo Montero on the defensive by revealing details of their October 12 one-on-one conversation. The transcript of the October 14 meeting, published in *La Prensa*, Oct. 15, 1960, revealed President Frondizi at his dialectical best, upholding the prerogatives of his office, agreeing to procedures for permitting military concerns to be voiced, but yielding very little in substance. The President's ability to stand firm rested in part on the expressions of support he received from business and labor groups, but more importantly on the fact that both the Navy and the Air Force refused to join the Army in disrupting the constitutional order. See the minutes of the military cabinet meeting that General Larcher leaked to the press, in *La Prensa*, Oct. 15, 1960.

[128] *Boletín Militar Público*, No. 3178, Oct. 15, 1960; *La Prensa*, Oct. 15, 1960. Toranzo Montero in an interview took the position that it was his recommendation that led the President to name General Fraga.

Toranzo Montero, it should be stressed, had not abandoned his goal of ousting Frondizi, and he continued to make plans in the belief that General Fraga, who had stood by him in the past, would do so in the future. The new Army Secretary, however, deftly turned aside his suggestions, and in the meantime took quiet steps to limit his influence. In one such move, he ordered the suspension of the periodic Monday morning meetings of generals that the Commander-in-Chief had been using to assert his influence. In the future, such meetings would be held only at the call of the Army Secretary.[129]

General Fraga moved very slowly and very discreetly in his efforts to reduce Toranzo Montero's hold on the loyalties of the generals. The year-end promotion list, for example, seems to have been agreed to readily by both the Secretary and the Commander-in-Chief and resulted in the elevation of several officers known to belong to Toranzo Montero's circle, including his brother Federico, who was one of only two promoted to the grade of major general. It is understandable, then, that Toranzo Montero continued to operate on the assumption that when the appropriate time came for the Army to move against the President, General Fraga and practically all of the generals would be at his side.[130]

The test of that assumption would come in mid-March 1961. Previous to this, and over a period of several weeks, events had been creating a sense of increasing alarm on the part of General Toranzo Montero and those political sectors that shared his staunch anti-communist, anti-Peronist, and pro-United States views. The fact that the winner in the February senatorial race in the Federal Capital was Alfredo Palacios, an old socialist who campaigned on a pro-Castro platform and received both Peronist and communist support, reinforced their fears that unless strong measures were taken, the country would slide irretrievably beyond their grasp. Their sense of unease was deepened by the release early in March of an announce-

---

[129] *Usted*, Año I, No. 5 (Nov. 19, 1960), p. 9; interview with General (Ret.) Rosendo Fraga, July 23, 1971.

[130] Interview with General (Ret.) Carlos Toranzo Montero. For the promotion of senior officers, see *Senadores* [3], 1960, III, 2784. Advanced to major general together with Federico Toranzo Montero was Florencio A. Yornet, hitherto a Toranzo supporter. Although it is not possible to classify all twelve newly promoted brigadier generals in terms of their support for Toranzo, certain names stand out, such as Carlos Ayala, Guillermo Salas Martínez, and Horacio Luis Scasso.

ment that the Frondizi administration was contemplating the lifting of the Conintes Plan. This would end the military's role in countering subversion and reduce its influence in those provinces where UCRI governors were still making deals with local Peronists. Behind-the-scenes pressures, presumably from within the Defense Ministry, postponed any final decision, but the indication that the administration was even considering the step was itself unsettling. So, too, was its resolve to hand over the CGT to trade union hands and thus fulfill a long-standing Frondizi promise to promote a united labor movement. After having been under continuous government intervention since 1955, the CGT was finally turned over on March 16 to a mixed committee representing twenty trade unions. Although ten of these were hardline Peronist, and the others independents of various orientations, the move was looked upon by Toranzo Montero as a shameful surrender of the CGT to "delinquents of the dictatorship."[131]

Although domestic considerations seem to have been uppermost in their minds, Toranzo Montero and like-minded elements in civilian and military circles were also upset by the administration's handling of foreign policy, especially as regards Castro's Cuba. Anything short of full support for the United States position was viewed by them as a betrayal of the national interest and an aid to extremism. It was in this light that they reacted to the Argentine Foreign Ministry's offer, made public on March 6, to have Argentina mediate the differences between the United States and Cuba. Toranzo Montero saw the offer, with its implication that Argentina was a neutral and the issues involved were not hemispheric but bilateral, as an "oblique international move . . . which opens the floodgates to the crudest leftism." Admiral (Ret.) Rojas, who shared his outlook, saw in the mediation offer a return to Perón's "discredited" third position.[132]

Under the impact of the series of events described above, General Toranzo Montero proceeded to sound out Secretary Fraga and their fellow generals about the need to terminate the Frondizi government. To his surprise, the Commander-in-Chief discovered that he

[131] The quoted words are from Toranzo Montero's post-resignation letter to Army Secretary Fraga published in *La Prensa*, March 26, 1961. For an interpretation that sees Toranzo Montero as the target of an administration trap, see *Usted*, Año II, No. 21 (March 14, 1961), p. 11.

[132] See Toranzo Montero's letter cited in the previous note; on Admiral Rojas's reaction, see his letter to Navy Secretary Clement, *La Prensa*, April 7, 1961.

no longer enjoyed the nearly unanimous support that had rallied behind him on the eve of the October 1960 confrontation. Indeed, over
the period March 10–22, he encountered traces of an organized effort
to discredit him as a politicized general and to bring about his
separation. Aware now that Secretary Fraga was flatly opposed to a
coup and that several quondam supporters, including General Poggi,
the First Army Corps head, and General Pablo Spirito, the Chief of
the General Staff, were also opposed, he asked to be relieved as
Commander-in-Chief on March 22. General Fraga, after a show of
reluctance, accepted the oral request and advised the Army that for
the time being, he was taking on the duties of Commander-in-Chief
himself.[133]

Because of the events of the next several hours, a question remained about Toranzo Montero's intentions. He did not follow up
his oral resignation with a statement in writing, as repeatedly requested by Secretary Fraga; meanwhile, rumors began to spread in
military circles that his resignation was involuntary. That night and
into the early morning hours of March 23, a gathering of generals
took place at the Palermo headquarters of the First Motorized Division with Toranzo Montero present. Its commander, General Fernando Elizondo, offered to support him by seizing the Casa Rosada
if he gave the order. Secretary Fraga, however, appearing at the
meeting, asked Toranzo Montero to concede that his request for relief was voluntary. The ex-Commander-in-Chief, aware that many
generals were now behind Fraga, that his own prestige had been
diminished by personal attacks, and that a seizure of power would
divide the Army and risk civil war, confirmed his earlier decision to
resign, and the meeting dissolved without further consequences.[134]

The resignation and prompt retirement of General Toranzo Montero must have come as a great relief to President Frondizi. He could
now make decisions with a greater sense of freedom and with less
concern for Army reactions than at any time over the past two

[133] Interviews with Generals (Ret.) Toranzo Montero and Rosendo Fraga;
Usted, Año II, No. 22 (March 21, 1960), p. 12, and No. 23 (March 28, 1961).
pp. 11–12.

[134] Interviews with Generals Toranzo Montero and Rosendo Fraga. Toranzo
Montero retired officially on April 18, 1961, with a total service record of 50
years, 10 months, and 24 days (*Boletín Militar Reservado*, No. 3911, April 19,
1961).

years.[135] In this spirit, Frondizi proceeded to shake up his cabinet, getting rid of Alvaro Alsogaray, whom he had reluctantly appointed to the Economy Ministry to assuage military opinion in June 1959, and whose failure to implement the developmentalist aspect of his economic program was a source of great exasperation.[136] The President also paid increasing attention to foreign affairs. Over the next eight months, Frondizi made five trips abroad, one of which was to address the United Nations in New York and meet with President Kennedy; another and more extensive one took him to Canada, Greece, and Asia, concluding with another meeting with the U.S. President. At no time did he seem preoccupied that his control of the government might be subverted in his absence. Yet, as the next chapter will discuss, his independent exercise of his constitutional authority over foreign policy making was to send tremors through the armed forces and pave the way for the final and fateful confrontation of March 1962.

[135] A coincidental development also contributing to the greater sense of freedom on the part of the President was a series of local electoral victories won by the UCRI. Its candidates came out ahead in Catamarca on March 5, Rosario on March 19, and Misiones and San Luis on April 9.

[136] For Frondizi's explanation of his decision to oust Alsogaray as given to a journalist in 1962, see Pandolfi [228], p. 89 and note 7. The date of the ouster was April 24 (*La Prensa*, April 25, 1961).

Chapter 9

Dangerous Games:
The Fall of Frondizi, 1961–1962

The encouragement taken by President Frondizi from the departure of General Carlos Toranzo Montero had to be qualified by the realization that the Army was still sharply divided in outlook. At best an uneasy balance existed within the officer corps in favor of supporting the constitutional government. The divisions within that corps were not simply of a political nature; professional values and personal ambitions were also involved. The challenge presented to Army Secretary Fraga was how to respond to the pressures emanating from the different groups while preserving the internal peace and unity of the institution.

On the one hand were the legalists, officers who supported the Frondizi administration without necessarily agreeing with its specific policies. In the immediate aftermath of Toranzo's departure, a group of such officers, dubbed by the media the "forty colonels," lobbied with the Army Secretary for a purge of those generals most closely associated with the former commander. Moreover, in a show of little confidence in the remaining senior officers, they recommended the recall from retirement of one or two prestigious generals to take over the topmost posts of commander-in-chief and chief of the general staff. These colonels, many of them cavalry unit commanders, saw themselves as highly professional officers who wanted to confine the Army to its institutional tasks and to purge it of its politicized elements. But in proposing that the resulting vacancies should be filled by "true professionals" regardless of whether they had the necessary rank, they were vulnerable to the charge that they were urging a course of action whose principal beneficiaries would be themselves, colonels seeking to fill the shoes of generals.[1]

Opposed to the legalists were the ex-Torancistas, officers who were still convinced that President Frondizi could not be trusted and that his continuation in office was a danger to the country. Such officers did not hesitate to seek adherents within the officer corps to their views or to give them public, if indirect, expression. Writing in the pages of the *Revista Militar*, the military circle house organ that circulated among hundreds of Army officers both active and retired, Colonel Rómulo Menéndez put the case for military intervention. While denying that the armed forces should take part in partisan or factional struggles, he bluntly proclaimed their obligation to act to safeguard the nation's highest interest: "Nevertheless, when the authorities of the state, through incapacity or conscious errors in the exercise of power, show themselves to be powerless or ineffective in halting the spread of evils that damage the highest values of the nation, endangering its very existence, the armed forces, in fulfillment of their specific mission, must intervene in defense of those values."[2] Citing various government actions that he claimed were promoting chaos, he concluded by stating: "The hour in consequence is one of profound and grave reflection."[3]

Army Secretary Fraga's response to the conflicting pressures within the institution was to move very discreetly. Despite the activities of the "forty colonels" and apparent urgings from the President himself, he avoided anything resembling a purge. His choice of Raúl Poggi, the senior major general, to be the new Commander-in-Chief, was made in part to avoid the requests for retirement that would have followed the appointment of a more junior general. The selection of Poggi, an engineering officer, did not fail to arouse criticism from other branches, but Poggi's experience both as a troop commander and in administrative services provided arguments that Fraga could use to defend his appointment.[4] The Army Secretary did, however, make concessions to the legalist cavalry officers. He appointed

---

[1] *Usted*, Año II, No. 25 (April 18, 1961), pp. 11–12, and No. 26 (April 25, 1961), p. 12. Among the spokesmen for the legalist viewpoint were Colonels T. Sánchez de Bustamante, Berrotarán, Caro, Aguirre, and General Enrique Rauch.

[2] Menéndez, "Las fuerzas armadas y la defensa nacional" [168], p. 14.

[3] *Ibid.*, p. 17.

[4] Interview with General (Ret.) Rosendo Fraga, July 23, 1971.

one of their number as a subchief of the general staff; and when given an excuse by the behavior of the Torancista commander of the First Armored Division at Campo de Mayo, he and General Poggi replaced him in that powerful post with Brigadier General Juan Onganía. Shortly thereafter, two other known Torancista generals were transferred out of their current posts, including the head of the capital-based First Motorized Division.[5]

Fraga's hope was to strengthen the cohesive forces within the Army. In his first general order, issued on April 13, he called on officers to put aside antagonisms and pledged his efforts to protect the Army from external influences that "disturb, divide, and weaken it." He promised, moreover, to be sensitive "to the important problems that affect the life of the institution and the country" and to be a "faithful interpreter of the just aspirations of the cadres."[6] To this end, with the consent of President Frondizi, he created a council of generals to serve as an institutionalized vehicle for expressing the concerns of Army commanders. Consisting of one-third of the generals of the command corps, chosen in order of seniority, the council, according to the April 14 decree creating it, was "to have as its mission to advise the Army Secretary on the fundamental problems of the institution."[7] Its original members were the fifteen top generals; at least four and possibly more of these officers were clearly identified with anti-Frondizi positions. Little wonder, then, that its meetings often deteriorated into political debates and that an institution intended to promote the cohesiveness of the Army did little to achieve that goal.[8]

Despite Secretary Fraga's institutional innovations, the Army remained a body that was as much divided as united. Its unity lay in

---

[5] Colonel Carlos Caro (see note 1 above) replaced General Salas Martínez as subchief of the General Staff; General Onganía replaced General Carlos Ayala at Campo de Mayo; General Enrique Maffei replaced General Fernando Elizondo at the First Motorized Division; and General Luis Estol took over from General Horacio Scasso at the Eighth Mountain Infantry Division (*La Prensa*, April 17, 20, 25, 28, 1961).

[6] *Boletín Militar Reservado*, No. 3910, April 14, 1961.

[7] *Ibid.*

[8] Interview with General (Ret.) Raúl Poggi, May 29, 1970. The original members were Generals Poggi, Sosa, Yornet, Federico Toranzo Montero, Ardanaz, Locatelli, Spirito, Morón, Landa, Naveiro, Cordes, Cecilio Labayru, Cordini, Turolo, and Martijena.

the agreement of practically all officers that a return of Perón or his system to power was not to be tolerated. This unity also extended to a common concern with the spread of communism, a concern that was being transformed into an obsession under the impact of events in Cuba. Army officers of all political hues perceived Castro's avowal of Marxism-Leninism, his acceptance of Soviet assistance, and the support expressed for Fidel in Argentine student, intellectual, and worker circles as a threat not only to national security, but to the very existence of the armed forces. The destruction of the pre-Castro Cuban officer corps at the hands of Fidel's firing squads did not pass unnoticed.

But while Argentine Army officers were united in their opposition to Peronism and communism, they were divided over whether these objectives could best be achieved by preserving President Frondizi in power and enabling him to implement his developmentalist policies or by seeking his ouster. And even among those advocating the latter course, differences existed over whether the successor government should be civilian in character, the product of a new election, or an outright military dictatorship.

As of May 1, 1961, the third anniversary of Frondizi's assumption of the presidency and the halfway mark of his elected term, the balance of forces within the Army, though not overwhelming, still favored his continuation in office. A similar distribution seems to have prevailed in the Navy and Air Force. It was up to the President to decide whether to tailor his future actions to strengthen that balance or to press ahead with policies that, however justifiable from his viewpoint, could well risk its collapse.

Though willing to listen to military concerns, President Frondizi was not prepared, especially in the field of foreign relations, to yield control over the determination of his policies. His conception of his authority in this field made seemingly little concession to the precariousness of his position or to the need to assess the impact of his acts on the military balance. He stated in a speech to the nation in August 1961:

I am the head of the Executive Branch, and I have the sole responsibility for fulfilling the duties which the constitution assigns to it. I accept that responsibility completely; I am not disposed to evade it, to delegate it, or to place it on the shoulders of officials who loyally carry out the President's instructions. Such conduct would be improper in a leader who aspires to the respect of his subordinates.[9]

This view of his powers and his penchant for keeping his foreign policy decisions secret from the military members of his cabinet were to precipitate over a period of seven months two major crises, either of which might have ended in his ouster.

Before examining those specific crises, it is important to note the conflict between President Frondizi's personal approach to foreign policy making and the historic claims of the Argentine military in this field. Involved were issues of both style and substance. Ever since the 1930's, and perhaps earlier, the Argentine armed forces had come to believe that they had an inherent right to play a major role in foreign policy decisions. In periods of military government, or when the chief executive was himself a military man, the differences that arose were settled within the military hierarchy. But even under civilian presidents (Ortiz, 1938–40, and Castillo, 1940–43), the military were able to exert significant influence on policy decisions. Under President Frondizi, it seems safe to say, the military leaders expected to be kept fully informed and have an opportunity to veto actions that in their view endangered national security.[10]

Frondizi, however, was determined to play his foreign policy cards close to his chest, even at the risk of alienating the military. Why did he do so? The explanation seems to lie in a mixture of considerations, political, practical, and even emotional. In his economic policy decisions and in other areas such as education, Frondizi, as we have seen, had broken with traditional Intransigent Radical positions, alienating in the process many of his former friends and supporters. He had also been forced to yield on several occasions to military pressures at a considerable cost to personal dignity and authority. The foreign affairs field, particularly after 1961, offered Frondizi an opportunity to recoup his image and, perhaps, also his self-esteem. He could demonstrate to fellow Intransigent Radicals, as well as to nationalists of the left or right, that he had lost none of his

[9] *La Prensa*, Aug. 22, 1961, p. 4. See also Casas [224], p. 123, where he is quoted as saying: "The management of foreign affairs belongs completely to me and in these problems I will not yield one iota."

[10] Potash, *The Army & Politics in Argentina, 1928–1945* [188], Chapters 4–6, for the development of the military view on the conduct of foreign affairs.

earlier dedication to an Argentina that refused to be taken for granted, a country that would insist on playing an independent role in hemispheric politics and even aspire to recognition on the world stage. He could at the same time demonstrate to other countries that Argentina was in the hands of a leader who knew what he wanted and who had to be taken seriously. In fact, as a result of his contacts with political and diplomatic leaders in other countries, Frondizi's prestige stood much higher abroad than it did at home.

The accession of John F. Kennedy to the United States presidency, coinciding with the challenge that Castro's Cuba presented to prevailing inter-American relationships, gave Frondizi the opportunity to play an enlarged role in hemispheric affairs. Invoking such traditional principles of Argentine foreign policy as respect for self-determination, nonintervention in domestic affairs of other states, and reliance on peaceful solutions to international disputes, President Frondizi formulated a subtle policy designed to demonstrate friendship to the United States while opposing precipitous action against Cuba. Frondizi apparently saw in the continued existence of Castro's regime a lever that could be astutely utilized to Argentine advantage. President Kennedy, in proclaiming the Alliance for Progress, committed himself in principle to providing assistance for peaceful economic and social change. Dedicated to his own developmentalist strategy, Frondizi hoped to persuade the Kennedy administration to augment the size of the economic aid component of the announced program and to allocate a major share of such funds to Argentine projects. Frondizi did, in fact, succeed in establishing a cordial relationship with President Kennedy, and Argentina was eventually selected as a major showcase for the Alliance for Progress. In this context, the Argentine President's Cuban policies seem to have been designed to secure an expanded flow of economic assistance from the United States while simultaneously demonstrating that his government was not its satellite. Frondizi, indeed, was determined to display his independence by taking initiatives to promote a common front of the countries that form the Southern Cone.[11]

[11] For a critical view of Frondizi's Cuban policy, see Conil Paz and Ferrari [230], pp. 188–222; Casas [224], pp. 129–60, provides a sympathetic interpretation. For evidence that Frondizi hoped to get a billion dollars in loans from President Kennedy for Argentine development projects, see John F. Kennedy Library, President's Office Files, Folder 12, Document 11a.

The most concrete result of these initiatives was the Uruguayana meeting with Brazilian President Janio Quadros in April 1961 and the signing of a vaguely worded treaty of friendship and consultation that committed both governments to coordinating their efforts in seeking concessions from the advanced world to promote the development of their respective countries. For a variety of reasons, Frondizi's policy of friendship with Brazil aroused the concern of the Argentine military. Quadros's public avowals of neutralism toward the United States–Soviet rivalry and his undisguised sympathy with developments in Cuba contributed to the uneasiness of the military, whose traditional perception of their huge neighbor was that of a permanent rival and potential foe. Still, it was one thing to express their concern, as they did in connection with the Uruguayana agreement, but quite another to mount organized resistance, as they were later to do on issues involving Cuba.[12]

Although Frondizi had a legitimate, if debatable, rationale for his Cuban-related policy, it was not one he could proclaim openly without reducing its effectiveness. It was, moreover, not one that many in the military were prepared to accept. Anything short of unqualified opposition to Castro's Cuba was seen as promoting the spread of communism in Argentina and the rest of Latin America. Given the suspicion that already existed in certain circles, especially the intelligence services, that close advisors to the President, and even Frondizi himself, were communists at heart, actions that might have been acceptable in another chief executive, served to arouse a hysterical response.[13]

Such was the case with the secret interview that Frondizi granted Ernesto "Che" Guevara at the Olivos presidential residence on August 18, 1961. Guevara, in his capacity as Cuban Minister of Indus-

[12] On the Uruguayana agreement, see Conil Paz and Ferrari [230], pp. 201–3, and Casas [224], pp. 135–40; for the Frondizi administration's defense of the agreement, see *Senadores* [3], 1961, II, 1078–79, and *Diputados* [2], 1961, VII, 4653–54.

[13] Interviews with Generals (Ret.) Pedro E. Aramburu, July 31, 1962, and Federico Toranco Montero, Feb. 24, 1970. Aramburu, while disclaiming it to be his view, stated that many in the military believed Frondizi to be a communist. Toranzo Montero, referring to the Che Guevara interview (see below), asserted: "If it were not Frondizi, no one would deny the President the right as president to do what he wanted; but this was the drop that sufficed to cause a general indignation in all the armed forces, even among those who were Peronists and even the semi, the lukewarm, Frondicistas."

try, had been attending the Punta del Este meeting of the Inter-American Economic and Social Council, the meeting that, over his opposition, had endorsed the concept of the Alliance for Progress and approved a mechanism for its implementation.

The preliminaries to the Frondizi-Guevara meeting are still shrouded in uncertainty, and it has not been definitively established who took the initiative to bring it about, or what the principals said to each other. Frondizi's decision to receive Guevara, however, was apparently related to his hope of serving as a mediator between Cuba and the United States. Had he succeeded, he would have pulled off a diplomatic coup with political benefits for his party in the forthcoming Argentine elections. What he produced, however, was a political crisis that came close to precipitating a domestic coup.[14]

Although Guevara's visit to Argentina lasted less than four hours, the precautions taken to assure its secrecy were not airtight. He was flown in a small plane sent over to Montevideo to a minor airfield in Buenos Aires province whence he was driven in a closed car to Olivos. Permitted by Frondizi to visit a sick relative in Buenos Aires, Guevara returned to Uruguay by the route he arrived although not without having been recognized prior to departure.[15]

The rumor of the Guevara visit, which the Casa Rosada press office subsequently confirmed, broke like a bolt of lightning preceding a storm. The storm in this instance was generated by the wave of emotion that swept through the armed forces and a good part of the public. For the next two days, military garrisons and headquarters were the scene of numerous meetings, while the Secretaries of the Army, Navy, and Air Force engaged in marathon discussions with their respective commanders, with one another, and with the President. Contributing to the problems of the military secretaries in restraining their subordinates was their own complete ignorance of the Guevara visit until after it happened. Frondizi's decision, taken allegedly for security reasons, to handle the arrangements the way

[14] For an account that ascribes the initiative to Guevara, see Pandolfi [228], p. 97; Casas [224], p. 143, ascribes it to Frondizi. Guevara for his part, on returning to Cuba, stated that he had been invited (*La Prensa*, Aug. 24, 1961), but Foreign Minister Mugica insisted that "he was not invited" (*ibid.*, Aug. 25, 1961).

[15] On the details of the visit, see Pandolfi [228], pp. 97–103.

he did, left the secretaries with little capacity to turn aside the protests of angry officers. Army Secretary Fraga, in particular, felt seriously compromised by the President's action and at one point was on the verge of resigning. Frondizi, however, was able to overcome his sense of distress and to win his continued support, without which an Army takeover might have been inevitable.[16]

As part of the process of restoring calm, President Frondizi on August 19 convoked a meeting of the high commands of the three armed services together with the entire defense cabinet. Following a lengthy exposition by the President and an expression by the military of their concerns, a mutually agreed upon communiqué was issued to the effect that the Guevara visit in no way altered Argentina's firm position in regard to Cuba and communism. It was also decided that Frondizi should make a nationwide address to spell out the aims and principles of his foreign policy. His speech of August 21 was a masterful presentation that combined a firm assertion of his presidential prerogatives with an appeal to nationalistic sensibilities. He linked Argentine concern over the defense of its own sovereignty with the need to respect the sovereignty of other nations and to accept peacefully the coexistence of divergent systems. At the same time, with an eye to those who cast doubt about his own political orientation, he emphasized his repudiation of totalitarianism, reaffirmed his commitment to Western values, and cited at length the high regard in which President Kennedy and other United States officials held his government.[17]

The furor aroused by the President's secret interview with Guevara eventually subsided, with the only visible casualty being the resignation of the Foreign Minister, Adolfo Múgica. As the official nominally responsible for issuing the entry visa to the Cuban revolutionary, Múgica submitted his resignation as a concession to appease military anger. In his place Frondizi appointed a well-known con-

[16] The military reactions filled the front pages of the daily press from August 18 to 23. On Fraga's near resignation, see Casas [224], p. 123. Highly critical of Frondizi's action in seeing Guevara but at the same time cautioning against a military takeover was General Pedro Aramburu. For his statement to the press, see *La Prensa*, Aug. 21, 1961; on his behind-the-scenes activities, see Toryho [79], pp. 110–12.

[17] *La Prensa*, Aug. 20, 22, 1961. The Frondizi speech quoted verbatim the May 24, 1961, statement of President Kennedy that stressed the relationship of friendship, partnership, and mutual respect of the two governments.

servative, Miguel A. Cárcano, whose social standing, political antecedents, and long-standing personal friendship with the Kennedy family were presumably regarded as assets that could strengthen the administration.[18]

The August crisis, however, did not fail to leave its hidden wounds. Even officers not opposed to the President found his actions puzzling.[19] Did he really expect to keep the interview secret, especially since the presidential aide who escorted Guevara to Olivos was himself a naval officer? And if not, was Frondizi deliberately seeking to provoke the military, or did he miscalculate the depth of their reaction? It was, after all, the President of the nation who tried to conceal the fact of the interview from the public eye, not some emissary whose actions could be officially denied. Whatever Frondizi's aim, "it is indisputable," as a writer friendly to him was to observe, "that the Guevara visit launched into conspiratorial activity hitherto reluctant officers and destroyed the will of some [other] officers to use their weapons to defend legality."[20]

The relative calm that descended over the relationship between Frondizi and the armed forces was to last less than five months. In this period the President continued to stress his foreign policy role, making a visit to New York in September to address the United Nations and meet for the first time with President Kennedy, and then in late November embarking on a month-long journey that would take him to Canada, Greece, the Far East, and again the United States. At his departure, the country was suffering from a prolonged railway strike called to protest his policy of reducing the state railway deficit by turning over repair and other auxiliary services to private hands. Ended during his absence through the mediation of the Archbishop of Buenos Aires, the 42-day strike frayed the nerves of the commuting public, aroused concern within the military, and served to demonstrate that serious social and economic problems still confronted the government whether the President was at home or abroad.

[18] *La Prensa*, Aug. 29, 1961. The Cárcano-Kennedy friendship dated from the eve of World War II when Cárcano and President Kennedy's father were serving simultaneously as ambassadors to London.

[19] Interviews with Admiral (Ret.) Jorge Perren, April 1, 1970, and General (Ret.) Alcides López Aufranc, March 23, 1977.

[20] Alonso [124], p. 20.

The crisis that erupted between the President and the military in late January 1962 was again related to differences over the conduct of foreign affairs. This time the spark that precipitated the controversy was the role of the Argentine delegation at the Eighth Consultative Meeting of Foreign Ministers held at Punta del Este under the aegis of the OAS to consider the Cuban problem.

How and to what extent President Frondizi consulted with the armed forces secretaries on the instructions to be issued to the Argentine delegation to the Punta del Este Conference is a matter of controversy. A recent study sympathetic to Frondizi contends that the "military secretaries pressured the President to spell out to them the position Argentina would assume at Punta del Este, and Frondizi, who was aware of their aims, acted in such a way that the armed forces only learned of the Argentine position when the sessions were under way, even though the Navy had sent over almost its entire intelligence service and the Chief of the General Staff, Admiral Palma."[21] The implication of this version is that Frondizi kept the military secretaries at arm's length until they could learn from events what his policy was.

A less charitable interpretation, however, emerges from other sources. According to the recollections of the then Navy Undersecretary Admiral Juan C. Bassi, the President invited the military secretaries in advance of the conference to express the opinions of their respective services; Foreign Minister Cárcano met with them and gave assurances that Argentina would take a position of frank opposition to communist Cuba. The subsequent behavior of the Argentine delegation, Bassi insists, belied these assurances, and the military felt deceived on a matter in which they, as guardians of the nation's defense, had a legal right to influence Argentine policy.[22] The Bassi version finds support not only in the recollections of other officers, but in contemporary documentary evidence. On February 1, the day after the Punta del Este Conference concluded, Frondizi presided over a meeting of the External Security Cabinet. The minutes taken at this meeting show Navy Secretary Clement stating without contradiction from the President or the Foreign Minister that "in ac-

21 Casas [224], pp. 155–56.
22 Interview with Admiral (Ret.) Juan C. Bassi, May 5, 1970.

cordance with reports received through various channels the conduct of the Argentine delegation contradicts the exchange of opinions that took place beforehand."[23] That the President did more than keep the military in the dark, that he deliberately undertook to deceive them, is the inescapable conclusion.

The real dispute between the President and the military, however, was not over honesty, but over policy. While the armed forces' leaders saw the Cuban problem essentially as a military threat to be countered by collectively endorsed sanctions, including Cuba's expulsion from the inter-American system, Frondizi saw the problem in a different light. To him, the real issue confronting the nations assembled at Punta del Este Conference was not Castro, but attacking the problems of underdevelopment. As he stated in a letter of instructions to Foreign Minister Cárcano,

It is up to us, the Argentines, to establish clearly that what is up for discussion in America is not the fate of an extremist caudillo who speaks in favor of a political system that has nothing to do with the reality of our peoples, but rather the future of a group of underdeveloped nations which have freely decided to climb to the highest levels of economic and social development. If that sovereign decision is not respected, if an attempt is made to hide or distort it in the ideological game of extremists, then indeed the evil will be difficult to conjure: an entire continent will give way to political and social convulsions.[24]

Frondizi obviously felt that preoccupation with militant responses to the Cuban problem would divert attention from long-term developmental needs and increase resistance within Latin America to peaceful social and economic change. In his letter of instructions to Dr. Cárcano, therefore, he made plain his attitude toward sanctions: "We wish to save the unity of the inter-American system and therefore we will abstain from voting sanctions that can hurt the principle

[23] Reunión del Gabinete de Seguridad Exterior, 1° de febrero de 1962, MS, Lockhart Papers. These are typed minutes based on the notes taken by Navy Captain Eduardo Lockhart, who as Chief of the Military Household served as the recording secretary for External Security Cabinet meetings. Present at this February 1, 1962, session, in addition to President Frondizi, were Foreign Minister Cárcano, National Defense Minister Villar, Navy Secretary Clement, Army Secretary Fraga, and Air Force Secretary Rojas Silveyra.

[24] Cited by President Frondizi in his Paraná speech, Feb. 3, 1962, and reproduced in Casas [224], p. 447, and also in Frondizi, *La política exterior argentina* [85], p. 189.

of nonintervention, that will aggravate existing political conditions, and that will contribute to intensifying extremist activities of the left and right."[25]

In presenting this rationale for opposing the sanctions permitted by the Rio Treaty, which served as the legal basis for convoking the Punta del Este Conference, Frondizi did not spell out what may have been another major concern: that if Cuba were excluded from the inter-American system, as Colombia, Peru, and a number of Central American states were advocating, Argentina and the rest of Latin America might well be the losers. If the sanctions voted against Cuba proved effective, and the United States concern over Castro dropped, the willingness of the U.S. Congress to vote the economic concessions and the massive sums needed for Latin America's development would also decline. The challenge to Argentine diplomacy at Punta del Este, therefore, was to find ways to damn Castro's Cuba without destroying it.

At Punta del Este, the Argentine delegation played what seemed on the surface to be an ambiguous role. At first it appeared to agree with the United States on the desirability of excluding Cuba from the OAS. On January 24, however, it joined Brazil, Mexico, Chile, and three other states in opposing Cuba's expulsion on the grounds that the Charter of the OAS would have to be amended first to permit such an action. The next day, Foreign Minister Cárcano, in a major address, deplored the Marxist-Leninist orientation of the Cuban authorities, but at the same time upheld the right of each country to determine its own government. The Argentine position on January 27 again seemed to favor expulsion, although not immediate, and its delegates worked with the U.S. delegation in seeking a formula that would declare Cuba's status as a Marxist regime incompatible with membership in the inter-American community.[26]

Of the nine resolutions finally adopted in the plenary sessions, Argentina voted in favor of eight. Several of these were clearly directed against the Castro regime, such as Resolution I that declared continental unity and democratic institutions to be in danger from an international communist offensive; Resolution II, that requested

[25] Frondizi, *La política exterior argentina* [85], pp. 189–90.
[26] *La Prensa*, Jan. 26, 1962, for Cárcano's speech; Conil Paz and Ferrari [230], pp. 216–17; for a U.S. account, Schlesinger [297], pp. 782–83.

the OAS Council to set up a special consultative committee on security against communist subversion; Resolution IV calling on all governments to hold free elections; Resolution VII that excluded Cuba at once from the Inter-American Defense Board; and Resolution VIII that called for the immediate ban on arms sales to Cuba and charged the OAS Council with studying the feasibility of extending the trade embargo to other items. In addition, Argentina voted readily for the resolutions that reiterated the principles of nonintervention and self-determination (III), emphasized the commitment to economic and social development (V), and called for a revision of the statute of the human rights commission (IX).[27]

It was Argentina's January 30 vote on the all-important Resolution VI, however, that revealed the contradiction within the Argentine position. Resolution VI consisted of four articles: first, a declaration that adherence by any member of the OAS to Marxism was incompatible with the inter-American system; second, that the present Cuban government, having identified itself as a Marxist-Leninist government, was incompatible with the principles and purposes of that system; third, that this incompatibility excluded Cuba from the inter-American system; and, fourth, that the OAS Council and other inter-American bodies should proceed at once to implement this resolution. On the article-by-article phase of the vote, the Argentine delegation voted yes on articles one and two, but abstained on articles three and four. On the vote on the resolution as a whole, Argentina abstained, together with Brazil, Mexico, Chile, Bolivia, and Ecuador.[28]

This refusal to associate Argentina with the United States and the thirteen other states that voted for Cuba's immediate exclusion—a refusal that Foreign Minister Cárcano tried to justify on the juridical grounds that the OAS Charter had no provision for excluding members—aroused the ire of the Argentine armed forces, brought denunciations from the opposition press and political parties, and precipitated the most serious crisis to confront President Frondizi since the Guevara visit. Again, as in the previous August, each service headquarters was the scene of stormy meetings. The Air Force was the first to take its case to the public. In a remarkable statement

[27] Department of State, *Bulletin* [36], Feb. 19, 1962, pp. 278–83.
[28] *Ibid.*; *La Prensa*, Jan. 31, 1962.

issued the afternoon of January 31, the Secretary repudiated the position of the Argentine delegation at Punta del Este, and in a general order distributed to all units, proclaimed the Air Force's solidarity with "all those countries that have assumed the defense of the free world."[29] The other military services were no less perturbed. That night the three military secretaries, on behalf of their respective high commands, submitted individual notes to President Frondizi. According to press accounts, these notes called on the President to calm public opinion by taking three steps: reassessing the government's foreign policy; breaking relations with Cuba; and shaking up the Foreign Ministry by asking for the resignations of Dr. Cárcano and certain other foreign policy advisors.[30]

President Frondizi's response was to convoke the February 1 meeting of the External Security Cabinet previously referred to so that Cárcano, who had returned from Uruguay just that noon, could "report at length on the development of the conference and explain the position adopted by the Argentine representatives." The Foreign Minister did in fact make a vigorous defense of the delegation. He claimed that it had shown "a firm anticommunist conviction" in the various votes it cast and that the "abstention in the voting on the third and fourth points of the Resolution [VI] was based exclusively on legal grounds." The Punta del Este meeting of consultation, he argued, had no juridical authority to exclude any of its members, and he challenged any jurist to prove the contrary. Cárcano, moreover, insisted that Argentine diplomacy had achieved a triumph in gaining acceptance for the thesis of Cuban incompatibility with the OAS and persuading Mexico and Brazil to abstain rather than vote against the resolution as originally intended. "With this," he asserted, "unanimity had been achieved since no one had voted in favor of the present Cuban regime." President Frondizi, in turn, endorsed this assessment of the Argentine performance, noted that Cárcano had always followed presidential instructions, and observed that President Kennedy had publicly praised Argentina's role at Punta del Este.[31]

The response of the three military secretaries was to urge the Pres-

[29] General Order No. 29, in *La Prensa*, Feb. 1, 1962, p. 20.

[30] *La Prensa*, Feb. 1, 1962, p. 20.

[31] Reunión del Gabinete de Seguridad Exterior, 1° de febrero de 1962 (see note 23, above), MS, pp. 1–4.

ident to break relations with the Cuban regime, both as a logical extension of the incompatibility thesis and as an essential step to restoring tranquility to the armed forces and the general public. Army Secretary Fraga and Navy Secretary Clement, deferring to the legal arguments presented by Dr. Cárcano, also asked whether Argentina could not then sponsor an amendment to the OAS Charter that would legally permit the exclusion of Cuba.[32] Air Secretary Jorge Rojas Silveyra, on the other hand, showing less sensitivity to the juridical aspect, argued that the danger of communism, which respects no legal restraints itself, made it necessary at times to subvert the law. "Democracies," he contended, "should not be so generous and should guard their existence even at the sacrifice of law so as to avoid the risk of collapsing into the hands of those who do not respect them."[33] No one else at the meeting endorsed this reasoning, but it represented a viewpoint that was not restricted to Air Force officers. Fifteen years later, under vastly different circumstances, it became the operating principle of an Argentine military government.

The three-hour meeting of the External Security Cabinet ended with Frondizi announcing the measures he proposed to take. He promised that Argentina would strictly implement all the resolutions adopted at Punta del Este and that the position of abstention on the two parts of Resolution VI in no way impaired Argentina's solidarity with the countries that voted affirmatively at Punta del Este. He also stipulated four steps to be taken by the Ministry of Foreign Affairs: the immediate recall of Argentina's ambassador to Cuba; the prompt initiation of a study of the possibility of reforming the Charter of the OAS; the study of the problem of a break in relations with the Cuban regime; and the preparation, for issuance by the presidency, of a communiqué explaining the actions of the Argentine delegation at Punta del Este.[34]

If the President hoped that with these decisions the crisis would

[32] *Ibid.*, pp. 4–6.
[33] *Ibid.*, pp. 6–7.
[34] *Ibid.*, p. 11. According to Captain Lockhart, President Frondizi asked after the meeting broke up to see the minutes and directed him to change the wording where he had the President saying "to study the break in relations" to the wording that now appears in the minutes: "to study the problem of the break in relations." This was the first cabinet session Lockhart had taken notes at in his new assignment, and at the time he gave no importance to the change (interview with Navy Captain [Ret.] Eduardo Lockhart, May 16, 1970).

dissipate, he was doomed to disappointment. The next day, February 2, saw, if anything, an increase in tensions, with the military services confining all their troops to barracks, and the Air Force going so far as to place units on alert. The central issue in the continuing crisis was the demand by officers of all three services for a prompt break in relations with the government of Cuba. The President's decision to order the Foreign Ministry to study the problem was insufficient to mollify military opinion. Indeed, tempers were running so high that when Foreign Minister Cárcano, at the invitation of Admiral Clement, visited the Navy Ministry to explain his role at the Punta del Este Conference, excited officers would not let him speak.[35]

The atmosphere of mounting tension put a particular strain on the loyalties of the military secretaries. Caught in the middle between Frondizi's determination to frame his own foreign policy and the pressures emanating from their subordinates, each Secretary found himself trying to represent the views of his respective force while defending the government against the machinations of coup-minded officers. The longer the crisis continued unresolved, the greater the danger that the golpista minority might attract enough support from the mainstream of officer opinion to topple the government. It was to prevent such an eventuality that the military secretaries gave assurances to their respective senior officers following the February 1 cabinet meeting that a break in relations could be expected. Moreover, as a substitute for the draft communiqué prepared by the Foreign Ministry that avoided reference to the diplomatic rupture, they drafted a text that embodied their own ideas. This text got into the hands of journalists who described it as an ultimatum served on the President.[36]

Understandably vexed, Frondizi convoked a new session of the External Security Cabinet on the evening of February 2. For several hours, he and the military secretaries wrangled over what was to be done. The President, complaining of the insult shown to his person, insisted that his was the power of decision and that, while willing to discuss his policies with them, he would not yield to an imposition. The military secretaries, for their part, disclaimed any intention of

[35] Interview with Admiral (Ret.) Bassi.

[36] Reunión del Gabinete de Seguridad Exterior, 2 de febrero de 1962, MS, Lockhart Papers. This is a handwritten document consisting of 35 small sheets.

insulting the President and insisted that they had been trying to strengthen his authority. Both Navy Secretary Clement and Army Secretary Fraga tried to make the point that they had come away from the previous cabinet meeting believing that the President reluctantly had accepted the necessity of the Cuban break and that the study requested of the Foreign Ministry dealt only with the form of implementing the break. The President, supported by Dr. Cárcano, took sharp issue with this, insisting that the decision to break, as well as the form it might take, was contingent on what the study would show. In the course of this heated exchange, the President cited the minutes of the February 1 meeting to prove that he had not agreed to a break in relations, but only to a study of the problem. He failed to mention that after that meeting he had asked the official charged with keeping the minutes to change the wording where he had written "to study the break in relations" to read "to study the problem of the break." The confusion of the military secretaries was understandable.[37] Faced with the President's unbending response, Clement and Fraga conceded that they had misunderstood. In the Navy Secretary's words, "I have interpreted badly, and reported badly, and this puts me in an untenable position."[38] As he and the other military secretaries pointed out, however, the problem remained: their forces were awaiting an acceptable statement of policy from the President. Here Interior Minister Vítolo, attending the meeting in his capacity as head of internal security, tried to find a compromise. Under his direction, a statement was prepared for publication that combined elements from both the military secretaries' draft and that of the Foreign Ministry. The carefully worded final paragraph hinted, without stating so, that a diplomatic break with Cuba was in the wind.[39]

President Frondizi, however, adamant to the last, announced to the cabinet that he would not feel bound by this statement; his decision would still depend on future study. At this point, Minister Vítolo lined up with the military secretaries in stressing the necessity of a prompt decision if the constitutional order were to be maintained.[40] Confronted, thus, with the possibility of revolt, and advised by the service secretaries that without a decision now they would

[37] *Ibid.*, pp. 1–7. See note 34, above.
[38] Reunión del Gabinete . . . 2 de febrero, p. 17.
[39] *Ibid.*, pp. 18–25.
[40] *Ibid.*, pp. 26–33.

have to resign, the President finally yielded. The handwritten notes on which this account of the February 2 cabinet meeting is based end with the following, almost plaintive, exchange: "Fraga: You have the wish to break relations; President: Yes, but as long as I don't take the decision under pressure; Fraga: I need to know your intention; President: Yes."[41]

The decree ordering the break in relations with the Cuban government was eventually issued six days later.[42] Before actually signing it, however, and thus abandoning under pressure a policy he believed to be best for Argentines, Frondizi gave vent to his feelings in a bitter speech delivered at Paraná on February 3. Yielding to the emotionalism that had characterized much of the criticism of his actions voiced in civilian and military circles, he denounced his opponents as enemies of Argentine democracy and as members of a world conspiracy of reactionaries opposed to Latin America's development and sovereignty.[43] The intemperate nature of these remarks did little to reduce the resentment and suspicion that existed among many men in uniform. With the signing of the decree, the immediate crisis eased, but the factors that gave rise to it did not disappear. The President's lack of frankness in his dealings with the military, combined with the latter's inability to understand his policy objectives, served to prevent any real improvement in their relationship.[44]

Foreign policy issues had precipitated the most recent crisis for President Frondizi, but his handling of the electoral matters and the results of the March 1962 elections would provide the most decisive test of his relationship with the military. At stake in these elections was control of the Chamber of Deputies—for the first time since 1958 the UCRI could be reduced to a quorumless minority—and control of the governorships of the various provinces. Moreover, over and above the specific offices to be won or lost was the vital matter

---

[41] *Ibid.*, pp. 33–35.

[42] Decree No. 1250, Feb. 8, 1962, in *Anales* [1], XXII A, 254.

[43] The full text of the Paraná speech is given in Frondizi, *La política exterior argentina* [85], pp. 186–95, with the denunciatory passages beginning on page 193.

[44] Relations between the President and his military secretaries were so cool after the February 2 meeting that the latter boycotted a state dinner for the King of Belgium on February 6 and did not step foot into the Casa Rosada until February 12. The military demand for a shakeup in the foreign policy sector led to the resignation of Undersecretary of Foreign Affairs Oscar Camilión and Economic Advisor Ambassador Arnaldo Musich (*La Prensa*, Feb. 7, 13, 15, 1962).

of Frondizi's survival in office; a clear-cut victory for administration candidates would enhance his prestige and reduce the capabilities of those who had been seeking his forcible overthrow; an electoral rebuff could well have the opposite effect.

In anticipation of the elections, Frondizi and the UCRI leadership gave serious attention to two major questions of political strategy. The first involved the possibility of changing the rules by which deputies were elected and, in presidential years, by which electoral college votes were assigned. Under the Sáenz Peña system introduced early in the century but altered by Perón, the political party with the largest plurality in any province (or the Federal Capital) received two-thirds of its seats in the Chamber of Deputies, and in a presidential election, of its electoral college vote; the runner-up party received the remaining third. The Radical Party had traditionally championed this system and after Perón's fall, its two offshoots, the UCRI and UCRP, both hoping to come in first, insisted on restoration of the system for the 1958 elections. Despite the objections from smaller parties, the Aramburu military government complied, and through the provisions of the Sáenz Peña law the UCRI had gained its initial dominance of the Congress.

Now, however, the UCRI had to face a different situation. It could no longer count on the support of Peronist votes as it did in 1958. Peronist abstentions in 1960 had enabled UCRP candidates to come in first in a number of provinces, substantially increasing that party's congressional representation. A repeat performance in the 1962 election might give the UCRP control of the lower house, unless, of course, the rules of the game were changed. By shifting to a system of proportional representation in the more populous provinces where the UCRI's prospects were most in doubt, the negative consequences of defeat could be minimized. If UCRI candidates lost by narrow margins, as some anticipated, they would receive almost as many seats as the victor; but if the UCRI ran badly and came in third, it would still receive some of the contested seats. The UCRP would lose the benefits of the Sáenz Peña law. Moreover, enactment of the new system now, while the UCRI still had a majority in both houses of Congress, might control the choice of a president in 1964. In a close race, the effect of the proportionate allocation of votes for the electoral college might well be to prevent it from reaching a decision.

The choice would then fall to the Legislative Assembly where deputies and senators each cast one vote. Here the UCRI senators who made up over 80 percent of the total could be expected to swing the result.[45]

It was calculations of this sort presented by Interior Minister Vítolo and other advisors that led President Frondizi to send an electoral reform bill to the Senate in November 1961. That body gave its prompt approval, but the Chamber of Deputies delayed final action until after the results of the December 17 elections in the provinces of Catamarca, San Luís, and Santa Fe could be analyzed. The UCRI victory in all three provinces gave less urgency to the arguments in favor of the electoral reform, and the administration decided to postpone bringing the bill to a final vote.[46]

These early elections, and especially the contest in Santa Fe province with its heavy working-class population, raised in urgent form the second major question of political strategy: Should the Peronists be allowed to present their own candidates? When Frondizi refused in 1958 to legalize the outlawed Peronist Party, Perón's supporters, acting under his orders, cast blank ballots in the 1960 congressional elections; later that year Peronist leaders adopted the tactic of throwing their support in selected elections to candidates running against the government. Now in 1961, for the first time since Perón's fall, they presented for approval by election authorities their own slates of candidates, using variously named neo-Peronist parties as the legal instruments for channeling the potential votes of their loyal followers. In effect, the Peronists were challenging the Frondizi administration to live up to its rhetorical commitments to legality and democracy by allowing them to participate in the elections on their own terms, or else by barring their candidates to give them an excuse for violence.[47]

The facts that only three provinces were involved and that in Santa

[45] This analysis of the implications of a shift to proportional representation is taken from the column "Panorama Político," *La Nación*, Nov. 15, 1961.

[46] On the Senate vote of Nov. 10 approving the bill see *Senadores* [3], 1961, III, 2432–83. The Chamber of Deputies considered the bill briefly on December 7, but when a move to take it up under suspended rules failed to get the necessary vote, the UCRI majority leadership never scheduled a further debate although special sessions were held later in December and again between January 17 and 31, 1962 (*Diputados* [2], 1961, IX, 5970–75).

[47] For an insider's view of the process that led to the resumption of Peronist electoral activity in 1961, see Guardo [60], pp. 301–46.

Fe province the UCRI gubernatorial candidate was especially popular among working-class people seem to have made the decision easier. Interior Minister Vítolo was highly optimistic that the UCRI would defeat the Peronist candidates in all three provinces, and events proved him correct. Yet it should be noted that President Frondizi had initially opposed allowing the Peronists to run. Away in New Delhi, India, when the decision had to be made, he had telephoned his views to the UCRI national committee, but finally accepted his Interior Minister's judgment to allow them on the ballot.[48]

The December elections were to exercise a fateful dual influence on the preparations for the more important March 1962 contests. First, in permitting Peronist candidates, they set a precedent which the administration would find very difficult to reverse. Without some external pressure or provocation, a change of course now would be politically embarrassing. The second, and related, consequence of those elections was to enhance Interior Minister Vítolo's credibility as a political manager and give his views a greater influence on the President than might otherwise have been the case.[49]

Yet the dangers of a miscalculation were far greater from the March elections, not only because more posts were at stake, but because control of the country's most important elective office after the presidency, the governorship of Buenos Aires province, was involved. This province, the largest and most populous in the entire country, contained the industrial belt where Perón had derived much of his strength and where loyalty to his wishes could be anticipated. An administration victory here over a Peronist candidate would deal a body blow to Perón's political influence and be a major step toward ensuring a UCRI victory in the 1964 presidential election. By the same token, a Peronist victory could be a disaster for Frondizi.

And here it was not simply votes that had to be calculated. If Buenos Aires province contained the core of Peronist support, it was also the location of numerous military bases of the Army, Air

[48] Interview with Roberto Etchepareborda, April 25, 1970. Dr. Etchepareborda was first vice-president of the UCRI National Committee in December 1961; see also his "Un poco de historia," pp. 1–2, an unpublished article-length memoir which he kindly made available to me.

[49] For evidence of the extent of Dr. Vítolo's influence, see the open letter of Felipe Díaz O'Kelly to Frondizi published in *La Nación* (edición internacional), Aug. 31, 1964. Díaz O'Kelly had been Minister of Government in Buenos Aires province prior to the March 1962 elections.

Force, and especially the Navy. In the ceremonial that constituted so much of military life, the election and installation of a Peronist governor would place military commanders under obligation to invite him to their installations and to show him the courtesies owed to the civilian leader of the province. Military bands might once again be asked to play the hated Peronista tunes that were banned after 1955. On emotional as well as institutional and political grounds, the seven years that had passed since these officers overthrew Perón were insufficient to erase their antipathy to him or to permit them to view with equanimity the election of Peronists to public office.

Why, then, did the armed forces not pressure Frondizi to proscribe the Peronists from running for office? After all, they did not hesitate to force his hand in questions of foreign relations. Why did they not act to prevent the possibility of a Peronist victory in the March elections by excluding their candidates from the polls? The answer may be found by examining the sequence of events from late January to the eve of the elections.

In January, the Argentine public, civilian and military, was startled to learn that the Popular Union Party had presented to the Electoral Tribunal the name of Juan D. Perón as its candidate for vice-governor of Buenos Aires province; at the same time, in the Federal Capital, Perón's name was included in that party's list of candidates for national deputy. This news understandably aroused concern in military circles. What they apparently did not know was that Perón himself was counting on their reaction. The exiled leader, under pressure from supporters in Argentina who wanted to participate in the elections, but himself fearful that if they emerged victorious the result would be a military takeover and a return to the even more repressive atmosphere of 1955, presented his own candidacy as a political ploy. His aim presumably was to goad the military into pressuring the authorities to proscribe not only his name, but those of other Peronist candidates as well. He could then justify asking his followers to abstain from the elections.[50]

What followed did not exactly coincide with these expectations. The three military secretaries and Interior Minister Vítolo, meeting

[50] "Asi cayó Frondizi" [128], p. 75.

in the Defense Ministry offices on January 29, engaged in an exchange of views that were incorporated in a confidential document. Vítolo declared that Perón could not be a candidate for any office because he was disqualified on legal as well as political and historical grounds. The Interior Minister, moreover, speaking for the President as well as himself, stated that the government "is firmly disposed to prevent any form of return to the system overthrown on September 16, 1955." However, he went on, this did not prevent the followers of the ex-dictator from organizing legally and participating in national life for peaceful and democratic ends. The three military secretaries, after disclaiming any intention of interfering with the government's political actions, made it clear that their forces were not disposed to permit Perón or those jointly responsible with him for the harm done to the nation by his regime to return to political life. These persons, they stated, are "criminals who cannot occupy elective posts, nor those of any other nature, without impairing national dignity."[51]

This January 29 exchange produced a meeting of the minds on the exclusion of Perón, but postponed for future consideration what, if anything, would be done with the other Peronist candidates. The importance of this issue was soon superseded by the crisis that arose over Punta del Este. As noted earlier, this crisis was resolved when the President finally broke relations with Cuba, but the bitterness engendered by his Paraná speech lingered on in military as well as civilian circles. Relations between Minister Vítolo and Secretaries Fraga, Clement, and Rojas Silveyra, however, probably improved, for he had taken their side in the tense cabinet discussions that preceded the break. It would not be surprising, then, if, as a result, Vítolo's optimistic view about the election influenced the attitudes of the military secretaries. Throughout the month of February and up to the very eve of the elections, he exuded confidence that the Peron-

---

[51] I am grateful to Admiral (Ret.) Jorge Palma for providing me a photostatic copy of the original of this document. Marked confidential and dated January 29, 1962, it consists of three pages, the first two of which have initials on the left margin and the third of which has the signatures of the following: Justo P. Villar, Minister of National Defense; A. R. Vítolo, Minister of Interior; R. M. Fraga, Secretary of the Army; G. Clement, Secretary of the Navy; and Rojas Silveyra, Secretary of the Air Force.

ists could not win and that it was therefore in the longrun interest of the country to allow them to run, and thus destroy the myth of Perón's power.[52]

The final phase of the election campaign, however, increased apprehensions in other quarters. Never as sanguine about the outcome as Vítolo, President Frondizi had been trying since January to negotiate with the Peronists to take themselves out of the race. If journalistic accounts can be believed, the President had sent intermediaries to talk with Perón in Madrid, then with the leaders of the Peronist Coordinating Council in the capital, and finally with the Popular Union candidate for governor in Buenos Aires province. This was Andrés Framini, leader of the national textile workers unions, who, together with a former Perón cabinet minister, Dr. Francisco M. Anglada, headed the Peronist slate in that province.[53] Perón, as noted earlier, shared Frondizi's desire to avoid an electoral confrontation that could precipitate a military takeover. If his followers could be persuaded to abstain in the March elections, thus enabling Frondizi to hold onto office, the exiled leader would be in a strong position to extract concessions for the 1964 presidential race.[54] But for all of his political acuteness, Perón found himself unable to refuse when a delegation of his main labor supporters came to Madrid specifically to pressure him into giving his blessing to the candidates of the several neo-Peronist parties now linked together in a "Justicialist Front." According to the recollections of one trade union leader, so great was the fear that Perón would later change his mind that the delegation got him to put into writing his approval of the Framini-Anglada ticket.[55]

With self-proscription by the Peronists ruled out, Frondizi found his alternatives limited in the last weeks of the electoral campaign. To be sure, he could appeal to independent voters to support the

[52] See note 40 above; Reunión del Gabinete Seguridad Exterior y Ministro del Interior 15 de marzo, MS, pp. 1–3.

[53] "Asi cayó Frondizi" [128], p. 75; Pandolfi [228], p. 136.

[54] To provide Perón with arguments he could use to overcome his followers' desire to participate in the elections, President Frondizi secretly requested the Buenos Aires provincial Minister of Government, Felipe Díaz O'Kelly, to ban a Peronist rally and to intervene with the provincial electoral board to get them to proscribe the Peronists. Díaz O'Kelly refused. See his letter, cited above in note 49.

[55] Domínguez [56], pp. 82–85; "Asi cayó Frondizi" [128], pp. 75–76.

UCRI as the only barrier to a Peronist deluge, an electioneering tactic that would be effective in districts like the Federal Capital where the middle classes comprised a large part of the electorate. But this did nothing to resolve the threat of a Peronist victory in other provinces, and especially Buenos Aires. The one option Frondizi steadfastly refused to take was to ban the Peronist candidates by presidential decree. To do so on his own initiative without being able to cite as justification a threat to domestic peace, or irresistible military pressure, would make a mockery of his public commitment to legality and democracy; it could antagonize the working-class vote beyond repair and thus negate all possibility of determining the results of the next presidential election; and it could provide his golpista foes with new pretexts for promoting his overthrow. But even if Frondizi had contemplated a belated move to outlaw the Peronists, the unexpected death on February 22 of the UCRP candidate for the Buenos Aires governorship made this all but impossible politically. In what was thereafter essentially a two-man race, the proscription of Framini would be tantamount to awarding victory by decree to the UCRI candidate.[56]

As the March 18 hour of truth approached, Dr. Frondizi probably would have welcomed a military pronouncement demanding elimination of Justicialist Front candidates. Indeed, on March 16, at the ceremonies commemorating the 150th anniversary of the founding of the San Martín Grenadiers regiment, Dr. Frondizi told the Army Commander-in-Chief, General Poggi, that there was still time to exclude the Peronists if he insisted. But neither Poggi nor any other high military officer chose to assume that responsibility.[57]

To what extent was this disinclination part of a deliberate military maneuver to unseat Frondizi? Certainly golpista officers who had tried so often in the past through crises of their own manufacture to oust the President had little incentive to help him escape now from a dilemma of his own making. And, indeed, there is evidence that on the eve of the election certain anti-Frondizi officers were hoping for a clear Peronist victory in Buenos Aires province, presumably in the belief that this would convulse public opinion and facilitate a coup.[58]

[56] "Así cayó Frondizi" [128], p. 74; Pandolfi [228], p. 137. Larralde died while campaigning on February 22, 1962 (*La Prensa*, Feb. 23, 1962).
[57] Interview with General (Ret.) Raúl Poggi.
[58] Admirals Palma and Sánchez Sañudo displayed such views at a private

But such golpista officers did not dictate the policies of their respective services. Ironically, greater responsibility for the military's
passivity may have rested with the officers of legalist outlook. Although they would like to have seen the Peronist candidates excluded, they went along with the government's position rather than
intervene openly to compel a change. In maintaining a low profile on
this issue, they tried to avoid having the armed forces become the
instrument of partisan politics. Aware that politicians of several sectors, Frondicistas, anti-Frondicistas, and even Peronists, were specu-
lating on military resistance to Peronism, they saw no reason to do
their dirty work for them.[59] In hindsight, this inhibition on their part
helped produce the post-election crisis and contributed to the disruption of the very constitutional order they had been supporting for
the past four years.

But although the military secretaries, as spokesmen for the prevailing opinion within their respective services, presented no ultimatum
to the President, they were deeply concerned with how the government proposed to fulfill the commitment made to them on January
29, the commitment embodied in the confidential document signed
by Vítolo "to prevent any form of return to the system overthrown
on September 16, 1955." This question was the object of an External
Security Cabinet meeting held at the request of the Defense Minister
on Thursday, March 15, three days before the scheduled election.[60]

In the presence of President Frondizi, Defense Minister Dr. Justo
P. Villar, Army Secretary Fraga, Navy Secretary Gastón C. Clement,
and Air Force Undersecretary Brigadier Juan C. Pereyra, Interior
Minister Vítolo reviewed the situation in the various provinces, dis-
tinguishing the independent parties that were receiving Peronist
electoral support, as in La Rioja, San Juan, and Entre Ríos, from
those that were genuinely Peronist, like the Union Popular and
Justicialist Front. Vítolo still insisted that the Peronists would run no
better than second countrywide, but he conceded that in Buenos

---

dinner held in the home of Admiral (Ret.) Jorge Perren (interview, April 1,
1970; also Perren Memoirs, p. 367).

[59] Guevara [153], pp. 134–38; interview with General Tomás Sánchez de
Bustamante, May 11, 1970.

[60] Guevara, a member of the Army General Staff, claims that it was as a result
of a memorandum he prepared on March 13 that the armed forces leadership
insisted on this meeting. See previous note.

Aires, Córdoba, and Tucumán provinces a victory on their part would have serious consequences. His proposal for this eventuality was to resort to the constitutional power of intervention, that is, to have the federal government take over direct control of the provincial administration.[61]

The minutes of this meeting spell out beyond any doubt the tactics Vítolo proposed to use in the nation's largest electoral district:

As regards the province of Buenos Aires, Framini is clearly Peronist. I believe that Framini cannot take charge of the government, just as I expressed in the January 29 meeting in the Defense Ministry, even though the procedure to be followed was not spelled out. I believe that if Framini wins, we should resort to the constitutional procedure of intervening the province, basing this on the evidence provided by the nature of his political campaign and statement of aims, which clearly indicate the chaos and retrogression which the province would experience. I believe we should not wait for the opening of Congress, but should proceed to order the intervention during the recess of parliament, giving it notification in due course. . . . With respect to Buenos Aires, I believe it is worth running the risk, and I consider that Peronism and its standard-bearers will be defeated definitively. I repeat, nonetheless, that if they win, we should intervene.[62]

Neither the Interior Minister nor President Frondizi attempted to argue the case for another alternative: allowing Framini to assume the governorship. The argument could have been made that Framini, as governor, would find himself with limited authority; the provincial legislature would be in the hands of parties hostile to him; the federal government and the armed forces would watch him closely; and at the first sign of arbitrariness or excesses against any sector of the population, the device of intervention could be used to oust him. Whatever the logic of such an argument, no one was prepared to make it at this time.[63]

Instead, the cabinet discussion focused on the timing and manner of ordering the interventions. The military secretaries were anxious to have the interventors take over as soon as possible to avoid disorders. But Vítolo and the President proposed an alternate course:

[61] Reunión del Gabinete . . . 15 de marzo, pp. 1–5.

[62] *Ibid.*, pp. 3–4.

[63] The case for this alternative had been presented in late January or early February by Felipe Díaz O'Kelly but to no avail. See his letter cited above in note 49. It was an alternative that Rodolfo Martínez (h.), a Christian Democratic politician, also favored (interview, Washington D.C., Oct. 29, 1970).

to issue the decrees of intervention the day after the election, but defer their date of effectiveness to May 1, when the governors-elect were to assume office. Otherwise, Frondizi argued, the interventions would apply to the incumbent governors and not to their successors. When asked whether the opening of Congress on May 1 might not create difficulties, since under the constitution when it is in session its approval is required to authorize an intervention, President Frondizi replied that "in case of necessity, and for the purpose of avoiding interference, the inauguration of the congressional sessions could be postponed for two or three days."[64] The conclusion of the discussion was that the announcement of the interventions, should they be required for Buenos Aires, Córdoba, or Tucumán provinces, would be made the day after the elections and that the appropriate decrees would be adopted in a full cabinet meeting.[65]

At no time in this last cabinet meeting prior to the Sunday, March 18, elections did President Frondizi admit to any doubts about the course he had followed. He defended the Interior Minister's handling of the question of Peronist participation and expressed confidence in the possibility of victory.[66] The military secretaries, on the other hand, did not disguise their concern. Navy Secretary Clement, in particular, expressed his worry at the "moral violence it signified for the armed forces to supervise an election in which, if Framini wins and intervention is decreed, they are moral accomplices in the resulting political fraud." Clement wanted it clearly understood that he had opposed having the armed forces guard the elections in the first place, and he reiterated his view that it was a political mistake for the government to allow the Peronists to run.[67]

At the close of this sensitive meeting, it was understood that the Minister of the Interior would inform the press that the President had convoked it to review the measures for guaranteeing the elections. He would also restate his previous declaration to the press that there would be no proscription of any party and "that the popular will which stays within democratic norms would be respected." On this note of calculated deception, these high officials of the Frondizi

[64] Reunión del Gabinete . . . 15 de marzo, p. 4.

[65] Ibid., p. 5.

[66] Ibid., p. 5. This may be contrasted with the pessimistic view ascribed to him by such writers as Pandolfi [228], p. 137, and Alonso [124], p. 25.

[67] Reunión del Gabinete . . . 15 de marzo, p. 5.

administration went off to their other tasks and to await the results of Sunday's election.[68]

Ironically, were it not for the political consequences, the March 18 election might be remembered as an example of Argentine civic culture at its best. Under the watchful eye of miliary detachments assigned to guarantee access to polling places and the honesty of the vote count, record numbers of men and women cast their ballots without a single reported disturbance. At nightfall, however, when the preliminary results showed the Justicialist Front clearly ahead in ten of the fourteen gubernatorial races, including the crucial one in Buenos Aires province, it was clear that the Frondizi administration was facing the most serious crisis of its history. It had gambled that it could nullify the Peronists as a political force by defeating them at the polls and had lost. The question now was what political price it would have to pay for this mistaken judgment.[69]

The search for an answer turned out to be an agonizing process that all but paralyzed the Argentine government. For the next ten days *and* nights the President and the military leadership, political figures of all hues, the Argentine press, and even the United States Ambassador all took part in the search that ended only in the early morning hours of March 29 when armed forces deposed Dr. Frondizi. At the start of the crisis, however, it was by no means certain that this would be the end result. Indeed, had the military leadership been decisive in seeking power, they would not have waited for ten days, nor acted finally in the manner they did.

The vacillation of the armed forces, a reflection of the divisions within and between each military service, created a fluid situation that allowed for attempts at compromise solutions. The first such attempt was made the very night of the elections, when Argentina's twelve top military men, the Army, Navy, and Air Force Secretaries, Undersecretaries, Commanders-in-Chief, and General Staff Chiefs, assembled at the Air Force Ministry to examine the situation created by the Peronist electoral victories. The all-night session of this committee of twelve produced a consensus on several points: that they would not accept Framini or other Peronists of his type; that they

[68] *Ibid.*, pp. 5–6. Vítolo's remarks to the press at the close of the meeting adhered to the agreed-upon explanation (*La Prensa*, March 16, 1962).
[69] On the absence of election irregularities, see *La Prensa*, March 19, 1962.

did not like interventions as a solution; and that the idea of nullifying elections their own men had guarded was distasteful. Nevertheless, if the alternative were ousting the President or going along with interventions, they would choose the latter.[70]

Accordingly, they drew up a four-point *planteo* (set of demands) that was delivered to Frondizi later that morning. The planteo called for federal intervention of all provinces where the Peronists triumphed except Salta, Jujuy, and San Juan; elimination of Frigeristas from all government posts; a direct assault against communism; and the proscription of Peronism, its emblems, and its activities, direct or indirect. In addition, they asked for the arrest of Peronist leaders to discourage acts of violence.[71]

Frondizi agreed only partially to the planteo, for while consenting to the intervention, he promised only to study the request for proscribing the Peronists and flatly refused to authorize any arrests.[72] His decree of intervention came out later that day, March 19, and applied only to five provinces: Buenos Aires, Chaco, Río Negro, Santiago del Estero, and Tucumán. The terms of the decree, however, went beyond the President's March 15 concept of deferring the effective date to May 1. Instead, the decree placed these provinces under immediate and complete federal control and stipulated that the intervention applied both to the existing executive and legislative authorities and to those elected on March 18. Moreover, by directing the federal interventors to plan for new elections for municipal and provincial authorities, the decree, in effect, nullified the March 18 results.[73]

Partisan accounts have tended to obscure the role of President Frondizi in the issuance of the decree. Writers sympathetic to him have tried to absolve him of responsibility and place the blame for this violation of democratic principle on unrelenting military pressure. Critics of Frondizi, on the other hand, have tended to downplay

[70] Interviews with Admiral (Ret.) Bassi, General (Ret.) Poggi, Air Force Brigadier (Ret.) Rojas Silveyra, General (Ret.) Fraga, and Admiral (Ret.) Palma.

[71] Dr. José Cáceres Monié, at that time Undersecretary of Defense, provided these details in a statement published in the press in April 1962 and reproduced in Luna, *Diálogos con Frondizi* [66], pp. 211–12.

[72] *Ibid.*

[73] Decree No. 2542, March 19, 1962, *Anales* [1], XXII A, 1962, 342–43.

the external factors and emphasize his personal responsibility. The truth of the matter is more complex.[74]

The idea of using federal intervention to deprive the Peronists of the fruits of victory was, as we have seen, the brainchild of Interior Minister Vítolo, not of the military, who had been critical of allowing the Peronists to vote in the first place. In the March 15 cabinet meeting, the President had given the intervention idea his explicit approval. That the military planteo of March 19 contained a request for provincial interventions could hardly come as any surprise. But there is additional evidence to indicate that, once the election returns were in, Frondizi deliberately encouraged the military to press for the interventions as a means of defusing the crisis atmosphere. Even before the military committee of twelve got down to work, he had begun to draft the intervention decree. Moreover, before that committee could decide on a course of action, Dr. Vítolo joined them in the Air Ministry and, in a telephone conversation to Olivos, which they could overhear, confirmed that the President was personally drafting the intervention decree.[75] It seems fair to conclude, then, that though military pressure, explicit or implicit, certainly influenced Frondizi's decision to promulgate the intervention decree, his role in the steps that led to its issuance was hardly that of an innocent bystander.

Whatever Frondizi may have hoped to accomplish with the intervention decree, far from putting an end to the crisis, it gave it new impetus. Opposition groups could now argue that, in rejecting the results of the provincial elections, the President was guilty of violating his constitutional oath to uphold the laws.[76] Within the ranks of the military, golpista elements used this argument to overcome the inhibitions of legalist officers, and nowhere more effectively than in

[74] For an example of an account that focuses on the military pressure, see Luna, *Argentina de Perón a Lanusse, 1943–1973* [112], p. 140; for an account that ignores the military pressure, see Toryho [79], p. 159.

[75] Navy Captain (Ret.) Lockhart recalls that when he reached the Olivos residence around 11:00 P.M.. Frondizi told him that he had already prepared the *fundamentos* of the decree (interview, May 6, 1970). On the Vítolo telephone conversation, interviews with Admiral (Ret.) Bassi and Air Force Brigadier Rojas Silveyra.

[76] For political party reactions to the provincial interventions see *La Nación*, March 20–25; also interview with Democratic Socialist leader Américo Ghioldi, March 20, 1970.

the Navy. As of March 20, the top Navy leadership decided to press for the voluntary resignation of President Frondizi and the installation of a constitutional successor or, if he refused, to proceed with the establishment of a new government. At Navy initiative, the committee of twelve was reconvened to consider this proposal.[77] Neither the Army nor Air Force leadership, however, was prepared to go along with it. Instead, they proposed that Dr. Frondizi be kept in the presidency, provided that he agree to the appointment of a coalition cabinet named by the three services and to follow a plan of government that they would dictate. Should Frondizi refuse to accept this arrangement, however, their position then would be to force him out and transfer control to the armed forces. The Navy representatives agreed to go along with the Army and Air Force in the interests of maintaining a united military front, but they reserved the right to review their position to meet changing circumstances. The twelve military men thereupon proceeded to affix their signatures to a secret *acta* that embodied the positions of their respective services.[78]

Golpista elements in the Navy, however, through their contacts with the political parties, may well have anticipated that the coalition cabinet idea would never succeed. This proved, indeed, to be the case. Although Frondizi readily agreed to the military proposal and accepted the resignations of his civilian ministers, his invitation to the leaders of seven non-Peronist parties to discuss the formation of a coalition cabinet met with insufficient response. Apart from his own party, the UCRI, only the small Christian Democratic Party and Alvaro Alsogaray's miniscule Civic Independents accepted his invitation. The leaders of the principal opposition party, the UCRP, as well as of the conservative Federation of Center Parties, the Progressive Democrats, and the Democratic Socialists refused even to talk with the President and demanded instead that he resign. So great was their distrust of Frondizi that they preferred to risk the breakdown of civilian government rather than do anything that

[77] Interview with General (Ret.) Poggi.

[78] I am indebted to Admiral (Ret.) Palma for providing me with a photostatic copy of the original. It is a five-page handwritten document initialed on the left margin of the first four pages and bearing twelve signatures on page 5: (Army) Fraga, Peralta, Poggi, Spirito; (Navy) Clement, Bassi, Penas, Palma; (Air Force) Rojas Silveyra, Pereyra, Cayo Alsina, and Romanelli. The last-named officer prepared the document in his handwriting.

would enable him to serve out his term. Army Secretary Fraga, who had been delegated by the committee of twelve to canvass the prospects for a coalition cabinet, was forced to report to his colleagues and to the President on March 22 that the plan had failed.[79]

Aware now that his presidency was close to collapse, Frondizi turned to the man who had come to his rescue many times in the past, the former president General Pedro E. Aramburu. Aramburu's prestige in military circles was still considerable, save of course among golpista elements, who never forgave him for turning over the presidency to Frondizi in the first place. Aramburu had demonstrated his commitment to constitutional government at that time by accepting the results of the 1958 elections, and while openly condemning many of Frondizi's policies, he had consisently opposed all efforts to oust him. That General Aramburu hoped to be elected President to succeed Frondizi was widely assumed, but that this was his overriding motive in discouraging coups over the past four years is too cynical a view to be accepted.[80]

Now, however, President Frondizi, at the moment of greatest threat to his presidency, invited General Aramburu to serve as a mediator and find a solution that would be acceptable to all interested parties, civilian and military. Aramburu consented without hesitation and proceeded to assist in the formation of a new cabinet by encouraging two of his political friends, Oscar Puiggrós and Rodolfo Martínez, to agree to serve when invited by Frondizi. As of the close of March 23, the President was able to announce the appointment of four new ministers, two of them anti-Frigerio UCRI members, the other two (Puiggrós and Martínez) affiliated with the Christian Democrats, all four selected from a list of individuals recommended by the military. General Aramburu, moreover, met at length with the committee of twelve to set forth his plan for solving the crisis and to ask for time to explore its feasibility.[81]

[79] Interview with General (Ret.) Poggi; Alonso [124], p. 28.

[80] The idea that Aramburu, if he could stave off a military takeover, might be the beneficiary of UCRI support in the 1964 presidential elections was very much in the minds of politicians (interview with Rodolfo Martínez; letter from Roberto Etcheparaborda, May 22, 1978).

[81] Interviews with Oscar Puiggrós, July 12, 1971, and Rodolfo Martínez (h). These men were selected to be Ministers of Labor and Social Security and National Defense, respectively; the other two choices were Hugo Vaca Narvaja for

Although the Army and the Air Force leaders were willing to wait, the Navy reverted to its earlier stance of insisting on the voluntary resignation of the President. Urged on by younger Navy officers impatient of the delay, the Navy leadership broke ranks from their Army and Air Force colleagues in publicly demanding a prompt solution of the crisis and in making a direct and personal appeal to the President to step aside. On the night of March 24–25, Navy Secretary Clement, accompanied by Admirals Bassi, Penas, and Palma, visited Frondizi at the Olivos residence. Secretary Clement, in very respectful fashion, suggested to the President that he should resign for the good of the country and to maintain a constitutional government. The other admirals, while denying that theirs was in any sense a planteo, also urged his resignation, or at the least, that he take a leave from office until the political atmosphere cooled. Frondizi rejected both proposals and made it abundantly clear that he had no intention of giving up his office voluntarily. Unable to obtain a voluntary solution, and finding himself in a conflict of loyalties, Navy Secretary Clement presented his own resignation.[82]

Although the Navy was the first of the services to come out openly for Frondizi's resignation, within the Army, pressure to adopt a similar stance was on the increase. General Franklin Rawson, normally stationed at Tandil in southern Buenos Aires province, moved up to the outskirts of the Federal Capital to encourage other generals to speak out against Army Secretary Fraga's policy of supporting the Aramburu mediation effort. By March 25, it was evident that the Army Commander-in-Chief, General Poggi, identified himself with the views of those officers and no longer agreed with the Army Secretary.[83] It was probably this shift in the balance of high-level Army opinion, together with the responses received from civilian poli-

---

Interior and Jorge Wehbe for Economy (*La Nación*, March 24, 1962; Alonso [124], pp. 29–30).

[82] Interviews with Admirals (Ret.) Bassi, Penas, and Palma. Palma recalls having said to the President: "What is the solution, then? You are responsible for the situation." Frondizi's reply was to outline three alternatives: that he continue in office as in the past; that he continue under a plan of conciliation such as Aramburu was working on; that the military having the force impose a solution (interview with Dr. Arturo Frondizi, April 14, 1970).

[83] For the Fraga-Poggi divergence, see the Army Secretary's radiogram to all units reproduced in *La Prensa*, March 26, 1962; also interview with General (Ret.) Carlos Caro, March 18, 1977.

ticians to his mediation effort and the advice obtained from his immediate circle of friends, that led General Aramburu to reconsider his own position. Although he refrained from making any public announcement until the night of the 26th, after he again had consulted with the military committee and made a personal call on Frondizi, it is clear that as of early that morning, he had made his decision to abandon the President.[84]

Among the first outside his immediate entourage to learn of this decision were the two men he had encouraged three days before to accept appointments to the new cabinet. Aware that Rodolfo Martínez and Oscar Puiggrós were to take the oath of office together with the other ministers-designate at a ceremony scheduled for noon that day, General Aramburu summoned them to his home that morning to tell them they should not swear in. He explained that he was going to announce the failure of his mediation effort that night and publicly call on the President to resign. Neither Puiggrós nor Martínez, however, having given their word to Frondizi to serve in the cabinet, was willing to follow Aramburu's advice. The meeting ended in angry exchanges, with Martínez telling Aramburu that if the plan was to execute the President and the cabinet members, to put his name down on the list.[85]

With General Aramburu now adding his voice to the growing clamor for the President's resignation, the latter's position as of March 26 was the most precarious it had been since the night of the elections. Still, it was not entirely hopeless. Within the Army, the Campo de Mayo garrison was still in legalist hands, and many unit commanders were prepared to defend the government if ordered to do so. President Frondizi, however, adamantly opposed to resigning, but equally determined to avoid bloodshed, preferred to rely on the persuasive powers of two men, who in separate ways were trying to

[84] For Aramburu's public statement calling on the President to resign, see *La Nación*, March 27, 1962. A major influence on Aramburu's decision may have been the advice received from his longtime associate General (Ret.) Bernardino Labayru, at whose home he dined the night of March 24 (*La Prensa*, March 25, 1962). Interview with Rodolfo Martínez.

[85] Interviews with Rodolfo Martínez and Oscar Puiggrós. Sworn in as cabinet members in addition to those cited in note 81 above were: Roberto Etchepareborda, Foreign Affairs and Worship; Miguel Sussini, Education and Justice; Tiburcio Padilla, Social Welfare and Public Health; and Pedro Petriz, Public Works and Services.

forestall his ouster, the new Defense Minister, Rodolfo Martínez, and the United States Ambassador, Robert McClintock.

The role of the United States in the events of these days has been variously interpreted. Authors sympathetic to Frondizi have claimed that the Pentagon, for reasons ranging from a desire to undermine President Kennedy's Alliance for Progress to anger at Frondizi's Cuban policy, deliberately orchestrated the coup to oust the Argentine President. No evidence is ever offered for this general charge, or for the more specific one that U.S. military personnel in Buenos Aires, during the ten-day crisis that began on March 18, egged on their Argentine counterparts to overthrow Frondizi.[86] Until such time as documentary evidence, or convincing oral testimony, becomes available, and thus far none has appeared, such charges may best be regarded as highly imaginative speculation. What can be established, in contrast, is the yeoman effort made by Ambassador McClintock to try to save the Argentine President.

Acting apparently in advance of specific instructions from Washington, McClintock made personal calls on top military leaders to warn them of the serious difficulties Argentina would face with the United States if President Frondizi fell. According to the recollections of the then Navy Undersecretary, Admiral Jorge Palma, the Ambassador asked to see him and the Chief of Naval Operations, Admiral Agustín Penas. At a meeting held in a private apartment, McClintock explained that President Kennedy was very much concerned with what was happening to his only friend in Argentina, Dr. Frondizi. To this Palma replied, not very enthusiastically, "I am sorry President Kennedy has such bad friends." McClintock proceeded to warn the two Admirals that if Frondizi were thrown out, Argentina would not get any economic support from the United States. Palma responded, according to his recollections: "I can't tell you whether Frondizi is going to go or not; but if he has to go, we will face the situation independently of the United States." The Navy leaders were obviously not to be deterred by the Ambassador's efforts, efforts that constituted United States intervention in Argentine affairs not to overthrow its government, but to save it.[87]

---

[86] For such allegations see Alonso [124], pp. 13 and 31; Casas [224], p. 173; also García Lupo [146].

[87] Interview with Admiral (Ret.) Palma. The date and nature of the instruc-

Defense Minister Rodolfo Martínez's contribution to the sequence of efforts to protect Frondizi took the form of an ingenious plan designed to reconcile the deep distrust of the President on the part of powerful military and political circles with his obstinate refusal to resign his office. Martínez proposed a reduction in the powers of the chief executive and his subordination to a council of government made up of the Ministers of the Interior and Defense. The naming of the Defense Minister would require the approval of the armed forces, and his consent would be necessary, together with that of the Interior Minister, to give legal status to any presidential decree, message to Congress, or promulgation of law. To enact the legislation that would establish the new power arrangements, Martínez proposed the summoning of a special session of Congress within 48 hours of the plan's approval. The Congress would also be asked to sanction a proportional representation law so that no party in the future could monopolize power, to outlaw totalitarian groups, and to prohibit the use of Peronist symbols and emblems. Defense Minister Martínez offered his plan as a middle course between entrenched positions, one that would maintain, in his words, "constitutional continuity, the only guarantee against the country marching toward anarchy or dictatorship."[88]

President Frondizi was quick to accept the Martínez plan despite the lowering of his authority its provisions implied. Indeed, the night of March 27, while Martínez was discussing the plan with Navy leaders, the President asked congressional leaders and cabinet members to stand by in the Casa Rosada until after midnight, ready to take the necessary steps to summon Congress into special session if the military agreed. Neither that night nor the following morning, however, was Martínez able to get the unanimous consent of the three services. Although the Army and Air Force secretaries gave it tentative support, in the Navy the plan was submitted to the Council

---

tions sent by Washington to McClintock are contained in State Department documents that have yet to be opened to the public. At 10:30 or 11:00 P.M. on March 27, according to Dr. Oscar Puiggrós (interview, July 12, 1971), Ambassador McClintock interrupted a meeting President Frondizi was holding with cabinet members to inform him that he had received instructions from Washington to support the Argentine President.

[88] *La Nación*, March 29, 1962. The quoted words are from the text of Martínez's televised address of the previous night.

of Admirals, where the hardliners talked it down. Rodolfo Martínez was left with the feeling that he had come within a millimeter of success, but an earlier understanding to proceed only if all three armed services approved it doomed the plan to failure.[89]

With the political crisis entering its tenth day, the Commanders-in-Chief of the Armed Forces, General Raúl Poggi, Admiral Agustín Penas, and Air Force Brigadier Cayo Alsina decided finally on the morning of March 28 to impose their own solution. Hitherto, for all of the clamor that Dr. Frondizi resign, they had been reluctant to assume responsibility for actually ousting him. Now, however, with impatient subordinates threatening direct action—at dawn the Third Motorized Infantry Regiment at La Tablada on the outskirts of the capital proclaimed itself in rebellion—the Commanders-in-Chief overcame their reluctance and moved to take control of the situation. The Plan Conintes was put into effect subordinating the police and all communications media to military control; and, just before noon, Poggi, Penas, and Cayo Alsina made the definite decision to demand Frondizi's resignation later that afternoon and to proceed with his ouster if he still refused.[90]

Before making what they knew to be a momentous decision, the three Commanders-in-Chief discussed the nature of the government that might have to take over. Whether for want of driving personal ambition, or in order to minimize military rivalries, or out of a sensitivity to international opinion, Poggi, Penas, and Cayo Alsina made a pledge to one another not to seek the presidency for himself and agreed in writing "that in case events produce extreme situations which make unavoidable the change of government, the new government will be civilian."[91] It is clear, then, that even before they

[89] Interview with Rodolfo Martínez; Roberto Etchepareborda, "Un poco de historia," p. 11 (see above, note 48); interview with Air Force Brigadier (Ret.) Jorge Rosas Silveyra. It was at this meeting of the Council of Admirals that the voices of the legalist admirals who had retired in 1959 were missed. See above, chapter 8 at note 92.

[90] Interviews with General (Ret.) Poggi and Admiral (Ret.) Penas. For the movements of the Third Infantry Regiment see *La Nación*, March 29, 1962. Its commander, Lieut. Colonel Amicarelli, was operating under the orders of General Franklin Rawson, who simultaneously ordered the units of his own Third Cavalry Division in southern Buenos Aires province to take up an insurrectionary stance.

[91] The text of this agreement, which has never been published, to my knowledge, reads as follows: "En Buenos Aires a los veintiocho dias del mes de Marzo

made any move to terminate the Frondizi presidency, they hoped to avoid the establishment of a military junta and to maintain at least the forms of constitutional government.

The final act in the prolonged drama proceeded in a surprisingly gentlemanly fashion to its ultimate conclusion. Although the Commanders-in-Chief had announced at noon their intention to demand the President's resignation, it was not until 5:00 P.M. that they received an audience with him at the Casa Rosada. In the ensuing conversation, that was not devoid of cordiality, they urged him, for the last time, to resign, or at the least to take a leave of absence. Once again, Frondizi refused, insisting that if he had done anything wrong, the proper remedy was to bring impeachment proceedings. The fact that his followers controlled both houses of Congress made this a less than satisfactory response to his military visitors. In any event, a few minutes after they withdrew, the President made a hasty exit from the Casa Rosada and drove to his official residence at Olivos, a location much closer to the big military encampment at Campo de Mayo, where he might hope for assistance.[92]

For the next ten hours, while the Commanders-in-Chief tried unsuccessfully to persuade Dr. José Guido, the Senate President and legal successor to Dr. Frondizi, to agree to assume the presidency, the Olivos residence was the scene of feverish efforts to save Frondizi. Defense Minister Martínez sought to resuscitate his plan, while other advisors offered their own solutions. Shortly after midnight, Navy Secretary Clement and Air Force Secretary Rojas Silveyra, their earlier offers to resign having been rejected by the President, appeared at Olivos to discuss a possible way out.[93]

It was in this conversation that Frondizi himself came up with the suggestion for ending the impasse. As conveyed by Admiral Clement

---

del año mil novecientos sesenta y dos, en Reunión celebrada en la Secretaría de Estado de Marina a once horas los Comandantes en Jefe de las tres Fuerzas Armadas, dejan expresa constancia, de que en caso que los acontecimientos lleven a situaciones extremas que hagan ineludible el cambio de Gobierno, el nuevo Gobierno será civil. [firmado] Raúl Poggi Cayo Alsina A. R. Penas." I am indebted to Admiral Palma for supplying me with a photostatic copy of the signed original.

[92] Interviews with General (Ret.) Poggi and Admiral (Ret.) Penas; on the President's departure for Olivos, see *La Nación*, March 29, 1962.

[93] On the efforts to persuade Dr. Guido, interview with him in Boston, Massachusetts, March 1, 1975; also interviews with General Poggi and Admiral Penas.

to the three Commanders-in-Chief, who were then waiting in Dr. Guido's office, and separately to his colleagues in the Navy ministry, Frondizi's words were: "If you ask me as Dr. Frondizi, not as the President, what should be done, I advise the following: (1) I should be detained at a military base. (2) My preference is for Martín García Island. (3) The detention should take place at 8:00 A.M., with the change of guard delayed for fifteen minutes so that the troops guarding the president should not feel compelled to fight."[94] The suggestion was accepted. At Admiral Clement's direction, Admiral Penas radioed the commandant of the naval base on Martín García Island, where Hipólito Yrigoyen, in 1930, and Juan Perón, in 1945, had also been confined, to prepare adequate living quarters. The Chief of the President's Military Household, Navy Captain Eduardo Lockhart, meanwhile, personally drafted the instructions that were to be given the base commandant to ensure that Dr. Frondizi would receive the considerations that befitted an ex-President.[95]

Captain Lockhart went out to Olivos around 4:00 A.M. to inform the President that he would be flown in a Navy plane later that morning to the island. Dr. Frondizi's response, as Lockhart recalls it, was "the sooner, the better." At 7:45 A.M., in the company of Captain Lockhart, and with only the usual security personnel, the President calmly drove off to the intown airport for the flight to Martín García. The embattled administration of Arturo Frondizi was at an end.[96]

But to understand fully the role of the military in his final day, one more question needs to be raised. Why did the substantial military forces opposed to a coup, the legalists, not intervene to defend the President? The answer requires an examination of Dr. Frondizi's

[94] Interview with Dr. Guido. A slightly different wording of Frondizi's suggestion was given by Dr. Guido to Felix Luna in a 1970 or 1971 interview that was later published in *Todo es Historia*, No. 99 (Aug. 1975), pp. 12–13. On Admiral Clement's report of the Frondizi suggestion to his colleagues at the Navy Ministry, interviews with Admirals (Ret.) Penas and Palma.

[95] Interviews with Admiral (Ret.) Penas and Navy Captain (Ret.) Lockhart. I am indebted to Admiral Penas for permitting me to see the original "Instrucciones para custodia del Dr. Frondizi." According to these instructions, the President's wife, daughter, and a valet were permitted to accompany him; he was permitted to have visitors with the approval of the Navy Secretary; he was to have the best furnished house on the base; and he was to enjoy freedom of movement on the island. The Navy was to assume the costs of his upkeep.

[96] Interview with Navy Captain (Ret.) Lockhart. The daily papers on March 29 have photographs of Dr. Frondizi, showing him fully collected on this emotion-packed day.

attitudes and actions as well as those of the one person who conceivably could have protected him, Army Secretary Rosendo Fraga. As in the case of earlier crises, the President wanted to avoid bloodshed and was therefore reluctant to permit military confrontations that could end up in shooting. Thus, during the early morning hours of March 28, he refused to allow Lieut. Colonel José Herrera, commander of the presidential escort regiment, the San Martín Horse Grenadiers, to move against the rebellious Third Infantry Regiment at La Tablada. Herrera had already alerted his unit for action and had the support of two tank-equipped units at Campo de Mayo, whose commanders had also placed their troops at the ready, when the President ordered Herrera to desist.[97]

A few hours later, General Enrique Rauch, Commander of Cavalry, tried to organize a separate move to defend the President. That also fell apart. With the consent of Army Secretary Fraga, with whom he had conferred that morning in the Ministry, General Rauch went out to Campo de Mayo to see if he could organize forces to repress the rebellion at La Tablada. Having received assurances of support from officers of the First Armored Division, he first telephoned the Commander-in-Chief, General Poggi, to tell him that he no longer acceped his orders, and then tried to get in touch with Secretary Fraga, only to learn that he was no longer at the Ministry and had resigned. At this point, General Rauch, considering himself relieved from his post as Cavalry Commander, abandoned his effort.[98]

While Dr. Frondizi and General Fraga, in their separate ways, frustrated the eagerness to act of the legalist elements mentioned above, it is also clear that the President and the Secretary failed to work out a coordinated plan between themselves for the defense of the government. Responsibility for this failure is a matter of dispute. A writer sympathetic to Frondizi contends that on March 27, he and Fraga reached an understanding that before events got out of hand,

[97] Interview with General (Ret.) Tomás Sánchez de Bustamante, May 11, 1970. In 1962, as a colonel, he commanded the Tenth Armored Cavalry Regiment at Campo de Mayo; aligned with him was General Carlos Caro, who headed the Escuela de Caballería. Their target, the Third Infantry Regiment, was the one that later that same day moved unopposed into the capital, seizing bridgeheads, and at one point threatening to occupy the Casa Rosada.

[98] Rauch [200], pp. 98–100; interview with General (Ret.) Tomás Sánchez de Bustamante.

the President would place himself at Olivos while the Army Secretary would go to Campo de Mayo and from there attempt to defend the government. This same writer asserts that Frondizi even drafted a note directing Fraga to defend the constitutional order. The Army Secretary, however, instead of going out to Campo de Mayo when the President made his hasty exit to Olivos the afternoon of March 28, went instead to the Army Ministry. There forces responding to General Poggi placed him under arrest, and he played no further role in the unfolding events.[99]

This version differs in several respects from what General Fraga himself was to relate in a personal interview. He denies that he ever agreed to go to Campo de Mayo and makes no mention of a note. As he explains it, the issue was first raised on March 28 when he came to the Casa Rosada around 1:00 P.M. to offer his resignation. When the President asked him whether he would go to Campo de Mayo, he replied that he would be willing to do so provided that Dr. Frondizi would accompany him. With the head of the government there, Fraga felt, the chances of retaining the loyalty of the bulk of the Army were good, and there could be no question of his own intentions. Otherwise, the situation could develop into an armed confrontation between the Army Secretary and the Commander-in-Chief, a situation that had happened several times before, and one he did not want to repeat. The President, however, refused to accept Fraga's idea and insisted that he would only go to Olivos. As a result, nothing firm was decided at this meeting, and Fraga, having presented his resignation, retired to his home.[100]

General Fraga also cites another effort to persuade the President to move to a military installation. That afternoon at his home, he received a visit from Lieut. Colonel Herrera, the Chief of the Grenadier regiment, unhappy at being a simple spectator in the unfolding drama. He wanted to fulfill his assigned mission of defending the

---

[99] Alonso [124], pp. 31–32.

[100] Interview with General (Ret.) Fraga. Why he resigned is a matter that needs explanation. Admiral Clement had presented his own resignation as Navy Secretary days before. Fraga and Air Force Secretary Rojas Silveyra decided to present their resignations also, and did so around 1:00 P.M. on the 29th, so as to enable the President to deal directly with the three Commanders-in-Chief who were coming to see him at 5:00 P.M. Dr. Frondizi, however, issued a statement around 4:30 P.M. that he had rejected the resignations of all three secretaries (*La Nación*, March 29, 1962).

government and proposed that the President and General Fraga install themselves at the Grenadier barracks. Fraga telephoned the President to convey the offer and received the same reply as before: they should go, but he intended to go only to Olivos.[101]

Whether, as the pro-Frondizi version claims, General Fraga promised to defend the government from Campo d Mayo, or whether, as he insists, he made no commitment, it is clear that his efforts to protect Dr. Frondizi were less vigorous than those of the military men who sought his ouster. To be sure, General Fraga had supported each of the compromise proposals put forth to preserve the constitutional order, the coalition cabinet idea, the Aramburu mediation, the Martínez plan; but he was loath to take action that would put himself in open confrontation with the Commander-in-Chief. One suspects that he remembered all too well the fate of his predecessors who had been sacrificed by the President to appease a rebellious commander-in-chief; and though the present situation was certainly different, unless he had full assurance that the President was with him—and his physical presence at Campo de Mayo or at the Grenadier barracks would provide such assurance—he preferred to avoid any action that would make him responsible for splitting the Army.

Still, one may wonder why around 6:00 P.M. of March 28, General Fraga returned to the Army Ministry where troops taking orders from General Poggi placed him under detention.. Did Fraga deliberately seek to put himself in a position where he could remain a simple spectator and disclaim any responsibility for the course of events? Such a judgment implies that he knew what would happen to him when he returned to the Ministry. There is evidence, however, that suggests this was not the case and that he was simply following bad advice. A caller at his home earlier that afternoon, Colonel Alejandro Lanusse, a legalist officer, had urged him to "go to the Ministry and take charge, because if you give orders, they will be carried out." Fraga waited until after Frondizi formally rejected his offer to resign, and then went to the Ministry only to find himself under arrest.[102]

---

[101] Interview with General (Ret.) Fraga.

[102] Interviews with General (Ret.) Alejandro A. Lanusse, Aug. 23–24, 1973, and General (Ret.) Fraga. Fraga recalls that General Poggi asked him to join the movement to oust the President but that he refused, stating that an Army Secretary is part of the Executive Power and in no way can join a revolution against

The detention of the Army Secretary undermined the final efforts made by Frondizi to seek military support. Late that night, he telephoned a number of officers to see if they would help him resist. One of those called was General Juan C. Onganía, commander of the First Armored Division at Campo de Mayo. According to an eyewitness, Onganía listened to the President and then replied: "No, no, Mr. President, this command obeys the orders of its natural superior."[103] At that hour his superior was General Poggi. Also receiving a midnight call from a presidential aide at the Olivos residence was Colonel Lanusse. His response was another piece of dubious advice: to tell the President that "if he wishes to resist, he can count on Lanusse, but he must call Lanusse from Government House."[104] By this time, however, it was questionable whether the forces under the three Commanders-in-Chief would have allowed the President to leave Olivos.

Had Frondizi really been serious about resisting, he should not have waited until it was too late. One is permitted to wonder, then, whether these belated calls were meant to produce results, or were designed instead to give satisfaction to his political followers that their President had not gone down without a struggle. In any event, Frondizi now had no option but to accept his ouster and try to salvage what he could for his party, his program, and his own political future.[105]

---

his own government. Detained with Fraga in the Ministry were several other officers including General Rauch, with whom, he says, he had lost contact since the morning.

[103] Interview with General (Ret.) Tomás Sánchez de Bustamante.

[104] Interview with General (Ret.) Lanusse.

[105] Once convinced of his ouster, Dr. Frondizi asked Rodolfo Martínez, the Defense Minister, and Admiral Clement to persuade Senate President Dr. Guido to fill the vacancy. Later on March 29, when Dr. Guido finally agreed to do so and took the oath at the Supreme Court, Dr. Frondizi—now on Martín García Island—gave his express approval to a group of UCRI leaders who flew out to see him on a Navy plane supplied by Admiral Clement (interviews with Rodolfo Martínez and José M. Guido). I am also indebted to Roberto Etchepareborda for providing me with a copy of the notes made by Senator Lucio Racedo of the points made by Frondizi on Martín García to the UCRI leaders.

Chapter 10

Epilogue

The collapse of the Frondizi administration destroyed the hopes that once existed that the installation of a popularly elected civilian president would initiate a prolonged period of constitutional rule. The democratic impulses that had underlain the uprising against Perón in 1955 and pressured the successor military regime to surrender power at the earliest opportunity proved insufficient to lay the bases for long-term political stability. Events revealed that the gulf between Peronists and anti-Peronists, a gulf that affected civilians and military alike, was too wide to be bridged by the policies and promises of the Frondizi administration. Despite his undoubted political skills, Arturo Frondizi failed to break Perón's hold over the working classes, exacerbated the fears of the anti-Peronists, and in the process managed to demoralize elements that belonged to neither camp.

It was perhaps a historic mistake for Dr. Frondizi, with his plans for integrating disparate sectors of Argentine society under the banner of developmentalism, to have sought and won the 1958 presidency in the first place. Three years after Perón's overthrow was too soon to erase the sense of grievance felt by those who had suffered under his regime. An intervening term under an administration more in consonance with the philosophy of the Liberating Revolution might have produced, if only by reaction, a more genuine acceptance of the Frondizi approach to economic and social problems in military as well as labor circles.

As it was, for many of the military men who had worked for the overthrow of Perón, Frondizi's integration policies seemed to mean the return to active service of ousted Peronist and nationalist officers and a threat to their own professional careers; and they acted accordingly. In contrast, years later, after this generation of officers was to yield control of the armed forces to younger men, it proved relatively easy to reincorporate into retired status all those officers whose political stances had led to their ouster and to reward them retroactively with promotions and increased retirement pay. But by then, of course, a dramatic new situation had developed. The rise of terrorist groups that attacked military men and their installations was to have a cohesive effect on officers' attitudes and to make past political differences seem far less meaningful.

In the late 1950's and early 1960's, however, these differences were very real and contributed directly to Frondizi's overthrow. That event, however, insofar as military unity was concerned, made matters worse. During the remainder of 1962, the Army was torn apart by a series of confrontations culminating in warlike acts. The ultimate victors in this struggle were the onetime legalists, now labeled the Azules (Blues), chiefly cavalry and artillery officers who henceforth looked to General Juan C. Onganía as a national leader. Viewing themselves as both more professional in a military sense and more committed to constitutional government than their Colorado (Red) rivals, they proceeded to impose on the latter a victor's peace, forcing hundreds of Colorado officers into premature retirement. At the same time, they gave tentative support to a political plan that envisioned the formation of a national front that would include Peronists but not Perón and would serve as an electoral vehicle for General Onganía.

In the face of internal resistance within Azul ranks from officers who had second thoughts, the national-front plan collapsed, and with it Onganía's candidacy. Ousted Colorado officers, for their part, anxious to forestall the plan, made one final attempt to seize control, launching a revolution early in April 1963. Forced to rely primarily on naval support, they experienced a new defeat, with the added consequence that the Navy now underwent a major purge and lost what remained of the political leverage it had enjoyed since 1955.

The Azul victory guaranteed in the short term one further experiment with civilian government in the July 1963 elections that gave rise to the People's Radical (UCRP) administration of Dr. Arturo Illia. Ironically, the chief civilian support of the defeated Colorado officers had come from members of this party. Dr. Illia's relations with the Azul-dominated Army were therefore anything but cordial. But it was not just past history that threatened the support the Illia administration needed from the military establishment. The very emphasis on professionalism that characterized the Azul officers led them increasingly to question the effectiveness of this civilian government.

A professional Army, in their view, had little purpose unless it served a country whose national objectives were clearly defined in terms of current realities, domestic and international. Military preparedness plans required a redefinition of national aims that the Illia administration was slow to provide. Moreover, this government seemed to them incapable of promoting economic growth or of overcoming the political and social divisiveness that was the legacy of the past.

The subsequent ouster of Dr. Illia in June 1966 and the elevation of General (Ret.) Juan C. Onganía to the post of a dictatorial President with unlimited powers was an act of exaggerated self-confidence on the part of these same military men; it expressed their belief that what civilian administrations had been unable to do to reverse long-standing patterns of inflation, low economic growth, and labor unrest and to move the national agenda beyond the Peronist–anti-Peronist issue, a revolutionary military regime, without obligation to any political sector, would be able to accomplish.

But it was not military men alone who subscribed to this view. Civilian intellectuals who had been associated with the Azul group, certain politicians and labor leaders, and even ex-President Arturo Frondizi contributed to the abrupt termination of the Illia administration and extended a welcome to the Onganía government. In the case of Dr. Frondizi, it was not simply a matter of political revenge against the UCRP, many of whose leaders had helped to bring down his own administration; it was rather that he had come to the conclusion that elected governments could not produce the far-reaching economic, social, and political changes he felt were essential. This loss of faith in the democratic process was one of the long-term consequences of the events described in the present volume.

The resumption of a military-based government under General Onganía was to mark a new chapter in the recent history of Argentina. Insufficient time has passed to determine whether this government was fated from its inception to defraud the expectations of those who created it, or whether in the hands of a more politically talented leader it might have been more successful. What is clear is that under this government the country's problems became more serious. In the absence of elections in which to direct their political energies, in the face of unpopular economic policies, and in reaction to heavy-handed intervention in the universities, the younger generation of Argentines was becoming increasingly radicalized.

The full significance of this process was not to be revealed until the Córdoba uprising of workers and students in May 1969, the kidnapping and execution of ex-President General (Ret.) Pedro Aramburu a year later, and the increasing incidence thereafter of political terrorism. Not even the decision of the military leadership associated with Army Commander-in-Chief Alejandro Lanusse to oust Onganía and to commit the country to a restoration of constitutional government could reverse the process whereby numbers of young men and women joined guerilla movements and sought to impose their views at the point of a gun.

Even the Peronist triumph in the elections of March 1973 and the return of an aging Juan Perón to the presidency failed to eliminate the propensity for violence. The conflicts between leftist youth groups, which had welcomed Perón's restoration as a stepping-stone to some kind of socialist state, and his more conservative supporters, interested primarily in the fruits of power, produced a spate of kidnappings and killings. Political violence reached unprecedented heights after his death, when his widow, the Vice-President Isabel Martínez de Perón, took over the presidency. Argentina began its descent into its own particular hell as guerrilla operations grew bolder and shadowy counterguerrilla groups carried on their own secret war of repression.

In March 1976, the armed forces once again stepped in and took direct control over the Argentine government. This was a move that was universally anticipated and generally welcomed by most sectors of opinion, including Peronists. Even the extremist groups that had most to lose apparently harbored the hope that another period of military government would further radicalize the Argentine populace and pave the way for transition to a revolutionary socialist regime. As of 1978, however, the armed forces had proceeded efficiently and ruthlessly to destroy the power of the guerrilla groups, driving many of their sympathizers and also other Argentines who were simply frightened into exile. Only the future can disclose what the long-term impact on Argentine society will be of this internal war whose casualties extended to many innocent individuals and already exceed those of any other conflict Argentina has experienced in the present century. And only that future will reveal when, and under what conditions, the armed forces will surrender power to a more broadly based constitutional regime.

The fact that they have periodically taken control—six times between 1930 and 1976—is more an indication of the failures of the civil sector to stand united in defense of constitutional government than it is of military lust for power. In every one of these six instances, a part, and sometimes a very substantial part, of public opinion has encouraged the armed forces to act. Leaders of practically every political party, trade union, and business organization have given their blessing on at least one occasion to the forcible ouster of an incumbent president. The notion that Argentine political parties or other important civilian groups have consistently opposed military takeovers bears little relation to reality.

It is true, however, that once in power, military regimes have come under public pressure to limit their tenure. The very civilians who have urged the military to step in usually have been interested in an act of political surgery, not a prolonged cure; and soon after the ouster of the incumbents, those civilians have stressed the return of power to their hands. This may explain why, prior to 1966, military governments never lasted more than three years, and why elected officials, despite the six military interventions between 1930 and 1976, governed the country for all but nineteen of those 46 years. Two recent variations in the pattern of alternating civilian and military regimes must be noted, however. The first is that the life span of elected governments has consistently declined; Perón served over nine years as constitutional president before he was ousted in 1955; Frondizi had only four, and Illia, less than three years in office before their respective removals in 1962 and 1966; and, most recently, the Peronist restoration of 1973 lasted only two years and ten months.

The second departure from previous patterns is the greater longevity of military governments. The regime established in 1966 lasted under different leaders for almost seven years, and there is reason to believe that the armed forces government that took control in 1976 may remain in power at least as long. What this suggests is a lowered confidence within Argentina among civilian as well as military elements in the capacity of elected administrations to solve the nation's problems. The disillusionment with the democratic process that was the legacy of events before 1962 recurred after each subsequent experience with elected government. This is not to deny that within both the military and the civilian population there is a strong desire to see a return to constitutional government, but that desire is accompanied, at least on the military side, by a determination to develop a set of institutional arrangements that will break with the past half-century's pattern of alternating civilian and military governments and assure long-term political stability, economic growth, and social harmony. This is a goal that Argentine civilians of various viewpoints share. It remains to be seen whether they will be able to agree with one another and with the military leadership on the steps to be taken to assure its achievement.

Bibliography

Bibliography

PRIMARY SOURCES

Unpublished Materials

The historian of contemporary Argentina cannot expect to find relevant materials in that country's public archives, partly because officials tend to take their papers with them on leaving public office, partly because the documents that find their way into such archives are usually withheld from scholars until several generations have passed. The task for the researcher, then, becomes one of seeking out papers that may lie in private hands. Gaining access to such materials is often a matter of luck, and the historian can never be certain that he has seen all, or even a substantial part, of the relevant papers.

For this study, I was fortunate enough to be given access to a variety of privately held materials. These included copies of *actas* (formal agreements), internal military memoranda, letters, position papers, and accounts of events prepared by participants or close observers. Among the various unpublished papers to which I had access, the most valuable were the following three: Admiral (Ret.) Jorge Perren's memoirs, a typed manuscript of almost 400 pages that covers the years 1943–66 and is especially useful for the Navy's role in the years 1955–62; Navy Captain (Ret.) Eduardo Lockhart's minutes of national cabinet meetings (Reuniones del Gabinete) that he took from February 1 to September 20, 1962; and the diary of the late Admiral (Ret.) Teodoro Hartung, a 493-page contemporaneous account of what he saw, heard, and did as a member of the Junta Militar from November 1955 through April 1958.

United States archives also furnished important materials. The General Records of the Department of State (Record Group 59) were examined at the National Archives, Washington, D.C., for the years 1945–49. The most useful of these records were the following: papers relating to Argentine internal affairs (U.S. State Department Decimal File 835), especially the political, military, economic, and petroleum sections; United States–Argentine relations (Decimal File 711.35); the Argentine Blue Book Files; and the Office of American Republic Affairs Memoranda on Argentina, a collection that ends in 1947. In addition to the above series, I was able to see the papers in the Argentine internal political affairs file (735.00) for the years 1950–52 by using the procedures of the Freedom of Information Act. The long delays encountered in getting access to these papers, however, led me to give up further efforts to explore post-1950 Department of State records and to rely on other sources. A few useful papers were found in the John F. Kennedy Library and Archive in Waltham, Massachusetts.

While the manuscripts mentioned above were of great value, this study has also relied heavily on the oral history approach. Data that could not otherwise have been obtained were secured through a series of interviews with Argentine political and military personalities. These interviews, many of them on tape, were conducted over a period of fifteen years in Argentina and this country. Wherever possible I have tried to check the information obtained in this manner with other sources, printed, manuscript, or oral, including the Oral History Collection at Columbia University. In some cases follow-up interviews and exchanges of correspondence were used to resolve contradictions or conflicts. I am deeply grateful to the 80 individuals listed below, some of them no longer alive, and to others who asked not to be named, for generously consenting to answer my questions. One final comment. The perspicacious reader will note the absence from the list of a central figure in this study. I can only state that it was not for want of effort on my part that I was unable to talk to Juan D. Perón.

Contributing through their interviews to this volume were:

Alsogaray, Ing. Alvaro C.
Alsogaray, General (Ret.) Julio
Apicella, Brig. Mayor (Ret.)
    Horacio
Aramburu, General (Ret.) Pedro E.
Arredondo, General (Ret.) Roberto
    J. M.
Avalos, General (Ret.) Ignacio
Bassi, Admiral (Ret.) Juan C.
Becerra, Dr. Olegario
Bléjer, Dr. David
Bramuglia, Dr. Juan A.
Cáceres Monié, Dr. José R.
Caro, General (Ret.) Carlos
Castiñeiras, General (Ret.) Pedro
Castro Sánchez, General (Ret.)
    Eduardo
Correa, Colonel (Ret.) Daniel A.
Embrioni, General (Ret.) José
Emery, Ing. Carlos
Estévez, Admiral (Ret.) Adolfo B.

Etchepareborda, Dr. Roberto
Fernández Funes, Colonel (Ret.)
    Jorge M.
Forcher, General (Ret.) Emilio
Fraga, General (Ret.) Rosendo
Frigerio, Sr. Rogelio
Frondizi, Dr. Arturo
Gallo, General (Ret.) Bartolomé
Garasino, Lieut. Colonel (Ret.)
    Alberto
Garrido, Dr. Jorge E.
Ghioldi, Prof. Américo
Gómez Morales, Dr. Alfredo
Goyret, General (Ret.) José T.
Grondona, Dr. Mariano
Guglialmelli, General (Ret.)
    Juan E.
Guido, Dr. José M.
Hernándaz, Sr. A. Aurelio
Illia, Dr. Arturo
Iñíguez, General (Ret.) Miguel A.

388   *Bibliography*

Ivaníssevich, Dr. Oscar
Labayru, General (Ret.)
  Bernardino
Lagos, General (Ret.) Julio A.
Lanusse, General (Ret.)
  Alejandro A.
Laprida, General (Ret.) Manuel A.
Lockhart, Navy Captain (Ret.)
  Eduardo
López Aufranc, General (Ret.)
  Alcides
Martínez, Dr. Rodolfo (h.)
Menéndez, General (Ret.)
  Benjamín
Molinari, Navy Captain (Ret.) Aldo
Morello, General (Ret.) José H.
Muñíz, Dr. Carlos M.
Ordóñez, Dr. Manuel
Palma, Admiral (Ret.) Jorge
Penas, Admiral (Ret.) Agustín R.
Peralta, General (Ret.) Carlos
Pérez Amuchástegui, Colonel
  (Ret.) Agustín
Pérez Leirós, Sr. Francisco
Perren, Admiral (Ret.) Jorge
Pistarini, General (Ret.) Pascual
Poggi, General (Ret.) Raúl
Pomar, General (Ret.) Manuel H.
Puiggrós, Dr. Oscar
Rattenbach, General (Ret.)
  Benjamín

Real, Dr. Pedro
Rial, Admiral (Ret.) Arturo
Rivera, General Auditor (Ret.)
  Román
Rivolta, Navy Captain (Ret.)
  Antonio
Rojas, Admiral (Ret.) Isaac F.
Rojas Silveyra, Brigadier (Ret.)
  Jorge
Sánchez de Bustamante, General
  (Ret.) Tomás A.
Sánchez Sañudo, Admiral (Ret.)
  Carlos A.
Shaw, Dr. José D.
Solanas Pacheco, General (Ret.)
  Héctor
Solari, General (Ret.) Angel
Toranzo Calderón, Admiral (Ret.)
  Samuel
Toranzo Montero, General (Ret.)
  Carlos S.
Toranzo Montero, General (Ret.)
  Federico
Uranga, General (Ret.) Juan J.
Uriondo, General (Ret.) Oscar A.
Vago, General (Ret.) Ambrosio A.
Varela, Colonel (Ret.) Eliseo
Videla Balaguer, General (Ret.)
  Dalmiro F.
Zavala Ortiz, Dr. Miguel A.

Printed Documents

Laws and Decrees

[1] Anales de legislación argentina, 1852–1973. 33 vols. bound in 70.
Buenos Aires, 1942–73.

Legislative Debates

[2] Congreso Nacional. Diario de sesiones de la cámara de diputados.
Años 1946–55, 1958–66. 117 vols.
[3] Congreso Nacional. Diario de sesiones de la cámara de senadores.
Años 1946–55, 1958–66. 55 vols.
[4] Convención Nacional Constituyente. Diario de sesiones año 1957.
2 vols. Buenos Aires, 1958.

[5] Junta Consultiva Nacional. Bases para la confección de una nueva ley electoral. Buenos Aires, 1956.

Reports of Executive and Legislative Bodies

[6] Comando en Jefe de la Armada. Secretaría General Naval. Departamento de Estudios Históricos Navales. Las primeras cien promociones egresadas de la escuela naval militar 1879–1971. Buenos Aires, 1972.

[7] Comisión de Estudios Constitucionales. Materiales para la reforma constitucional. 7 vols. Buenos Aires, 1957.

[8] Comisión Especial Investigadora Sobre Petróleo. Dictámenes de mayoría y minoría. Cámara de Diputados de la Nación. Sesiones de Prórroga 1964. Orden del Dia N⁰ 394.

[9] Comisión Investigadora de los Servicios Públicos de Electricidad de la Ciudad de Buenos Aires. Informe. Superiores decretos 4,910 y 6,961 del 6 y 28 del agosto de 1943 respectivamente. Buenos Aires, 1959.

[10] Comisión Nacional de Investigaciones. Documentación, autores y cómplices de las irregularidades cometidas durante la segunda tiranía. 5 vols. Buenos Aires, 1958.

[11] Libro Negro de la segunda tiranía. Buenos Aires, 1958.

[12] Ministerio del Interior. Subsecretaría de Informaciones. Las fuerzas armadas restituyen el imperio de la soberanía popular. 2 vols. Buenos Aires, 1946.

[13] Ministerio de Guerra (also known as Ministerio de Ejército). *Boletín Militar Público*, 1946–63.

[14] ———. *Boletín Militar Reservado*, 1945–63.

[15] ———. Dirección General de Difusión. Manual de doctrina y organización nacional. Buenos Aires, 1953.

[16] ———. Escalafón del ejército argentino . . . hasta 1 de julio de 1946. Buenos Aires, 1946.

[17] ———. Escalafón del ejército argentino . . . hasta 31 de diciembre de 1952. Buenos Aires, 1952.

[18] ———. Escalafón del ejército argentino . . . hasta 31 de diciembre de 1954. Buenos Aires, 1955.

[19] ———. Memoria presentada al honorable congreso de la nación correspondiente al año 1940–1941. Buenos Aires, 1941.

[20] ———. Memoria . . . 4 de junio 1945–4 de junio 1946. Buenos Aires, 1946.

[21] ———. Memoria . . . 4 de junio 1946–4 de junio 1947. Buenos Aires, 1947.

[22] ———. Memoria . . . 4 de junio 1947–4 de junio 1948. Buenos Aires, 1948.

[23] Ministerio de Hacienda. Dirección Nacional de Estadística y Cen-

sos. Informe demográfico de la república argentina, 1944–54. Buenos Aires, 1956.

[24] Ministerio de Marina. Memoria correspondiente al ejercicio 1945. N.p., n.d.

[25] ———. Memoria . . . al ejercicio 1946. N.p., n.d.

[26] ———. Memoria . . . al ejercicio 1947. N.p., n.d.

[27] ———. Memoria . . . al ejercicio 1948. N.p., n.d.

[28] Ministerio de Relaciones Exteriores y Culto. La república argentina ante el "Libro Azul." Buenos Aires, 1946.

[29] Presidencia de la Nacion. Secretaría de Prensa y Difusión. Doctrina nacional. Buenos Aires, 1954.

[30] ———. Gobierno Provisional de la Revolución Libertadora. Memoria 1955–1958. Buenos Aires, 1958.

[31] ———. Subsecretaría de Informaciones. Doctrina Peronista. Perón expone su doctrina. N.p., n.d.

[32] ———. Subsecretaría de Informaciones. 2^0 Plan quinquenal. N.p., n.d.

[33] Ratificación del informe producido por la Comisión Investigadora N^0 58 de la Policía Federal, sobre la muerte de JUAN DUARTE. Buenos Aires, 1956.

Other Printed Documents

[34] Council on Foreign Relations. Documents on American Foreign Relations. New York, 1962.

[35] United Nations. Departamento de Asuntos Económicos y Sociales. Análisis y proyecciones del desarrollo económico. Part Five, El desarrollo económico de la argentina. 3 vols. Mexico, 1959.

[36] U.S. Department of State. Bulletin. Washington, D.C., 1949–55, 1962.

[37] ———. Consultation Among the American Republics with Respect to the Argentine Situation. Washington, D.C., 1946.

[38] ———. Foreign Relations of the United States: Diplomatic Papers, 1945. Volume IX, The American Republics. Washington, D.C., 1969.

[39] ———. Foreign Relations of the United States: Diplomatic Papers 1946. Volume XI, The American Republics. Washington, D.C., 1969.

[40] ———. Foreign Relations of the United States 1947. Volume VIII, The American Republics. Washington, D.C., 1972.

[41] ———. Foreign Relations of the United States 1948. Volume IX, The Western Hemisphere. Washington, D.C., 1972.

[42] ———. Foreign Relations of the United States 1949. Volume II, The United Nations; The Western Hemisphere. Washington, D.C., 1975.

[43] ———. Foreign Relations of the United States 1950. Volume I, Na-

tional Security Affairs; Foreign Economic Policy. Washington, D.C., 1977.

Memoirs, Dialogues, Letters, and Apologias

[44] Alende, Oscar. Entretelones de la trampa. Buenos Aires, 1964.
[45] Amadeo, Mario. Ayer, hoy, mañana. 3d ed. Buenos Aires, 1956.
[46] Antonio, Jorge. Y ahora qué? Buenos Aires, 1966.
[47] Arce, José. Cartas y escritos inéditos. Buenos Aires, 1958.
[48] Braden, Spruille. Diplomats and Demagogues: The Memoirs of Spruille Braden. New Rochelle, 1971.
[49] Bruce, James. Those Perplexing Argentines. New York, 1953.
[50] Bustos Fierro, Raúl. Desde Perón hasta Onganía. Buenos Aires, 1961.
[51] Carril, Bonifacio del. Crónica interna de la revolución libertadora. Buenos Aires, 1959.
[52] Carulla, Juan E. El medio siglo se prolonga. Buenos Aires, 1965.
[53] Corbière, Emilio J. Conversaciones con Oscar Alende. Buenos Aires, 1978.
[54] Correspondencia Perón–Frigerio 1958–1973. Análisis crítico de Ramón Prieto. Buenos Aires, 1975.
[55] Díaz, Fanor. Conversaciones con Rogelio Frigerio. Sobre la crisis política argentina. Buenos Aires, 1977.
[56] Domínguez, Nelson. Conversaciones con Juan José Taccone sobre sindicalismo y política. Buenos Aires, 1977.
[57] Galíndez, Bartolomé. Apuntes de tres revoluciones (1930–1943–1955). Buenos Aires, 1956.
[58] García, Eduardo A. Yo fui testigo. Antes, durante y después de la segunda tiranía (Memorias). Buenos Aires, 1971.
[59] Gómez, Alejandro. Política de entrega. Buenos Aires, 1963.
[60] Guardo, Ricardo C. Horas difíciles. Buenos Aires, 1963.
[61] Ibarguren (h.), Carlos. Respuestas a un cuestionario acerca del nacionalismo, 1930–1945. Buenos Aires, 1971.
[62] Irazusta, Julio. Balance de siglo y medio. Buenos Aires, 1972.
[63] Lanusse, Alejandro A. Mi testimonio. Buenos Aires, 1977.
[64] Luca de Tena, Torcuato, et al., comps. Yo Juan Domingo Perón. Relato autobiográfico. Barcelona, 1976.
[65] Lucero, Franklin. El precio de la lealtad. Buenos Aires, 1959.
[66] Luna, Félix. Diálogos con Frondizi. Buenos Aires, 1963.
[67] Martínez, Rodolfo. Grandezas y miserias de Perón. Mexico, 1957.
[68] Olivieri, Aníbal O. Dos veces rebelde: Memoria . . . julio 1945–abril 1957. Buenos Aires, 1958.
[69] Pastor, Reynaldo. Frente al totalitarismo peronista. Buenos Aires, 1959.
[70] Pavón Pereyra, Enrique. Coloquios con Perón. Buenos Aires, 1965.
[71] Perina, Emilio. Detrás de la crisis. Buenos Aires, 1960.

[72] Perón-Cooke correspondencia. 2 vols. Buenos Aires, 1973.
[73] Perón, Juan. Del poder al exilio. Cómo y quiénes me derrocaron. Buenos Aires, 1973.
[74] ———. La fuerza es el derecho de las bestias. Montevideo, 1959.
[75] ———. Tres revoluciones militares. Buenos Aires, 1963.
[76] Plater, Guillermo D. Una gran lección. La Plata, 1956.
[77] Prieto, Ramón. El pacto. 8 años de política argentina. Buenos Aires, 1963.
[78] Real, Juan José. Treinta años de historia argentina. 2d ed. Buenos Aires, 1976.
[79] Toryho, Jacinto. Aramburu; confidencias, actitudes, propósitos. Buenos Aires, 1973.
[80] Viñas, Alberto. Celda 43. Treinta y dos meses de cautiverio (1951–1953). Buenos Aires, 1956.

Speeches, Messages, and Leaflets

[81] Centro de Documentación Justicialista. Diálogo entre Perón y las fuerzas armadas. Buenos Aires, 1973.
[82] Descartes (pseud. for Juan D. Perón). Política y estrategia (no ataco, crítico). Buenos Aires, 1953.
[83] Farrell, Edelmiro J. Discursos pronunciados por el excelentísimo señor presidente de la nación argentina durante su período presidencial, 1944–1946. Buenos Aires, 1946.
[84] Frondizi, Arturo. Petróleo y nación. Prólogo y notas por Arturo Sábato. Buenos Aires, 1963.
[85] ———. La política exterior argentina. Ordenación y prólogo de Dardo Cuneo. Buenos Aires, 1962.
[86] Lafiandra, Felix (h.). Los panfletos. Su aporte a la revolución libertadora. Buenos Aires, n.d.
[87] Manual práctico del 2⁰ plan quinquenal. Buenos Aires, 1953.
[88] Partido Peronista Consejo Superior. Manual peronista. Buenos Aires, 1954.
[89] ———. El movimiento peronista. Orígen, ideal, síntesis de la doctrina, realizaciones y soluciones universales. Buenos Aires, 1954.
[90] Perón, Eva. "Representamos el ejemplo de la cooperación social," *Hechos e Ideas*, Vol. XX, No. 79 (Oct. 1950) pp. 25–28.
[91] Perón, Juan D. Discursos del excmo. señor presidente de la nación . . . dirigidos a las fuerzas armadas 1946–1951. Buenos Aires, n.d.
[92] ———. "En el quinto aniversario del 17 de octubre," *Hechos e Ideas*, Vol. XX, No. 79 (Oct. 1950), pp. 19–24.
[93] ———. "Hablando a los intelectuales," *Hechos e Ideas*, Vol. XIX, No. 77 (Aug. 1950), pp. 406–18.
[94] ———. "Informando al pueblo sobre los alcances del 2⁰ plan quin-

quenal," *Hechos e Ideas*, Vol. XXIV, Nos. 106–9 (Jan.–Apr. 1953), pp. 397–430.

[95] ———. "Lineamientos del plan económico para 1952," *Hechos e Ideas*, Vol. XII, No. 95 (Feb. 1952), pp. 483–96.

[96] ———. "Normas de gobierno y directivas políticas," *Hechos e Ideas*, Vol. XXIV, No. 103 (Oct. 1952), pp. 177–88.

[97] ———. "La organización del gobierno, del estado y de la nación," *Hechos e Ideas*, Vol. XIX, Nos. 74–75 (May–June 1950), pp. 193–206.

[98] ———. Perón expone su doctrina. Buenos Aires, 1948.

[99] ———. Perón habla a las fuerzas armadas, 1946–1954. Buenos Aires, 1954.

[100] ———. El pueblo ya sabe de que se trata. Discursos 1944–1946. Buenos Aires, n.d.

[101] ———. "Principios doctrinarios que orientaran la política social del gobierno y declaración de los derechos del trabajador," *Hechos e Ideas*, Vol. VI, No. 42 (Aug. 1947), pp. 51–61.

[102] ———. Síntesis del mensaje presidencial pronunciado . . . el dia 1⁰ de mayo de 1954 ante el honorable congreso nacional, al inaugurar el 88⁰ período de sesiones. Buenos Aires, 1954.

[103] La revolución de los tres tanques. Buenos Aires, 1951.

Secondary Sources

General Works

[104] "Los años críticos 1955–1970. De Perón a Onganía," *Panorama Semanal*, Vols. VI–VII, Nos. 79–134 (1968–69).

[105] Cantón, Dario. Materiales para el estudio de la sociología politica en la argentina. 2 vols. Buenos Aires, 1968.

[106] Ciria, Alberto, et al. New Perspectives on Modern Argentina. Latin American Studies Program, Indiana University. Bloomington, 1972.

[107] Ferns, H. S. Argentina. London, 1969.

[108] Floria, Carlos A., and Cesar A. García Belsunce. Historia de los argentinos. 2 vols. Buenos Aires, 1971.

[109] Germani, Gino. Estructura social de la argentina. Buenos Aires, 1955.

[110] "La historia del peronismo," *Primera Plana*, Vols. III–VII, Nos. 136–55, 175–392 (1965–69).

[111] Imaz, José Luis de. Los que mandan (Those Who Rule). Translated and with an introduction by Carlos A. Astiz. Albany, 1970.

[112] Luna, Félix. Argentina de Perón a Lanusse, 1943–1973. Barcelona, 1972.

[113] Magnet, Alejandro. Nuestros vecinos justicialistas. 10th ed. Santiago, 1955.

[114] Rock, David, ed. Argentina in the Twentieth Century. Pittsburgh, 1975.

[115] Santos Martínez, Pedro. La nueva argentina, 1946–1955. 2 vols. Buenos Aires, 1976.

[116] Whitaker, Arthur. Argentina. Englewood Cliffs, N.J., 1964.

[117] ———. The United States and Argentina. Cambridge, Mass., 1954.

[118] ———. The United States and the Southern Cone. Cambridge, Mass., 1976.

[119] Zuleta Alvarez, Enrique. El nacionalismo argentino. 2 vols. Buenos Aires, 1975.

Publications Relating to the Military

[120] Abrahamsson, Bengt. Military Professionalization and Political Power. Beverly Hills, 1972.

[121] "A diez años de un intento para derrocar la dictadura," La Prensa, Sept. 28–30, Oct. 10, 1961.

[122] Albariño, General Ramón A. "La contribución de las Fuerzas Armadas al desarrollo industrial en el 2^0 Plan Quinquenal," Hechos e Ideas, Vol. XXIV, Nos. 106–9 (Jan.–April 1953), 687–94.

[123] ———. Verdad y justicia (documentos que revelan los móviles políticos de una imputación calumniosa). Buenos Aires, 1947.

[124] Alonso, Enrique. "Hace diez anos: La caída de Frondizi," Todo es Historia, No. 59 (March 1972), pp. 8–35.

[125] Anaya, General Laureano. "El ejército: Factor ponderable en el desenvolvimiento económico social y político de la nación," Hechos e Ideas, Vol. XVI, Nos. 62–63 (May–June 1949), pp. 188–234.

[126] ———. La nacionalización de los transportes y servicios públicos. Su significado desde el punto de vista de la defensa nacional. Conferencia. Buenos Aires, 1951.

[127] Arditi, Leon. "Frondizi y los militares," El Príncipe, Vol. 3, No. 9 (March 1962), pp. 8–10.

[128] "Así cayó Frondizi," Atlántida (April 1966), pp. 74–83.

[129] Astiz, Carlos. "The Argentine Armed Forces: Their Role and Political Involvement," Western Political Quarterly, Vol. 22, No. 4 (1969), pp. 862–78.

[130] Becke, Lieut. General Carlos von der. Destrucción de una infamia: Falsos 'Documentos oficiales.' Buenos Aires, 1956.

[131] Beltrán, Virgilio R. "El ejército y los cambios estructurales de la argentina en el siglo XX," Revista de Estudios Políticos (Madrid), Nos. 171–72 (1970), pp. 173–99.

[132] Bortnik, Ruben. El ejército argentino y el arte de lo posible. Buenos Aires, 1967.

[133] Botana, Natalio, Rafael Braun, and Carlos A. Floria. El régimen militar, 1966–1973. Buenos Aires, 1973.

[134] Burzio, Humberto F. Armada nacional. Reseña histórica de su origen y desarrollo orgánico. Número extraordinario del Boletín del Centro Naval. Buenos Aires, 1961.

[135] Cantón, Darío. La política de los militares, 1900–1971. Buenos Aires, 1971.

[136] Cardoso Cuneo, Captain Raúl E. "El concepto marxista ante las fuerzas armadas," *Revista Militar*, No. 651, (Jan.–March 1959), pp. 58–65.

[137] Carreras, General Marino B. "La mentira," *Revista Militar*, No. 659 (Jan.–March 1961), pp. 41–42.

[138] Castiñeiras, Pedro F. Esto lo hicieron los argentinos. Buenos Aires, 1972.

[139] Ceresole, Norberto. Ejército y política nacionalista. Buenos Aires, 1968.

[140] Cerro Fernández, Patricio. En defensa de la libertad. Crónica de un movimiento terrorista. Buenos Aires, n.d.

[141] Chinetti, Jorge A. "Historia política del ejército argentino," *Leoplan*, Nos. 740, 741, 742 (1965), pp. 42–50, 54–60, 60–64.

[142] Fayt, Carlos. El político armado. Dinámica del proceso político argentino, 1960–1971. Buenos Aires, 1971.

[143] Ferla, Salvador. Mártires y verdugos. 3d ed. Buenos Aires, 1972.

[144] Fernández Alvarino, Próspero. Argentina, el crimen del siglo: Teniente general Pedro Eugenio Aramburu. Buenos Aires, 1973.

[145] Florit, Carlos A. Las fuerzas armadas y la guerra psicológica. Buenos Aires, 1963.

[146] García Lupo, Rogelio. La rebelión de los generales. Buenos Aires, 1962.

[147] Garimaldi, General Eduardo A. "La defensa nacional y el progreso industrial," *Hechos e Ideas*, Vol. XIX, No. 77 (Aug. 1950), pp. 331–52.

[148] ———. "La industria siderúrgica argentina," *Hechos e Ideas*, Vol. XXII, Nos. 90 and 91 (Sept. and Oct. 1951), pp. 19–38, 153–70.

[149] Gazzoli, Colonel Luis. ¿Cuándo los militares tenemos razón? Buenos Aires, 1973.

[150] Ghioldi, Américo. Ejército y política. El golpe del 28 de junio de 1966. Buenos Aires, 1967.

[151] Godio, Julio. La caída de Perón: De junio a setiembre de 1955. Buenos Aires, 1973.

[152] Goldwert, Marvin. Democracy, militarism and nationalism in Argentina, 1930–1966: An interpretation. Austin, 1972.

[153] Guevara, Colonel Juan F. Argentina y su sombra. Buenos Aires, 1970.

[154] Guglialmelli, General Juan Enrique. 120 días en el gobierno. Buenos Aires, 1971.

[155] Güiraldes, Commodore Juan José. "Fuerzas armadas y desarrollo," Temas Militares, Vol. I, No. 1. (Sept.–Oct. 1966), pp. 51–57.

[156] Grand d'Esonin, Lieut. Colonel Henri. "Guerra subversiva," Revista de la Escuela Superior de Guerra, Vol. XXXVIII, No. 338 (July–Sept. 1960), pp. 339–63.

[157] Heare, Gertrude. Trends in Latin American Military Expenditures, 1940–1970. Department of State Publication 8618. Washington, D.C., 1971.

[158] Lanús, Roque. Las fuerzas armadas en los regímenes democráticos. Conferencia pronunciada en San Nicolás de los Arroyos el 8 de julio de 1949. Buenos Aires, 1949.

[159] Leoni, Major Luis A. "Encuadre de la institución ejército en el estado moderno," Revista Militar, No. 657 (July–Sept. 1960), pp. 29–43.

[160] "Las logias militares: Otra vez la fantasía," Confirmado, Vol. I, No. 8 (June 25, 1965), pp. 12–13.

[161] Lonardi, Luis Ernesto. Dios es justo. Lonardi y la revolución. Buenos Aires, 1958.

[162] López, General Adolfo Cándido. Ideas políticas. Buenos Aires, 1969.

[163] López Aufranc, Lieut. Colonel Alcides. "Estados mayores mixtos," Revista de la Escuela Superior de Guerra, Vol. XXXVIII, No. 339 (Oct.–Dec. 1960), pp. 588–601.

[164] Lozada, Salvador M. Las fuerzas armadas en la política hispano-americana. Buenos Aires, 1967.

[165] McAlister, Lyle N., Anthony Maingot, and Robert A. Potash. The Military in Latin American Sociopolitical Evolution: Four Case Studies. Washington, D.C., 1970.

[166] McKinlay, R. D. "Professionalism, Politicization and Civil-Military Relations," in M. R. van Gils, ed., The Perceived Role of the Military. Rotterdam, 1971, pp. 243–65.

[167] Marini, Colonel Alberto. "El ejército en los últimos cincuenta años," Revista Militar, No. 656 (1960), pp. 357–62.

[168] Menéndez, Colonel Rómulo F. "Las fuerzas armadas y la defensa nacional," Revista Militar, No. 660 (April–June 1961), pp. 13–17.

[169] ———. "Papel político del ejército en la historia nacional, 1806–1820," Revista Militar, No. 659 (Jan.–March 1961), pp. 76–81.

[170] Millington, Thomas M. "President Arturo Illia and the Argentine Military," Journal of Inter-American Studies, Vol. VI, No. 3 (July 1964), pp. 405–24.

[171] Mom, Colonel Manrique M. "Guerra revolucionaria," *Revista de la Escuela Superior de Guerra*, Vol. XXXVII, No. 334 (July–Sept. 1959), pp. 489–515.

[172] Montemayor, Mariano. Presencia política de las fuerzas armadas. Buenos Aires, 1958.

[173] Nun, Jose. "The Middle-Class Military Coup." In Claudio Veliz, ed., The Politics of Conformity in Latin America. London, Oxford, New York, 1967, pp. 66–118.

[174] Nunn, Frederick. "The Latin American Military Establishment: Some Thoughts on the Origins of Its Socio-Political Role and an Illustrative Bibliographical Essay," *The Americas*, XXVII (1971), 135–51.

[175] Ochoa de Equileor and V. R. Beltrán. Las fuerzas armadas hablan. Buenos Aires, 1968.

[176] O'Donnell, Guillermo A. Modernización y golpes militares. (Teoría, comparaciones y el caso argentino.) Instituto Torcuato Di Tella Centro de Investigaciones en Administración Pública. Documento de Trabajo. 1972.

[177] Orona, Juan V. La dictadura de Perón. Buenos Aires, 1970.

[178] ———. La revolución del 16 de septiembre. Buenos Aires, 1971.

[179] Orsolini, Lieut. Colonel Mario. La crisis del ejército. Buenos Aires, 1964.

[180] ———. Ejército argentino y crecimiento nacional. Buenos Aires, 1965.

[181] Páez, Juan L. "Idea general de la doctrina nacional," *Revista de la Escuela Superior de Guerra*, Vol. XXXII, No. 313 (May–June 1954), pp. 63–82.

[182] Panaia, Marta, and Ricardo Lesser. "Las estrategias militares frente al proceso de industrialización (1943–1947)." In Miguel Murmis et al., Estudios sobre los orígines del peronismo. II, 81–164. Buenos Aires, 1973.

[183] Pandolfi, Rodolfo, and Federico Mittelbach. "Los golpes en la argentina (1930–1976)," *Carta Política*, No. 38 (Dec. 1976), pp. 30–36.

[184] Pérez Tort, Lieut. Colonel Miguel A. "El potencial económico-industrial argentino y la defensa nacional," *Revista de Informaciones*, Vol. XXVI, No. 279 (Sept.–Oct. 1948), pp. 610–36.

[185] Perez Tort, General Miguel A. "La siderúrgia en la Argentina," *Revista de la Escuela Superior de Guerra*, Vol. XXXVIII, No. 337 (April–June 1960), pp. 147–64.

[186] Politi, Lieut. Colonel A. S. Pasqualis. "El problema marxista y su incidencia en nuestra resolución de estrategia general," *Revista Militar*, No. 661 (July–Sept. 1961), pp. 45–79.

[187] Potash, Robert A. "Argentina's Quest for Stability," *Current History*, Vol. 42, No. 246 (Feb. 1962), pp. 71–76.

[188] ——. The Army & Politics in Argentina, 1928–1945. Yrigoyen to Perón. Stanford, 1969.

[189] ——. The Impact of Professionalism on the Twentieth Century Argentine Military. Program in Latin American Studies Occasional Papers Series No. 3. University of Massachusetts at Amherst, 1977.

[190] "Las proclamas militares," *Confirmado*, Vol. I, No. 12 (July 23, 1965), pp. 12–13.

[191] Queral, Colonel Horacio E. "Acción comunista en el campo educacional," *Revista Militar*, No. 663 (Jan.–March 1962), pp. 59–69.

[192] Ramos, Jorge Abelardo. Ejército y semi-colonia. Buenos Aires, 1968.

[193] Rattenbach, Lieut. General Benjamín. *Estudios y reflexiones*, Buenos Aires, 1955.

[194] ——. "Fenómenos post-revolucionarios," *Revista Militar*, No. 636 (March–April 1956), pp. 6–8.

[195] ——. "El profesionalismo militar en el ejército argentino," *Temas Militares*, Vol. I, No. 3 (March–April 1967), pp. 9–16.

[196] ——. El sector militar de la sociedad. Principios de sociología militar. Buenos Aires, 1965.

[197] ——. El sistema social-militar en la sociedad moderna. Buenos Aires, 1972.

[198] ——. Sobre el país y las fuerzas armadas. Buenos Aires, 1975.

[199] ——. "El Telón," *Revista Militar*, No. 633 (Sept.–Oct. 1955), pp. 6–11.

[200] Rauch, General Enrique. Un juicio al proceso político. Buenos Aires, 1971.

[201] "Reestructuración. El ejército de la legalidad," *Primera Plana*, Vol. III, No. 108 (Dec. 1, 1964), p. 8.

[202] Rivera Echenique, Silvia. Militarismo en la argentina. Golpe de estado de junio de 1966. Mexico, 1976.

[203] Romero, Luis A. Los golpes militares, 1812–1955. Buenos Aires, 1969.

[204] Roth, Roberto. El país que quedó atrás. Buenos Aires, 1967.

[205] Rouquié, Alain. "Adhesión militar y control político del ejército en el régimen peronista," *Aportes*, No. 19 (Jan. 1971), pp. 74–93.

[206] Salvadores, Lieut. Colonel Julio C. "Defensa nacional. Algunos conceptos sobre política general vinculados con la defensa nacional," *Revista de Informaciones*, Vol. XXXI, No. 310 (Nov.–Dec. 1953), pp. 643–55.

[207] Sánchez de Bustamante, Lieut. Colonel Tomás A. "La guerra revolucionaria," *Revista de la Escuela Superior de Guerra*, Vol. XXXVIII, No. 339 (Oct.–Dec. 1960), pp. 602–14.

[208] Sanguinetti, Colonel Julio. "La metalúrgia y la defensa nacional,"

Revista de Informaciones, Vol. XXVI, No. 278 (July–Aug. 1948), pp. 500–534.

[209] Sanguinetti, General Julio. "Nuestras fuentes de energía eléctrica y la política nacional de energía," *Revista de Informaciones*, Vol. XXXI, No. 303 (July–Aug. 1953), pp. 357–70.

[210] ———. "El problema de la movilización industrial," *Revista de Informaciónes*, Vol. XXX, No. 302 (July–Aug. 1952), pp. 299–348.

[211] ———. "El problema nacional de los combustibles y las previsiones del 2⁰ plan quinquenal," *Revista de Informaciones*, Vol. XXXI, No. 307 (May–June 1953), pp. 237–51.

[212] Saravia, José Manuel (h.). Hacia la salida. Buenos Aires, 1968.

[213] ———. "La nueva naturaleza de la guerra," *Revista de la Escuela Superior de Guerra*, Vol. XLIII, No. 361 (Sept.–Oct. 1965), pp. 63–73.

[214] Senen González. Santiago and Juan C. Torre. Ejército y sindicatos. Los 60 días de Lonardi. Buenos Aires, 1969.

[215] Silvert, Kalman H. The Conflict Society. Rev. ed. New York, 1966.

[216] Springer, Philip B. "Disunity and Disorder: Factional Politics in the Argentine Military." In Henry Bienen, ed., The Military Intervenes: Case Studies in Political Development. New York, 1968.

[217] Uriburu, General Eduardo J. El Plan Europa. Un intento de liberación nacional. Buenos Aires, 1970.

[218] Villegas, General Osiris G. Guerra revolucionaria comunista. Buenos Aires, 1963.

[219] ———. Políticas y estrategias para el desarrollo y la seguridad nacional. Buenos Aires, 1969.

[220] Walsh, Rodolfo J. Operación masacre. 3d ed. Buenos Aires, 1972.

[221] Zabala, Arturo J. La revolución del 16 de setiembre. Buenos Aires, 1955.

Biographical Studies

[222] Anzoategui, Yderla. Crisólogo Larralde. Paladín de la democracia. Buenos Aires, 1965.

[223] Barrera, Mario. Information and Ideology: A Case Study of Arturo Frondizi. Sage Professional Papers in Comparative Politics, IV, No. 01–044. Beverly Hills and London, 1973.

[224] Casas, Nelly. Frondizi: Una historia de política y soledad. Buenos Aires, 1973.

[225] Firpo, M. Eduardo. Perón y los peronistas. Buenos Aires, 1965.

[226] Newton, Jorge. Perón el visionario. Buenos Aires, 1955.

[227] Otelo Borroni, Roberto V. La vida de Eva Perón. Testimonios para su historia. Buenos Aires, 1970.

[228] Pandolfi, Rodolfo. Frondizi por el mismo. Buenos Aires, 1968.
[229] Sebreli, Juan José. Eva Perón. ¿Aventurera o militante? Buenos Aires, 1966.

International Relations

[230] Conil Paz, Alberto, and Gustavo Ferrari. Argentina's Foreign Policy, 1930–1962. Translated by John J. Kennedy. Notre Dame, 1966.
[231] Green, David. The Containment of Latin America. A History of the Myths and Realities of the Good Neighbor Policy. Chicago, 1971.
[232] Peterson, Harold F. Argentina and the United States, 1810–1960. New York, 1964.
[233] Rodríguez, Celso. "Después de Braden," *Todo es Historia*, No. 127 (Jan. 1978), pp. 28–41.
[234] Scalabrini Ortiz, Raúl. "Perspectivas para una esperanza argentina," *Hechos e Ideas*, Vol. XIX, No. 78 (Sept. 1950), pp. 447–60.
[235] Scenna, Miguel A. "Braden y Perón," *Todo es Historia*, No. 30 (Oct. 1969), pp. 8–30.
[236] ———. Como fueron las relaciones argentino-norteamericanas. Buenos Aires, 1970.
[237] ———. "Frondizi y las cartas cubanas," *Todo es Historia*, No. 48 (May 1971), pp. 8–31.

Economics, Labor, and Political Parties

[238] Baily, Samuel L. Labor, Nationalism and Politics in Argentina. New Brunswick, N.J., 1967.
[239] Belloni, Alberto. Del anarquismo al peronismo. Buenos Aires, 1960.
[240] Bowen, Nicholas. "The End of British Economic Hegemony in Argentina: Messersmith and the Eady-Miranda Agreement," *Inter-American Economic Affairs*, Vol. 28, No. 4, (Spring 1975), pp. 3–18.
[241] Cafiero, Antonio F. 5 años después. Buenos Aires, 1961.
[242] Cantón, Darío. Elecciones y partidos políticos en la argentina. Historia, interpretación y balance: 1910–1966. Buenos Aires, 1973.
[243] Cárdenas, Gonzalo, et al. El peronismo. Buenos Aires, 1969.
[244] Ceresole, Norberto, et al. Peronismo: De la reforma a la revolución. Buenos Aires, 1972.
[245] Ciria, Alberto. Perón y el justicialismo. Buenos Aires, 1971.
[246] Cuneo, Dardo. Comportamiento y crisis de la clase empresaria. Buenos Aires, 1967.
[247] Díaz-Alejandro, Carlos F. Essays on the Economic History of the Argentine Republic. New Haven, 1970.
[248] Doyon, Louise M. "Conflictos obreros durante el régimen peronista (1946–1955)," *Desarrollo Económico*, Vol. 17, No. 67 (Oct.–Dec. 1977), pp. 437–73.

[249] Drosdoff, Daniel. El gobierno de las vacas (1933–1956) tratado Roca-Runciman. Buenos Aires, 1972.

[250] Durruty, Celia. Clase obrera y peronismo. Córdoba, 1969.

[251] Eshag, Eprime, and Rosemary Thorp, "Las consecuencias económicas y sociales de las políticas económicas ortodoxas aplicadas en la república argentina durante los años de postguerra," *Desarrollo Económico*, Vol. 4, No. 16 (Jan.–March 1965), pp. 287–343.

[252] Fayt, Carlos S. La naturaleza del peronismo. Buenos Aires, 1967.

[253] Frigerio, Rogelio. Crecimiento económico y democracia. Buenos Aires, 1963.

[254] ———. Los cuatro años (1958–1962). Política económica para argentinos. Buenos Aires, 1962.

[255] ———. Petróleo. Versión taquigráfica completa de las declaraciones prestadas ante el Comisión Especial Investigadora. Buenos Aires, n.d.

[256] Frondizi, Arturo. Petróleo y política. Buenos Aires, 1954.

[257] Gazzera, Miguel, and Norberto Ceresole. Peronismo: Autocrítica y perspectivas. Buenos Aires, 1970.

[258] James, Daniel. "The Peronist Left, 1955–1975," *Journal of Latin American Studies*, Vol. 8, Part 2 (Nov. 1976), pp. 273–96.

[259] Kenworthy, Eldon. "The Function of the Little-Known Case in Theory Formation or What Peronism Wasn't," *Comparative Politics*, Vol. 6, No. 1 (Oct. 1973), pp. 17–45.

[260] Little, Walter. "Electoral Aspects of Peronism, 1946–1954," *Journal of Inter-American Studies*, Vol. 15, No. 3 (Aug. 1973), pp. 267–84.

[261] Llorente, Ignacio. "Alianzas políticas en el surgimiento del peronismo: El caso de la provincia de Buenos Aires," *Desarrollo Económico*, Vol. 17, No. 65 (Apr.–June 1977), pp. 61–88.

[262] Luna, Félix. El 45. Crónica de un año decisivo. Buenos Aires, 1969.

[263] Mallon, Richard D., and Juan V. Sourroille. Economic Policymaking in a Conflict Society: The Argentine Case. Cambridge, Mass., 1975.

[264] Mazo, Gabriel del. El radicalismo: El movimiento de intransigencia y renovación (1945–1957). Buenos Aires, 1957.

[265] ———. El radicalismo: Ensayo sobre su historia y doctrina. Tomo II. Buenos Aires, 1959.

[266] Murmis, Miguel, Juan C. Portantiero, Marta Panaia, and Ricardo Lesser. Estudios sobre los orígines del peronismo. 2 vols. Buenos Aires, 1971–73.

[267] O'Donnell, Guillermo A. "Un 'juego imposible': competición y coalición entre partidos políticos en Argentina, 1955–1966," *Revista Latinoamericana de Sociología*, VII (1970), 103–31.

[268] Senen González, Santiago. El sindicalismo después de Perón. Buenos Aires, 1971.

[269] Silberstein, Enrique. ¿Por qué Perón sigue siendo Perón? (La economía peronista). Buenos Aires, 1972.

[270] Silverman, Bertram. "Labor Ideology and Economic Development in the Peronist Epoch," *Studies in Comparative International Development*, Vol. IV, No. 11 (1968–69), pp. 243–58.

[271] Silvert, K. H. "Economics, Democracy and Honesty: An Assessment of the Frondizi Regime," American Universities Field Staff Report. East Coast Series VII, No. 1 (1960).

[272] Smith, Peter H. Argentina and the Failure of Democracy. Madison, Wis., 1974.

[273] ———. "Las elecciones argentinas de 1946 y las inferencias ecológicas," *Desarrollo Económico*, Vol. 14, No. 54 (July–Sept. 1974), 1974), pp. 385–98.

[274] ———. "The Social Base of Peronism," *Hispanic American Historical Review*, Vol. 52, No. 1 (Feb. 1972), pp. 55–73.

[275] ———. "Social Mobilization, Political Participation and the Rise of Juan Perón," *Political Science Quarterly*, Vol. 84, No. 1 (March 1969), pp. 30–49.

[276] Snow, Peter G. Argentine Political Parties and the 1966 Revolution. Report from the Laboratory for Political Research. No. 15. University of Iowa, Iowa City, 1968.

[277] ———. "Argentine Radicalism, 1957–1963," *Journal of Inter-American Studies*, Vol. V, No. 4 (Oct. 1963), pp. 507–31.

[278] Solberg, Carl. Oil and Nationalism in Argentina. Stanford, 1979.

[279] Stickell, A. Lawrence. "Peronist Politics in Labor." In Alberto Ciria et al., New Perspectives on Modern Argentina. Bloomington, Indiana, 1972.

[280] Sylvester, Hugo L. Historia viva de la legislación del trabajo. Buenos Aires, 1968.

[281] Wright, Winthrop R. British-Owned Railways in Argentina. Austin, 1974.

[282] Zuvekis, Clarence. "Economic Growth and Income Distribution in Post-War Argentina," *Inter-American Economic Affairs*, Vol. XX, No. 3 (Winter 1966), pp. 19–38.

Other Works Consulted

[283] Alexander, Robert. The Perón Era. New York, 1951.

[284] Bearn, Georges. La décade péroniste. Paris, 1975.

[285] Domingorena, Horacio O. Artículo 28. Universidades privadas en la Argentina. Buenos Aires, 1959.

[286] Escudé, Eduardo A. Por dios y por la patria. Buenos Aires, 1968.

[287] Esquema para un prontuario (Libro negro del frigerismo). N.p., n.d.

[288] García de Loydi, Ludovico. La iglesia frente al peronismo. Bosquejo histórico. Buenos Aires, 1956.

[289] García Flores, José I. Frondizi: Estrategia del desarrollo argentino. Rosario, 1967.

[290] Grondona, Mariano. La argentina en el tiempo y en el mundo. Buenos Aires, 1967.

[291] Irazusta, Julio. Perón y la crisis argentina. Buenos Aires, 1956.

[292] Merchensky, Marcos. Las corrientes ideológicas en la historia argentina. Buenos Aires, 1961.

[293] Odena, Isidro J. Libertadores y desarrollistas, 1955–1962. Buenos Aires, 1977.

[294] Palenque Carrera, Arturo. La revolución que nos aguarda. Buenos Aires, 1967.

[295] Quinterno, Carlos A. Historia reciente. La crisis política argentina entre 1955 y 1960. Buenos Aires, 1970.

[296] Rabinovitz, Bernardo. Sucedió en la Argentina (1943–1956): Lo que no se dijo. Buenos Aires, 1956.

[297] Schlesinger, Arthur. A Thousand Days. Boston, 1965.

[298] Uzal, Francisco H. Frondizi y la oligarquía. Buenos Aires, 1963.

[299] Viñas, Ismael. Análisis del frondizismo. Buenos Aires, 1960.

[300] Waldmann, Peter. "Las cuatro fases del gobierno peronista," *Aportes*, No. 19 (Jan. 1971), pp. 94–106.

[301] Zalduendo, Eduardo. Geografía electoral de la Argentina. Buenos Aires, 1958.

NEWSPAPERS AND PERIODICALS

1. Newspapers: *La Capital* (Rosario), 1951; *Clarín*, 1955, 1956, 1962; *Correo de la Tarde*, 1962; *Democracia*, 1951, 1955; *El Laborista*, 1951; *El Mundo*, 1947, 1955; *La Nación*, 1949–57; *La Nación* (international edition) 1962–66; *New York Times*, 1945–62; *La Prensa*, 1946–49, 1956–62; *La Razón*, 1961–62; *The Standard*, 1955; *The Times* (London), 1945–46; *La Vanguardia*, 1945–47.

2. Military journals: *Estrategia*, 1969–77; *Gaceta Marinera*, 1967; *Revista Militar*, 1946–64; *Revista de Informaciones* (title changed to *Revista de la Escuela Superior de Guerra* in 1954), 1946–77; *Temas Militares*, 1966–67.

3. News magazines: *Confirmado*, 1965–66; *Esto Es*, 1954–56; *Extra*, 1966; *Panorama Semanal*, 1968–69; *Primera Plana*, 1963–70; *Qué*, 1946–47, 1956–59; *Usted*, 1960–61.

4. Political weeklies: *Adelante,* 1957; *Afirmación,* 1958–60; *Azul y Blanco,* 1956–59; *El Leñador,* 1957; *La Lucha,* 1949–50; *Mayoría,* 1957; *Mundo Peronista,* 1955; *Nuevas Bases,* 1950–52; *País Unido,* 1957–58; *Rebeldía,* 1957; *Resistencia Popular,* 1957; *El Socialista,* 1948–49; *La Vanguardia,* 1957–60.

5. Other periodicals: *Desarrollo Económico,* 1961–78; Foreign Broadcast Information Service. *Latin America Daily Report,* 1955–62; *Hechos e Ideas,* 1945–55; *Review of the River Plate,* 1945–55; *Todo es Historia,* 1967–78.

Index